SPIRITUALITY AND COUNSELLING

EXPERIENTIAL AND THEORETICAL PERSPECTIVES

EDITED BY
JUDY MOORE
AND
CAMPBELL PURTON

PCCS Books
Ross-on-Wye

First published in 2006

PCCS BOOKS
3 Thomas Row
Alton Road
Ross-on-Wye
Herefordshire
HR9 5LB
UK
Tel +44 (0)1989 763 900
contact@pccs-books.co.uk
www.pccs-books.co.uk

Spirituality and Counselling:
Experiential and Theoretical Perspectives

British Library Cataloguing in Publication Data.
A catalogue record for this book is available from the British Library.

ISBN-10 1 898059 74 8
ISBN-13 978 1 89805 974 5

Cover design by Geraint Roberts
Cover artwork by Tess Sturrock
Printed by The Bath Press, Bath, UK

CONTENTS

ACKNOWLEDGEMENTS

Many people have contributed to the creation of this book, which is based on a selection of papers from a conference, 'The Spiritual Dimension in Therapy and Experiential Exploration' held at the University of East Anglia, Norwich in July 2004. To some individuals we are indebted for their contribution to the conference itself; to others for their assistance in the process of compiling, editing and designing the book.

Two individuals deserve particular mention. The first of these is Brian Thorne, a key figure in the planning of the conference, whose advice with regard to conference organization was invaluable at every stage. Sadly, a week before the conference was due to take place, Brian had a heart attack serious enough to prevent his attendance, apart from a brief appearance at the final plenary. At the time his absence felt like a great blow, but, in retrospect, there was a curious appropriateness about the quality of space we were left with, wholly in keeping with the nature of Brian's facilitation of the spiritual growth of others. Never seeking to impose his own Christian framework, one of his greatest skills is his ability to open up a safe space for others to explore their own intimations of and deepest longings for 'something more' in their own experiencing. The conference was just such a safe space, characterized by a collective generosity of spirit that was undoubtedly fed by concern for Brian and an awareness of the fragility of human life that his sudden illness forced us to confront. Many conference presenters paid warm tribute to his role in keeping exploration of the spiritual dimension high on the agenda of the person-centred approach. Others acknowledged the role he had played in their own personal journey of spiritual growth as trainer, therapist or friend. Fortunately, Brian has made a good recovery from a coronary bypass operation and we are indebted to him for his translation from the German in Jan van Blarikom's chapter.

The other figure deserving of particular mention is our colleague, Jane Ramsbottom, to whose phenomenal organizational skills the conference owed a significant part of its success. Jane's dedication, thoughtfulness and attention to detail at every stage meant that conference delegates could relax into the experience, confident that all practical matters were in extremely good hands.

Jane was ably assisted by Ros Montague, who dealt competently with all the conference bookings and was a calm and efficient presence throughout the conference itself. We are also extremely grateful to Julie Game, Robina Scott and Deanna Skittrell, the other members of the committee besides ourselves, for their hard work and generous support both before and during the conference. We would also like to thank the team of helpers who ably supported delegates and presenters throughout the week: Lynne Booker, Sheridan Chaffe, Kumi Fukuda, Jane Gutteridge, Ruth Mackintosh, Hélène Rankin, Marian Thomas and Trevor Wood. We are grateful to Makiko Mikuni for additional help with Japanese conference participants. We would like to thank all involved in enabling the daily Christian Eucharist to take place; for leading the early morning Sōtō Zen meditation we are very grateful to Reverend Master Daishin Morgan.

The success of the conference also depended upon the support of other colleagues at UEA and we are particularly indebted to the following: to the then Dean of the School of Education and Lifelong Learning, Anne Cockburn, who warmly encouraged us in the project at every stage; to our colleagues in the Counselling Service who ensured that the Service continued to function as normal throughout the conference; to other colleagues at UEA, far too numerous to mention individually, who worked cooperatively both before and during the conference to ensure that everything ran as smoothly as possible. We are also grateful to the Norwich Centre for early financial support. The conference was a massive feat of organization and cooperation and, it is in honour of that hugely successful collaborative enterprise that we have chosen to dedicate this book to all who contributed to its success.

We would like to thank Sandy Green at PCCS Books for her patient and supportive editorial work, and Pete Sanders for his tolerance of our ignorance of the publishing world and his endeavours to accommodate our more idiosyncratic requests. Finally, we would like to thank Tess Sturrock for her encouragement to include some illustrations to represent the experiential dimension of the conference and for her supportive and enthusiastic engagement with the project over the past eighteen months. We would particularly like to express our gratitude to Tess and Geraint Roberts for designing the cover of the book.

The authors, editors and publisher wish to acknowledge the following sources for permission to quote:

Yehuda Amichai, Doubts and Loves, from *Selected Poetry*, London: Faber & Faber, 1996. Reprinted by permission.

PRH International, diagram of the Pivotal Centres of the Person, in *Persons and Their Growth: The anthropological and psychological foundations of PRH education*, (1997: 53). Reprinted by permission.

Vera Sinton, *Encounter with God*, Milton Keynes: Scripture Union, 2003. Reprinted by permission.

ASJ Tessimond, *The Collected Poems of ASJ Tessimond*, with translations from Jacques Prévert, edited by Hubert Nicholson, Reading: Whiteknights Press, 1985. Reprinted by permission.

RS Thomas, Children's Song, from *Collected Poems*, London: JM Dent, Division of the Orion Publishing Group, 1993. Reprinted by permission.

INTRODUCTION

JUDY MOORE AND CAMPBELL PURTON

THE CONFERENCE

This book is a selection of papers from an international conference held at the University of East Anglia, Norwich, England in July 2004. The conference theme was 'the spiritual dimension in therapy and experiential exploration' and it was advertised as a gathering for 'counsellors, psychotherapists and other professionals concerned to explore the significance of spirituality in their life and practice'. We had initially expected that the conference might attract seventy or eighty people, but we eventually achieved the maximum numbers we could accommodate and the attendance was over one hundred and fifty.

The contributors to the conference came from many countries, mainly the UK and mainland Europe, but there were also delegates from as far afield as Japan and the US, and from different spiritual and therapeutic allegiances. The Christian tradition was the spiritual tradition most strongly represented and the person-centred approach the most widely represented in terms of therapeutic orientation.

It is hard to convey a felt sense of the conference solely in the printed word. Along with versions of the papers collected here (and many others) there were sessions devoted to Hawaiian Kahuna dance, poetry reading, expressive arts, experiencing through doodling, 'godly play', and the therapeutic power of ritual in psychotherapy. The conference was designed to reach deeply not only into the philosophical and theoretical aspects, but also into the lived experiencing of 'the spiritual dimension'. A number of delegates began each day with Sōtō Zen Buddhist meditation; others attended Christian Eucharist in the University Chaplaincy. It was our aim to enable participants to feel physically nurtured and 'held' so that, free as far as possible from practical concerns, they would be able to give themselves over to individual experiencing and be open to the sense of 'interconnectedness' that can develop in large groups when there is a collective openness to self and other.

THE STRUCTURE OF THE BOOK

In our compilation of material from the conference we have been limited in a number of ways. The Christian tradition is strongly represented and the Humanist view explored in some depth in the final section of the book, but, apart from Reverend Daishin Morgan's keynote address which explores the Buddhist perspective, none of the other major faiths is represented, although some papers and workshops acknowledge the influence and importance of other Eastern traditions, and Buddhism was much more strongly represented at the conference itself. Within psychotherapy, the person-centred approach is most strongly represented in the book, although at the conference there were significant inputs from cognitive-behavioural and psychodynamic practitioners. The book is based on papers that were offered and accepted for publication. Some presentations that we would have liked to include were not available for publication; others were not recorded in such a form as would lend themselves to adaptation for the purposes of this book. We are fortunate to have the input of several philosophers, whose contribution is invaluable in terms of opening up new ways of thinking.

The conference structure involved keynote speeches and invited addresses, as well as submitted papers and experiential workshops. We have retained the keynote addresses as a separate section, the first of the book, and they are here presented in alphabetic order of author. We have structured the rest of the book in terms of broad fields of interest: 'Philosophy', 'Presence and the Core Conditions', 'Christian Perspectives' and 'Humanism'. There were many possible ways of organizing the material; we have chosen a particular structure, but we would encourage readers to explore connections *between* the various sections as well as within them. For example, the theme of 'presence' appears in many of the presentations besides those that appear in the 'Presence' section; an exploration of language is a striking feature of several of the papers, and writers again and again make it clear that spiritual experiencing often cannot be expressed adequately in words. It is in acknowledgement of the importance of 'wordless' expression that we took the decision to represent some of the experiential sessions in the 'Personal Reflections and Workshops' section. We were strongly encouraged in this respect by Tess Sturrock, one of the workshop presenters, and it is to Tess that we owe the inspiration of the 'pink page', the decision to include illustrations of some of the artwork that was produced during the conference, and the cover design of the book.

Each of the six sections of the book begins with a brief introduction to the individual papers or workshops in which we endeavour to draw out some key points. In the rest of this general introduction we will consider briefly some recent definitions of 'spirituality' and draw out some of the main threads to emerge in the book as a whole. Each writer or presenter has struggled with their own thoughts or experiencing around the nature of the theory or practice of spirituality, but the collective expression of these reflections leads to the emergence of common themes that offer ways forward not only for a deeper appreciation of spirituality in relation to counselling, but for our understanding of how we may live meaningfully as human beings.

One theme that follows from the changed social context in which we now live our spiritual experiencing is the wide range of spiritual traditions available to us at the start of the twenty-first century. The theme of the adequacy or inadequacy of language to express spiritual experience recurs in several of the presentations, and related to this is the theme of how religious language functions, and also the theme of mysticism in religious thought. Other themes are the question of the 'self' and whether the self is viewed differently in therapeutic as contrasted with spiritual traditions. This leads to consideration of the interconnectedness of people, both with each other and with the larger world. The thinking of Carl Rogers features strongly in many of the presentations, and the final section in this general introduction is devoted to looking at some aspects of how spirituality has come to be regarded, specifically within the person-centred approach.

WHAT IS 'SPIRITUALITY'?

Western culture is no longer strongly identified with its Christian roots and individuals are now free to choose their own path towards what expresses their deepest longings to find a 'home' in what Richard Holloway terms a world of 'humanistic homelessness', characterized by 'religion without religion' (p. 23). With so many options to choose from in this 'homeless' world the term 'spirituality' has come to replace 'religion' in a way that would simply not happen in a culture such as that of Saudi Arabia, where all aspects of daily life are regulated by a shared Islamic faith (Al-Bahadel, 2004).

Edward Bailey has noted that a significant change in the public attitude towards 'spirituality' occurred in British culture in the 1970s. He observes that terms such as 'pastoral', 'myth' and 'spiritual' became 'no longer seen as purely religious' and began to be appropriated into secular society to the extent that today the 'spiritual' aim of education is now monitored in schools and the 'spiritual needs' of patients are considered in the provision of health care (1999: 1). The shift of spirituality from being seen in terms of the secular rather than the religious he identifies as being part of a broader social trend 'from the (self-styled) rational to the emotional, from the intellectual to the intuitive, from the mechanical to the mythical, from formula to fable' (1999: 2). Bailey points out that this shift raises many difficult questions for organized religion. It also leaves individuals in confusion as to where and with whom spiritual issues should be raised: with the priest, the minister or with the teacher, the health worker, or the counsellor? Some of the issues arising from the overlap of traditional pastoral care within the religious context and counselling as a secular activity are explored later in this book in the dialogue between Chris Jenkins and William West and in the research into differing perceptions of a Christian counselling centre presented by Jack Earl.

In their recent sociological study of the community of Kendal in Cumbria, Paul Heelas and Linda Woodhead (2005) link contemporary talk of spirituality with what they call the 'massive subjective turn of modern culture'. It is, they write:

> a turn away from life lived in terms of external or 'objective' roles, duties and obligations, and a turn towards life lived by reference to one's own subjective experiences (relational as much as individualistic) ... the turn is away from worlds in which people think of themselves first and foremost as belonging to established and 'given' orders of things. (Heelas & Woodhead, 2005: 2–3)

Heelas and Woodhead associate the term 'religion' with established orders of things, with scriptures, dogmas, rituals and so on, and 'spirituality' with those new forms which connect primarily with subjective experience. There is a huge variety of these latter forms. Amongst the groups and activities surveyed in Kendal were aromatherapy, astrology, circle dancing, craniosacral therapy, energy management workshops, healing, kinaesiology, massage, meridian therapy, paganism, rebirthing, reiki, Sai Baba teachings, Taizé singing, Tarot card reading, a wild women group, and yoga. That each of these may be defined as 'spiritual' points to one of the central problems that we face in addressing this area of human experiencing: it is only subjectively meaningful and can easily be dismissed by those who have not shared such experiencing or give credibility to the particular framework within which it occurs. The term 'spiritual' is both too broad and too vague and yet, in the West, we no longer inhabit a cultural framework that will permit a general use of the word 'religious' to capture the nature of experiencing that contributors to this book are seeking to express. A century ago William James (1902) endeavoured to capture something essential within the variety of what he then termed 'religious' experience; today, despite its negative connotations for many through its association with New Ageism, the term that best fits the general area under consideration in this book, and the one we have chosen to use, is 'spirituality'.

THE VARIETY OF TRADITIONS AND THE LANGUAGE OF SPIRITUAL EXPERIENCING

Holloway, from a Christian perspective and van IJssel from a Humanist perspective, draw attention to the wide range of spiritual traditions which are open to us today. Our 'postmodern' situation is one in which we can draw significantly not just on traditions such as Christianity or psychoanalysis, but also on Native American culture, Islam, Indian and Chinese traditions, spiritual paths growing out of the cultures of Africa and South America, together with a huge range of more recent 'New Age' traditions, such as those described by Heelas and Woodhead in the preceding section. This is a relatively new situation, though not one that is entirely unprecedented. There have been earlier times when a whole range of different spiritual paths were open to people. For example in Hellenistic Alexandria could be found followers of the ancient Egyptian religion, Christians, Jews, Gnostics and Stoics. At times such as these, it would seem that there is the need for an acceptance of the reality that there are many valid paths, but also the need for attention to individual experiencing, for it is to that to which one must turn in choosing between the various paths and authorities which present themselves.

The nature of experiencing that underlies the spiritual quest is a 'longing', a theme touched on by several authors and most fully explored by Mary Hill and Suzanne Keys in their workshop, 'Longing in Practice: Prayer and Therapy'. But what is this longing?

> I long for God, but does that longing come from within me or is it sparked by God's longing for me? Am I longing for or in response to? The answer is that it has to be both. This longing comes from deep within me as well as in response to a calling from without. (Keys & Hill: 183, this volume)

Discursive language cannot fully capture the quality of 'longing', nor of 'wonder', another term that appears in some of the more personal accounts of individual experiencing of spiritual openness. Such experiences are more likely to be communicated through metaphor, in poetry, for example, or in scripture. Mary Green and Stephen Platten explore, through a variety of individual experiences, what is, in effect, an elaborated metaphor of the cathedral as 'a route to God'.

All this points to a central difficulty we encounter when trying to describe spiritual experiencing: that it always contains more than can be expressed. It is helpful in this respect to consider the central argument of Jon Sharp's paper 'Towards a Phenomenology of the Divine', which is that we are capable of receiving direct experiencing, including experiencing of a spiritual nature, through our senses, unmediated by language or social context. Such experiences can only be received and not explained, either they are 'known' to us or not 'known'. Paradoxically, they also often involve, as many presenters observe, being in a state of 'unknowing', a state which finds its best-known metaphorical expression in the medieval text, *The Cloud of Unknowing* (Anon, 2001). As Peter Schmid observes:

> We cannot think or talk 'about' God; any endeavour to do so can only be an attempt to 'ask and think towards' God ... in other words, to seek God. Any conversation about God is more wrong than right or it is only analogous, i.e. similar, illustrative, metaphoric, symbolic. (Schmid: 228, this volume)

Each tradition has its own language, its own ways of expressing what it takes to be true and valid in the spiritual sphere. But what can be expressed in language has often been held to be less important than the 'unknown' or the inexpressible. This is the theme of mysticism, which is explicitly addressed by Ellingham and Sharp. The conceptual forms of the different traditions may be less important than the lived experiencing which we try to formulate, and our lived experiencing may in the end be the only means we have of assessing the validity of competing traditions. This theme of language and its relation to the non-linguistic is addressed in three of the philosophical papers (Ellingham, Schneider and Sharp), but is also raised in a more down-to-earth context by Earl (p. 291), and approached in a different way again by Luczaj. Both Schneider and Earl draw on Wittgenstein's view that 'language only has meaning in the stream of life'. From that point of view it is misleading to think of language as primarily labelling objects in the world; instead we need to understand how linguistic expressions work in practice. It is also important to acknowledge, as Schneider points out, that the language of spirituality, because of the elusive nature of spiritual experiencing, is, and will always be, 'a language for "insiders"' (p. 63).

ATTITUDES TOWARDS THE 'SELF'

An important theme running through many of the papers is that of 'the self'. Some of the participants suggest that there can be a tension between therapeutic positions which take an affirming or 'positive' view of the self, and encourage people to 'be themselves' or 'find themselves', and spiritual positions which take an apparently 'negative' view of the self, encouraging a 'transcending' or 'dissolving' of the self.

Speaking from the Buddhist perspective, Daishin Morgan begins his address by saying: 'Therapy and religion seem to me to be part of one continuum, yet their aims may not be the same'. He explains that the 'aim of Buddhism is enlightenment', which he defines as follows:

> Enlightenment is coming to see things as they are without the overlays that result from experiencing the world from the perspective of a separate self .... Enlightenment can be summarized as the release from our own greed, anger and delusion that can happen when we come to know our true nature. (Morgan: 26, this volume)

At the therapeutic end of the continuum the aim is to come to know and accept the self as it is in order to live more effectively. In terms of the presentations gathered in this book, differing attitudes to the self appear, reflecting different points on the continuum, as one might expect given the conference theme.

On perusing the various contributions we find at the 'self-acceptance' end of the spectrum:

van Blarikom's view (p. 257, quoting Rogers and Kierkegaard): one needs to 'will to be that self which one truly is';
Thorne's view (p. 44) of 'the unremitting task of seeking to embrace and then to hold on to so profound a level of self-acceptance that I am no longer a problem to myself';
Leonardi's person-centred view of the importance of self-actualization and self-acceptance (p. 206);
van Kalmthout's account (p. 156) of 'one's own inner appreciation of oneself'.

A rather different view of this layer of self is, however, given by Luczaj (p. 139), speaking from her experience of facilitating creative writing, she remarks that 'attempts at accurate "self-expression" have cathartic value for the writer, but do not tend to open out for others, and create new meanings .... The kind of poetry I refer to, however, relies on the assumption of a fixed, authentic self.'

At the other end of the spectrum we find the following references to a point at which the known or 'fixed' self dissolves:

Morgan (p. 27) speaks of 'an encounter or realization of one's true nature. It is a meeting in which one's self, as one believes oneself to be, falls away';

van Kalmthout (p. 158) says: 'When we discard this self-structure we indeed enter a deeper layer of experiencing … The discarding of the self-structure is described in some religious or spiritual circles by "the transcendence of the self" or "the dissolution of the ego"';

Thorne (p. 44), continuing the sentence quoted earlier, speaks of '… so profound a level of self-acceptance that I am no longer a problem to myself and can therefore be utterly self-forgetful';

Ellingham (p. 89), quoting Underhill, suggests that in mysticism the self needs to be 'remade, transformed';

Nimetz (p. 149) suggests that 'The "I" transforms itself into something beyond itself which is its non-existence as I know it when I live within duality/separation';

Scott suggests (p. 197) that '… in our depths all is positive … this constitutes our intact, essential self, our *being* which is a concrete reality that we can access in ourselves, and which is an autonomous centre'.

Several of the participants comment on the tension between these attitudes to the self:

Leonardi (p. 206) distinguishes a sense of deeper self from ego, linking the ego with the structures set up by introjected values;

Morgan says (pp. 26, 27) that we need to get away from 'the perspective of a separate self… There is this great need to know the true self, yet to find it one must let go of the self';

Ellingham (p. 84) quotes Underhill's view of the mystical position in which 'the pure soul' is one 'from which … all the beams and motes of egotism and prejudice have been removed';

Thorne (p. 44) remarks: 'This is a self-love which is the very contrary of selfishness';

van Kalmthout says (p. 156): 'The true self points to an inner, unconditioned dimension of existence that stands in opposition to an outer, conditioned dimension that is sometimes referred to as the false self' and adds (p. 158) that 'the term "true self" is nothing more than a pointer …'.

A broad consensus could be seen to emerge from all this. We might say that human beings range from being relatively fixed, structure-bound, prejudiced, conditioned, separated from others and the world, to being relatively flowing, open, unprejudiced, unconditioned, self-giving and open to others and the world. Where therapists *value* 'the self' they are usually valuing the person as a free, changing, interactional being who is able to let go of fixed ways of thinking and being. When they appear to *devalue* 'the self' they are usually devaluing those aspects of the person which have become rigid, closed to experience, separated from others. Those aspects they may call 'the ego', and it can be said that, in the course of therapeutic or spiritual development, if the person stays with acceptance of what is and then lets go of that (as opposed to clinging to any 'current' version of the self), the ego is gradually 'dissolved' or 'transcended'. The person is then open to what is 'unconditioned' within them, to a transcendent or spiritual dimension of existence.

If we adopt this kind of position then we are seeing the self as an interactional process rather than as any kind of *thing*. In this connection Ellingham (p. 96) refers to Whitehead's philosophy in which 'we view ourselves as process immersed in process beyond ourselves'. We become more 'thing-like' as we lose our sense of our interconnection with others and with the world. The ego is then a reification or solidification of the self, a falling of that which is beyond forms into the realm of the formed.

Yet we need to bear in mind the kind of warning which Schmid issues in connection with overbalancing in favour of the *multum* over the *unum*. Schmid acknowledges that the *unum* (the individual) has its own specific value, just as has the *multum* (the interactional community). It is important to value what *is* valuable in the ego. The ego with its logic, structures, concepts and linguistic forms is not necessarily at odds with the interactional flow of the self. As Luczaj (p. 140) puts it, drawing on Gendlin's philosophy, 'the forms require attention, and effort to maintain, and they are needed in order for us to think'. The forms (words, logic, structure, theories, models, formulations ...) may *further* the interactional flow rather than block it, as when the words of a poem carry us deeper into our experiencing, or when a therapist's formulation of a client's situation elicits the response 'Yes, that's exactly it!', or when a scientist hits on just the right model—such as the DNA double helix—which will explain the data.

It is not the forms that create the difficulties, but our rigid holding to the forms. Mountford (p. 108) draws attention to Rogers' remark that theories should be thought of as 'gossamer threads' which we weave around our experiencing, not as iron-clad structures which imprison that experiencing. If 'ego-self' refers to our tendency to hold rigidly to our ways of seeing things, then the ego-self needs to be transcended or dissolved. But that does not mean there is no place left for language or conceptual structures. Rather, in the words of Master Shen Yeng, quoted by Luczaj (p. 140) 'it is not like monism, is not like a big cosmic ONE where there is no duality at all, no more difference at all. It is just the realization that all individualities are interdependent, empty of *inherent* existence' (our emphasis).

It is important to recognize the fact that the egocentric self is not 'the enemy' of the fluid, open 'self as process'. Gradual acceptance of the egocentric self and self-knowledge are vital to the spiritual path and this is where therapy and religion meet. Self-knowledge, acceptance of 'what *is*' is vital both to emotional well-being and to spiritual growth.

This brings us to the importance of being fully present to oneself and others. On a personal basis this means that we need to accept who we are without distortion, accepting all that is there, not judging, not blaming. Being present to 'what is' can be developed by different means: by participating in an encounter group (Prüller-Jagenteufel); through spiritual practice (Prüller-Jagenteufel and others); through the repeated experience of listening with the whole of one's being to individuals in therapy or groups (Carl Rogers, see p. 10 below); through the experience of childbirth (Iseli Schudel); through the practice of meditation (Morgan). The current interest in 'mindfulness' as a psychological therapy (e.g. Segal, Williams & Teasdale, 2002) is based on a recognition that being fully present to 'what is' in the present moment can reduce anxiety and help individuals who are severely depressed. It is through the act of being present to ourselves that we may become open to a sense of something more, whether it be 'a profound sense of totality and connectedness' (Sharp: 68), a deep appreciation of the Trinity and of our participation in 'God as group' (Schmid: 228ff), the 'lost dimension' of ourselves (van Kalmthout: 156), the non-human world (Mountford: 101), a realization of 'the emptiness of things' (Morgan: 28). Seeking more than 'what is' blocks the openness that comes, paradoxically and inexplicably, from simply being present. Therapeutically, this paradox is clear: '... only what is allowed to be, can change' (Prüller-Jagenteufel: 126), but it also has implications for spiritual practice: one presenter comments on the significance of the name of God in the Jewish tradition—'Yahwe', 'the one who is present' (Prüller-Jagenteufel: 123), another on the Kabbalistic title of the Godhead on the Tree of Life—'*Eheieh* which translates as "I am that which is"' (Sharp: 78). Wherever one is in terms of the therapy–religion continuum, or however one regards 'the self', the value of acceptance of 'what is' is a unifying theme.

CARL ROGERS AND THE PERSON-CENTRED APPROACH

As mentioned above, the thinking of Carl Rogers was prominent in the conference papers. His 'core conditions' of genuineness, unconditional positive regard and empathy are explored throughout the book in a rich variety of contexts. Van Kalmthout argues that each of the conditions has a spiritual aspect; Hitchcock relates them to a series of Christian metaphors; Leonardi sees them as leading to an emptying of self that is characteristic of both Buddhism and mystical Christianity; Mountford extends them to the non-human world. In a sense, the core conditions represent an 'ideal' way of being that in itself may, for some, including it would seem Carl Rogers himself, constitute the beginning of a spiritual path.

As is well known, Rogers himself had ambivalent feelings about religion. It is to the more negative connotations of the word that he refers in his statement, quoted by Martin van Kalmthout, 'I am too religious to be religious ... I have my own spirituality' (Baldwin & Satir, 1987: 35; p. 155, this volume).

The person-centred approach, for some, including van Kalmthout, offers 'a system of meaning' (van Kalmthout, 2004 and p. 155, this volume). This is not surprising. It is a carefully researched therapeutic orientation, based on meticulous observation of the human being over many years. It is undoubtedly the case that it expresses many truths about humanity that are easily demonstrable in practice (for example, if the core conditions are offered a person will grow and change). Carl Rogers never ceased observing human beings and, in his later years in particular, extended this observation to himself, reaching an understanding of the spiritual nature of existence that it is difficult to comprehend with the thinking mind alone. Brian Thorne claims that 'Fifty years from now it is likely that Rogers will be remembered ... as a psychologist whose work made it possible for men and women to apprehend spiritual reality' (Thorne, 1992: 105–6). It is certainly true for many individuals that the self-exploration encouraged by their experience of person-centred counselling has led to the opening up of an inner world that may be regarded as partaking something of a spiritual reality.

When Thorne describes 'the practice of person-centred therapy [as] a profound spiritual discipline' (2002: ix; quoted in Ellingham, p. 88) he is saying something important about the nature of spiritual practice, a point drawn out by Ivan Ellingham where he quotes Rogers on his method of working with individuals:

> I let myself go into the immediacy of the relationship where it is my total organism which takes over and is sensitive to the relationship, not simply my consciousness. I am not consciously responding in a planful or analytic way, but simply react in an unreflective way, my reaction being based (but not consciously) on the total organismic sensitivity to this other person. (Rogers, 1967: 202; quoted p. 88, this volume)

Ellingham points out that Rogers' ability to focus his attention at this deep level is the result of many years of disciplined professional practice. This is not a religious discipline, but one that partakes of aspects of a religious discipline. Here we have a glimpse of the path, a very important insight when we bear in mind that so much attention is focused on the apparently 'spiritual' place where Rogers eventually arrived rather than how he actually got there. This statement demonstrates, in effect, how Rogers seems to have developed his own ability to be present to 'what is' (see above; p. 88 this volume).

This view is corroborated by Jan van Blarikom, who demonstrates how the particular nature of Carl Rogers' Protestant upbringing imbued him with certain values that are integral to the person-centred approach. Van Blarikom writes:

> The reformed-Christian character of Rogers' upbringing is voiced in his work through his emphasis on realness. 'To be who you really are', that is Rogers' credo; his belief in man as he really is ... His concept of realness is an appeal for presence: an appeal to be there for the other as you really are. (van Blarikom: 260, this volume)

It was towards the end of his life, after many years of developing his ability to be present, that Carl Rogers writes what is probably his best-known pronouncement on the spiritual dimension:

> When I am at my best, as a group facilitator or as a therapist, I discover another characteristic. I find that when I am closest to my inner, intuitive self, when I am somehow in touch with the unknown in me, when perhaps I am in a slightly altered state of consciousness, then whatever I do seems to be full of healing. Then simply my *presence* is releasing and helpful to the other. There is nothing I can do to force this experience, but when I can relax and be

> close to the transcendental core of me, then I may behave in strange and impulsive ways in the relationship, ways which I cannot justify rationally, which have nothing to do with my thought processes. But these strange behaviors turn out to be *right*, in some odd way: it seems that my inner spirit has reached out and touched the inner spirit of the other. Our relationship transcends itself and becomes a part of something larger. Profound growth and healing and energy are present. (Rogers, 1980: 129; original emphasis)

This very personal statement clearly strikes a chord in many and will be found repeated several times in the course of this book. An error into which one may easily fall, however, is that of seeking 'presence' as a goal or as a 'fourth condition'. In a late interview, quoted by Geller and Greenberg, Rogers returns to what may happen in an interaction when he is fully present:

> I am inclined to think that in my writing I have stressed too much the three basic conditions (congruence, unconditional positive regard, and empathic understanding). Perhaps it is something around the edges of those conditions that is really the most important element of therapy—when my self is very clearly, obviously present. (Baldwin, 2000: 30; quoted in Geller & Greenberg, 2002: 73)

Geller and Greenberg cite this as an example of Rogers' view of the healing quality of 'presence', but the nouns that Rogers uses are, in fact, 'something (around the edges)' and the 'self'. What we suggest Rogers is saying here is that 'something around the edges' enters the interaction as a source of growth or healing *when* his 'self' is fully present. It is not simply his presence that is healing: it is *what comes* when he is present to himself and to the other. Rogers' language both here and in his earlier statement is hesitant—'when I am somehow in touch with the unknown in me …', 'when perhaps I am in a slightly altered state of consciousness …', 'it seems that my inner spirit has reached out …', '[p]erhaps it is something around the edges …'—and characteristic of articulations of religious experience as described by Hans Schneider (see Chapter 4, pp. 50–64). The danger, Schneider makes clear, in terms of all spiritual experiencing, lies in applying an 'over-belief' to what is emergent in terms of spiritual awareness that loses the quality of the original experience. For Rogers and his followers, the 'over-belief' is likely to be expressed in terms of the theory that underpins the person-centred approach and it is tempting to think in terms of a 'fourth condition', be it 'presence' or, as Brian Thorne has differently expressed his own version of this quality of experiencing, 'tenderness' (Thorne, 1985; see also pp. 37, 38 and 39, this volume).

Rogers is saying nothing more than that if he is fully present to himself and the other then 'something' may happen 'around the edges'. This is the case for all of us. The papers in this book represent a rich cross-fertilization of exploration of this 'around the edges' territory.

REFERENCES

Al-Bahadel, D (2004) The Feasibility of Introducing Counselling for Women and Family Therapy within Saudi Society in Saudi Arabia. Unpublished PhD thesis, University of East Anglia, Norwich.

Anon., translated with an introduction and notes by Spearing, A (2001) *The Cloud of Unknowing and Other Works*. Harmondsworth: Penguin.

Bailey, E (1999) 'What has Spirituality got to do with the Church?' quoted with permission of the Bible Society, <www.biblesociety.org.uk>.

Baldwin, M & Satir, V (1987, 2nd ed, 2000) Interview with Carl Rogers on the Use of Self in Therapy. In *The Use of Self in Therapy*. New York: Howarth.

Geller, S & Greenberg, L (2002) Therapeutic Presence: Therapists' experience of presence in the psychotherapy encounter. *Person-Centered & Experiential Psychotherapies, 1* (1&2) 144–55.

Heelas, P & Woodhead, L (2005) *The Spiritual Revolution: Why religion is giving way to spirituality*. Oxford: Blackwell.

James, W (1902) *The Varieties of Religious Experience: A study in human nature*. London: Longmans Green.

Rogers, CR (1980) *A Way of Being*. Boston: Houghton Mifflin.

Segal, Z, Williams, J & Teasdale, J (2002) *Mindfulness-based Cognitive Therapy for Depression*. New York: Guilford.

Thorne, B (1985) *The Quality of Tenderness*. Norwich. Norwich Centre Publications.

Thorne, B (1992) *Carl Rogers*. London: Sage.

Van Kalmthout, M (2004) Person-centered psychotherapy as a modern system of meaning. In *Person-Centered and Experiential Psychotherapies 3* (3) 192–206.

KEYNOTE ADDRESSES

INTRODUCTION

During the conference there were three keynote addresses, held on consecutive evenings and presented by invited speakers who represented between them a deep understanding of particular religious and therapeutic traditions. Richard Holloway is an author, broadcaster and former Bishop of Edinburgh; Reverend Master Daishin Morgan is Abbot of Throssel Hole Buddhist Abbey in Northumberland, England; and Professor Brian Thorne, former Director of Counselling at the University of East Anglia, is both one of the most influential figures in the person-centred approach today and a devout Anglican Christian. Unfortunately, as previously mentioned, Brian Thorne was, at the time of the conference, in hospital recovering from a recent heart attack and unable to deliver his own address. It had fortunately been written in advance and was presented by Jeff Leonardi.

Richard Holloway's unscripted address provides an overview of the contemporary religious scene. It was recorded and transcribed, but has not been significantly adapted for publication. Holloway addresses the prevailing atmosphere of contemporary religious discussion, which he characterizes as essentially secular. Several aspects of this secular paradigm create difficulties for the more traditional forms of religion: one is the emphasis on consent rather than on authority, another is the element of hedonism, and a third is the element of tolerance for plurality. This third element—associated with 'postmodernism'—Holloway sees as crucial to where we stand today, and he goes on to sketch four ways in which people respond to it. The first option is that of fundamentalism, the response of 'holding to tradition in a traditional way'. The dangers of this are clear enough: Holloway quotes from the Israeli poet Yehuda Amichai, 'From the place where we are right/ flowers will never grow/ in the Spring'. The second option is to hold to a tradition, but provisionally, with lightness. The third is to see religion as having made itself redundant, having usefully performed the function of establishing the values of justice, mercy, adoration and so on. These are deep and real values, but the tradition in which they are embedded can continue without the support of a religious framework. The fourth option Holloway calls 'humanistic homelessness', in which we stand outside any tradition: 'there is no one but us, there never has been'. In the modern world, Holloway concludes, we have to live with this diversity of options, but to do so itself requires certain qualities which could themselves be seen as spiritual: magnanimity, honesty and a 'kind of practical love'.

Daishin Morgan's address, again unscripted and kindly adapted by the author for publication from the original transcript, is entitled 'The Process of Transformation within Buddhism'. While acknowledging that therapy and religion form part of 'one continuum', he addresses himself specifically to the religious end of this continuum as expressed through Buddhism. One of the most fundamental ways in which Buddhism differs from therapy is in its view of the self. 'Enlightenment', Morgan explains, 'is coming to see things as they are without the overlays that result from experiencing the world from the perspective of a separate self.' He describes the five stages of transformation, or enlightenment, as understood in Sōtō Zen: hearing the call to train; making the commitment to following the path of training; the encounter with or realization of one's true nature; going into a deep understanding of what is known as 'emptiness'; and, finally, 'returning to the world'. Each of these stages is explained in some detail and then the 'how' of training is explored. Morgan focuses particularly on the practice and process of meditation and the importance of letting go of generating a 'me' by attaching to the thoughts and feelings that arise naturally in meditation. The Buddha nature within us all, he explains, '*is* compassion, love and wisdom' and all we need to do is to get '[ourselves] out of the way'. This deeply positive view of the person is akin to the view held by the person-centred approach, but the view of the self could not be more different. The comparison is one we need to make for ourselves, but Daishin Morgan's exposition of the process of transformation through Buddhist practice makes it clear that there is a practical and viable way forward that can take us far beyond the 'separate self'.

Brian Thorne begins with Auden's words 'We must love one another or die', and recalls a lecture that he gave over twenty years ago in which he particularly emphasized that aspect of love which we call 'tenderness'. He connects the quality of tenderness closely with the quality that Carl Rogers called 'presence' and defined as a state of being involving heightened awareness, a high degree of contact with the intuitive side of one's being, the risking of being fully alive, a sense of being caught up in a stream of love, and 'an overpowering sense of energy, well-being and healing'. Such tenderness has a strongly physical aspect which is emphasized more by Thorne than by Rogers. Thorne reflects on the personal implications of having publicly advocated the need to develop such a way of being, and on the parallel experience of Rogers who, in consequence of his later writings, was often seen as naïve and idealistic. In Thorne's case the problems have been compounded through his commitment to Christian spirituality; he found himself criticized for his 'bad theology' as well as his 'bad psychology'. Since the time of his original lecture on the quality of tenderness, Thorne has experienced current developments in society, such as the ubiquity of the mobile phone, as further weakening the bonds of tenderness between human beings. In response he advocates a form of spiritual discipline founded on self-acceptance and self-forgetfulness, which for him connects deeply with his own childhood experiences of profound love.

Chapter 1

LOOKING IN THE DISTANCE: SPIRITUALITY IN GOD'S ABSENCE

Richard Holloway

I would like to begin by reminding those of you who live in Britain, of the Bristol Heart Baby inquiry of a few years ago, when there was a great medical scandal in Britain. A hospital in Bristol that did paediatric cardiac surgery, operating on babies' hearts, found that too many babies were not surviving; they were coming out of the theatre dead, and the young anaesthetist who was on the staff at the hospital 'blew the whistle' on this fact. He, of course, lost his job over it and is now working in Australia because the establishment closed ranks. But the government did set up an inquiry which sat for a long time, and during the inquiry one of the witnesses, one of the learned witnesses, one of the medical witnesses, let loose an extraordinary fact that to him seemed of no importance or interest at all: he revealed quite casually that the Royal Liverpool Children's Hospital had the biggest collection of children's hearts in the country. There was a bit of a pause, and it gradually became obvious to this guy that he had revealed something that the public didn't know, and it led to another scandal, and yet another inquiry, which was called the 'stolen organ inquiry'. It was discovered that for the last fifty years in Britain doctors had been taking the organs out of children when they died, and returning incomplete corpses to their parents to bury, without anyone's consent or permission. The doctors were puzzled by the outcry at the scandal: they were learned and revered, and of course they were doing this for our benefit, and were gaining nothing from it except new knowledge that would help us in being healed. They couldn't quite come to terms with the fact that people were outraged that no consent had been given; and in the inquiry that followed lots of horrible statistics were revealed. It was discovered that there were about 100,000 livers, kidneys and hearts of children, up and down the country. The most revolting item discovered in this grisly landscape was that they actually had the head of an eleven-year-old boy in one hospital. And of course there was a colossal uproar in the country because all these parents who had buried incomplete corpses lost what I think in the therapy profession you call 'closure' on their grief, and they had to get organs back if they were still available, and do little burials. During the inquiry one mother whose child had been so used said, 'If only they had asked' and when I read those words I realized that a highly significant seismic shift had occurred in British culture: something had happened that moved

This is a lightly edited version of a recording of Richard Holloway's keynote address at the conference.

people from a culture of authority to a culture of consent. We were no longer prepared simply to take it on the basis of the reverence we owed to this great profession, this godlike profession—the medical profession. We were no longer simply prepared to let them patronize us by doing good to us without our consent; we expected to be asked.

Philosophers would describe that as a paradigm shift; they would say that something profound had happened to the culture of Britain. In fifty years no one, in a sense, checked this, no one took a temperature, but in that moment during that scandal, during that investigation, with the words of that young woman whose child had been returned to her divested of various organs, it became obvious to the country that we had moved; we had made a massive paradigm shift.

Now I want to spend some time this evening thinking about this theory called 'Paradigm Theory' because I want to use it to try and describe what I think has happened to religion and culture in today's world, certainly in the developed world, and 'Paradigm Theory' is one appropriate and useful way into it. I know I am teaching my grandmother and a few grandfathers to suck eggs here, but I want to remind you of the history of the 'Paradigm Theory'. A young physicist at Harvard in the sixties called Thomas Kuhn was invited by the president of Harvard to give a lecture to science and humanity students on the history of science, and in his research he made an interesting discovery. He assumed that science was a linear kind of horizontal incremental discipline; it simply chomped its way through the facts of the universe like those coal-mining machines that cut their way through a seam of coal. He thought it was a non-interruptive, undramatic, linear, horizontal process; that you simply crawled your way through the facts of the universe, and you revealed them. But not at all: he discovered that it was much more dramatic than that, much more interruptive than that, and he used paradigms as a way of explaining what actually happened. He said that the scientific community would create a constellation of theories and explanations and techniques that actually worked, and explained the world, and performed useful technological techniques, and he called this a 'paradigm' and it worked until it stopped working, until new knowledge either challenged its basis or new questions were asked (which couldn't actually fit into the paradigm used), until it couldn't be used any longer. And then there was what he called a paradigm revolution. It was never easy because people get fond of their paradigms, even scientists get fond of their paradigms, and that's actually quite a good thing; stability is important, if a thing is working you let it work—'if it ain't broke, don't fix it'. So there is a natural kind of rooted inertia to hold onto the thing that is actually doing the business until it becomes obvious that it no longer can do the business. The classic example of the paradigm shift is the shift from Aristotelian astronomy to Copernican astronomy. Aristotelian astronomy, a version of the nature of the universe on which most of the ancient scriptures are based, is the 'three-deck' universe with the pot lid. Incidentally it still works: you can still navigate by the Aristotelian picture of the heavens. But of course with new knowledge, with telescopes gradually showing that in fact the earth was not the centre of the system, that indeed it went round the sun, there was this great paradigm shift and gradually the Copernican model took over. There have been lots of paradigm shifts since then, for instance the

Newtonian, and the Einsteinian. We are in the midst of a whole new way of understanding astronomy at the moment and that was what Kuhn (1962) wrote up in a seminal little text called *The Structure of Scientific Revolutions*—a thin book but a very, very hard read, which came out in the sixties.

Now the point about this book is that not only did it help inform people who wanted to know about the history of science, it was actually used and taken up by philosophers, by culture critics, by people who studied religion. There are religious paradigms, and religious paradigms very rarely shift and change. Hans Küng, the great Catholic theologian, doesn't have an official Catholic theological driving licence but he writes more prolifically than any other theologian in the world. He has used 'Paradigm Theory' in his vast study of the religious situation of our time. Only two volumes are out, one on Christianity (Küng, 1995), one on Judaism (Küng, 1992); the one on Islam is on its way. He says there are five Christian paradigms and we are on the cusp of a sixth. That's interesting, because the difference between a scientific paradigm that is replaced, and a religious paradigm that is modified, is that a dead scientific paradigm is as dead as Monty Python's parrot—it just doesn't work any longer. If you study science today you don't start with Aristotle, you start with the going paradigm, you start with the living thing that is working, unlike religion which never lets go of anything. (You know those places where we put our trays in the Sainsbury's eating hall, that's what you do with religious paradigms, you simply stack them up in formation, so there is always the paradigm of your choice available.) If you want the religion of the sixth century, fine, there's a sixth century paradigm. But religious paradigms do adapt and I would like to spend a little time exploring how they come to adapt.

Paradigms, scientific, religious, cultural, or political, are all power systems, and the thing you ask about a power system is, 'Who are the victims here?' Change in religious paradigms comes much more slowly; they don't change as rapidly as science does because we don't like giving them up. But they do change, and the elements that create the change I think are best interpreted by the last and greatest of the Hebrew prophets, Karl Marx. Karl Marx pointed out that all power systems, including religious power systems, create victims, and the things that cause their overthrow is the revolt of the victims, and a number of interesting things happen when victims revolt. Another one of Marx's insights was that, unlike the Romans that Nietzsche loved because they were honest about their hold of power: 'We're in charge and, by God, we're going to stay here, so push off!'—since those happy days, people in positions of power have been reluctant to express their naked ambition about holding on to power so they developed what Marx called an 'ideology' which is the respectable, spiritual, intellectual way of justifying the fact that they're in power. And it always comes down to 'It's for your own good that we've got the stretch limousines and all of that, we're doing this for you, it's tough, it's hellish up here'. The classic example of a paradigm shift, it's hardly a shift, let's call it a wee stagger, was in the Anglican Church's attitude towards women. Women caused the biggest paradigm shift in the last fifty years. After two thousand years of changeless male dominance, women said 'Enough already, we are joining the power system.' And note what Marx would have described as the ideological response of the male power structure. It didn't say 'Push off sister, we don't want you in the Sanctuary.' It said: 'We'd love to have you in the Sanctuary sisters, but it's the law, it's the Bible that tells us you are created to be subordinate to men, and we can't change that.' And an interesting thing happens, and it illustrates that although religious paradigms do shift, they never shift honestly, and it's worth understanding this if you want to actually change a religion. Now you can't actually go up to a religious paradigm that you think is operating unjustly and say 'This is unjust, subordinating women is unjust, stoning sodomites is unjust', you can't do that. What you have to do is to find some way within the scriptural paradigm to do it, to give a paradigmatic permission to do it. So what you would do then is a thing called 'the canon within the canon': God said 'That isn't possible', but, you go on, 'He said something else'—which, in a sense, trumps the argument. It's a kind of bad faith really, it's a kind of dishonesty. You would never actually say God is wrong, or God got it wrong, or we got God wrong, or let's forget it and be good human beings and make this thing right for justice's sake. You never actually get that, but you do get shifts.

There has been a shift in Christianity, and the other element in the shift is actually very interesting. Remember I said that Marx said, 'It is the revolt of the victims, which is opposed by ideology or by theology.' But then there's this other, this very, very interesting little group, the most interesting group in human cultural history, what Nietzsche called 'the degenerates'. I'm a degenerate; degenerates are people who find that they are incapable of fidelity to system. Now you need people to be faithful to systems because you do need stability, you need fidelity as an important virtue, but Nietzsche made a very interesting point. He said 'The danger to these stable systems to which people are faithful'—it's working, it's been around for two thousand years, it's mandated by God or whomever—'the danger to these stable systems, is increasing stupidity'. Now OK, maybe two thousand years of female subservience is a bit long, but when all the changes—the discovery of birth control, the liberation of women from their biological destiny, the decision grudgingly to educate them, the discovery that they actually had brains—when all of those things actually came up, it made men opposing the liberation of women look stupid and this is Nietzsche's way. He said, 'The danger to all these stable systems to which people faithfully adhere is stupidity, increasing stupidity' and he said that the people who bring the future to these stable systems are the unfaithful, the heretics, the degenerates, the people who are not persuaded, the people who never settle for any system because they're always looking in the distance, they're always wanting to find out what the future is. And these degenerates, like a kind of small touch of the disease, inject the stable community with the future. What happened in the paradigm example—still going back to women—is that there were enough men within the citadel who felt uneasy about the paradigm of male dominance, who revolted against it, and they allied themselves with the sisters and changed the lock on the cage. It's not complete yet, and it certainly isn't throughout in the Christian community, but it is an example that religious paradigms do shift.

Bearing all that in mind, the fact is that religious and cultural paradigms never really go away, though some of them do. There are very few people who actually perform sacrifices (though there may well be some, somewhere in Norwich, in a back street somewhere!). However, it's unlikely, partly because of legislation on slaughtering practices in England, but on the whole, religious paradigms hang around, and what gets added on is the kind of prevailing paradigm on top of all these other options that are available to you (that structure in Sainsbury's dining hall that has all those trays in it). There's always a dominant paradigm that stands above all the others and in a sense, influences them, and upsets them.

The dominant paradigm today is the secular paradigm, and I want to suggest that it influences all of us, even if we are comfortably or uncomfortably ensconced in one of the other paradigms, because it creates a kind of prevailing atmosphere. I want to suggest three elements in the prevailing secular paradigm that create lots of problems for people trying to hold on to one of the traditional spiritualities or religions and I want to look back at the way I opened tonight.

A fundamental element in the contemporary secular paradigm is that the principle of consent is the most important ethical principle that we can operate in society today, and it applies not only to medical care, things that doctors will get your consent for before they operate on you, or take this out, or make this move. And in some ways we've probably overcorrected there; legislation has come in to make consent 'de rigueur' and it's almost so minutely tuned that you're probably going to have to get a judge's permission to have your toenails cut the next time you're in hospital, because we tend always to overcorrect. But consent is a fundamental ethical principle in secular ethical thinking and it applies not only to medical ethics; it applies above all to sexual ethics. The old paradigm, the old moral paradigm, religious paradigm, was a paradigm of authority. It was essential to have ethical authority—you got permission to do it. You got your licence, you got married. Today's prevailing ethic is an ethic of consent. The central, essential element in any sexual transaction is consent. Both parties have to agree to it, and it has to be informed consent, which is why we are so hot against sex with children, or sex in which power is an element. It may appear to be consensual, but in fact there's a power play going on, but that's a very important element in all of the professions that have access to situations which might engender a sexual relationship; consent has become the fundamental principle.

I think increasingly it will be a fundamental principle in the ethics of war. I think it will be very difficult for a Prime Minister of Britain ever to lead Britain into an unwanted war again without our consent. Consent has become a dominant ethical law, and it's a good one; and it's an ethical law for grown-up people who no longer have to be told what to do, who no longer have to obey some superior godlike figure or a person standing in the place of God. So consent is a fundamental element in the new secular paradigm that we're all living in, around and within.

The second element, and this is a very glamorous and dramatic element, is that it's very hedonistic. Most of the old religious paradigms believed in the indefinite delay of gratification. Gratification was essentially an eschatological concept which God gave after death, not this side of it, and in fact if you got too much pleasure this side of death, you might have a very bad time on the other side. You remember that hymn,

'Brief life is here our portion, Brief sorrow, short-lived joy.' My God, you came out on your knees when you sang that. And it was all about how this was not the real life, this was merely a gloomy prelude to the life to come. Today, it's NOW, we WANT IT NOW. I like that about today's society, because having been brought up in the Christian paradigm I feel I didn't get enough pleasure. We were taught to delay gratification, but it always took revenge. Duodenal ulcers used to be prevalent among the clergy, for whom a dry sherry on a Sunday was the nearest they got to Rabelaisian excess. By that standard, the prevailing secular norm, that pleasure is good, is a good thing; but there's always a cost. You get more out of pleasure if you balance it, as Aristotle, with his middle-way between extremes, well knew. But don't knock pleasure; don't use that as simply a grudging way of saying human beings want to keep enjoying themselves. We need to develop in Britain, an ethic of pleasure. We need to help our young people to enjoy themselves with appropriateness, and with a kind of responsibility to their own pleasure, to the goodness of pleasure.

The third characteristic of the prevailing secular paradigm is that it has an enormous tolerance for plurality, for multi-value systems. Indeed, one of the definitions of contemporary society—you've heard that terrible generic phrase 'postmodernism'—the characteristic of postmodernism is that there is no single system that everyone adheres to. We're in a plural, multicultural society where there are lots of systems, where you will have people following a very, very rigid form of religiosity, right over to people following a very abandoned form of secularity. And young people today have an enormous tolerance for that need, for that kind of multiplicity. But it's new to people, or it's comparatively new, to older people who were brought up in a rather more homogenous culture, and it can be very disturbing for them. What I want to suggest now is that we're all living in this churning kaleidoscope of multiple paradigms and we're confused.

The people that come to you for therapy, they don't know which paradigm to cling to, whether there is one at all that is available to them any longer that will endure, that will give them some kind of stability. It's working through you as well. It's impossible not to be affected by this, because the whole world has become a big, big mixing bowl of cultures and religiosities and political systems. The world has become a village, that important cliché, the global village; we now encounter all this. You can't get away from it.

This is the context in which we are existing. And one way of defining it is that there is no God. There is no prevailing system; there is no absolutely obvious, overpowering authoritative system that compels obedience and consent. There are many that claim to, but no single one does. Nietzsche saw all this coming, he prophesied the death of God—I prefer the phrase 'the absence of God'. There is a sense in which in European culture today, certainly, God is a very uncertain, elusive reality, if God is a reality at all; and there are theologians who now have a theology of the unreality of God. God seems to be disappearing round the corner before we can ever catch up with him. So we're all in a state of confusion. And there are many ways of handling this, but I think there are four big options that people seem to be going for and I suspect that at least three of them are represented among you here tonight.

Probably the most dramatic and the most volatile and the most disturbing of the options is fundamentalism, which is an increasing phenomenon everywhere in our world. But it's an obvious recourse for people who can't cope with this churning kaleidoscope of paradigms, this incessant change, this acceleration of different points of view; they say 'Enough!' The interesting thing about fundamentalism is that it refuses or rejects paradigm thinking; it says *only this* is the truth. Giddens' (1994) definition of fundamentalism is 'holding to a tradition in the traditional way'. Before we understood that there were multiple traditions, and that if you're really embedded in the paradigm, you don't know you're in a paradigm, you thought this is the truth, you thought this is the way it is. 'It's not the way it is *for us*, it is the way it *is*, it is the truth, and all others are outside the truth, they're in danger', and that's very tempting to people in our world. So it's not a surprise that people are stampeding into Christian fundamentalism, Islamic fundamentalism. Even Hinduism now has a fundamentalist wing and that is a notoriously inclusive form of religion. And there are doubtless various other forms of fundamentalism. There may even be fundamentalisms in the therapy rooms. I mean, I've met therapists who hold their particular tradition with something that seems to me fairly close to fundamentalism, but I wouldn't dare to suggest that to this audience here.

I think there are therapeutic possibilities in fundamentalism and this may surprise you. I think there are some people for whom fundamentalism is the answer, they need to be contained. They're afraid of their own inner chaos, they can't cope with the chaos of the external world and this is a refuge for them, and I'm not going to deny anyone a refuge that will keep them in some kind of integrity. I have known people who have been saved from terrible, chaotic lives by converting. I've known heroin addicts who've become Jesus addicts, a far better drug to get off on. I've known prisoners who've been converted by the prison bible fellowship and they've been young people with no hope or pattern to their lives at all, not very intelligent, not very educated, hardly literate, but they've bought into religion, a very simplistic form of Christianity; that's done it for them. Now I don't want to deny that the trouble with fundamentalism is that it can, when it goes political, become extremely dangerous. Malise Ruthven (2004) has written a very interesting book about it, and he says the trouble with fundamentalists in the political sphere is that they transcendentalize conflict. You may have a conflict, a territorial conflict, a political conflict, and you can maybe work it out on immanent grounds, on human grounds, but if you bring the transcendent God into it, how can you negotiate that? God says we have a claim to this, there's no way, that's why Giddens says another definition of fundamentalism is 'refusal to negotiate', because how can you negotiate away God? That's a terrible kind of danger in our world. I spent an afternoon with Yehuda Amichai, a wonderful Israeli poet. I spent an afternoon with him in Jerusalem, two years ago, just before he died of cancer. An enormously humane man, a humanist, an atheist, sitting in that city which is driven mad by religion. In one of his poems he said that all the prayers in Jerusalem created a kind of fog above the city, like the fog over industrial cities he says, it's hard to breathe. And he wrote a wonderful poem (Amichai, 1996) and it seems to me to be the antidote to the temptation to bad fundamentalism:

From the place where we are right
flowers will never grow
in the Spring.

The place where we are right
is hard and trampled
like a yard.

But doubts and loves
dig up the world
like a mole, a plough.

And a whisper will be heard in the place
where the ruined
house once stood.

That spirit of a proper kind of reverent doubtfulness, a loving hesitancy, brings me to the second option of the four that I'm suggesting to you as a way of dealing with this bewildering circus of paradigms that we're living through. And that is to cleave to one of the traditions with a certain lightness, in the spirit of Amichai's poem—doubts and love digging up the world like a mole. Many people manage to hold on to one of the paradigms, one of the religious traditions with a certain lightness, a certain provisionality. They know all about the horrors that this particular paradigm has perpetrated in history. They understand that; they know they are capable of horrors themselves, but it has taught them a little bit about love and mercy, and they want to cleave to it as long as they can. But they want to hold it with a kind of lightness of touch. They don't want to ram it down other peoples' throats; they don't want to be evangelical about it unless they're asked. It's as if you've seen a good movie and you want to share that—if you're in a good set-up you want to share that, but you don't hammer it. That is the way a lot of my Christian friends are holding on to Christianity. Many of them describe it as holding on with their fingernails, because a lot of people find that the infection of fundamentalism is seeping into Christianity, even in groups that are not themselves paid-up fundamentalist, because they think it works, gets bums on seats, gets money in the bank. (The business side of Christianity is something that those of you who have not been in the ordained ministry will be deliciously innocent of, but it's a very important part of keeping the show on the road.) And what seems to keep the show going today is converting people to a hard gospel: which is why it's very difficult to hold on to the tradition today with this kind of gentleness and lightness and tolerance—but it's beautiful when you see it. It used to be the main characteristic of dear old Anglicanism, but I fear that there's a kind of evangelicalism in Anglicanism today that may change the personality of the church that nurtured and nourished me. I hope not, I hope there's some kind of fight back, but it does rather look that way at the moment.

So that's the second of the options. The first is fundamentalism, the second is holding to a tradition with lightness, with hesitancy, even with a kind of insecurity. There's an anxiety about this way of holding it, but it can have a gentleness and a beauty to it.

The third is what, after Derrida, we might call 'religion without religion'. And I want to spend a few minutes' time to unpack this. The way I try to explain this way of relating to religion and the great spiritual traditions is by using the metaphor of the rocket that gets the payload into space. Derrida, and those who share this view, think that the great religions have carried fundamental human values for the rest of us, which are now, as it were, delivered into the human orbit, so the delivery vehicle, the great institutional apparatus that carried them through time, can fall away, leaving behind the great values of justice and mercy and forgiveness and attention and adoration and awe and presence. All of these wonderful words that religion has carried and sometimes loaded with too much doctrinal meaning, you can separate them from the container and value them for their own sake. You can have a kind of religion after religion; a religion without religion. It is a way of being in continuity with the best of the religious traditions without throwing them overboard, but taking the best of them on with you. And I suspect that a lot of that has been going on here in this conference these last few days.

The fourth option, the one that I want to conclude on, I call 'humanistic homelessness'. This is where you honestly accept that you have been nourished, nurtured and loved in the tradition you've come from, but you can no longer be at home there, so you leave home, go outside, come out. We shouldn't let our gay and lesbian brothers and sisters monopolize that wonderful expression, because lots of us have to come out of all sorts of wardrobes and closets and dungeons that we've inhabited for too long. We need to open the door and simply step outside and say 'I'm out now, I'm on my own'. It can be quite frightening, coming of age in this way. People in this position now view all religious traditions as human constructs. We're extraordinary creatures, we humans, and we create these wonderful dreams and theories and visions, some of which liberate us, some of which oppress us. It can be liberating to know that they are constructed by us and therefore they can be abandoned by us or they can be reformed by us; they can be changed radically or changed in tiny but significant ways. This is how Annie Dillard (1999) expresses it:

> There is no one but us. There is no one to send, nor a clean hand nor a pure heart on the face of the earth, nor in the earth, but only us, a generation comforting ourselves with the notion that we have come at an awkward time, that our innocent fathers are all dead—as if innocence had ever been—and our children busy and troubled, and we ourselves unfit, not yet ready, having each of us chosen wrongly, made a false start, failed, yielded to impulse and the tangled comfort of pleasures, and grown exhausted, unable to seek the thread, weak and involved. But there is no one but us, there never has been.

'There's no one but us, there never has been'—when you recognize that, a kind of relief can come. It's OK, I'm on my own, there's no big Daddy in the sky disapproving of me now. I am on my own to make it or break it, for myself and for lots of other people. That attitude is an important element in humanistic spirituality in our day. It's where a lot of people are, people you know, and they don't want to be hectored out of it. They don't want to be accused of not having a container or a community, because they've reached that stage where this is who they are. This is honestly who they are and you have to say yes to that, it's all right to be outside and on your own.

Living with this pluriformity, this multiplicity, calls for enormous magnanimity. In the emergence, the evolving, of a new spirituality, a secular spirituality for our time, one of the key elements is going to be magnanimity, the ability to allow others to be different, and say 'Yes' to the way they are. I'm going to have to learn to accept the fact that in our culture young Muslim women may want to cover their hair with headscarves, because it expresses something important about their religious self-understanding. We're going to have to avoid the mistakes that France made, because it applied its secular paradigm maybe too stringently. Living in this kind of mix requires enormous magnanimity. Because a lot of the things that you'll be seeing around you may not be sympathetic to your point of view, and you may not understand in the slightest how anyone could get into that. But you're going to have to be more than glumly tolerant, you're going to have to learn to tolerate the fact that this is the way things now are in the human community, and it's glorious in its way.

I think the second thing we're going to have to learn is honesty towards ourselves. You're going to have to know your inner paradigm. I mean you're going to have to know—am I really a closet fundamentalist, is that really where I want to go, will I not be happy until I get in there? Go! It's all right. Everything is permitted as long as it doesn't make you a hater, as long as it doesn't make you cruel. If it helps you to go into that particular container—and many of them are beautiful containers—then go. And the same is true of the other paradigms, the other places we find ourselves: know where you are and say 'Yes' to it: it's OK.

The third thing I want to suggest—and I know that it's tough for you because therapists are the lightning rods for the kind of spiritual weather systems that swirl round the culture, and you have to process a lot of this stuff, sometimes physically as well as mentally—but I think that what you need to do also is to learn an ethic of love, though not the big supernatural kind of love. I'm going to read you a poem, because I want it to become the anthem for the therapy movement; it's by a sad old guy called A. S. J. Tessimond. I think what we need is love: The Beatles were right; Brian Thorne is right. We need the ability to be openly affectionate towards the other for no benefit towards the Self: what the New Testament calls *agape*, pure love, like a fountain giving out, not a sponge soaking up. Sometimes I know that in a therapy situation you are bathing your clients with that kind of love: because you're so willing them to get on, and get up, and get out, and get well, and get with it, and maybe even get angry. So love is the third element in this little handbook of spirituality. We need magnanimity, honesty and this kind of practical love. Let me end by reading you the poem by Tessimond I mentioned, 'This is not love perhaps' (Tessimond, 1985). When I read this it makes me think of your work, and the work of lots of clergy I know who do the same kind of listening, and trying to be present, and trying to hold the wounded, the broken, the shattered of the world whom no one else is regarding.

> This is not Love perhaps—Love that lays down
> Its life, that many waters cannot quench, nor the floods
> drown
> But something written in lighter ink, said in a lower tone:
> Something perhaps especially our own:
> A need at times to be together and talk—
> And then the finding we can walk
> More firmly through dark narrow places
> And meet more easily nightmare faces:
> A need to reach out sometimes hand to hand—
> And then find Earth less like an alien land:
> A need for alliance to defeat
> The whisperers at the corner of the street:
> A need for inns on roads, islands in seas, halts for discoveries
> to be shared,
> Maps checked and notes compared:
> A need at times of each for each
> Direct as the need of throat and tongue for speech.

That's you, brothers and sisters: I salute you.

REFERENCES

Amichai, Y (1996) Doubts and loves. In *Selected Poetry*. London: Faber & Faber.
Dillard, A (1999) *Holy the Firm*. London: HarperCollins.
Giddens, A (1994) *Beyond Left and Right*. Cambridge: Polity Press.
Kuhn, T (1962) *The Structure of Scientific Revolutions*. Chicago: Chicago University Press.
Küng, H (1992) *Judaism*. London: SCM.
Küng, H (1995) *Christianity: Its essence*. London: SCM.
Ruthven, M (2004) *Fundamentalism*. Oxford: Oxford University Press.
Tessimond, ASJ (1985) *The Collected Poems of ASJ Tessimond* with translations from Jacques Prévert, Hubert Nicholson (ed). Reading: Whiteknights Press.

Chapter 2

THE PROCESS OF TRANSFORMATION WITHIN BUDDHISM

Reverend Daishin Morgan

Therapy and religion seem to me to be part of one continuum, yet their aims may not be the same. The aim of Buddhism is enlightenment, and so it is necessary for me to offer some explanation of what that means before we can explore the process of transformation that is the heart of Buddhism. Enlightenment is coming to see things as they are without the overlays that result from experiencing the world from the perspective of a separate self. As human beings, we tend to distort reality by grasping after external things—whether that is money, fame or the love of another—often out of an underlying sense of incompleteness. We believe ourselves to be separate beings and experience loneliness and isolation. Then seeing ourselves as separate, we have to defend ourselves against the intrusions of others and so we justify anger. Enlightenment can be summarized as the release from our own greed, anger and delusion that can happen when we come to know our true nature. To know that we are not separate from the universe as a matter of direct experience takes away the impulse towards greed, anger and delusion.

Buddhism looks at human experience in terms of those things that lead to enlightenment and those that do not. Enlightenment is a very high ideal. When a person stops creating the causes of delusion, there emerges a deep sense of peace and, most importantly, a knowledge of one's connection with others that leads to compassion. As the individual is always going deeper in this process, even though they may appear to be enlightened to someone looking on, it is unlikely that they would see themselves as enlightened. They would no longer be thinking in terms of having a self to be enlightened. There is just a great sense of ease and openness about them that is somehow selfless.

In the Sōtō Zen tradition, we sometimes speak of the process of transformation as being in five stages. This process begins with a recognition of the need to train oneself. This arises from the realization that we are all subject to suffering. We experience isolation, fear and inner pain, and those we love pass away. It seems that suffering is inherent in existence and so we awaken the wish to do something about it. There is a recognition that while we cannot control the world, we can do something about our own way of being in the world. So the first step is to hear the call to train our minds.

The Zen tradition points to the fundamental nature of all beings and all existence, which we refer to as the Buddha nature. There is something more than suffering and it is found right here in the present moment. To know this fundamental existence, it is necessary to let go of adding anything or taking anything away, when we look into ourselves. All our ideas and opinions, all our views, all these things we have to let go of. But first of all, there is the call, the inner sense that there is something more; there has to be some kind of purpose, and so one is launched on the path.

The second step is taken when we really begin to answer the call by developing a commitment to following the path. The more clearly we see the inner causes of suffering and how unnecessary they are, the greater becomes the commitment to living in a manner that gradually eliminates them. When that commitment grows into a certainty that compassion and wisdom lie at the heart of our being and our lives centre around the commitment to realize the Buddha nature directly, then we come to the third stage in the process. This takes the form of an encounter or realization of one's true nature. It is a meeting in which one's self, as one believes oneself to be, falls away, and in that falling away one discovers what was there all along: the heart of compassion and wisdom. This encounter fundamentally changes one's whole approach to life. In Zen terminology, this experience is often referred to as a 'kenshō'. It can be a sudden realization or it can appear gradually over time. People will sometimes train in order to achieve this realization, yet by doing so they shoot themselves in the foot. To experience kenshō, one has to let go of grasping after anything, even kenshō itself. What is needed here is an utter willingness to let go, where the wish to answer the call is greater than anything else. If you're looking for some external validation, then it will not happen. So long as you believe there is something missing, you spend your life trying to fill a hole; however much you shovel in, the hole never gets filled. It needs another kind of approach, one that involves letting go of oneself. There is a paradox here: there is this great need to know the true self, yet to find it one must let go of the self. So coming to this third step is not easy. In my experience of working with people, and for myself too, this realization most often comes gradually.

It is here that people often stop and make a place for themselves based upon the fruits that come at this stage. But they have only reached step three: the fundamental causes of suffering have been reduced, not eliminated; if one does not keep going, one can get lost in them again. Even though it has been hard to get this far, the next step is, are you willing to let go of what you have found? Zen is not about substituting one position for another; it comes down to letting go of everything.

Step four is to go into a deep understanding of what we call emptiness. The idea of emptiness is easily misunderstood. It is realizing that you know nothing. Even though there is some understanding, there is no permanent person inside, nobody to know anything. It is the realization that everything changes and that we are intimately connected with everything. When we say things are empty, we mean that they are empty of intrinsic existence. That is to say nothing exists on its own, most especially that I don't exist on my own. I only have this form because everything else has the form that it has. We know that with our minds and we live it to some degree, but to really understand that the self is empty: this is something else and the people who go that far are rare.

After realizing the emptiness of things comes step five, sometimes called 'returning to the world'. To utterly let go of clinging to any idea of oneself and discover that all things are empty and pure, even that is not enough: if one stays there, what of compassion, what of love, what of the application of wisdom? Buddhism suggests that real compassion is inseparable from wisdom. We can only really know what helps when we have experienced the fundamental nature for ourselves. Before that we are trying to do good, but our motivation may still be entangled with our own desires. We are still within the heart of compassion and wisdom, but we do not recognize it clearly and so find ourselves scratching at the edge all the time. To really let go of one's self is a tall order. Having done so, it's not enough just to let go: there is then the ongoing discovery of what it means to live from this place and embrace the world. This is the work of a Bodhisattva, a being who devotes their life entirely to the welfare of others.

Although these five stages can seem like huge steps, the process is more like going round a spiral where each step contains something of all the other steps. So there is some understanding of emptiness as soon as we seriously begin to look within. However, to arrive at a deep understanding takes a great deal of time and training and there are no short cuts.

I would now like to focus more on the 'how'. What does it mean to answer the call? The process begins for most people by learning how to meditate. In the Zen tradition, meditation is called 'zazen'—a term that literally means 'sitting meditation'. Although traditionally done in a cross-legged position, today many people sit on a chair or meditation bench.

Eihei Dōgen was a monk who brought Sōtō Zen to Japan in the thirteenth century. He wrote a famous text on how to meditate called the *Fukanzazengi,* which contains a very pithy statement of what meditation is. My teacher, Reverend Master Jiyu-Kennett, translated it as 'neither trying to think, nor trying not to think, just sitting with no deliberate thought is the important aspect of zazen'. Neither trying to think, nor trying not to think is the essential element which I'll try to describe.

When you sit down and meditate and become aware of your mind, you find that thoughts, feelings, ideas, worries, memories all tend to run on in a continuous stream. Meditation consists of being aware of the stream and learning how to refrain from feeding it or getting caught up in it. It is helpful to distinguish between what we might call deliberate thought and natural thought. Natural thought is the arising of memory or a spontaneous idea or reflection. Deliberate thought occurs when we apply volition to the process of thinking. It often feels like we are at the mercy of our own thoughts, that we sit down and, whoosh, we're away. However, we can take control of our deliberate thinking. Whether we take that control or not is up to us. At any time a memory can arise; how I respond to that memory depends upon my own volition. The arising of the memory is natural thought, the response to it is deliberate thought. Emotions work in a similar way. For most people, anger can arise just like that. Somebody treads on your toe and before you realize what has happened, you are caught up in it. The more you meditate, if you're doing it properly, the more you learn to see the gap between a stimulus and your response. There is a moment of choice and that option gradually becomes clearer. That is, of course, if you *want* to give up your anger. Or would you rather say, 'Well, damn it, they should have been more careful!' That is awfully seductive. Commitment is very important here and if we're really committed, then it is possible to eventually let go of anger entirely. It takes some doing.

Greed, anger and delusion have to be converted, yet I take the view that this process is hindered if we see ourselves as a septic tank containing loads of gunk that has got to be emptied. There is gunk, but only when it arises. I need to choose to let it go, but there is no reserve pile of gunk inside me. This is one of the meanings of emptiness—that gunk appears yet has no self-nature. We are not stained, but the choices we make are critical. Do I choose the direction of enlightenment or that of continuing the anger? This choice has nothing whatever to do with how justified I think my anger is. Anger is regarded in Buddhism as an afflicted state. That is, a state that tends to take you away from enlightenment, rather than a state that helps you achieve it. This goes for everything from mild irritation to murderous rage. Anger, greed and delusion all begin with deliberate thought, or the application of volition within the mind. When I am sitting there fuming about someone treading on my toe, I am applying volition and continuing a state of anger. It is a kind of fantasy that I create in which I am an injured party persecuted by a cruel world.

Meditation requires a willingness to let go of fantasies. Some fantasies may seem harmless or even beneficial in certain circumstances. But from a point of view of trying to pursue this process of enlightenment, fantasy is a rather destructive thing, as one is applying volition to that which is not true and making an unreal inner world for oneself, rather than living with what is here and now. Everyone who tries to meditate finds that their mind wanders into fantasy—perhaps imagining what they are going to do when on holiday. A pleasant dream, but time enough for that when you're on holiday. It doesn't mean you can never plan; if now is the time to plan, then plan. Such is the right use of the mind from the point of view of zazen. When we just chunter on to ourselves rehashing old hurts or speculating about the future, we create a world of delusion in which we become trapped.

You gave me a warm welcome this evening and that was very helpful. Your welcome, to a degree, changed my mind. Had you all started throwing things at me, that would have changed my mind in another way. So my mind is conditioned by circumstances. One might say that conditions *are* the mind; the mind is conditions. Depending on what volition we apply to the mind, we alter the conditions of our life. We all know those who see everything as a problem—their life is a certain way. Those who tend to take an optimistic view of life—their life is another way. The volition to change that orientation may be quite deeply buried and actualizing it is no easy matter, but ultimately we can choose the way our minds behave. To believe otherwise is to believe we are less than human.

When sitting in meditation seeing all these thoughts, fantasies and feelings arising, if we add volition to them we generate a person, a 'me'. The aim in meditation is not to add anything to the naturally arising thoughts and feelings so that there is no extra layer of 'me'. It is to just sit and allow the mind to be as it is. When this happens, the mind remains very aware and also very still. This is neither trying to think nor trying not to think, just sitting.

To sit up straight with body and mind together as one is to recognize the presence of the Buddha within and around you, the Buddha nature. Even when mistakes are made, sit up straight in the presence of the Buddha. It is necessary to trust that one's true nature is Buddha nature. When you let go of constantly generating a me, then there is no obstruction to the compassion, love and wisdom that are the characteristics of our true nature. To allow these virtues to manifest, we have to entrust our fearful selves to the meditation. In practice this means being willing to meditate without carrying on a running commentary, without trying to be in control of what's going on all the time. It doesn't matter how profound and wonderful one's thoughts may be, nor how great a vision may arise; it is simply another movement of the mind. The thought may have a message for you, but you still need to let it come and let it go. You don't need to grasp hold of it. If it has a message for you, that will stay of itself for as long as it is needed. You entrust yourself to the process and then, within the stillness, there is insight.

When I was young, I grew to six feet three-and-a-half inches fairly quickly. Our family moved to a cottage in Sussex, one of those old cottages built at a time when people must have been a lot shorter. My father was also fairly tall and his strategy of dealing with banging his head, which we both did regularly, was to turn around and thump the door lintel and swear. I thought this was pretty good so I started thumping the door lintel and swearing too. As I learned to meditate, I realized that when you bang your head, as you are reeling back there's a second when you can choose to let the anger pass by. It doesn't really matter. The lintel didn't mean it and even if the lintel did mean it, what difference would that make? So, if somebody comes along and wallops you, you experience the effects, but you don't have to add anything to it. Anger is an affliction that we need like a hole in the head. The situation may call for some action and we will discern what that may be far better without the fantasies of anger.

When someone becomes a monk (we use the term for both men and women), they sit next to the person who entered the monastery before them, and the one who enters after them sits on the other side, so you don't have any choice about who you sit next to or who you sit opposite. When I became a monk, the person who sat opposite me had some dire table manners. I found the way she ate porridge revolting and one morning I saw myself hating this person. Things can get pretty wound up in a monastery. You live a very intense existence in quite a confined space. Each monk has a space in the meditation hall six feet by three feet with a cupboard at the end where you keep your bedding and possessions. You meditate and sleep in that space and sometimes you eat there as well. At night the hall is divided by a big curtain with women sleeping on one side and men on the other. This lack of privacy can be tough. Monks usually live in this way for a good few years at the beginning of their training and learn how little they actually need. And it has its moments—this porridge-eating monk was mine; there I was hating her. I had been doing a bit of meditation and it really hit me what it is to hate. This was a turning point. I didn't want to hate ever again. I wish I could say I was unable to hate anymore, but that takes longer. Gradually, as we go on meditating, these kinds of connections happen. You can't teach it, you can only point out the direction. If someone truly does the meditation, then the wish to eliminate greed, anger and delusion gets stronger by developing insight into what they truly are. In Buddhism, we have the precepts: cease from evil, do only good, do good for others. It is said that the precept cease from evil is the source of all the teaching of the Buddha.

In the Zen tradition, we don't focus much on developing the positive, because we have a deep faith in the presence of the positive as fundamental. The Buddha nature *is* compassion, love and wisdom. That is the heart of our being. So cease from evil is basically get yourself out of the way. If you get out of the way, it's all there. I find it a little toe-curling when people try to generate the positive virtues. It feels like a façade. We do need to have a deep faith in the presence underneath and to express that faith through our efforts to keep the precepts. In the end, the precepts and Buddhahood, or enlightenment, are one and the same thing. It's necessary to act like a Buddha, in order to understand what a Buddha is. If we keep acting in ways that are contrary to Buddha nature, we can't expect to understand it.

Through meditation and the precepts, we have a basis for understanding who we are, or perhaps for beginning to really ask the question. To look at oneself is to realize that nothing is fixed. I'm British, I grew up in a fairly happy, middle-class family. I have all the benefits of that and yet what does that count for in the end? What am I? There's a subjective paradox that I encounter when I seek to know who I am. To look at myself, I have to split into the observer and that which is observed. This cannot work as I am not two people. Knowing oneself has to come in a different way. I have to let go of wanting to know who I am. This does not mean giving up. It means realizing that it has to be the universe knowing itself through this body and mind, rather than me gaining something. Enlightenment can be realized, but it comes only when we let go of our previous ways of knowing and being. Such letting go expresses real faith.

One of the things I have to be willing to do is to let go of being a monk. When I was about to come back to England from America in the early 80s to take on the job of abbot, I knew I had not yet fully dealt with ambition. I went to my teacher and said I should not take on the job. Her response was, 'Well, in that case, you will be defeated by ambition'. We can be defeated by not doing that which is good to do and we can be defeated by indulging in what we want. We must have the courage to go ahead and keep letting go of the ambition, or whatever the problem may be. To let go is to be willing to enter death right now. What would hold me back? Right now it is not time, nor will it be until the very last moment. So now is the time to live and that is to do the work that comes. Part of doing that work is to let each thing go as it arises in the deep faith that all will continue to arise as long as it is good. When life comes to an end, then the next thing is death, the unknown, and there is a going on even then, adding nothing and taking nothing away. You can be a much better therapist or a much better monk when you are willing to let go. If you are willing to die right now, then the ambition stuff doesn't grab you, because in the context of life and death it is sad to hold on to such things. These days I don't assume ambition has gone, nor do I assume it hasn't; if it arises, I know what choice I wish to make.

After a while you start to forget about enlightenment and so it becomes possible to move through this subjective paradox. What really matters is to do that which needs to be done and that doesn't have much to do with what I want. Ultimately, what I want is that which is good to do. If I go for some imagined desire, I know where that leads and I don't want to go there. To ask what is good to do simplifies one's choices and the old conflicts dissolve.

What is good? Well, that which is in tune with Buddha nature. One has to trust one's intuitive sense of that which is good. This trust is expressed in Buddhism as taking the Three Refuges—that is taking refuge in the Buddha, the Dharma, and the Sangha. Refuge in the Buddha is finding the Buddha within oneself and all beings; refuge in the Dharma is seeking help from the teaching, which is everything that leads towards enlightenment; refuge in the Sangha means seeking help from others who have more experience in this process. It is necessary to check one's understanding with others in order to put it into perspective. If you don't have enough knowledge of the Dharma, you can be at step three and imagine you are at step five and get very stuck.

The process of transformation in Buddhism requires one to take refuge in the present moment, which means accepting whatever conditions constitute this moment. It is, of course, important to cultivate whatever supportive conditions we can, both externally and internally, but to depend upon externals is a mistake. For example, when I read Carl Rogers' descriptions of empathy and unconditional positive regard, something in me craves that. To be touched by the transcendent, to be held in unconditional love are things probably everyone yearns for. However, when we seek these things out of a sense of inadequacy or dissatisfaction, we create a problem. We end up wanting Carl Rogers in our pocket ready to give us a fix of unconditional positive regard whenever external circumstances are not to our liking. To desire enlightenment in this kind of way leads to the same problem.

As a conclusion, I would like to affirm that there is such a thing as liberation from greed, anger and delusion. The path towards it seems to involve a daunting level of renunciation, until you actually begin to let go. Then it dawns on you that you are given everything you need. There comes a gratitude for life and a deep engagement with it as long as it lasts, with no worries about its end. This is to know that this moment is all there is and that it is enough, which leads to a deep sense of inner peace and stability. One is no longer charging about the place trying to fill holes. The gratitude that comes is the song of the heart and the rising up of compassion, the life of Buddha nature. When you know Buddha nature, you know a luminous brightness even within grief and pain. One can know this luminous brightness in one's life even though the process of training is not yet over.

I will stop here and ask for questions and other contributions.

Q: What is the Buddhist outlook on sexuality?

A: I'm a celibate monk, which is not a popular style of life these days. I think it comes down to what are we going to do with desire? In the beginning of the process of training, we are in a different place with regard to sexuality than we are at the end. Our sexuality needs to be considered along with every other part of our lives. The starting point is to do no harm. In other words, take the greatest care, be considerate, make your sexuality an expression of compassion, love and wisdom, rather than greed and desire. Leaving aside some of the commentaries, the Buddha himself doesn't get into defining which sexual practices are OK and which are not. For example, homosexuality is not really an issue. The Buddha's concern is to help us understand how we can get lost in our sexuality, if we insist upon it or are ruled by it. In Buddhism, nothing comes above seeking the Buddha nature. If you say that sexuality is more important, then you will remain the slave of desire. Our following of the way must, in the end, be unconditional. I am not saying that at some stage everyone has to become celibate; rather if there is anything we are unwilling to let go of, then it will eventually become an obstacle.

Q: Could I expand on the question about sexuality: is it possible to see Buddha nature within sexuality?

A: Yes.

Q: And to practice sexuality with that mindfulness?

A: Yes, by respecting the Buddha nature in one's partner and oneself.

Q: How do Buddhists regard creativity? By creativity I mean the need within oneself to create, not just art and music but the things we use as well—houses, plates, knives and forks, whatever they may be?

A: Whatever we do should be done with all the creativity we have. We need to be fully committed to our actions, so when making things, decorating our houses and living our lives, creativity naturally plays a part. If we get very self-conscious about being creative, or set up the ideal of creativity, it can be an obstacle. One of the things we try to do at the monastery is to create a wonderful space. The art work we produce is part of that, but the real thing is our commitment to training. Without that, the rest is surface dressing. I enjoy doing some sculpting and usually have some kind of project on the go and I have to keep it within certain bounds. For me I suppose the real creativity is in finding ways to answer the calls that arise. There are those for whom art is more than a hobby, and for them it becomes a way in itself. If you feel you have to follow that way, then do it with great devotion. At the same time, I think it is a mistake to identify artistic endeavour with spirituality. There is nothing more intrinsically spiritual about painting, sculpting, creative writing or even meditating than doing the washing up. True creativity is to do that which needs to be done, and to discern what that may be one has to cultivate a truly open heart and mind.

Q: How do the concepts of original sin and guilt relate in your form of Buddhism?

A: They don't. We do have the idea of karmic consequence, which is that you are responsible for what you do. Earlier on I was talking about volition and the effect it has on the mind. When we act with volition, we condition the nature of our mind. If I steal, I condition myself to have the mind of a thief. So there is a very direct cause and effect relationship between my volition and the world that I experience. Buddhism is quite unequivocal: you cannot avoid responsibility for what you do and nobody can take that responsibility away. That makes what you do very significant. If I act in a way that causes harm to myself or to others and then I realize what I am doing and begin to change, then that sets in train another positive force of karma that can counterbalance the negative.

One of the signs of someone who is taking training seriously is that they do not complain about the consequences of their actions. There is a very deep teaching in being content. This is different from being complacent: you commit yourself utterly to the work that comes to you and you are responsible for the decision you make about where to draw the line between what is your work and what is not.

CHAPTER 3

THE GIFT AND COST OF BEING FULLY PRESENT

BRIAN THORNE

Peter Senge is an American organizational change guru who wrote a highly influential book entitled *The Fifth Discipline* in which he explores those moments when individuals and organizations tap into deeper capacities for creative transformation. In a more recent book, co-authored with three colleagues and significantly entitled *Presence: Human purpose and the field of the future*, Senge is quoted in the radical magazine *What is Enlightenment?* as he reflects with his co-authors on the dinosaurs:

> Isn't it ironic the way people talk about dinosaurs? Today we say an organization is 'just like a dinosaur' when we mean it's slow and can't adjust to change. But, you know, the dinosaurs did manage to survive over a hundred times longer than humans have so far. Whatever beings might take our place here in the future will probably say, 'Just like the human beings—too bad they didn't have the adaptive capabilities of dinosaurs!' (Senge et al., 2004: 32)

This comment sends a shudder of horror down the spine of one of his listeners, Betty Sue Flowers, a specialist in myth. She replies with a statement which I should like you to consider as a backdrop to all I shall attempt to explore in this opening keynote address at what I believe to be a conference of some significance not only for the lives and work of those of us assembled here but on the much broader canvas of the spiritual, psychological and political challenges facing our planet. Betty Sue, then, in horrified reaction to Peter Senge's dinosaur reflections says:

> Hearing human beings talked about in the past tense like that is terribly chilling. I guess we all know that since we have the means to destroy ourselves, it's possible that we will. The unthinkable is possible, but it's still very difficult to consider. The poet Auden said, 'We must love one another or die'. No one thinks we're very close to loving one another just yet, but we also don't seem willing to consider the consequences of not doing so. (Senge et al., 2004: 32)

The words of W. H. Auden have haunted me ever since I came across them in this dialogue between Peter Senge and Betty Sue Flowers and they are with me now as I embark on this lecture: *we must love one another or die.*

It was over twenty years ago that in this same lecture block I gave a public lecture which has turned out to be, I believe, one of the most influential contributions I have made to the world of counselling and psychotherapy. What I did not realize at the time was that the lecture was in large measure a kind of statement of belief and a plan of action for my own life. My personal and professional existence were somehow fused in that lecture and I have had to live with the outcome ever since. Put like that it sounds a heavy burden and one which I would sooner be without. That is certainly not true: I have come rather to think of my lecture—whatever else it might be—as a costly gift which I made to myself and, in almost equal measure, I have been continually aware ever since I delivered it of its preciousness and of its cost to me both in terms of the meaning it has given to my existence and of the demands to which it has subjected me.

In retrospect, I have come to realize that the form of therapy which I practise, person-centred therapy, and my relationship with its originator, Carl Rogers, are central to my personal odyssey. Indeed at precisely the same period that I was struggling with the experiences and ideas which eventually found shape in my lecture of twenty years ago, Carl Rogers, too, was grappling with the implications of his recent experience which was taking him into an area which was new and, for him, both exciting and unnerving. In his last book, *A Way of Being* (1980), he is fascinated by both experience and research which suggests that human beings are moving toward the more complete development of awareness. 'It is at this level', he says 'that new forms are invented, perhaps even new directions for the human species' (Rogers, 1980: 129). As he warms to his theme, Rogers describes the person who is moving towards ever greater awareness and thus becomes potentially conscious not only of his or her external world with all its stimuli but of thoughts and dreams and of the flow of feelings, emotions and physiological reactions that he or she senses from within. What is more, such a person is free to live a feeling subjectively as well as be aware of it. In a key sentence Rogers concludes:

> The crucial point is that when a person is functioning fully, there are no barriers, no inhibitions, which prevent the full experiencing of whatever is organismically present. This person is moving in the direction of wholeness, integration, a unified life. (Rogers, 1980: 128)

Empirical scientist as he was to the end of his life, Rogers was at pains to seek support for his emerging ideas from research studies and, above all, from his own experience. Of the former he was able to conclude:

> They picture the individual self as being dissolved in a whole area of higher values, especially beauty, harmony and love. The person feels at one with the cosmos. Hard-headed research seems to be confirming the mystic's experience of union with the universal. (Rogers, 1980: 128)

Of his experience both with individuals and in intensive groups, he writes even more compellingly:

> When I am at my best, as a group facilitator or as a therapist, I discover another characteristic. I find that when I am closest to my inner, intuitive self, when I am somehow in touch with the unknown in me, when perhaps I am in a slightly altered state of consciousness, then whatever I do seems to be full of healing. Then, simply my *presence* is releasing and helpful to the other. There is nothing I can do to force this experience, but when I can relax and be close to the transcendental core of me, then I may behave in strange and impulsive ways in the relationship, ways which I cannot justify rationally, which have nothing to do with my thought processes. But these strange behaviors turn out to be *right,* in some odd way: It seems that my inner spirit has reached out and touched the inner spirit of the other. Our relationship transcends itself and becomes a part of something larger. Profound growth and healing and energy are present. (Rogers, 1980: 129, original emphasis)

This, then, was the man whose work has had such a profound impact on my own life and whom I met for the first time in 1978 at an extraordinary eleven-day cross-cultural event in Spain. For me that was a privileged time in many ways but not least because it afforded me the opportunity to spend many hours with Rogers, often in private intimate discussion, as we struggled together to make sense of experiences which seemed to defy most psychological explanations. Rogers certainly found my Christian commitment difficult to stomach but this was readily explicable against the background of his own experience as a child and adolescent of a well-nigh fundamentalist brand of Christianity which had been deeply guilt-inducing and had left him psychologically crippled until well into middle age. I was deeply moved when on Easter Sunday he actually attended an eccentric Eucharist conducted by a Presbyterian minister and a Jesuit priest assisted by Jewish and humanist readers. In a taxi together on Easter Sunday afternoon on our way to The Prado, he told me that it was the first Eucharist he had attended for fifty years and he said it in such a way that I knew he was glad to have been there.

So much, then, for an introductory context for what I wish to present this evening and now to the previous lecture to which I have somewhat hermetically alluded thus far. It was on March 18th, 1983 that I delivered 'The Quality of Tenderness' here at the University having first given it a trial run at the Norwich Centre the previous December. I must confess that there was a point in the run-up to this conference when I considered simply repeating the lecture in its entirety this evening for it is, after all, in many ways a discourse precisely on what it means to be fully present in the world. To do so, I concluded, would nonetheless be a cop-out and in any case it would only deal with half of my current title. Instead, I have decided to use key extracts from the 1983 lecture as my point of departure. I shall present to you what I suppose could be termed my manifesto of twenty years ago and then explore with you the agony and the ecstasy of my inadequate attempts to live it out.

After a lengthy opening section in which I reflect on the many meanings of the word 'tender', I arrive at the point when I attempt to describe what it means for a person to possess the quality of tenderness in all its fullness. I recall even now the immense struggle I had at the time to find the words to give expression to so elusive a state of being. Here, then, is what finally emerged:

> What does it mean for a person to possess the quality of tenderness in all its fullness? In the first place it is a quality which irradiates the total person—it is evident in voice, the eyes, the hands, the thoughts, the feelings, the beliefs, the moral stance, the attitude to things animate and inanimate, seen and unseen. Secondly, it communicates through its responsive vulnerability that suffering and healing are interwoven. Thirdly, it demonstrates a preparedness and an ability to move between the worlds of the physical, the emotional, the cognitive and the mystical without strain. Fourthly, it is without shame because it is experienced as the joyful embracing of the desire to love and is therefore a law unto itself. Fifthly, it is a quality which transcends the male and female but is nevertheless nourished by the attraction of the one for the other in the quest for wholeness.
>
> It will be evident that so breathtaking a quality is rare. What is more no one person can hope to embody it more than fleetingly and intermittently, for to be irradiated by it is to achieve a level of humanness which belongs to the future and not to now. It is precisely for that reason, however, that those of us who have chosen to dedicate our lives to counselling and to the education of the person have the awesome responsibility of developing this quality in ourselves and others now. If we can do this in our generation then we can have hope that there will indeed be a future and that it will be a time in which something qualitatively different can happen between human beings. (Thorne, 1985: 7–8)

A little later I go further and put myself on the line as I describe the nature of the fleeting moments when I believe that this quality of tenderness is present in my own interactions as a therapist. It is perhaps this passage which is the most frequently cited in the literature and which has provoked the most comment and controversy. I am aware as I speak that, even today, I feel anxious as I present it but here goes:

> Inwardly I feel a sense of heightened awareness and this can happen even if I am near exhaustion at the end of a gruelling day. I feel in touch with myself to the extent that it is not an effort to think or to know what I am feeling. It is as if energy is flowing through me and I am simply allowing it free passage. I feel a physical vibrancy and this often has a sexual component and a stirring in the genitals. I feel powerful and yet at the same time almost irrelevant. My client seems more accurately in focus: he or she stands out in sharp relief from the surrounding décor. When he or she speaks, the words belong uniquely to him or her. Physical movements are a further confirmation of uniqueness. It seems as if for a space, however brief, two human beings are fully alive because they have given themselves and each other permission to risk being

> fully alive. At such a moment I have no hesitation in saying that my client and I are caught up in a stream of love. Within this stream there comes an effortless or intuitive understanding and what is astonishing is how complex this understanding can be. It sometimes seems that I receive my client whole and thereafter possess a knowledge of him or her which does not depend on biographical data. This understanding is intensely personal and invariably it affects the self-perception of the client and can lead to marked changes in attitude and behaviour.
>
> For me as a counsellor it is accompanied by a sense of joy which when I have checked it out has always been shared by the client. The difficulty lies in trusting such experiences for there seems to be in all of us a *deep and almost pathological distrust* of something which brings such joy and such clarity. It is as if *joy and knowledge are forbidden fruits* and the experience of them must therefore be evidence of dubious motives and unhealthy desires or of insanity. Or to put the matter into slightly different terminology, 'If I am full of understanding and of the joy of desiring then it can only be that I have fallen into the hands of a demonic or perverse power.' If, however, both the client and I are able to trust the moment, that is to trust the working of tenderness, then a number of things can happen and I have come to recognise a whole range of possibilities. Tears, for example, may flow without warning and without apparent cause or there may be a sudden release of laughter. There may be an overwhelming desire for physical contact which can result in holding hands or in a close embrace. There may be an urgent need to talk about death or God or the soul. There may be a desire to walk around or lie down ... Always there is a sense of well-being, of it being good to be alive and this in spite of the fact that problems or difficulties which confront the client remain apparently unchanged and as intractable as ever. Life is good and life is impossible, long live life. (Thorne, 1985: 9–10)

If you recall the earlier passage in which Rogers spoke so eloquently of the quality of presence in a relationship I do not believe it at all fanciful to conclude that my wrestling with the concept of tenderness is an attempt to do battle with the same phenomena. The two descriptions are strikingly parallel in a number of significant respects. In the first place they speak of a high level of consciousness in the therapist, of a 'heightened awareness' or 'a slightly altered state of consciousness', of 'being in touch with the unknown'. Secondly, there is a sense of the therapist being responsive to the intuitive rather than the powerful rational part of his being and as a result being endowed with new and often complex understanding. Thirdly, there is a powerful experience of relating at a new and deeper level: Rogers speaks of 'inner spirit' reaching out to 'inner spirit' while I speak of two persons giving themselves and each other permission 'to risk being fully alive'. Fourthly, there is the experience of the transcendent, that is to say, of two people being linked into something greater than themselves: Rogers states explicitly 'Our relationship transcends itself and becomes a part of something larger', while I speak of being 'caught up in a stream of love'. Fifthly, in this transcendent state there is an overpowering sense of energy, well-being and healing.

A little later in the same chapter from *A Way of Being*, as he reflects on the experience he has attempted to describe, Carl Rogers wrote:

> I realize that this account partakes of the mystical. Our experiences, it is clear, involve the transcendent, the indescribable, the spiritual. I am compelled to believe that I, like many others, have underestimated the importance of this mystical, spiritual dimension. (Rogers, 1980: 130)

For me, of course, the certainty of being hoist with my own petard was sealed when I authoritatively proclaimed—speaking of the quality of tenderness:

> Those of us who have chosen to dedicate our lives to counselling and to the education of the person have the awesome responsibility of developing this quality in ourselves and others now. If we can do this in our generation then we can have hope that there will indeed be a future. (Thorne, 1985: 8)

With those words I threw down a gauntlet principally to myself and I had done it in public, a public which has grown in numbers over the years as the original lecture has been published, re-published and translated. I had, if you like, put my own life under the spotlight and landed myself with an awesome agenda. And yet to duck the self-imposed challenge would be to render all my fine words, and those of Carl Rogers, too, so much hot air, an idealistic fantasy bearing little or no relation to the conduct of therapy let alone to the living of a human life in an increasingly desperate age.

For Rogers, his ability to be fully present was a gift to others which could have immense healing potential; for me the ability to embody the quality of tenderness similarly constituted a gift which could transform the other's experience of his or her reality. The impact of the gift, then, is potentially enormous and its offering the trigger for untold blessings. But this says nothing of the cost to the giver and neither Rogers nor I in our respective treatises pay much attention to this darker aspect of the whole mysterious process. We record the ecstasy but have little to say about the agony. I wish now in the second part of my lecture to redress that balance.

Before embarking on my own experience let me say a word or two about Carl Rogers. These are, of necessity, somewhat sketchy reflections but they are based on some personal knowledge of Rogers' last years as well as on what I have observed since his death. It is my belief that Rogers paid quite a heavy price for having written *A Way of Being* and more particularly for having attempted to articulate his experience of the quality of presence in human interactions. For many of his erstwhile colleagues, what they perceived as his flight into mysticism and the spiritual terrain was altogether misguided. They were embarrassed by it and feared that it would undermine completely both Rogers' and their own credibility as empirical scientists and clinicians worthy of respect in the world of the psychological therapies. They accused him of grandiosity, of trying to save the world and—a somewhat malicious innuendo—of having fallen victim to the wiles of women. It is true that in the final decade or so of his life Rogers' closest colleagues were mainly women including his own daughter, Natalie, and that he was much influenced by the more expressive, intuitive and embodied apprehension of experience which is perhaps more characteristic of the female psyche. It is also true that after the death of his wife Helen in 1979, Rogers became much freer in his personal response to women and in his closing years enjoyed several intimate relationships which gave him profound satisfaction. The point I am making, however, is that both personally and professionally Rogers paid a heavy cost for these late developments. He was criticized and attacked by members of his own profession for having gone off the rails and betrayed the cause of empirical science and there were those who were also prepared to accuse him of encouraging a loose morality which threatened conventional wisdom and constituted a danger to traditional society. While he was winning accolades in other quarters for his work in intensive groups, both small and large, and for his determined commitment to the world peace movement, there were many who were only too ready to snipe, to undermine and to accuse him of naïveté, false idealism and worse. And this hurt Rogers—sometimes deeply—and the more so when it resulted in both *A Way of Being* and his previous book *On Personal Power* (1977) receiving scant attention in the professional journals. Indeed *On Personal Power* was never reviewed at all in the United States and had to wait for a British edition before it received any attention from clinicians and educators. For me, one of the saddest outcomes of this rocky professional ride was the publication of a posthumous essay on person-centred therapy by Rogers and Sanford (1989) which contained no reference to the later discoveries so enthusiastically described in *A Way of Being*. Whether this was the result of a heavy editorial hand or of Rogers himself having grown weary of presenting such controversial material, I do not know. Either way it is a gloomy reflection on the apparent unwillingness of professional psychology and psychotherapy to engage with what Rogers had prophetically referred to in 1980 as 'the cutting edge of our ability to transcend ourselves, to create new and more spiritual directions in human evolution' (Rogers, 1980: 134). The situation since his death has scarcely improved and those in the person-centred international community who take Rogers' late work with the seriousness which I believe it deserves often find themselves in a somewhat embattled minority and regarded as something of a nuisance in the competitive world of the therapeutic orientations where person-centred therapy strives to make itself acceptable in the market place.

In exploring the cost which I myself have paid for my own commitment to what I will for the moment call 'the path of tenderness' I will only briefly allude to the public arena. My main concern is to explore with you the strains and stresses which it has engendered in my personal life and within the deeper recesses of my inner world. But just a word about the public domain.

I am somewhat unusual in that over the years I have made contributions to both the literature of counselling and psychotherapy and that of pastoral theology. As a result I have not infrequently found myself under attack from both camps. Curiously enough, although these attacks are couched in different language as one might expect for different disciplines, they tend to focus on the same issues. In brief I am taken to task—as was Rogers—for having far too optimistic a view of human nature, for underrating the dark forces or the shadow side, or, in Christian terms, the power of evil and the reality of the Fall. The outcome of my bad psychology or bad theology is that I advocate ways of relating which are far too risky and in any case make demands on priests and therapists alike which are unrealistic and are likely to lead to an early grave. More recently I have made sorties into the theology of the Eastern Orthodox Church and have attempted to explicate the doctrine of *theosis* or divinization in which I find a view of human nature which takes as its basic assumption that we have within us the seeds of our divinity. Such a theology is for me entirely in harmony with the insights of our local fourteenth century mystic, Julian of Norwich, and in both my psychological and theological writings I have attempted to draw out the implications of conceptualizing men and women as beings capable of the divine activity of loving and being loved. What is more, I have concluded that there is little else under heaven or earth worth doing. Auden, you will remember, put the whole matter into a much more dramatic and urgent context when he stated 'We must love one another or die'.

The riskiness—perhaps foolhardiness—of promulgating such views is perhaps best illustrated by noting the kind of things which are said by reviewers of my books. The latest volume, *Infinitely Beloved* (2003), which attempts to move across the boundaries of psychology and theology, received the lead review in the *Church Times* last autumn. The review was highly critical and suggested, *inter alia*, that I had confused love of God with adherence to a psychological theory, that my real saviour was Carl Rogers and not Jesus Christ.

In all fairness to the reviewer he has since described himself in a letter to me as a 'chastened man' and has made a generous gesture of reconciliation towards me but the comments were painful at the time and seemed unwarranted by the actual text. A previous book, *The Mystical Power of Person-Centred Therapy* (2002) was recently reviewed in the *British Journal of Guidance and Counselling* (Vol. 32 No. 2, 2004, pp. 249–50). In what is basically a laudatory and sympathetic review there appears the following cautionary comment:

> Even within the family of person-centred counselling there are many who would deny any spiritual content. Outside the fold, in the mainstream body of helping approaches, any suggestion of mysticism is met with reactions from deep scepticism and scorn to the accusation of naiveté. Hippie-dom and the New Age beckon. (*British Journal of Guidance and Counselling*, 2004)

The concluding sentence is perhaps even more revealing: 'This is a humane and beautiful book which makes the heart sing, even though at the same time the head is whispering caveats.' It is difficult to avoid the thought that the reviewer might really be thinking: 'Watch it when the heart sings in the presence of something which is humane and beautiful. It probably means that the thinking is awry and it's all too good to be true.'

The accusation of being 'too good to be true' has not only been thrown at my writings but has been directed at me personally. And here lies the core of the inner torment by which I am so often afflicted. Let me attempt a kind of explication *de texte* of the passage which I quoted earlier from *The Quality of Tenderness*:

> I feel in touch with myself to the extent that it is not an effort to think or to know what I am feeling. It is as if energy is flowing through me and I am simply allowing it free passage. I feel a physical vibrancy and this often has a sexual component and a stirring in the genitals. I feel powerful and yet at the same time almost irrelevant. (Thorne, 1985: 9)

Immediately, you see, the doubts come pouring in. What claims are these? I am describing myself as a channel of energy or is it of grace? I am also claiming a level of self-awareness which is exceptional. And then, to crown it all, I talk about physicality and sexuality. I am embarrassed and within my own head I hear the accusation of arrogance and even of perversity. How can I hold my head up and confidently affirm that I am reporting lived experience when in that same head there are whispers of self-delusion or even of madness? And I have gone public—I have nailed my colours to the mast and must now endure not only the scepticism and criticism from without but also the conflicting voices from within. Later on in the same passage I make what can seem even more extraordinary or outrageous statements. In the environment of tenderness—or put it another way, when I am able to be fully present to the other—I identify a whole range of possible outcomes:

> Tears, for example, may flow without warning and without apparent cause or there may be a sudden release of laughter. There may be an overwhelming desire for physical contact which can result in holding hands or in a close embrace. There may be an urgent need to talk of death or God or the soul. There may be a desire to walk around or lie down ...
>
> Always there is a sense of well-being, of it being good to be alive and this in spite of the fact that problems or difficulties which confront the client remain apparently unchanged and as intractable as ever. Life is good and life is impossible, long live life. (Thorne, 1985: 10)

Earlier I had summed it all up in the sentence: 'It seems as if for a space, however brief, two human beings are fully alive because they have given themselves and each other permission to be fully alive.'

What is immediately evident is that this quality of tenderness, this ability to be fully present, can lead to startling results. In 1983 it felt risky enough to describe them but twenty years later it seems even more frightening. I would suggest that in the intervening years our culture in Britain has become much more cynical, cautious and distrustful. Risk assessment, accountability, and, above all, the threat of litigation permeate the very fibre of our communal life. What is more the rapid advance of technology has made for greater impersonality and arm's-length dealings. The mobile phone, symbol par excellence of the technological revolution, has at one and the same time put us all much more in contact with each other and fostered a climate where those who are absent can seem more worthy of attention than those who are physically present. How often are conversations in the flesh interrupted or dramatic or musical performances contaminated by the rings of a mobile phone? I have even been in a church when the moment of consecration was punctuated by the inane melody of a phone's intrusion.

In brief, to be fully present person-to-person in the moment and in the flesh seems now almost counter-cultural and the outcomes of such encounters, when they do occur, are more readily susceptible to misunderstanding and condemnation. There are times, indeed, when the potential cost of risking such intimate involvement seems far too high. And yet, in 1983 I claimed that to embody such tenderness and thus to be fully present can lead to moments of transcendence which are life-transforming. If my courage fails me so that I am no longer able or willing to be present in this way, then it would seem that I am not only refusing the challenge I had issued to myself so publicly but also failing to be the channel through which healing and transformative energy can flow out to suffering individuals in an anguished world. If it is possible to gain access to a stream of love much greater than anything I can myself embody and then I consciously decide to inhibit such access, the consequences of such blatant cowardice are too terrible to contemplate.

The task, it gradually became clear, was of a very different order: how could I discover and submit to a discipline which would strengthen this capacity rather than abdicating from exercising it because it was simply too dangerous and too costly in terms of the potential loss of self-esteem and public reputation? In short, I had to become a kind of secular monk and discover an appropriate rule of life. Put like that it sounds very businesslike, almost a matter of operational efficiency. The reality, however, has proved to be very different. It has involved quite simply the unremitting task of seeking to embrace and then to hold on to so profound a level of self-acceptance that I am no longer a problem to myself and can therefore be utterly self-forgetful. This is a self-love which is the very contrary of selfishness for it does not desire self-aggrandisement but wishes rather to be the servant whose reputation is of no account.

Of course, I don't manage it most of the time. Anxiety prevails, self-concern invades me, the potential judgement of others stops me in my tracks. Only too often I am a disappointing model of the self-forgetfulness which I yearn to embrace. And I of all people have the least of excuses for such failure in my observance of the rule of life which if only I could be obedient to it would ensure that I was fully present in the world and a source of healing and transformative energy for others. Born just before the Second World War and, as a child, constantly aware of imminent danger and possible death, I so often forget what I knew then.

I want to end this lecture by recalling with you what, as a child, I received. I know that if only I could really accept those childhood gifts I would be free to be present to all I meet and I would know, as Julian of Norwich puts it, that God is closer to me than my own soul and is the foundation on which my soul stands. With such knowledge I could trust my own desiring. Death would not be a problem, nor would the body, nor would sexuality. I would be free at last to harness the energies of love and, in the marvellous words of Pierre Teilhard de Chardin, 'for the second time in the history of the world, human beings [would] have discovered fire' (Teilhard de Chardin, 1975: 87).

Come with me first, then, to Chappells' grocers shop in 1941. I am four-and-a-half. Chappells' grocers shop, as I remember it, was a rather dark place although the assistants were always friendly and, despite the wartime shortages, my mother usually managed to find what she needed. It was also something of a community centre and the women of the district would congregate there to exchange gossip. A little later on in the war, when the American servicemen had arrived on the scene, Chappells' also became the place for swapping scandal about illicit amorous activities in the neighbourhood. My mother was to have her own contribution to make to these stories when our house became the temporary refuge for a series of American soldiers. Victor, of Italian descent, seemed to attract many of the prettiest young women, most of whom my mother feigned to despise. I recall with most pleasure a fat, red-faced sergeant who seemed to have an endless supply of large bars of dark, delicious chocolate with which he quickly won my affection. The day I saw her, however, preceded the arrival of the Americans and I can only imagine that the subject of my mother's conversation at that time was of insufficient interest to capture the imagination of a four-and-a-half-year-old. My attention was elsewhere and I was staring at the glass-panelled door of the shop, perhaps to see if it had begun to snow again.

What happened next has remained imprinted on my memory for sixty-two years. I do not know if it was 'real', 'imagined', a 'fantasy', a 'dream', an 'hallucination'. All I do know is that I remember it still and that it entered the core of my being and lodged there. It was and is a milestone in the journey of a soul.

As I stared at the shop door I became gradually aware of a figure standing outside. At first there seemed nothing exceptional about this occurrence and, in any case, I could not see clearly because of condensation on the glass. Nonetheless my gaze remained fixed on the door as if some sixth sense compelled me to keep watching. Whether the condensation cleared I do not know but, within a minute or two, the figure outside became increasingly visible. Framed in the glass panel, almost like a photographic model, there stood a little girl dressed in a white coat with a fluffy hat perched somewhat jauntily on her head. Her beauty was spellbinding and the feelings I experienced in that moment can never be expressed for no adequate words were available to a child of four-and-a-half. Certainly I was transfixed, unable to move, unable to speak. My adult mind tells me that if I had died in that moment I should not have noticed for I was already in heaven. Much later I was to study the poetry of William Wordsworth and knew what he meant when he wrote that 'Heaven lies about us in our infancy'. And then the little girl smiled at me and waved. As if awoken from a trance, I tugged at my mother's arm and pleaded with her to stop her chatter and come home. Reluctantly she allowed herself to be dragged to the door and as she opened it I ran out into the street. The little girl was nowhere to be seen. Only her smile continued to accompany me as we made our way home beneath a threatening sky. I never saw her again but I knew that, like Dante, I had met my Beatrice.

Less than five years later as a nine-year-old I am playing cricket on a sunny spring afternoon. I quote now from *Behold the Man* published in 1991.

> Good Friday 1946 found me playing cricket in a Bristol park which was still full of air-raid shelters and all the bric-à-brac of war. Suddenly there appeared in the street at the side of the park a procession of witness, headed by a crucifer, candle bearers and a thurifer swinging a censer. The effect on me was instantaneous. I left my friends, ran all the way home and shut myself in my bedroom and sobbed for what seemed like hours. In the midst of this overwhelming distress I encountered the living Jesus and from that day until this I have had an unshakeable conviction that love is the primary force in the universe no matter how great the evidence may seem to the contrary. Looking back on it, the events of that Good Friday afternoon probably determined the direction of my life because they impinged on me at so many different levels. In the first place, the initial incident was visually stupendous: the contrast between the solemn beauty of the procession and the barrenness of the park still ravaged by war could not have been greater. Secondly, the experience established in a moment an order of values. I suppose I felt mildly guilty that I was playing cricket on Good Friday but the main feeling was one of quite overwhelming gratitude that I could be so incredibly loved. In that moment I knew that in the last analysis all that matters is loving and being loved. I also knew that the love I had experienced brought with it a sense of being fully and profoundly understood. It followed therefore that to love in this way must involve the deepest commitment to understanding. I have since discovered that love devoid of understanding, although it can bring comfort and solace, can never heal. Thirdly, the incident endowed me with an intoxicating sense of my own unique value. At a wholly conscious level I knew that something special had happened to me which I would never be able to deny or eradicate. (Thorne, 1991: 5–6)

I do not know why I was privileged to have such experiences at a time when the world was caught up in the ravages of a terrifying war and its aftermath. Certainly there was no personal virtue involved and no personal merit. If in those experiences I glimpsed that I was beloved for all eternity by the God who dwells within and without, that suffering is the gateway to glory, that death is not to be feared, that sexuality and desire are a key to the transformation of love so that passion can serve spirit, then what I glimpsed *must be true for us all*. We are all infinitely beloved; our suffering is the material for wounds of glory; our physical and sexual desiring is the key to our spiritual membership one of another and not the stumbling block; death can offer us the faith and the audacity to love life to the full rather than paralyzing us.

These are the gifts which are ours for the taking: the cost lies in receiving them, believing them and living them in a world where as yet there are many whose hearts of ice dare not melt to reveal the hearts of flesh on which depends the future of our world and of our humanity.

REFERENCES

Baker, K (2004) Review of 'The mystical power of Person-Centred Therapy'. *British Journal of Guidance and Counselling, 32* (2), 249–50.

Rogers, CR (1977) *Carl Rogers on Personal Power: Inner strength and its revolutionary impact.* New York: Delacorte Press.

Rogers, CR (1980) *A Way of Being.* Boston: Houghton Mifflin.

Rogers, CR & Sanford, R (1989) Client-centered psychotherapy. In H Kaplan & B Sadock (eds), *Comprehensive Textbook of Psychiatry 5* (pp. 1482–501). Baltimore, MD: Williams & Wilkins.

Senge, P, Scharmer, C, Jaworski, J & Flowers, B (2004) *Presence: Human purpose and the field of the future.* USA: Society for Organizational Learning. (Quoted in *What is Enlightenment?* (2004) *25,* 32)

Teilhard de Chardin, P (1975) *Toward the Future.* London: William Collins & Sons Co Ltd.

Thorne, B (1985) *The Quality of Tenderness.* Norwich: Norwich Centre Occasional Publications.

Thorne, B (1991) *Behold the Man.* London: Darton, Longman & Todd.

Thorne, B (2002) *The Mystical Power of Person-Centred Therapy.* London: Whurr Publishers.

Thorne, B (2003) *Infinitely Beloved.* London: Darton, Longman & Todd.

SECTION 2

PHILOSOPHY

INTRODUCTION

Some of the issues involved in reflecting on the relationship between spirituality and counselling are of a philosophical nature. A widespread—though not uncontested—view of philosophy is that it is essentially concerned with the clarification of concepts. **Hans Schneider** takes this view of philosophy, and his paper 'William James and Ludwig Wittgenstein: A philosophical approach to spirituality' provides an illustration of the power of this approach. Schneider begins with the work of William James, perhaps the earliest psychologist to be seriously concerned with religious experiences. A large part of James' classic book *The Varieties of Religious Experience* consists in simply describing experiences which in current terminology might be called 'spiritual', but he then proposes a quasi-scientific explanation of such experiences in terms of a transcendent reality that is neither material nor psychological. Schneider, following Wittgenstein, suggests that rather than move in this speculative direction we should reflect on the way in which religious language actually works. Just as the use of words for numerals such as 'three' need not commit us to the existence of a transcendent realm of mathematical entities, so the use of spiritual language need not commit us to the existence of a transcendental realm of spiritual entities. Schneider shows well how nothing is lost through this kind of approach, apart from fruitless discussions about whether certain things 'exist' or not.

Jon Sharp's intricate paper grows out of a rather different philosophical tradition, that of phenomenology. 'Phenomenology' here means not the kind of description of experience found in William James, but a distinctive approach to philosophy originating in the work of Edmund Husserl. Phenomenology is concerned with experienced meanings, and has led to the current postmodern concern with the question of whether there are *any* objective meanings outside of particular linguistic and cultural frameworks. Reality—including anything which might be termed 'spiritual reality'—has come to be seen as 'socially constructed' and language-dependent. What is then at stake is whether there is any aspect of our experience which is *not* socially constructed, since it seems of the essence of the spiritual or mystical that it cannot be adequately rendered in the language forms which are available. Husserl wanted us 'to go back to the things themselves', and Sharp argues that a *perceptual* rather than a conceptual form of consciousness is possible. In articulating our experiencing, that experiencing is inevitably changed, yet we need the concept of that which is articulated. As Sharp notes, Gendlin's philosophy of experiencing and meaning-creation is very relevant to these issues, which inevitably lie right at the limits of what can intelligibly be said. This latter point is elaborated in Sarah Luczaj's paper in the following section.

Ivan Ellingham's paper is also concerned with mysticism, and with the attempt to provide a scientific explanation of the phenomenon. He examines Carl Rogers' ideas in connection with mysticism and goes on to suggest how they could be augmented to provide such an explanation. Ellingham draws a parallel between the Rogerian theme of therapeutic movement from rigidity to flux, and the mystical theme of release from the ego. At the same time, he suggests that Rogers' view of scientific discovery involves the sensing of patterns which lie beyond what is present to our senses; hence scientific knowledge is not to be sharply set apart from mystical awareness. With this background, Ellingham develops Rogers' hypothesis of a whole-making 'formative tendency' at work in the universe, which he sees as providing a foundation for a scientific explanation of mysticism. Understood in this way, the mystical vision consists in the direct apprehension of the formative tendency.

Finally, in this section, **Clive Perraton Mountford** argues that Carl Rogers' principles of therapy can be extended in a way that leads to our treating the non-human world with respect. There has been a long tradition in which it is assumed that only human beings fall under what Mountford calls 'the moral umbrella'. There are traditional arguments for human beings treating each other with respect, but how can we justify extending the moral umbrella to the non-human world? The utilitarian philosophers brought under the umbrella any creature which can suffer, but more recently some philosophers have wanted to enfranchise all living things, and even what is non-living. Mountford discusses a possible justification through the 'sensible', but essentially self-centred, policy of protecting the ecosystem in the interests of long-term human benefit, but notes that 'prudence is a cheap and shabby substitute for moral status'. Instead, he suggests, we might begin from the intrinsic value of certain attitudes, especially those which are central to person-centred therapy: empathy, acceptance and authenticity. In adopting these attitudes towards others we not only help them, but are changed in ourselves; in adopting the attitudes towards ourselves we help not only ourselves but others; in adopting these attitudes towards the world we change in ways that not only—in some sense—benefit the world, but also enhance the lives of ourselves and of others. Mountford suggests that this deep interconnection between people, and between people and the world, is something which has to be felt rather than argued for. Through adopting Rogers' 'conditions' we open ourselves to the experience of the interconnectedness of things, and then we have less need for an argument to justify extensions of the moral umbrella.

CHAPTER 4

WILLIAM JAMES AND LUDWIG WITTGENSTEIN: A PHILOSOPHICAL APPROACH TO SPIRITUALITY

HANS JULIUS SCHNEIDER

INTRODUCTION

First of all I would like to thank the organizers of this conference for accepting a philosopher as a speaker.[1] I am very glad to be here, among a majority of therapists, because members of this profession have something to rely on which philosophers normally lack. This is the experience of accompanying real people when they take real steps towards a better life, while philosophers in most cases restrict their activities to speculations about what the good life could be. So it is the experiential side stressed in the title of this conference that I hope to learn something more about on this occasion.

But of course I also hope to give something. Firstly, my aim is to contribute to a clarification of the concept of spirituality. And secondly I will try to defend what is designated by this term against charges of irrationality and esotericism. My main inspiration comes, as far as the phenomenology is concerned, from William James, but I will interpret his descriptions not in the way he himself does, but with the help of ideas developed by Ludwig Wittgenstein.

I think it is the clarification of concepts in which the genuine work of philosophers consists. And when I take a closer look at the title of this conference I have the impression that it *does* signal a need for clarification. It carefully speaks of a 'spiritual dimension' of psychotherapy. It thereby circumvents the noun 'spirit' and thus avoids a reference to objects. This might be felt to be necessary in order not to invite the association with 'spiritualism', i.e. the belief in ghosts, which seems to lurk in the background.

When I was reading some material in the preparation of my talk, I found a paper in which Harry Van Belle (Van Belle, 1990: 47) expressed his unhappiness with Carl Rogers' 'move toward mysticism'. And in a more recent paper about 'Therapeutic Presence' Shari Geller and Leslie Greenberg (Geller & Greenberg, 2003: 79) quote a therapist who expresses some uneasiness about his or her use of esoteric language. I hope that I will be able to dispel some of the uneasiness and fear connected with the charges of esotericism.

But I think that there indeed is a danger of going astray here. Given a broad

1. An earlier and much shorter version of this paper has been published as Schneider (2003). Once more I would like to thank my friend John Granrose for checking my English.

enough concept of rationality, I suppose we all want to avoid a sacrifice of our intellects on the altar of an esoteric creed that would have to be rejected when examined by the court of reason. But what is a broad enough concept of rationality? And what is a rational goal of psychotherapy to be formulated inside the boundaries of a broad enough field of reason? Sigmund Freud's double specification that, as an effect of his cure, the patient should regain her ability to work and her ability to love, seems to be too modest, not only for person-centred therapy, as I understand it, but also for that part of the *philosophical* tradition that has for long been concerned with the 'highest good', not to speak of the ambitions of our religious traditions. Sanity seems to lie on a road that many see as leading on to some kind of 'salvation', some 'spiritual' well-being that it is hard to be clear about. So opinions differ over how we could and should describe it without becoming esoteric or mystical (in the negative understanding of these terms which reduces them to synonyms for 'irrational' and 'unclear'). So my aim in this paper is to present a proposal as to how a certain understanding of the 'spiritual dimension' of life can be defended against charges of irrationality.

As I have indicated, my proposal will consist of two steps. The first is a sketch of what I take to be the main points we can learn from William James' famous book *The Varieties of Religious Experience* (James, 1982). Arguing from the stronger to the weaker, I want to say that if we can accept as rationally accessible what James describes as religious experience (and I think we can), then we should have no difficulty with what is called the 'spiritual dimension', for this latter way of speaking will probably involve weaker claims than James'. So in my first step I want to take the phenomena described by James as circumscribing the 'spiritual dimension' of human life. Accordingly, when (following James) I will speak of religion, I will use this term in a very broad sense, including, for example, Buddhism as a non-theistic religion. I have the impression that it is the broader, more inclusive sense of the word 'spirituality' that makes some people prefer it to the terms 'religious' and 'religion'. A second reason why James fits well into the frame of this conference is that methodologically one can well say that his approach is (in its descriptive or phenomenological part) an 'experiential' one.

I will part company with James, however, when it comes to the metaphysical conclusions he is drawing. James thinks that, given the phenomena he has described so carefully, we are rationally justified in entertaining the hypothesis that there exists a transcendent being that causally affects happenings in our world. This is the point at which critics like Van Belle, Geller and Greenberg would (I suppose) see mysticism and esotericism at work. They hesitate to take the step from certain kinds of experience to existence claims about transcendent beings. For many people such beings are too much like ghosts and spirits, so they fear to end up in spiritualism after all. Accordingly, I will try to develop the idea of a 'spiritual dimension' of our lives in such a way that such reference is clearly excluded.

So my main point in this paper is to show that metaphysical conclusions of the type tentatively proposed by James are unnecessary if we have a good philosophy of language. And furthermore I also think that it is against the spirit of religion to couch what it has to say in the terms of hypotheses, however well-meaning William James might have been when he did so. So this move of his is for my understanding both inadequate to religion and unnecessary to safeguard its meaning. One way of expressing the first point would be to say that James here missed the difference between an 'experiential' and an 'empirical' approach. Surely spirituality should be related to our experience as human beings and should in this sense be approached 'experientially'. But from this it does not follow that it can or should be treated with the methods developed in the empirical sciences. Only in the very loose sense of 'turning to the real world' can empirical or scientific methods be applied to the subject matter of spirituality, it seems to me. One reason why this point is not appreciated more clearly, I think, is the fact that university psychology has a strong tendency towards desiring for itself the status of a science like physics; as a result, psychologists are often very uncertain about their methods (see Bruner, 1990).

Consequently, in the second part of my paper I will offer an alternative philosophical interpretation of William James' phenomenological material, one that avoids his metaphysical conclusions as well as his understanding of the spiritual as something that is accessible for scientific hypotheses. This alternative is inspired by the work of Ludwig Wittgenstein, on the one hand by his thoughts about the subject, and on the other by his method, namely a reflection on the language involved in the area under discussion. More specifically: I claim that if religious language is able to articulate an experience that has a deep and decisive significance for the person concerned, this very fact, this success in articulating and guiding the experiences of the persons concerned, is sufficient to secure its meaning. An additional reference claim for the expressions involved is superfluous. But if this is correct, an hypothesis about causal influences producing these experiences is unnecessary. The *experiential* activity of articulating, sharing, and guiding experience has to be differentiated from the *scientific* activity of reporting an empirical observation that can be repeated at will in the laboratories around the world, independently of differences in forms of (spiritual) life. Both uses of language have to do with experience, of course, but in very different ways. And only the latter has to involve a reference to objects whether they are literally observed, like the moon, or only postulated as theoretical entities with a place in a scientific model, like some subatomic particles or entities in outer space.[2]

So my way of avoiding James' belief in a transcendent world that is causally effective in our world rests on observations in the philosophy of language. Certain expressions of language that according to a common understanding refer to peculiar (in our case: transcendent) objects will in my interpretation be deprived of such a referential function. What appeared to be a reference to a peculiar kind of object will instead be understood as a peculiar kind of using our language, a usage that only on the grammatical surface appears to be a kind of reference. Actually, so the claim goes, there is as little 'reference to something' as we see in the use of the word 'it' in the phrase 'it is raining'; there is no 'something' that the 'it' of this phrase refers to.

2. The difference between experiential and theoretical entities in psychology is worked out more fully in Schneider, 2000.

By this methodological turn to the philosophy of language, the *explanandum*, i.e. that which has to be explained, is shifted from the allegedly designated transcendent object to the workings of language, understood as an integral part of the forms of practical human life. With Wittgenstein's help I think we can see that this peculiar kind of depriving the act of reference of its object does not make the linguistic articulations empty and irrelevant. The non-existence of the object as object does not transform the corresponding utterances into purely ritualistic pieces of language that are isolated from the rest of life. Therefore it is not 'only language' that we are left with when we give up transcendent entities, as it seems to be in some conceptions of language developed by proponents of postmodernism. As I understand it, the interpretation proposed here can preserve the importance that is traditionally given to the forms of speech under discussion.

I would like to conclude my introduction by mentioning two facts about my background: as is visible in what I have said so far, my main fields of work are epistemology and the philosophy of language. But I would not dare to speak about the topics raised here if I were without any experience in the field of spirituality. So I might mention that I have been a practitioner of Zen meditation for many years now, and this experience has certainly influenced my reading of William James as well as Wittgenstein.

WILLIAM JAMES AND 'THE VARIETIES OF RELIGIOUS EXPERIENCE'

THE PROBLEM AS SET BY JAMES AND HIS METHOD OF TREATING IT

James' book grew out of his Gifford Lectures and these stand under the general title of a 'Natural Religion'. In order to see the specific character of his approach it will be helpful to set it against the one chosen by David Hume in his *Dialogues Concerning Natural Religion* (Hume, 1980). Hume's project was to inquire into the chances of a 'reasonable' religion in the sense that, firstly, all reference to special religious sources of knowledge (revelations like holy scriptures) should be excluded and secondly (and here he differs from the first steps taken by James) the appeal to reason is understood by him as an appeal to the methods of the *sciences* that began to flourish in his days.

Hume takes as his starting point certain articles of faith (notably: that a benevolent god has created the world) and then proceeds to inquire whether they can be validated by a kind of experience that would be accepted by the sciences. The result is very meagre indeed. Hume sums it up in the words: '... the cause or causes of order in the universe probably bear some remote analogy to human intelligence' (Hume, 1980: 227).

James, on the other hand, does not begin with a religious statement and then ask for its empirical justification, but he proceeds in the opposite order. He starts with a large and generously chosen number of reports about candidates for religious experiences; he brings them into some order and tries to give a general characterization of their main traits. Only then does he proceed to investigate whether it is possible to develop on this basis a convincing concept of the realm of the 'religious'. So for James the question is: Can it be made plausible that in human life as we know it (i.e. in our life, as we experience it) there are episodes that might be felt and understood as forming the occasions around which the realm of the religious may crystallize and develop?

It is noteworthy that James himself once had an experience that he felt was religious (James, 1982: 160–1). It was on an occasion when he suddenly remembered being confronted in an asylum with an epileptic patient, an 'entirely idiotic' youth, 'looking absolutely non-human', when a sudden awareness struck him, that the self-assured attitude he had developed as a trait of character was without foundation. He was different from this poor creature, no question, but it was not by his own merit that he was, and it occurred to him that he could in no way make sure that this difference would remain stable, would be guaranteed. A panic fear took possession of him, and later he had the impression that only his spontaneous prayers had saved him from becoming insane. This experience was of major importance for his whole life; so when he gave his lectures, James felt that he knew what he was talking about.

His method is the following: from a huge bulk of reports of life-changing events of different kinds from very different people he derives general characteristics of a subgroup of his material that might meaningfully be described as religious in a sense that is not tied to a particular religion. As was customary in his time and for the members of his social background, he often uses Christian terminology or words that were commonly used in Christian contexts, like 'god', 'godhead', 'godlike object', 'the cosmos', 'the universe', 'the invisible order'. But he makes it clear that he means to refrain from dogmatic claims and from an exclusively Christian terminology. This is why I think we can at many places substitute the expression 'spiritual' where James uses the word 'religious'. Accordingly, the 'spiritual dimension' of life would be the realm that traditionally has been expressed in words at home in one of the existing religions.

It is James' aim to interpret the reports of his witnesses as far as possible in a 'natural' way. This term is understood by him to refer to common sense, not to the methods of the natural sciences. So James' understanding of these reports rests on his (and his readers') own experience. This ensures that religious experience is not understood as something that occurred only in the old days. He makes it plausible that the kind of experience he is looking for does indeed exist and that in principle such an experience can happen to anybody. It is not restricted to 'special' people and in this sense it is nothing esoteric. It normally has a decisively positive effect on the lives of the persons who do have such an experience.

In a second step, James tries to state the core characteristics of the specifically religious or spiritual variant of these experiences and thereby makes a proposal for differentiating them from related forms and optional but not universal phenomena that might accompany them. This then is his phenomenological basis, the richness and liveliness of which, together with his systematization, constitute the main value of his book for me. In a third step, finally, James steps back from his material and tries to formulate a philosophical interpretation of it.

According to his original plans, this last part of the project was meant to have the same quantity, to cover roughly the same amount of pages, as his systematized collection of reports. In its actual form, however, it is much shorter. What he has to say in it, he calls his personal 'over-belief'. He makes it clear that concerning this part of his investigations it is not his intention to convince his audience. So he explicitly allows different 'over-beliefs' to be formed by different readers on the basis of the same material. The phenomenological facts are indubitable for him, but on their basis a reader of James might, with his explicit encouragement, form his or her own 'over-belief'. This invites the question, whether there are systematic reasons for the rather slim character of this part of the book, and more specifically, whether and in what sense it is possible to do without any 'over-belief' as far as it involves a belief in certain causally effective entities. My own interpretation tries to answer this last question in the affirmative.

THE CONCEPT OF 'RELIGIOUS EXPERIENCE'

The most important traits of James' concept of a religious experience are the following: Firstly: The experience is one that relates to the attitude the person undergoing it has to the whole of his or her life and the surrounding world. What is meant here is a whole as experienced (an 'experiential whole', one could say), not a spatial or temporal whole as a collection of entities in the sense at home in a scientific cosmology.

Secondly: This whole includes suffering and evil, like loss, pain, sickness, and death. A sober comprehension and a practically effective integration of these aspects of life into the attitude to the whole is the core of religious experience. The experience is always a positive turn in the way in which the aspect of suffering is perceived and accepted. Using a modern philosophical distinction one might say that the result of a religious experience in James' sense is an improvement in the province of *knowing how* (to live) rather than an addition to the stock of items of *knowing that* or of information.

Thirdly: A closer look at this turn reveals three steps. Its starting point is the experience of a total defencelessness against suffering and evil, often accompanied with a feeling that everything in one's life has lost its meaning. When this helplessness is admitted, the person concerned will (in the second step) give up the impulse to be in complete control of his or her life. And then the third step is a (subjectively surprising) experience: this giving up or 'letting go' does not result in catastrophe, in a kind of 'drowning'. On the contrary, the person concerned will experience being a part of an 'invisible order' and she will experience this not as a (moral) yoke, but as the 'highest good'.

For appreciating the religious (or spiritual) character of the phenomenon it is important that it is the giving up of one's own impulses that brings rescue, and that this is experienced as the feeling that there are processes at work which are outside one's own little conscious self. So the encounter is not the result of one's own practical activity or one's own thinking, rather it is something that 'befalls' one, which comes to the person as a surprise.

Such an encounter has a deep significance for the person concerned. It is experienced like a 'second birth', as a step from the unreal (naïve, deceitful) to the real life. In its highest form, its result is 'a superior denomination of happiness, and a steadfastness of soul with which no other can compare' (James, 1982: 369).

Characteristically this kind of state is constituted by a loss of fear and solicitude and a belief that one's situation is agreeable at a deep level, regardless of what will happen.[3] After this 'second birth' the world is seen in a positive light without having undergone any objective change. The suffering aspects of life are neither denied, nor is the positive attitude a result of the fantasy that higher powers will by their special intervention keep unpleasant or painful events from the particular person concerned.

And as a fourth trait of the concept of religious experience James mentions that in most cases the described change lasts; it brings a lasting mental equilibrium.

I would like to quote one articulation of such an experience from James' book. The linguistic expressions we find here often have the form 'it was as if', followed by the description of an episode, of an element in a story, that speaker and hearer are supposed to be able to share, i.e. that the hearer is supposed to understand. My example will show how freely and individually chosen phenomenological language can go hand in hand with established religious forms of expression. We read:

> Suddenly there seemed to be a something sweeping into me and inflating my entire being—such a sensation as I had never experienced before. When this experience came, I seemed to be conducted around a large, capacious, well-lighted room. As I walked with my invisible conductor and looked around, a clear thought was coined in my mind, 'They are not here, they are gone'. As soon as the thought was definitely formed in my mind, though no word was spoken, the Holy Spirit impressed me that I was surveying my own soul. Then for the first time in all my life, did I know that I was cleansed from all sin, and filled with the fullness of god. (James, 1982: 253)[4]

We have to keep in mind that for James it is the change in attitude, and this means the practical ability of the person concerned to come to terms with her life, that is at the centre of religious experience and that he does not call into question. This is what makes such religious experiences important. Only in a second step James turns to what he calls his 'over-belief', i.e. to what he thinks he can conclude from such experiences as a philosophically minded psychologist.

James' 'over-belief'

I think that one of the advantages of James' method is that it invites and enables us to regard the traditional religious articulations primarily as expressions of the just discussed very special life-enhancing quality of this kind of experience. Theoretical aspects of traditional religious articulations (for example, cosmological claims) can then be

3. Here we are reminded of Wittgenstein's reference to the formulation 'nothing bad can happen to me'; see Malcolm 1984: 58.

4. From a Buddhist perspective one might want to discuss whether the experience described as 'they are gone' (the sins, the ego-worries) bears a family resemblance to 'emptiness'.

interpreted as results of secondary interests, for example the interest in explaining phenomena in the world of nature, like the coming of day and night. Accordingly it would be in the religious experience as described by James where one would look for the key for understanding religious or spiritual articulations, not theoretical claims about matters like the origin of the universe. It is interesting to note that the older traditions of Buddhism explicitly attempt to dissuade us from trying to find out the answers to cosmological or metaphysical questions, because they are largely irrelevant for the character of our lives.

When I now turn to the philosophical interpretation of these experiences, I see two possibilities. The first, more traditional approach (which I will call the 'referential') presupposes that the referring expressions of religious language (for example the words referring to divine beings like the Holy Spirit)—that such words have independent meanings of the same kind as the meanings of other referring expressions, for example for persons, rivers or cities. The meaning of a referring expression is accordingly taken to be the object denoted. So in the religious case, the meanings of religious expressions are taken to be known to the members of the linguistic community, for example from stories they have heard or read. Loosely speaking, this view can be expressed as: in principle we know what kind of things gods and spirits are, today we are just not sure whether they exist. So for this approach (as for Hume) the next questions to be posed would be: do the relevant expressions indeed have a reference and if so, how would one go about finding out whether the pertinent sentences about the objects referred to are true or false?

As far as his 'over-belief' is concerned, James sticks to this traditional referential understanding. But since his book leaves no doubt that the experiences he has collected and systematized are much more important to him than their philosophical interpretation, the reader in our days may at this point take a different route without hurting the spirit of James' project, as we shall see presently. Knowing the materialist and reductionist tendencies in the sciences of his day, however, James seems to fear that his colleagues would want to deny the reality and importance of the experiences he had described if he did not insist on extra-psychological entities referred to by the terms used to express them. Otherwise, he seems to have feared, they would be placed under the same category as dreams experienced in a fever. This he certainly wants to avoid; he wants to secure the special importance he himself had felt of his own experience. And he seems to think that the only possible remedy against a devaluation is the claim that there exist transcendent entities which either themselves are the objects of the pertinent experience (they are that what is experienced), or are what is causally responsible for the occurring of the experience.

This leads him to a rather traditional picture that differentiates between three worlds, a world of material objects, a world of subjective psychological objects like impressions and feelings, and a transcendent or spiritual world of objects which are neither material nor psychological. To say of something that it exists by itself, that it is independent of us (especially, that it is more 'real' than the 'merely psychological' objects of our dreams and fictions), means to say (according to this position) that it belongs to a world outside our sensory and mental apparatus, and this means either to the material or to a transcendent, spiritual world. Admittedly, both of these worlds we are able to know only via our sensations, feelings, thoughts, etc. But what is only in the world of felt experience and does not point to something 'exterior' (i.e. to a member of either one of the other two worlds, the material or the transcendent) is taken to be 'only psychological', in a devaluating sense. Again I would like to remark that here it would have helped to make a difference between the experiential (the sphere of the full ordinary life, with real experience, not only hallucinations) and the empirical as the sphere of the science laboratory, and this means of the material world. Without this distinction James is lost between either denying the importance of his findings or of trying to save them by binding them to independently existing transcendent entities.

AN ALTERNATIVE INTERPRETATION INSPIRED BY LUDWIG WITTGENSTEIN

WITTGENSTEIN'S UNDERSTANDING OF RELIGION

Wittgenstein's philosophy of language opens an alternative view which I will call the 'criterial'. This word is meant as a contrast to the word 'referential' in the view just discussed.

First of all, Wittgenstein has an understanding of what religion is according to which it would constitute a grave mistake to think that it puts forward hypotheses about the existence and the nature of 'transcendent objects' like gods. For Wittgenstein (and here his position differs sharply from views such as put forward by David Hume) religions are not theories. Especially, they should not be seen as early and immature attempts of mankind to practice science. Such a view would imply that religious objects would be only a little different from but still of the same kind as other objects like trees and rocks. Instead, the very status of 'being an object' has to be called into question when we look at what religious expressions are taken to mean or to 'refer to'.[5]

I think that Wittgenstein here is in harmony with the pragmatic spirit of the phenomenological part of James' book. His view is that an understanding of religion that treats it as a kind of theory would not do justice to the role of religious ideas in the lives of the people having these ideas. In the relevant case, a believer would have (I quote Wittgenstein) 'what you might call an unshakable belief. It will show, not by reasoning or by appeal to ordinary grounds for belief, but rather by regulating for in all his life' (Wittgenstein, 1966: 54). Unshakable beliefs, so we think after Karl Popper, are impossible in science. It follows that if such beliefs are typical for the realm of the spiritual, this realm cannot be understood as having to do with hypotheses in a sense we know from the sciences.

---

5. For a more comprehensive treatment of Wittgenstein's understanding of religion see Canfield, 2004. A considerably extended version is Canfield, 2005.

THE LANGUAGE GAME APPROACH AND ITS APPLICATION TO THE PROBLEM OF EXISTENCE

The positive side of Wittgenstein's criterial view is an application of his language game approach to problems of (purported) reference. The language game view can be characterized as the claim that the general picture according to which words stand for things and these things are what gives meaning to them is wrong. This picture has to be substituted by the view that the meaning of a word is its use, that is to say, it is the way in which the word functions in practical and social activities. It is true that the use of words in many cases does involve things, like when we speak of flowers and cars, but often it does not, and this absence of corresponding things does not have the consequence that the words concerned have no meanings. Wittgenstein seems to have first discovered this for the logical connectives, i.e. for words like 'and' or 'if'. They clearly do not stand for anything but they are far from meaningless. There are clear criteria for their correct application, but there is no reference.

Much of Wittgenstein's philosophy of language of his later period is captured in the following quotation. On occasion of a discussion of the mind–body problem and traditional paradoxes associated with it he writes:

> The paradox disappears only if we make a radical break with the idea that language always functions in one way, always serves the same purpose: to convey thoughts—which may be about houses, pains, good and evil, or anything else you please. (Wittgenstein 1953: § 304)

In our context we can add to this list: thoughts about God or other transcendent powers or persons. His claim here is that we do not have one semantic relation, a word standing for an object, and an admitted plurality of kinds of objects, but that there are many semantic relations which are of radically different kinds. Gods are not peculiar objects, but the language games involving 'talk of god' are peculiar language games, differing deeply from language games concerned with trees and cars.

What this means for the question of reference can be easily understood from a comment Wittgenstein makes in the field of mathematics. It is especially apt for our context, because mathematicians are not normally taken to be likely subjects for charges of mysticism or esoteric language.

The problem is whether numerals like 'one', 'two', 'three', ... can be meaningful only if there exist objects to which such expressions refer, objects that we normally call 'abstract' and refer to as numbers: the number two, for example, to which we can refer using signs in Arabic or Latin or in any other suitable script. The German logician Gottlob Frege (Frege, 1960) was convinced that when we pose this question ('what kinds of entities are the numbers?') we are confronted with the following alternative (since Frege excludes psychologism, the claim that numbers are psychological entities, as obviously wrong, he is left with only two possibilities); either (this is the first horn of the dilemma) we take the material sign tokens (i.e. the traces of ink on a piece of paper or the chalk left on a blackboard) to be the numbers the mathematician is talking about. If for example he claims that two is even he is referring to a material sign token '2' that he has produced on this occasion. Or (and this is the second horn) we postulate the existence of an extra realm of transcendent entities, as Plato had done with his realm of ideal forms. Immaterial objects like 'propositions' and also numbers would be taken to be located in this 'third realm', which has to be postulated as existing beside the material and the psychological realms.

Now the first horn of this dilemma is obviously absurd in the mathematical case. Ink and chalk do not have mathematical properties like being even or giving four when multiplied by itself. Consequently Frege decided for the second option, the existence of a transcendent world of numbers. This choice is quite in line with that of William James when he opted for transcendent entities in order to guarantee the meaningfulness of religious language and the importance of the involved kinds of experience. He could not think of securing their significance without postulating that there must be 'something' that the words used in articulating these experiences refer to.

It is in this situation that Wittgenstein sees a third possibility. He comments on Frege's view of the dilemma about numbers with the following words:

> For Frege the alternative was this: either we deal with strokes of ink on paper or these strokes of ink are signs *of something* and their meaning is what they go proxy for. The game of chess itself shows that these alternatives are wrongly conceived—although it is not the wooden chessmen we are dealing with, these figures do not go proxy for anything; they have no meaning in Frege's sense. (Wittgenstein, 1979: § 105)

(Meaning in Frege's sense is reference; the object referred to.) And then Wittgenstein adds his own claim: 'There is a third possibility, the signs can be used the way they are in the game' (ibid.). And this means: they have a significance, a role, an importance, although there is no object (in the usual sense of 'object') referred to.

Transferred to the realm of religion, the first horn of the dilemma corresponds to the claim that what religious articulations are talking about is something 'merely' psychological or (from a different perspective) even neurological, something happening 'inside' an individual person in a metaphorical or material sense that is relevant only to the person concerned and to nobody else. This would be a radical devaluation as in the mathematical case would be the proposition that numbers are nothing but ink and chalk (or, even more absurd for Frege, that numbers are psychological entities). In this view, only the mental (or neural) states of experiencing are real, there is no way in which the experience points to something other than its individual occurrence. So the content of religion would consist in 'mental episodes' (for example in 'nice feelings') and would therefore be of the same kind as 'mere fantasies'. It is clear that William James, with all the understanding and empathy that shows in his phenomenological account and that is rooted in his own experience, could not opt for such a position. From his point of view it must look as absurd as the claim that the objects of our mathematical knowledge are traces of ink. It is for this reason, I suppose, that James (like Frege in the realm of mathematics) opted for the existence of a 'third', a transcendent world, beyond the material and the psychological.

Now in contradistinction to James and Frege, for Wittgenstein *both* horns of the dilemma are unacceptable for his understanding both of mathematics and of religion. His analogy to the game of chess is meant to open a third option for mathematics: numerals are meaningful, but not thanks to special 'third realm' objects of reference (and not because they denote psychological or neurological entities), but thanks to their role in our activities. It is with respect to this role (and not to problems of the existence of special entities) that we must in a particular case of utterance decide whether in the case at hand the sign token has a meaning or not. It has no meaning, for example, when it is an empty repetition or blind copying of a traditional piece of language. The meaning stems from the role of the word in our life (its 'experiential role'), not from a transcendent entity of which the word is the name and about which there could be empirical research of the type conducted in the sciences.

LESSONS FOR THE FIELD OF SPIRITUALITY

I think that this solution can be transferred to the field of spirituality. The occurrence and the life-changing importance of the experiences described by James suffice for giving a meaning to their articulations in religious language. Hypotheses about the existence of transcendent entities are unnecessary. That does not mean, however, that cases of empty copying, of meaningless babble, of mere traditional talk unconnected to important aspects of life are impossible. It is the context, the use of language in the particular situation that allows us to distinguish meaningful from empty speech; it is not the question of whether there is an entity referred to. There are independent criteria for this distinction that are not in need of special entities.

Here it is important to avoid a misunderstanding of what is called a 'pragmatic approach to language'. Sometimes Wittgenstein compares words with tools in order to say that they have a function in our lives. But this comparison does not mean that when one speaks of language games the words concerned must always be interpreted to have a technical function. Not all linguistic functions can appropriately be described as technical functions. In the case of religious experience, language works in the context of encounters, of what befalls a person, similar to the case of words like 'pain'. James and Wittgenstein agree that words get their meaning through their role in practical contexts or episodes, but these need not be activities, they include the more passive aspects of life.

It is also important to see that Wittgenstein's talk of 'language games' is not meant to suggest that language use is always playful. Accordingly, if we apply the concept of a language game to religion (which is, as we have been taught by James, concerned with a person's life as a whole, with all its suffering included), this does not mean not to take religion seriously. So again, if one wants to secure a deep significance for religious language and wants to avoid the impression that it consists of 'playing games', one is not forced to postulate special 'objects of reference'. My impression is that many theologians would be ready to agree to this claim and would confirm that in their field 'reference' has always been a debated concept. The Christian God is no object or person like other objects and persons and 'talk about God' (*theo-logia*) has always been a problem that demanded extra considerations.

The situation can be compared to one mentioned by Wittgenstein on an occasion when he comments on the expression 'to describe the state of my mind'. He thinks of a case of silently beckoning to someone and then (for some reason or other) having occasion to explain this act retrospectively, for example with words like 'I did not want you to come, but him'. Wittgenstein writes: 'One can now say that the words "I wanted N. to come to me" describe the state of my mind at that time; and again one may *not* say so' (Wittgenstein 1953: § 662). So on the one hand it is legitimate to talk in the traditional way about a 'state of mind' as if it were (the state of) an object. Turning to religion, we can say that the Christian tradition (among others) has shown that it is possible to articulate the content of a religious experience in theistic terms, i.e. as if one would refer to a person. But when one thinks that God is a person like other persons (or, returning to Wittgenstein's example, that the mind is like a physical object which has states, like the lung when it is fully inflated or less so, or that the mind really or 'lastly' is identical with the brain), then, I think, the other half of Wittgenstein's comment has to be applied, namely '... one may *not* say so'. The reason is that these ways of expressing oneself invite and encourage illegitimate (i.e. meaningless) ways of carrying on. These can be even funny, as when someone would not only speak about the eyes of God that see everything, but would go on from there to speak about God's eyebrows (Wittgenstein, 1966: 71). Or such a move can result in what one could call 'esoteric language' in a derogative sense, meaning a language that purports to speak about hidden entities that are like material entities or objects, but are at the same time hidden from the eyes of science. What is claimed here is that, in the religious case, 'speaking about' means something different from the case of 'speaking about objects', whether these are common material things or entities imagined to be similar but (in a way left unclear) also not similar to them.

In a fashion parallel to the quoted comments about a person's 'states of mind' Wittgenstein treats pain. He insists that my toothache is not an object like my tooth. And then in his typical dialogical style he develops the following argument:

> 'But you will surely admit that there is a difference between pain-behaviour accompanied by pain and pain-behaviour without any pain?' Admit it? What greater difference could there be? 'And yet you again and again reach the conclusion that the sensation itself is a nothing.' Not at all. It is not a *something*, but not a *nothing* either ...We have only rejected the grammar which tries to force itself on us here. (Wittgenstein, 1953: § 304)

Similarly, returning to William James and the topic of religious experience, one could say: when we compare a life that is felt as empty and meaningless (like James' own life in his long period of crisis) to a life felt (despite the full acknowledgement of its suffering aspects) as enlightened and unified by the kind of experience he describes in his book, it is quite appropriate to exclaim as Wittgenstein did in the case of pain: 'What greater difference could there be!' But this does not force us to entertain an hypothesis about transcendent objects. This is so, I believe, because we can say with respect to religious language what Wittgenstein says about sensations like pain: what we are (grammatically) talking about '... is not a *something*, but not a *nothing* either'. It is not a thing (not something), not an object. But still the language concerned has deep experiential relevance; it has a practical relation to our whole lives, to our knowing how to live. But meaning, as we have seen in the simple case of numbers, does not always demand objects and entities talked about in more than a merely grammatical sense.

If this point is overlooked, we easily get into empty quarrels that Wittgenstein describes in the following way: 'The one party attack the normal form of expression as if they were attacking a statement; the others defend it, as if they were stating facts recognized by every reasonable human being' (Wittgenstein, 1953: § 402). For my understanding quarrels about 'the existence of God' often have this character. Does He exist or not? Is the person who answers negatively arguing against a way of expression or against a substantial claim? It seems to me that the question to be treated first is: what would it mean to advance either claim? How do the relevant language games function? How would a difference show in our experience? Here we need the 'experiential' approach and nothing like experimental science could help us, as our glimpse at Hume's futile attempt was meant to show. We can find that our life as we know it indeed has a 'spiritual dimension'. Only after we have experienced this can we discuss the advantages and disadvantages of different religious language games (Christian, Buddhist) to articulate this dimension. If we follow Wittgenstein at this point in that we are ready to accept a great variety of semantic relations, we can avoid unnecessary quarrels about 'designated objects'. For example we can avoid 'esoteric language' if by this expression we mean a purported quasi-scientific 'reference' to 'ineffable objects'. Instead we can use a language of experiential articulation for which the problem of 'reference to an object' does not arise. With this understanding in place we no longer postulate dubious entities and this means we leave esotericism and spiritualism behind. There are no ineffable ghostlike entities about which there is a secret teaching, reserved for special people.

The spiritual dimension of our lives is no secret but it is open to the experience of everybody. Of course, for a person unaware of such experiences it is difficult to understand what people who are familiar with them are talking about. In this completely harmless sense the language of religious experience is a language for 'insiders', as is the language of wine connoisseurs. In this sense it can be called 'esoteric'. But in our days we are in the lucky situation that in both cases nobody (or more carefully speaking: probably no one among the readers of this paper) is excluded from the relevant experiences.

REFERENCES

Bruner, J (1990) *Acts of Meaning*. Cambridge, MA: Harvard University Press.

Canfield, JV (2004) Wittgenstein's religious point of view. In W Löffler, P Weingartner (eds), *Knowledge and Belief* (pp. 90–9). Vienna: öbv&hpt-Verlagsgesellschaft.

Canfield, JV (2005) Der Grund des Seins. Wittgensteins ‚religiöse Betrachtungsweise'. In *Deutsche Zeitschrift für Philosophie 53* (2), 257–75.

Frege, G (1960) *Translations from the Philosophical Writings of Gottlob Frege* (ed and trans by P Geach and M Black) (Revised edition). Oxford: Blackwell.

Geller, SM & Greenberg, LS (2003) Therapeutic presence: Therapists' experience of presence in the psychotherapy encounter. In *Person-Centered and Experiential Psychotherapies, 1* (1&2), 71–86.

Hume, D (1980) *Dialogues Concerning Natural Religion* (NK Smith, ed). Indianapolis: Bobbs-Merrill.

James, W (1982) *The Varieties of Religious Experience. A study in human nature*. Harmondsworth: The Penguin American Library.

Malcolm, N (1984) *Ludwig Wittgenstein: A memoir* (new edn). Oxford: Oxford University Press.

Schneider, HJ (2000) Metaphors and theoretical terms: Problems in referring to the mental. In M Carrier, GJ Massey & L Ruetsche (eds) *Science at Century's End. Philosophical questions on the progress and limits of science* (pp. 193–216). Pittsburgh: University of Pittsburgh Press/Konstanz: Universitätsverlag.

Schneider, HJ (2003) Der Begriff der religiösen Erfahrung bei William James und seine Weiterentwicklung nach Wittgenstein. In W Löffler & P Weingartner (eds), *Wissen und Glauben. Beiträge des 26. Internationalen Wittgenstein Symposiums, vol. XI*, (pp. 320–2). Kirchberg am Wechsel: Österreichische Ludwig Wittgenstein Gesellschaft.

Van Belle, HA (1990) Rogers' later move toward mysticism: Implications for Client-Centered Therapy. In G Lietaer, J Rombauts & R Van Balen (eds) *Client-Centered and Experiential Psychotherapy in the Nineties* (pp. 47–57). Leuven: Leuven University Press.

Wittgenstein, L (1953) *Philosophische Untersuchungen / Philosophical Investigations*, Oxford: Blackwell. (References are given by paragraph number, indicated §.)

Wittgenstein, L (1966) *Lectures and Conversations on Aesthetics, Psychology, and Religious Belief* (C Barrett, ed). Oxford: Blackwell.

Wittgenstein, L (1979) *Conversations Recorded by Friedrich Waismann* (B McGuinness, ed) (trans J Schulte and B McGuinness). Oxford: Blackwell.

CHAPTER 5

TOWARDS A PHENOMENOLOGY OF THE DIVINE

C. J. SHARP

INTRODUCTION

For many individuals a spiritual dimension is essential to any full account of how the meaning of their life is experienced and understood. There is growing need for new methodologies with which to explore and conceptualize subjective consciousness (Shear, 1997), and this includes the spiritual dimension. This paper seeks to construct a valid theoretical framework within which we can begin to adequately engage with and explore the potential that experiential spirituality has to impact on our sense of life-meaning. The term, 'life-meaning' refers to an individual's felt sense of their own meaning in the world and in relation *to* the world; the sum of all the aspects that I might include when I identify what it is that constitutes that 'I-ness'.

It is not the intent of this paper to argue for the validity of the spiritual origins attributed to these 'peak' experiences, to try and establish the existence of a Divine or to make a claim for the transcendence or immanence of a Divinity that may or may not exist, but to explore them from a phenomenological perspective.

THE DESTRUCTION OF MEANING

In constructing a phenomenological approach to experiential spirituality and its impact on our life-meaning, we must first address the thorny problem of meaning itself. In a broad overview of twentieth-century philosophy Graham Priest convincingly argues that the key philosophical problem of the last century has been 'the nature of representation in language and thought' (Priest, 2002). As noted by Priest, among others, a significant move in twentieth-century philosophy was, 'in a certain sense, the destruction of the very possibility of meaning' (Priest, 2002: 93; McDonald, 2002). If we are to claim that life-meaning exceeds its linguistic expression, we must first reclaim the possibility that meaning itself is more than a pipe dream.

As Mark Bevir notes, 'According to Derrida, we cannot have knowledge of anything beyond language because language cannot represent the world' (Bevir, 2000). Derrida's claim is based on the argument that in any sequence of signifiers the signified is only available to us through the construction of another signifier string and so on ad infinitum

(Derrida, 1982). If we accept this argument then being itself becomes textual and presence is replaced by a doomed attempt at reflection on our contingent being; this leads to a location of the mysterious within writing, rather than the world and certainly not in any notion of the Divine (McDonald, 2002). However, as Bevir argues, this self-enclosed view of language was utilized by Saussure in order to advance the science of linguistics, and so cannot simply be applied to the life-meaning of individuals. Saussure concentrated on *langue*, the structure of language, rather than *parole*, the application of language in speech acts. However, while *parole* requires *langue* in order to achieve meaning, *parole* itself in part emerges from our embodied status and relationship to referents in the world. Derrida's theory of language ignores this embodied element of language. The claim that signifiers can indicate what a referent *is* as well as sometimes achieving this end by clarifying what it is not allows us to re-establish the possibility of a meaning that is not endlessly deferred.

While it may seem somewhat removed from the immediacy of the spiritual experience, the establishment of some stability for meaning is an essential foundation to any claim for a meaningful sense of felt subjectivity. Bevir is right to point to Derrida's 'epistemological modesty' (Bevir, 2000: 420), but misses the opportunity to make the simple but accurate argument that faced with this radical epistemological uncertainty Derrida's own carefully constructed claims must lose any validity by virtue of his commitment to the instability of meaning. Paradoxically, if the claims of indeterminacy are true, they immediately lose any force. This same seemingly trite argument can be used to counter attempts to extend Baudrillard's notion of the *simulacrum* to a statement about reality as opposed to a particular reality (Baudrillard, 1998). While contemporary culture manifests a social reality that inhabits traces and images of reality rather than a solidity of content, this does not imply that reality itself can be regarded as only ever accessible as a simulacrum.

THE SOCIALLY CONSTRUCTED SELF

When we consider meaning in the context of counselling we are concerned with meaning as it relates to the meaning that people find within and about themselves. In looking at meaning in this broader and more holistic sense we come to engage with issues that are not always primarily linguistic either in how they are experienced or in how they are understood by individuals. As a social practice the very issues that are often explored by counsellors and their clients call into question the validity of the deconstructionist attack on meaning as anything more than a formal exercise. In reducing experience to the text, the deconstructionist project has little to offer those experiences which are manifestly extra-textual.

Counselling theory has historically focused on the personal phenomenological experience of selfhood, while not seeing the self as exclusively socially constructed. The debate around the way in which self-meaning is understood within counselling does need to include recognition and exploration of the arguments that even spirituality is, at least in part, socially constructed. In 'Beyond Empathy' Dan Zahavi ties together the self, others and world as necessarily interconnected (Zahavi, 2001). Although not the purpose of his article, we can unproblematically move from a 'world' conceived of as the arena within which the intentional contents of subjective consciousness are ultimately located, to a recognition that those contents are informed by the forces that partly delineate the transcendent objects which are the focus of the intentional consciousness. The forces recognized in this move will include socio-cultural factors as well politically neutral forces such as colour or temperature.

If we are to have a view of the 'sacred' that corresponds to the experiences of a broad cross section of society it is important that we recognize the social context in which the sacred is experienced and interpreted (Heimbrock, 2004). A socially grounded approach need not be reductive in terms of the integrity of the individual experience and hunger for a personal sense of self which is established through a development of a meaning for that self. Heidegger's development of *Dasein*, the sense of being within the world, led the way for the ascendance of a hermeneutic and existential approach to the phenomenological project (Priest, 2002). Since most of our conscious life is mediated through our status as embodied and social beings (McDonald, 2002: 22), it is through socially grounded theories of life-meaning that we will best understand the felt significance of those aspects of our lived experience.

Both Gadamer and Habermas developed their philosophy out of a phenomenological framework and they recognized the social nature of all dialogue. Habermas provides us with a philosophical model that sees language as the root of intersubjectivity and draws attention to the dual role in informing our consciousness of both our individual life-world and the social community which we inhabit (Habermas, 1984). Gadamer explored in detail the nature of understanding and the dependence of the synchronic response of an individual subject on the history of understandings out of which that individual response emerged (Gadamer, 2001). Counselling occurs as a dialogue between the client and counsellor and awareness of the socially grounded nature of both speakers can help to tease out the truly personal by ensuring that some attention is paid to recognizing those elements of the dialogue that reflect prejudice rather than immediate experience.

In the counselling process we are concerned with the discovery and construction of meaning for the client and by the client. By taking a dialogic approach we are innately recognizing the social nature of at least some aspects of identity since all conversation is social. The question 'what does my life mean?' is bound up with the question 'who am I?' This second question can only be fully answered by looking at the relational aspect of identity and this is inevitably a socially constructed element of identity. Unless we bring the socially constructed aspect of identity to conscious attention then we risk imposing a meaning on the client that comes from our own ontological framework. In other words if we are not focused on the factors that influence the 'what' of who we think we are, we may find ourselves unwittingly imposing that same sense of being on the client. This danger extends to our spiritual ontological framework; in William West's recent book which applied the theory of spiritually aware counselling to practical settings, he is very careful to rehearse a number of different and competing spiritual frameworks that one might associate with as a model of inner development (West, 2004).

While I will disagree below with Bevir's exclusion of perceptual contents of consciousness, I would agree with him that conceptual contents of consciousness (contextualized signifieds) should be conceived of as 'products of a social practice' (Bevir, 2000). This suggests that while we may need to move beyond a social constructivist view of the self when approaching the holotropic (moving towards wholeness) consciousness, we do also need to be focused on the socially constructed nature of 'normative' consciousness, otherwise the concept of life-meaning that is created by the client may be restricted by the boundaries that have been constructed around the socially determined limits of possible being. The holotropic consciousness refers to a state of consciousness which might be best referred to as mystical; a moment of awareness that is felt as a profound sense of totality and connectedness. Although the holotropic consciousness does not appear to be inscribed by social contexts, a failure to address and as far as possible neutralize the socio-cultural structures effecting the construction of concepts within a counselling dialogue can have an impact on emergent spiritual processes within a counselling session (Hinterkopf, 1998).

In agreeing that we do need to socially contextualize our sense of self and our reflections on our understanding of the world, I would not submit to Bourdieu's claim that our *habitus* necessarily leads us to accept unthinkingly our social conditions and their impact on our agency (Bourdieu, 1999). We cannot regard our identity as wholly constructed by external factors unless we wish to remove any claim to individual agency. I would concur with John Myles that in developing Husserl's concept of *doxa* (originally a Platonic concept referring to the natural attitude, used by Husserl to refer to the ground in which consciousness occurs) Bourdieu is mistaken in locating agency only in the arena of discourse and denying it to praxis, largely as a result of oversimplifying the multilayered nature of the movement from multivalent doxic states to reflective consciousness (Myles, 2004).

A concern with the societal context in which our experiences are situated can also be a basis for broadening the scope of those experiences which might be labelled as spiritual (Bailey 1998, 2001). It is important to recognize that while the label 'Divine' is used within this paper for many people a holotropic experience is not referenced to any theistic concept (Hinterkopf, 1998). Additionally, the resistance to notions of the spiritual can also be better understood by reference to our current social context which combines, '[a] lack of respect for wisdom, and a concentration on immediate and material gratifications' (Donaldson, 1992 cited in Lewis, 2000), particularly if we agree that 'to free oneself from a purely materialistic concept of humanity, to see its relativity, is an important aim of spiritual development' (Reich, 2001).

BEING AND/OR MEANING

Our sense of being and our sense of life-meaning are in a constant dialogue with each other, and in situating the notion of the holotropic consciousness within a phenomenological framework, the nature of this interaction needs to be carefully explored. Our identity can be seen as the sum of meanings understood through the framework created by our being. Our identity is constantly moving since each new experience increases the sum of meanings and so our identity needs to be seen as a process rather than as a fixed idea or state (Depraz, 2001: 170). As we gain a new self-understanding this changes the self that is being understood (Poellner, 2003).

If during a counselling session I am trying to focus on the meaning of my life, this act of reflection will lead to changes into what I see as my beingness in the world. Similarly, if I try to think about how I locate myself in the world this will inevitably have implications for the life-meaning which I can construct. At the actual point of focusing on my sense of being I can only do this in relationship to the meaning senses that I have available at the time of that act of focusing and so will not be reflectively aware of the shifts in meaning that occur during that act of focusing. This notion of flux or oscillation is also referred to, but in terms of Taoist conceptions, by Jeff Lewis in his exploration of spiritual education (Lewis, 2000).

If we come to see our beingness and our sense of meaning as being in a constant dialogue then this has implications for how we come to view the nature of meaning.

If our sense of life-meaning influences our sense of being then we can more clearly see the way in which our life-meaning acts not only to reflect our conscious contents but also to feed them through its impact on our concept of what we are. This highlights our potential to actively determine our being in the world as active possessors of agency. We can then apply this viewpoint to spirituality: its meaning is felt not just in terms of how we approach knowing the world but also in terms of how we view our status as being in the world. Thus it is both ontological and epistemological in nature. The spiritual experience offers a useful example of the problem that exists in trying to understand both our knowledge of ourselves and our sense of being in the world. The spiritual informs our sense of meaning in that it plays a part in how we determine both what we know about our selves and who we feel our selves to be.

We have said earlier that what marks out the spiritual is that it impacts on both our sense of who we are and also what our life means. It is not just that the spiritual impacts on both these aspects of our identity (Hinterkopf, 1998), but that it affects both simultaneously. Ironically although we often lose a sense of self in the direct spiritual or holotropic experience, there is also an awareness of the enormous significance of the experience and so by implication within the spiritual experience both our life-meaning and our sense of being are being simultaneously shifted. This is a rather prosaic way of describing the sort of experiences that we refer to as 'total' or 'profound'.

FELT-EXPERIENCE AND PERCEPTUAL CONSCIOUSNESS

Phenomenology post-Heidegger has made much of the importance of the situated status of all subjects. When considering the experience of individuals it has become generally accepted that no individual's experience is ever 'pure' in the sense of being wholly their own, but is inevitably mediated through the various influences of society and culture (Gadamer, 2001). The focus on our embodied status, powerfully developed by Merleau-Ponty among others has led to claims that the Husserlian approach to consciousness is solipsistic (McDonald, 2002), while others have more recently pointed to his awareness of the embodied subject (Dodd, 1997 cited in Myles, 2004). While the early Husserl does present a Cartesian paradigm, I would agree with Nathalie Depraz that his concept of intentionality is directed to the world and its contents and the process of bracketing is not seen as a negation of the existence of transcendent objects but an attempt to better apprehend the given nature of those objects (Depraz, 2001). Moreover Dan Zahavi argues convincingly that Husserl's concept of the subject's relationship to the world cannot be satisfactorily categorized as either externalist (consciousness as environmentally determined), or internalist (consciousness as wholly constituted within the subject) but can only be fully understood within Husserl's own phenomenological terms (Zahavi, 2004).

As noted above we cannot ignore the socially contextualized nature of selfhood. However, we should also maintain a strong commitment to the uniqueness of each individual. This is partly supported by the presence of felt, non-conceptual experience discussed below, but also by a factor that is fundamental to the notion of subjective consciousness. The basis on which my self-awareness is grounded is not the difference in my articulated responses to shared experiences to other individuals who have shared that experience, but on the very fact that I experience my conscious contents as mine (Zahavi, 1998). The awareness that I have of being in a first-person relationship to that which is given to consciousness is both a given of my status as a subject and the grounds on which I can be certain that said status accurately reflects the nature of my conscious experience. The presentation of any experience linguistically immediately shifts the experience to a socially constructed act of representation rather than a personal holistic felt meaning. At that point it could perhaps be argued that the meaning of my experience is now a public, socially determined sequence of signs, but at the point of being experienced it has an *intrinsic myness* [original italics] (Zahavi, 1998).

The argument for felt-experience, a perceptual aspect to consciousness, is implicit in the analysis of self-awareness offered by Zahavi. In the same article he argues that consciousness is coincidentally intentionally directed towards objects and is self-aware. He goes on to distinguish between pre-reflective awareness which corresponds to perceptual consciousness and reflective awareness which is conceptual (Zahavi, 1998: 696).The hermeneutic approach to experience, the notion that we can only interpret experience rather than accessing an unmediated experience is perfectly appropriate for conceptual modes of consciousness where our situated and socially embodied nature is active. However, the key defining feature of moments of spiritual experience is the sense of 'presence' and of totality. They are moments where our sense of being and our sense of meaning are mutually present to us. While we have no difficulty in attesting to the actuality of such experiences we find it extremely difficult to communicate these experiences linguistically, and this is because such experiences are given to consciousness perceptually.

In contrast to Bevir's claim that, 'Theories are implicit in all the objects that appear before consciousness' (Bevir, 2000), Peter Poellner argues that conscious intentional contents are not necessarily conceptual (Poellner, 2003). The possibility of a non-conceptual consciousness, or a consciousness content that exceeds the conceptual is also suggested by Depraz's definition of 'transcendental genesis' (Depraz, 2001), which draws on Focusing theory for the structure of its argument (Gendlin, 1997). Poellner draws on Husserl's thesis of presence to argue that 'there is always more to our experienced selves at any moment than what we are capable of articulating at the time' (Poellner, 2003: 32). Husserl's 'operative consciousness' thesis claims that experiences as experienced are not identical with experiences as re-identified (Husserl, 1970). This thesis is intrinsically supportive of perceptual consciousness and indeed goes further than we are seeking in this paper in its extreme rejection of the possibilities for reflection on lived experience.

In claiming a place for perceptual contents of consciousness Poellner references the problematic nature of self-interpretation and the way in which the articulation of self is always at some distance from the experience of self (Taylor, 1982 cited in Poellner, 2003). In his 2003 article Poellner suggests that in articulating perceptual contents our experience itself is transformed, which is to say that the significance of felt-experience does not correspond exactly to its post-hoc conceptualization. Naturalist or physicalist theories of mind have often tended to strongly argue against the validity of felt-experience or *qualia* (Vadén, 2001). However, in the arena of cognitive science it is argued by some that all conceptual knowledge emerges from those felt-experiences that we are referring to as perceptual consciousness (Crane, 1992; Myles, 2004), or that there are definite conscious subjective experiences that are non-conceptual (Nagel, 1998). Additionally, Vadén argues that *qualia* are only excluded by the application of algorithmic explanations of consciousness, explanations that are by no means the only means of accounting for consciousness even within a Naturalistic framework (Vadén, 2001). Poellner's concentration on the felt-experience as it is felt rather than what that experience is about provides us with a theory of perceptual consciousness that is ideally suited to describing the holotropic experience.

It is important to note that non-conceptual consciousness is not necessarily merely simple pre-conscious awareness. As Poellner demonstrates with his example of the non-trained listener's response to music, our perceptual contents can be rich and complex (Poellner, 2003). Gendlin presents possibly the best-known case for perceptual consciousness, what he refers to as 'experiential meaning' (Gendlin, 1997). While I find the term experiential meaning problematic, preferring experiential significance, because 'meaning' implies a relationship necessitating conceptual consciousness, the argument that Gendlin constructs is both philosophically coherent and demonstrated through the application of Focusing techniques. Of course the holotropic consciousness when viewed as a genuinely spiritual encounter involves perceptual contents that are transcendent in the sense that they originate outside the subject. The argument that a subject experiences perceptual concepts does not in itself imply that such contents emerge from anywhere other than within the subject; De Wit, who accepts perceptual consciousness, describes it as wholly internal to the subject (De Wit, 1999 cited in

Reich, 2001). It is the totality of the holotropic and its extreme resistance to adequate articulation that is suggestive of a transcendent dimension. That said, Poellner's article is suggestive of a spiritual potential for perceptual consciousness when he writes of the effect of perceptual conscious contents:

> It may for instance motivate an effort on the part of the subject to grasp it conceptually and thus to attain the sort of 'deeper' self-comprehension which Taylor, standing in this respect in a long tradition initiated by Plato, regards as highly important. (Poellner, 2003: 45)

THE SPIRITUAL DIMENSION

The quest for the articulation and self-understanding of meaning is fraught with dangers. The whole process becomes more problematic when we include the notion of a spiritual dimension. However the exploration of consciousness has historically been associated with mysticism and the spiritual, and a significant number of those working in the field of transpersonal psychology see their role as engaging with paths of spiritual transformation (Lancaster, 2004). The inclusion of a spiritual dimension within the field of counselling creates a fundamental shift in the significance of personal meaning. The question becomes as much about our being and its significance as it is about the meaning of that state of being.

The difficulty in representing the spiritual comes not only from the resistance of spiritual experiences to articulation, but also from the growth in felt spiritualities which are no longer tied to any recognized religious system or institution (Luckmann 1967; Rudge 1998, 2004). According to Fredric Jameson, 'Spirituality virtually by definition no longer exists: the definition in question is in fact that of postmodernism itself' (Jameson, 1991). If we agree with the postmodernist view that we are beings wholly constructed by language, then in view of the innately social nature of language, we do indeed remove the possibility of the spiritual. While postmodernism has proclaimed spirituality as being virtually unthinkable in our postmodern culture with its virtual and even 'hyper-realities' (Baudrillard, 1998; McDonald, 2002: 11) other parties have been recording a growth in popular spiritual interest, especially in areas of New Religious Movements (Bellah, 1970; Cox, 1977; Eliade, 1976; Green, 1992; Roof, 1993). This suggests that we are some way off from having to accept Jameson's rather dramatic claim, provided that we can satisfy ourselves that our life-meaning consists of more than an endless regress of content empty signifiers (Derrida, 1977).

I think it is possible to accept the existence of the spiritual or 'peak' experience without altogether denying the claim that our experience is informed by our position within the society in which our experience occurs, or indeed that language may well be the source of rather than the expression of our experience. As William James would have it, the fact that people feel that they have spiritual experiences warrants the study of such experiences (Lancaster, 2004). The spiritual certainly includes factors such as social position, culture and so on, but cannot be reduced to these factors alone (Lewis, 2000). It may be that the socially constructed nature of language provides us with an explanation of the difficulty in articulating the spiritual experience. If language is indeed a wholly social construct it is capable only of giving voice to experiences that have a social dimension.

Bevir states that objective knowledge must depend on theorizing activity rather than on the experience of objects being present to consciousness (Bevir, 2000). However, the holotropic experience is wholly subjective and the 'knowledge' that it provides is not of a theoretical nature. Grof separates objective knowledge that is conceptual from the knowledge that we can experientially gain through holotropic consciousness in moments where we have an immediate experience of non-ordinary dimensions of reality (Grof, 2000). If we seek to articulate the holotropic experience we must also remember that since it is not constructed through language in the way that objective knowledge is, it may not be possible to build an accurate picture of such experiences through the medium of language (Grof, 2000; Reich, 2001; Heimbrock, 2004; Poellner, 2003; Hinterkopf, 1998). Bevir derives the claim that not only meaning but also truth must exist within a theoretical context from the idea that conceptual meaning is relational (Bevir, 2000: 424). In so doing he falls prey to allowing his own, in part socially constructed, paradigm of 'truth' to inform his judgement. If we take truth at its most basic level to mean 'that which is' then there is no reason to assume that some aspects of truth cannot be given to consciousness perceptually, through a spiritual experience.

HOLOTROPIC CONSCIOUSNESS

The key feature of spiritual experiences is their totality, the sense of a loss of personal identity in the felt vastness of the moment. Han F. De Wit refers to the spiritual as an '"egoless" open space of experience' (De Wit, 1999, quoted in Reich, 2001). For Grof the holotropic is characterized by feelings of oneness with other people but also with the Divine (Grof, 2000). These are experiences that are more than difficult to communicate linguistically in any detail—they are impossible to render through the medium of language simply by dint of being spiritual in nature. It may seem paradoxical to recognize these features and yet argue that in the holotropic moment both our being and meaning sense are shifted. Yet, although there is a sense of ego-loss there is also an attendant recognition of the profundity and significance of the moment which implies that the totality of our identity, both our meaning sense and our sense of being, are being adjusted. Heimbrock, in exploring the spiritual development of children and adolescents refers to the sacred as, '[that which] seems to correspond to the ultimate mystery that you may contact sometimes, but that cannot be possessed in the form of a picture or words' (Heimbrock, 2004: 123). A spiritual experience is usefully described by Shafranske and Gorsuch as 'a unique, personally meaningful experience' (quoted in Hinterkopf, 1998). The preferred term within this paper for the spiritual experience is holotropic, meaning 'towards wholeness' (Grof, 1976).

As well as contributing a single term that summarizes the totalizing nature of the direct spiritual experience Stanislav Grof defines the transpersonal as experiences which seem to extend our consciousness beyond the confines of either our individual ego or our temporality (Grof, 1976). This definition of the transpersonal includes the spiritual or holotropic moment and accepting this definition immediately hints at the difficulty of fully articulating such experiences. K. Helmut Reich also suggests that we can view the spiritual as an experience that goes beyond normative consciousness to the extent that we transcend the biological (Reich, 2001). If the spiritual is to mean something other than a set of value positions constructed within a societal context, if we are to accept the possibility of a divine and the further possibility of an experience of that divinity, then given the societal limits of language it is inevitable that the holotropic cannot be adequately voiced.

It has been argued by some, such as S. T. Katz and Flanagan, that mystical experiences are socially constructed and this argues against their validity as holotropic experiences (Lancaster, 2004). In order for experience to be conscious it must be possible for an individual to conceptualize from or about that experience (Poellner, 2003). In this paper I am arguing that spiritual experiences are perceptual contents of consciousness and so to meet the criteria for consciousness an individual must be able to construct conceptually out of the experience. When conceptualizing from a holotropic experience it is almost inevitable that an individual will draw on known spiritual concepts and belief systems. However, such post-hoc conceptualizations are a representation of the experience and not the experience itself. As we have said above, once one moves into the medium of language one's position with regard to one's experience is immediately interpretative and that interpretation will always be framed by the social context in which one's language use has developed. In Foucault's terms we will speak our spiritual experiences within the framework provided by the discourse community that we inhabit.

I would suggest that in order to approach a phenomenology of the Divine we need to look further back to the phenomenological ideal put forward by Husserl and the notion of the eidetic level of perception. Husserl wanted us to go back to the things themselves. He argued for the possibility of describing pure consciousness or experience. Our aim in returning to the things themselves though is to concentrate on our consciousness of these things without reference to any pre-judgements we may have of that object given to consciousness (Husserl, 1931). Myles notes that Husserl was committed to maintaining a hypothetical space in which consciousness could function free from external inscriptions (Myles, 2004: 101). I would argue that it is within the holotropic moment that such a mode of perception becomes possible.

While it seems reasonable to maintain that this is not possible in what we would call normative states of consciousness, our perceptions being informed by all manner of extra-personal factors, it seems to offer an appropriate way of understanding the spiritual experience. Bevir strongly argues that Husserl's concept of the immediacy of presence is wholly invalid within a relational theory of meaning:

> A metaphysics of presence postulates a one-to-one correspondence between concepts and their referents. It implies that signifieds do not need a theoretical context to bind them to their referents. Some signifieds are given to consciousness as brute facts independent of all else. A relational theory of meaning implies that this is not so. If all signifieds are relational, they all require a theoretical context to bind them to their referents. (Bevir, 2000)

This argument functions well within the constraints that Bevir has applied. However, Husserl's claim that the eidetic mode of perception is possible does not speak directly of 'meaning'. Rather it speaks in terms of apprehending the 'being' of that which is immediately given to consciousness. Bevir is also assuming that consciousness is of necessity conceptual and never perceptual. If we allow that a subject can experience perceptually and consciously, that such experiences carry a felt significance, if not a fully symbolized meaning, then we can also allow for the immediacy of presence without contradicting our acceptance of a relational theory of meaning. Any meaning that is ascribed to the experience, in our case that of a holotropic moment, will indeed be relational and require a theoretical context. The experience itself does not require the context since it is directly and perceptually given to consciousness.

HOLOTROPIC CONSCIOUSNESS AND THE EIDETIC MODE

In the spiritual experience moment we are a state of 'totality'; our sense of self is 'suspended' and we feel unable to adequately relate the content of that experience using language. Husserl argued that we have access to a direct experience of the world as opposed to a mediated representation thereof (Husserl, 1970). Although it is unlikely that this can be defended in the context of our normative consciousness as socially situated and embodied subjects, recognized by Depraz as a problem that needs to be addressed in considering the *epoché* (Depraz, 1999), it does offer a useful approach to spiritual experiences. Poellner describes the way in which our 'normal intentional comportment' allows us to direct our attention to a particular aspect of what is given to consciousness at any given point (Poellner, 2003). In the holotropic experience by contrast it feels as though our attention is being directed in all directions equally and extremely intensely. If we believe in the possibility of such moments of peak experience as genuinely spiritual then we can see these moments as rare points in our lives when that moment of *epoché* is achieved. Natalie Depraz explores the possibility of achieving the phenomenological reduction 'as a disciplined embodied practice' and in so doing references this praxis to a range of spiritual traditions (Depraz, 1999).

The association of the *epoché* with spirituality is also indicated by others, for instance Lewis argues that such moments of suspension are a key aim of meditative practices that are intended to achieve holotropic consciousness (Lewis, 2000). While Depraz (1999) presents the experience of the reduction as impartial and disinterested, I would argue that the moment of suspension cannot fully occur while one is occupying a conceptual framework since that framework will in some part be constructed from pre-judgements. Our attempts at impartiality will always fail as long as they are organized by our ego-self. Additionally, when reflecting on the nature of spiritual experiences we cannot bracket out our ontological framework (Lancaster, 2004). Consequently, for me the moment of reduction needs to be reconsidered as a state of consciousness that goes beyond an attempt at impartiality and enters the non-ordinary holotropic state of consciousness. Phenomenology has been utilized in theological systematization and the exploration of religious consciousness (MacDonald, 2001), and so its use in the understanding of peak spiritual experiences is in a sense a natural development.

The phenomenological project was committed to a concern with direct experience. This led to a recognition that the actuality of experience is one in which our understanding of our experience is always mediated, if by nothing else, then by language. However, it is in the apprehension of that which we may call the Divine that the mediated mode of experience is suspended. Somewhat strangely this leads us to what might be regarded as a phenomenological metaphysics. Although such a concept does not sit well with established philosophical 'genres' it does make sense when considered from the perspective of a number of mystical traditions such as Kabbalah which see the Divine as both immanent within the Universe and transcendent in essence.

It is far from usual for academic discourse to propose anything approaching a mystical paradigm. However as Grof claims: 'The data from research on non-ordinary states of consciousness represents a critical conceptual challenge for the scientific paradigm that currently dominates psychology, psychiatry, psychotherapy, and many other disciplines' (Grof, 2000).

Grof is supported in this claim by recent empirical research into the physiological and psychological effects of spiritual experiences (Lancaster, 2004). Husserlian phenomenology may provide us with an academic discourse with which to approach the holotropic experience. However, on our journey back towards Husserl we carry with us the insights of later philosophers on the socially contextualized nature of language and the way in which we perceive and understand our life-world. In the context of such developments it is extremely difficult to regard objects as being possessed of an essence that is potentially available identically to any subject (Depraz, 1999; Husserl, 1982), partly because as Gadamer would argue, in terms of our normative consciousness, it is our prejudices that significantly constitute our sense of self (Gadamer, 2001).

It is worth noting that in her conclusion to her paper on the phenomenological reduction Depraz is at pains to argue that the reduction 'has nothing to do with anything mysterious or esoteric' (Depraz, 1999). I would argue that if we accept the deeply ingrained socially constructed and psychologically influenced nature of our perceptions, the achievement of a genuinely complete bracketing or *epoché* does require an experience of the holotropic type.

Retaining Husserlian typology we can regard the socio-cultural framework within which our normative consciousness operates as part of our *habitus* that feeds the *urdoxa* and its socialized form, the *doxa* (Myles, 2004). The *epoché* can be visualized as an instantaneous dismantling of this framework, caused by the non-ordinary state of consciousness brought about in the holotropic moment (Grof, 1976), thus the eidetic mode of perception does not require a determination to engage in the bracketing activity since the *epoché* is not deliberately effected, rather it erupts within the subject uncontrollably. Freeing ourselves from phenomenological terminology we could restate this in a directly spiritual lexicon and say that at peak moments of deep experience we are able to temporarily leave behind our ego-awareness and inhabit a consciousness that approaches the universal.

Although we have proposed conceptualizing the holotropic experience as a type of eidetic perception, we are left in something of an impasse in that we can attach a label to the experience and yet the moment we begin to talk about the experience itself we lose that which fundamentally defines it—its unmediated character. The labelling of an experience as holotropic suggests that something is being experienced within the consciousness which is outside the normal run of experience, beyond an idea or a thought and partly categorized as spiritual by its perceptual status. Gendlin's Focusing approach (Gendlin, 1997) offers us an avenue by which as individuals we can better attend to the felt aspect of our experiences, and its particular use in terms of spiritual experiences is proposed in detail by Elsie Hinterkopf (1998). We find similar approaches to felt-experience in De Wit's concept of 'contemplative psychology' for instance, which suggests a range of ways in which we can consciously attend to the nature of our inner experience (De Wit, 1999, cited in Reich, 2001). However, none of these approaches can fully remove the problem caused by the fact that once the perceptual is reconstituted as conceptual by its articulation the possibility of a one-to-one correspondence with the experience itself is lost.

CONCLUSIONS

It is because of the resistance to articulation of holotropic consciousness that this paper talks in terms of moving 'towards' a phenomenology of the Divine. We can only ever move towards it, but until some hypothetical future point where we are the possessors of a value-neutral mode of discourse we cannot fix it linguistically, or talk about such experiences as they are for the subject. The nature of the holotropic moment is that it defies location as either object or as the project of a subject and so cannot be conceptually manipulated. Moreover, to seek to specifically define the nature of the sacred would be oxymoronic (Heimbrock, 2004: 128; Winnicott, 1951/1958). This should not necessarily be regarded as problematic. The desire to fix experience through language and in so doing assign it to certain categories is just that—a desire, and it has often been said that desire is always a block to spiritual understanding.

As other philosophical paradigms, from a non-Eurocentric perspective, are increasingly accepted (Priest, 2002: 95, 99) and the historically contingent nature of epistemology is exposed (Foucault, 1970) we may see a general retreat from the focus on meaning-extraction. This is not to say that the holotropic experience does not deepen our sense of self-understanding. To paraphrase Levinas on our awareness of others

(Levinas, 1979, quoted in Zahavi, 2001): it is in the absence of ego-self that the presence of ego-self is given to consciousness. In other words, a holotropic experience removes me temporarily from my sense of ego, and having experienced that removal I am better placed to explore my sense of ego when I return anew to a normative state of consciousness not least because self-knowledge is 'intrinsically transformational' (Lancaster, 2004: 12).

I would also argue that in framing the holotropic within a philosophical discourse we can begin, as Grof advocates, to examine the spiritual as a legitimate aspect of the psyche and the world (Grof, 2000). Such examinations should perhaps not simply focus on the individual experience, but also on the innate connections between selves, the given capacity for intersubjectivity described by Merleau-Ponty, Meltzoff and Moore among others (Zahavi, 2001). It is even possible to read Husserl's own words as unwittingly pointing to the spiritual when he writes in his *Cartesian Meditations* that true being and consciousness are 'essentially interdependent and united' (Zahavi, 2004: 52).

If 'peak' experiences are moments of totality and universality perhaps we should not even be seeking a 'meaning' for them. If the holotropic experience represents a genuine encounter with Divinity, then the meaning of meaning as intended within the title of this paper is not relational at all, and so is neither conceptual nor susceptible to articulation. In this regard I would disagree with Brian Lancaster who argues for a conceptual approach to spiritual experience (Lancaster, 2004). It may in fact be that the spiritual experience is one in which we are able to experience pure 'beingness', which when experienced in an unmediated manner does not require any definition, any meaning, in order to be fully understood. Perhaps the closest we can come to representing this experience would be in the Kabbalistic title of the Godhead on the Tree of Life—*Eheieh* which translates as 'I am that which is'.

REFERENCES

Bailey, E (1998) *Implicit Religion: An introduction*. London: Middlesex University Press.

Bailey, E (2001) *The Secular Faith Controversy: Religion in three dimensions*. London: Continuum.

Baudrillard, J (1998) *Symbolic Exchange and Death* (trans I Hamilton Grant). London: Sage.

Bellah, R (1970) *Beyond Belief.* New York: Harper and Row.

Bevir, M (2000) Meaning, truth, and phenomenology. *Metaphilosophy, 31* (4), 412–16.

Bourdieu, P (1999) *The Weight of the World*. Cambridge: Polity.

Cox, H (1977) *Turning East: The promise and peril of the New Orientalism*. New York: Simon and Schuster.

Crane, T (ed) (1992) *The Contents of Experience*. Cambridge: Cambridge University Press.

Depraz, N (1999) The phenomenological reduction as praxis. *Journal of Consciousness Studies, 6* (2), 95–110.

Depraz, N (2001) The Husserlian Theory of Intersubjectivity as Alterology-Emergent Theories and Wisdom Traditions in the light of Genetic Phenomenology. *Journal of Consciousness Studies, 8* (5), 169–78.

Derrida, J (1977) *Of Grammatology* (trans G Spivak). Baltimore: Johns Hopkins University Press.

Derrida, J (1982) *Margins of Philosophy* (trans A Bass). Brighton: Harvester Press.
Eliade, M (1976) *Occultism, Witchcraft, and Cultural Fashions*. Chicago: University of Chicago Press.
Foucault, M (1970) *The Order of Things*. London: Routledge.
Gadamer, H (2001) *Truth and Method* (trans J Weinsheimer & D Marshall). London: Sheed & Ward Ltd.
Gendlin, E (1997) *Experiencing and the Creation of Meaning—A philosophical and psychological approach to the subjective*. Illinois: Northwestern University Press.
Green, M (1992) *Prophets of a New Age*. New York: Scribner's.
Grof, S (1976) *Realms of the Human Unconscious*. New York: EP Dutton.
Grof, S (2000) *Psychology of the Future. Lessons from modern consciousness research*. Albany: State University of New York Press.
Habermas, J (1984) *Theory of Communicative Action*. Cambridge: Polity Press.
Heimbrock, H-G (2004) Beyond secularization: Experiences of the sacred in childhood and adolescence as a challenge for RE development theory. *British Journal of Religious Education, 26* (2), 119–31.
Hinterkopf, E (1998) *Integrating Spirituality in Counseling: A manual for using the Experiential Focusing Method*. Baltimore: American Counseling Association.
Husserl, E (1931) *Ideas: General introduction to pure phenomenology* (trans W Gibson). London: George Allen and Unwin.
Husserl, E (1970) *Logical Investigations, Vols I & II*. London: Routledge.
Husserl, E (1982) *Ideas Pertaining to a Pure Phenomenology and to a Phenomenological Philosophy. First Book* (trans F Kersten). The Hague: Nijhoff.
Jameson, F (1991) *Postmodernism, or, The cultural logic of late capitalism*. Durham: Duke University Press.
Lancaster, B (2004) *Approaches to Consciousness—The marriage of science and mysticism*. Basingstoke: Palgrave Macmillan.
Lewis, J (2000) Spiritual education as the cultivation of qualities of the heart and mind, a reply to Blake and Carr. *Oxford Review of Education, 26* (2), 264–83.
Luckmann, T (1967) *The Invisible Religion: The problem of religion in modern society*. New York: Macmillan.
MacDonald, P (2001) Current approaches to Phenomenology. *Inquiry, 44*, 101–24.
McDonald, H (2002) The ontological turn: Philosophical sources of American literary theory. *Inquiry, 45*, 3–34.
Myles, J (2004) From doxa to experience—Issues in Bourdieu's adoption of Husserlian phenomenology. *Theory, Culture & Society, 21* (2), 91–107.
Nagel, T (1998) What is it like to be a bat? In N Block, O Flanagan and G Güzeldere (eds) *The Nature of Consciousness*. Cambridge, MA: MIT Press.
Poellner, P (2003) Non-conceptual content, experience and the self. *Journal of Consciousness Studies, 10* (2), 32–57.
Priest, G (2002) Where is philosophy at the start of the twenty-first century? Presented at a meeting of the Aristotelian Society held at the University of London.
Reich, K (2001) Spiritual development: Han F De Wit's and Stanislav Grof's differing approaches. *Zygon, 36* (3), 509–20.
Roof, W (1993) *A Generation of Seekers*. San Francisco: Harper Collins.
Rudge, L (1998) 'I am nothing'—Does it matter? A critique of current religious education policy

and practice in England on behalf of the silent majority. *British Journal of Religious Education, 20* (3), 155–65.

Rudge, L (2004) [unpublished] Implicit religion, secular faith and religious education. Presented to a symposium on implicit religion at University of East Anglia.

Shear, J (ed) (1997) *Explaining Consciousness: The 'hard problem'.* Cambridge, MA: MIT Press.

Vadén, T (2001) Qualifying qualia through the Skyhook Test. *Inquiry, 44*, 149–70.

West, W (2004) *Spiritual Issues in Therapy: Relating experience to practice.* Basingstoke: Palgrave Macmillan.

Winnicott, D (1951/58) Transitional objects and transitional phenomena. *DW Winnicott Collected Papers.* London: Tavistock.

Zahavi, D (1998) Phenomenal consciousness and self-awareness: A phenomenological critique of Representational Theory. *Journal of Consciousness Studies, 5* (5), 687–705.

Zahavi, D (2001) Beyond empathy: Phenomenological approaches to intersubjectivity. *Journal of Consciousness Studies, 8* (5), 151–67.

Zahavi, D (2004) Husserl's noema and the internalism–externalism debate. *Inquiry, 47*, 42–66.

SECONDARY REFERENCES

Bell, D (1990) *Husserl.* London: Routledge.

Bourdieu, P (2000) *Pascalian Meditations.* Cambridge: Polity.

De Wit, H (1999) *The Spiritual Path: An introduction to the psychology of the spiritual traditions* (trans H Jansen). Pittsburgh: Duquesne University Press.

Dodd, J (1997) *Idealism and Corporeality: An essay on the problem of the body in Husserl's phenomenology.* Dordrecht and London: Kluwer.

Donaldson, M (1992) *Human Minds: An exploration.* London: Penguin.

Levinas E (1979) *Les Temps et L'Autre.* Paris: Fata Morgana.

Shafranske, E & Gorsuch, R (1984) Factors associated with the perception of spirituality in psychotherapy. *Journal of Transpersonal Psychology, 16* (1), 231–41.

Taylor, C (1982) Responsibility for self. In *Free Will* (ed G Wilson). Oxford: Oxford University Press.

CHAPTER 6

TOWARDS A ROGERIAN THEORY OF MYSTICISM

IVAN ELLINGHAM

THE NATURE OF MYSTICISM

Mysticism is a term used with reference to certain out-of-the-ordinary human experiences, experiences of a powerful nature belonging to that category of human experience that we label 'spiritual'. Mystical experiences, that is to say, are powerful versions of experiences in which the individual knows that they, the world and those around them are seamlessly embedded in, and manifestations of, a unitary and ultimate, transcendent cosmic reality, a reality that F. C. Happold describes as 'a *beyond* ... something which, though it is interwoven with it, is not of the external world of material phenomena ... an *unseen* order over and above the seen' (1970: 18–19; original emphasis)—'an actuality', as Evelyn Underhill further elucidates, that is 'beyond the reach of the senses'(1915/2000: 5).

Such a spiritual actuality is deemed, too, to be beyond the logic of discursive language and the categories that such language mediates in our everyday consciousness (James, 1902/1982: 380; White, 1972: x; Zaehner, 1957/1961: 198), an actuality, in other words, that is beyond such categories as 'interior' and exterior'; 'presence and absence'; 'personal' and 'impersonal'; 'subject' and 'object'; 'me', 'you', and 'it'; 'sameness' and 'difference'. In mystical experience this 'beyond in the midst' (Bonhoeffer, 1959) is said to be apprehended in a direct and unmediated manner; in a modality of experiencing that itself transcends the discursive categories of 'thought' and 'emotion'. Operative in mystical experience, that is, is a form of intuition or insight of a feeling/knowing kind, a manner of apprehending in which a sense of certitude regarding the truth-value of one's apprehensions is infused with the aura of profound and blissful meaning, awe-full and wonder-full love.

Mystical literature gives various names to the transcendent actuality so apprehended, names that usually begin with capital letters: viz., Reality, Absolute Reality, Divine Reality, Transcendent Reality, Ultimate Reality, the Ultimately Real, the Absolute, the Good, the One; not to mention Brahman and God. Here the use, in particular, of Divine Reality, Brahman, and God calls attention to the intimate relationship of mystical experience with religious and spiritual traditions. As Nona Coxhead notes:

> [T]he 'mystic element' can be traced in records of all primitive religions. It is present in most of the Eastern spiritual philosophies such as Hinduism, Buddhism, Taoism; in the Hellenic 'Mystery Religions'; in the Hebrew and Jewish Old Testament and Christian New Testament of the Bible; in Eastern Christianity and Western Catholicism and Protestantism; in Islamic Sufism. (Coxhead, 1985: 5)

For Margaret Smith, though, 'Mysticism ... is not to be regarded as religion in itself, but rather as the vital element in all true religions, rising up in revolt against cold formality and religious torpor' (1980: 20). Smith's view echoes that of William Inge, who declares that 'mysticism ... that dim consciousness of the beyond is ... the raw material of all religion' and as such 'the fresh springs of inner life' that foster 'a revival of spirituality in the midst of formalism or unbelief' (1899/1956: 5).

When we use the term 'mysticism', it is usually this close connection between religion and mystical experience that is uppermost in our minds. But, as Inge himself points out, mystical experience is not limited to the domain of religion and spiritual traditions; it also serves as the wellspring 'perhaps of all philosophy and art' (ibid: 5)—an opinion other authorities definitively endorse (Coxhead, 1985; Gilbert, 1991; Happold, 1970).

Neither is science to be left out of this bigger mystical picture. Michael Polanyi, especially, strongly argues:

> The discovery of objective truth in science consists in the apprehension of a rationality which commands our respect and arouses contemplative admiration; that such discovery, while using the experience of our senses as clues, transcends this experience by embracing a vision of a reality beyond the impression of our senses, a vision which speaks for itself in guiding us to an ever deeper understanding of reality. (Polanyi, 1964: 5–6)

So we see that mystical experience has not just been considered the fount of established religions and spiritual traditions, but of the other cultural enterprises of philosophy, art and science.

Another cultural domain with which mysticism is said to have a similar relationship is the domain of ethics and morality, that domain concerned with the art of living and rightful conduct. Mystically apprehending oneself to be part and parcel of a transcendent order in which one is one with the world and the other exercises a galvanizing and transformative effect upon individuals. They experience understanding who they truly are and how best to conduct themselves in their relationships with the world and with others.

Established religions and spiritual traditions greatly concern themselves, of course, with the nature of human identity and with what is or what is not proper conduct. However, mystical experiences that so transform a person's 'way of being' need not occur within any formal religious or spiritual context. Such experiences frequently occur outside these formal contexts, seeming to come from out of the blue in a powerful manner—a number of adults relate enjoying 'spontaneous' mystical experiences of this kind in childhood (Robinson, 1977a). Various phenomena 'trigger' them, e.g., having sex, being depressed, appreciating art. When such experiences occur in relation to nature, though, they are referred to as 'nature mysticism', although a more general term, 'cosmic consciousness', is also used, a term used to connote that 'without and within are one' (Zaehner, 1957: 41). Irish novelist Forrest Reid gives us a flavour of such an experience when he writes, 'It was within me that the trees waved their green branches, it was within me that the skylark was singing, it was within me that the hot sun shone, and that the shade was cool' (in Zaehner, 1957: 41).

Contrasting with 'spontaneous' mystical experiences are those described as 'induced', experiences that arise in formal religious or spiritual contexts. In these contexts, past knowledge of what has facilitated the occurrence of mystical experience has led to the development of a discipline of specific beliefs and practices geared to such an end. Individuals who have committed themselves to these disciplines and enjoyed mystical experience record undergoing a roller coaster emotional journey; of travelling a developmental highway wherein, according to Evelyn Underhill, 'the stages of its slow transcendence of the sense-world [are] marked by episodes of splendour and of terror' (1912/1955: 445). 'It is,' says Underhill, 'an organic life-process' (1915/2000: 81–2).

Christian literature terms this organic sequence of peaks and troughs the *Mystic Way*, whereas Buddhists speak of the *Path to Enlightenment*. With some form of meditation a key rite of passage (and sometimes the taking of drugs), progress along this developmental pathway is proportional to a person's fitness as a traveller, fitness involving the purging of those aspects of her or his way of being that prevent them attuning themselves to the transcendental spiritual order.

Those who successfully travel the *Mystic Way* encounter experiences of oneness with others and the cosmos in general. But they are likely to encounter, too, strange and unusual experiences, including heightening of the five senses, extrasensory perceptions, and inner visions and auditions. When the term 'mysticism' is broadened to characterize disciplined pursuit of the mystic pathway, such bizarre experiences also tend to be dubbed 'mystical'. Most scholars, though, prefer to stick to deploying the term 'mysticism' where there is a more direct relationship to the final goal of the mystic path. This final goal or stage is that in which the being of the mystic pilgrim is so purified as to constitute oneness with the Ultimate, existential union apprehended in a direct and unmediated fashion devoid of any image or specific perceptual content.

Differences exist between spiritual traditions in describing and conceiving a condition wherein 'The knower and the known are one' (Meister Eckhart, in Huxley, 1946/1958: 25). So, for instance, 'in Christian terminology', informs R. Zaehner, 'mysticism means union with God; in non-theistical contexts it also means union with some principle or other' (1957: 32). It is a matter of academic debate whether such differences are (a) simply different interpretations of the same experiential condition—i.e., whether in experiencing a condition that does not fit the discursive categories of everyday consciousness, of 'personal' or 'impersonal', one tradition interprets things in terms of the category of the personal and the other in terms of the impersonal; or (b) indicative of a more fundamental difference.

However, whether the descriptions refer to a theistic, 'I–Thou' encounter (to a communion of one person with another), or to a monistic oneness with an infinite principle, the admonitions of William Blake and Evelyn Underhill still apply: that reaching the final goal of the mystic path involves some kind of cleansing or purification process, of eliminating the negative to become more whole and wholesome. 'If the doors of perception were cleansed', Blake famously recounts, 'everything could be seen as it is, infinite' (Huxley, 1946/1958: 197). For, describes Underhill, 'the pure soul is like a lens from which all the irrelevancies and excrescences, all the beams and motes of egotism and prejudice have been removed; so that it may reflect a clear image of the one Transcendent Fact within which all other facts are held' (1915/2000: 8). In other words, as Jesus divined: 'Blessed are the pure in heart, for they shall see God'.

Terms that mystics employ to portray the character of that which they apprehend in the final Unitive state include the Void, the Divine Nothing, and the Dazzling Darkness. Buddhism with its emphasis on monistic oneness uses the term 'Emptiness', the nature of which is described by Daisetz Suzuki. Declares Suzuki:

> In Buddhist Emptiness there is no time, no space, no becoming, no thing-ness, it is what makes all these things possible; it is a zero full of infinite possibilities, it is a void of inexhaustible contents. Pure experience is the mind seeing itself as reflected in itself, it is an act of self-identification, a state of suchness. This is possible only ... when the mind is devoid of all its possible contents except itself. (Suzuki, 1957: 19)

By contrast, Christians speak of the blissful experiencing of the living and loving presence of the imageless Other, of two becoming one in a 'spiritual marriage'.

To denote the contentless experience of Union, modern students of mysticism employ the term 'the pure consciousness experience', PCE for short (Foreman, 1990). The claim is that the PCE is an apprehension of reality as it truly is, one unconditioned and free from the categories of sense-making that constitute our cultural heritage.

As the lives of great mystics such as Buddha and St Teresa of Avila bear witness, attainment of the peak mystical experience serves not for detachment from the everyday world—even if the mystic has transcended the 'attachments' of everyday consciousness—but for energetic, fruitful and creative activity in the world, often performed with childlike spontaneity and gaiety. Robert Foreman (1990: 8) thus posits that such individuals enjoy a form of the PCE of an enduring, not transient, nature, one that is maintained in everyday activities. Conceivably this is what Martin Buber means when he declares that 'we can stand in the *I–Thou* relationship not merely with other men [*sic*] but with beings and things which come to meet us in nature' (1958: 124–5). Certainly it is a relationship with the world wherein individuals feel they are personally attuned to a transcendent order and acting in harmony with a power greater than themselves—a state of affairs that prompts Evelyn Underhill to aver that 'broadly speaking' she understands mysticism 'to be the innate tendency of the human spirit towards complete harmony with the transcendent order' (1912/1955: xiv). Harmony with the transcendent it may be, but there are times when such harmony leads to disharmony and even conflict with the existing world order. For the reliance by mystics upon private inspiration and personal creativity 'often puts them on a course that defies traditional practices, and they may find themselves at war with established authority' (Committee on Psychiatry and Religion, 1976: 719).

Such a brief overview of mysticism's main features fails to adequately portray the extent of academic disagreement over its precise definition and nature. What, for instance, is the meaning of the differences between Eastern and Western spiritual traditions in characterizing mystical experience? Is it fair to speak of a common experience across such traditions? What of the relationship between mysticism and madness? Like mystics, 'psychotic' individuals are convinced that their visions and auditions provide true knowledge. Are we to say that mysticism is a form of madness, or that madness is a form of mysticism?

As Frits Staal points out in his book *Exploring Mysticism* (1975), 'A rational explanation of a phenomenon requires the formulation of a theory which purports to explain that phenomenon' (1975: 17). Academic disagreement over the nature of mysticism indicates that we do not possess such a theory. Thus, Staal elucidates, 'since we do not have a theory of mysticism, we do not know precisely what mysticism is and we are not in a position to provide a definition' (1975: 18). The way to remedy such a state of affairs, according to Staal, is first to recognize that 'whatever it may turn out to be in addition, the study of mysticism is at least in part the study of certain aspects of the mind' (1975: 186). 'Mysticism and mystical experience', he asserts, 'cannot be understood in isolation from the more general problem of the nature of mind. Conversely, no theory of mind which cannot account for mystical experience can be adequate' (1975: 186).

On such a premise the kind of individual Staal considers best positioned to provide a rational, theoretical explanation of the nature of mysticism is a psychologist, an individual who seeks scientific understanding of the mind. But not any kind of psychologist; rather someone who has an open-minded attitude towards mysticism; someone who has engaged in spiritual practices and undergone mystical experiences first hand.

Such a someone, to my mind, is humanistic psychologist Carl Rogers, founder of person-centred therapy. Rogers, I contend, not only was open-minded towards mystical experience, not only enjoyed mystical experiences through engaging in spiritual practices, but provided us with the conceptual foundation for the development of a rational/ scientific understanding of mysticism. Below I examine Rogers' ideas vis-à-vis mysticism and go on to suggest how they might be augmented to furnish the kind of explanation that Staal envisions.

CARL ROGERS AND THE MYSTICAL, SPIRITUAL DIMENSION

At the end of his life, having spent over a quarter of a century engaged in scientific research into the nature of psychotherapy, Carl Rogers published an article entitled 'The Foundations of a Person-Centered Approach' (1980), an article singularly significant apropos developing a rational/scientific understanding of mysticism.

In this article, reflecting upon his work as an individual therapist and as a group facilitator, particularly on those moments when he was at his best, Rogers remarks that:

> Our experiences in therapy and in groups, it is clear, involve the transcendent, the indescribable, the spiritual. I am compelled to believe that I, like many others, have underestimated the importance of this mystical, spiritual dimension. (Rogers, 1980: 131)

This pronouncement is specially meaningful due to the fact that in his twenties Rogers had decisively turned his back on religion. After initially setting out to train as a Christian minister, Rogers forsook his Christian faith to qualify instead as a clinical psychologist. Thereafter he never again devoted himself to formal religious practices; and even after his re-estimation of 'the mystical, spiritual dimension' still confessed to only employing 'the word "spiritual" ... reluctantly' and not to 'like using religious terminology' (1984: 417). Thus, despite his own and others' experiences of a mystical, spiritual nature, and despite being prepared to accept others' judgement that he himself was 'very spiritual', Rogers still maintained that 'to talk about spirituality and God is not what gives life its religious or spiritual quality' (1984: 418).

If, then, Rogers came to enjoy mystical/spiritual experiences and was himself recognized as 'very spiritual', if he achieved such experiences and such a way of being without indulging in formal religious/spiritual activities, and if he did not explain such matters in traditional religious or spiritual terms, it seems reasonable (a) to appraise those practices through which he came to experience and exemplify the 'mystical, spiritual dimension', and (b) to examine his theoretical explanation of such matters in areligious and would-be scientific terms.

Rogers' 'Foundations' paper (1980) serves as a rich resource when it comes to furthering such investigation. For in this paper Rogers not only presents his key hypothesis apropos explaining mystical experience, but he makes reference to the two disciplinary practices that facilitated his personal development of 'mystical' abilities: the practice of psychotherapy and the practice of science.

In the succeeding discussion I consider in turn the 'mystical/spiritual' element in Rogers' characterization of the disciplines of psychotherapy and of science. Following which, I elaborate upon Rogers' concept of the formative tendency as the key hypothesis for the development of a rational/scientific explanation of mysticism.

THE PRACTICE OF PSYCHOTHERAPY

Regarding the practice of psychotherapy, as early as 1955 we find Rogers referring to the 'almost mystical subjectivity of myself as therapist ... when I am at my best in this function' (1967: 200). Familiarity with the ideas of the Jewish philosopher Martin Buber leads Rogers at this time to propose that in these 'deepest parts of therapy ... there is, to borrow Buber's phrase, a real 'I–Thou' relationship, a timeless living in the experience which is *between* the client and me' (1967: 202). 'When', he expands, 'there is this complete unity, singleness, fullness of experiencing in the relationship, then it acquires the "out-of-this-world" quality which many therapists have remarked upon, a sort of trance-like feeling.'

Buber, for his part, goes beyond portraying the 'I–Thou' relationship as the most loving, open and intimate of relationships between human beings. He also construes it as the relationship that obtains between the person and God. Rogers, to an extent, mirrors Buber in this respect, since, in tracing Rogers' thinking after 1955 we discover that, like Buber, he places the 'I–Thou' moments of therapy within a transcendental context. In 1955 Rogers describes 'the deepest parts of therapy' as those in which 'I do not *know*, cognitively, where ... [the] relationship is leading' since 'it is as though both I and the client ... let ourselves slip into the stream of becoming [or life], a stream or process which carries us along (1967: 202). Whereas in his 1980 Foundations article, he associates his best moments as group facilitator or therapist with being in touch with a transcendent, spiritual order. 'When', he says,

> I am closest to my intuitive self, when I am somehow in touch with the unknown in me, when perhaps I am in a slightly altered state of consciousness ... when I can relax and be close to the transcendental core of me, then I may behave in strange and impulsive ways in the relationship, ways that I cannot possibly justify rationally, which have nothing to do with my thought processes. But these strange behaviors turn out to be *right* in some odd way: it seems that my inner spirit has reached out and touched the inner spirit of the other. Our relationship transcends itself and becomes a part of something larger. (1980: 129)

That it is attunement to a transcendental order that sways his behaviour in such moments is underscored by Rogers through his witness to the 'peculiar satisfaction' and enrichment he experiences in 'really hearing someone', in 'resonating' to them 'at all levels' (Rogers, 1980: 8–9). Beyond his previous assertion that 'what is most personal is most general' (1967: 26), Rogers now boldly proclaims that such in-depth listening involves 'feeling one's self in touch with what is universally true' (1980: 8). Rogers avers:

> It is like listening to the music of the spheres because beyond the immediate message of the person, no matter what that might be, there is the universal. Hidden in all of the personal communication which I really hear there seem to be orderly psychological laws, aspects of the same order we find in the universe as a whole. (Rogers, 1980: 8)

In terms of spiritual traditions, what Rogers is describing here is 'mystical enlightenment'. For, states John White, 'Enlightenment reveals that *what is most deeply personal is also most universal.* In the mystical state, reality and ideality become one' (1972: xiv, my emphasis).

Accepting, then, that Rogers was privy to mystical experience vis-à-vis his person-centred practice of psychotherapy, what of the spiritual discipline he pursued that facilitated his development of this capacity? In other words, if 'the practice of person-centred therapy is a profound spiritual discipline' (Thorne, 2002: ix), what *specifically* is it that makes it so?

Thus far we have seen that for Rogers the discipline of practising person-centred therapy involves him relaxing and 'tuning in to his transcendental core'. That Rogers became capable of this depth of attunement seems to have been the reward for many years of determinedly refining a mode of interpersonal knowing that transcends the discursive knowing of everyday consciousness. Describing his method, Rogers says:

> I let myself go into the immediacy of the relationship where it is my total organism which takes over and is sensitive to the relationship, not simply my consciousness. I am not consciously responding in a planful or analytic way, but simply react in an unreflective way, my reaction being based (but not consciously) on the total organismic sensitivity to this other person. (Rogers, 1967: 202)

This description by Rogers appears to match what Freud terms 'evenly suspended attention', the successful exercise of which, according to Rogers, requires a person to be 'without any cognitive or emotional barriers to a complete "letting go" in understanding' (1967: 202).

Such a notion of cognitive and emotional barriers getting in the way of true and full knowing of the other obviously parallels the views expressed in spiritual literature referred to earlier: that spiritual purification is a necessary prerequisite for true spiritual perception to be achieved, especially Underhill's pronouncement that 'the pure soul' is one 'from which … all the beams and motes of egotism and prejudice have been removed' (1915/2000: 8).

Freud used the term 'fixations' for the kind of barriers that Rogers refers to; and it is exactly this Freudian term that Michael Whiteman employs in declaring that 'we are all a mass of fixations, and essentially the mystical way is to release these fixations one by one until there comes a time when they are released without effort, because our response has become open and unified' (Whiteman in Robinson, 1977b: 154). Janet Malcolm (1982: 26) makes a similar linkage in testifying to a kinship between Freud's 'evenly suspended attention' and Zen meditation, a discipline that Zen abbot Daishin Morgan (2004) emphasizes is specifically concerned with 'letting go'.

When it comes to explaining how an individual comes to develop psychological barriers to fulsome understanding and knowing, Rogers (like Freud and his account of fixations) focuses his attention primarily upon the experience of the child.

As an infant, says Rogers, a person starts life relying totally on the inner wisdom of her organism as the means by which to make sense of what she encounters. She deals with the world in a flexible and fluid manner, in process terms; she knows nonverbally 'what is good for her and what is not'; 'she is the center of the valuing process' (1983: 258). Unfortunately, cautions Rogers, this open and unsullied apprehending of self, world and other can become dimmed and distorted under circumstances in which 'love from a parent or significant other is made conditional' on the child introjecting 'certain constructs and values' belonging to that parental figure. 'These values', Rogers explains, 'are rigid and static since they are not part of the child's normal valuing process of his experience' (1963: 19). As alien introjects, they stand in the way of our appreciating reality for what it is and of our becoming integrated human beings. They thus reinforce the impact of the development, particularly in the West, 'of static concepts—in the formation of our language, in our thought, in our philosophy' (ibid.). Here, in his focus upon culture, Rogers acknowledges that he is serving as the mouthpiece for Lancelot Whyte and Whyte's hypothesis that 'though nature is clearly process, man [*sic*] has been caught in his own fixed forms of thought' and thereby comes 'to lose his proper organic integration' (ibid.).

Viewed from a 'spiritual' perspective, the pattern Rogers posits—of initial integration and undistorted apprehension of reality subsequently becoming sullied by the influence of society—obviously reprises the familiar religious theme of paradise lost. Likewise, when Rogers portrays the attributes of the individual who has wrestled free from such alien conditioning, his account closely resembles spiritual narratives of 'paradise regained'. Paralleling the description in spiritual literature of the mystic as one who enjoys re-found bliss and a re-found original vision, Rogers provides us with an account of the 'psychologically mature adult', or 'fully functioning person' (1967, 1983), where what is noteworthy about such a person is that in 'functioning fully there are no barriers, no inhibitions, which prevent the full experiencing of whatever is organismically present' (1980: 128). In consequence, just as the high functioning mystic is said to be childlike, so, 'like the infant', asserts Rogers:

> the psychologically mature adult trusts and uses the wisdom of her organism, with the difference that she is able to do so knowingly. She realizes that if she can trust all of herself, her feelings and her intuitions may be wiser than her mind, that as a total person she can be more sensitive and accurate than her thoughts alone. (Rogers, 1983: 264)

Clear comparisons can therefore be drawn between Rogers' characterization of the fully functioning person as one who is 'free from introjects' and thereby 'a unity of flow, of motion', 'an integrated process of changingness' (1980: 127, 1967: 158), and descriptions in spiritual literature of the way of being of the mystic: with, for example, Underhill's portrayal of the unitive mystic as one in whom 'the self is remade, transformed, [and] has at last unified itself' (1912/1955: 416); or Roger Westcott's (1972: 30) account that such an individual enjoys 'a state of consciousness' called '*moksha*, "released"'. Elaborates Westcott:

> In the released state the waking intellect no longer attempts to stay the cosmic process by chopping it into segments or rigidifying it into an entity. Instead it flows—like the world movement of which it is part. (1972: 30–1)

Such 'released' freedom, Rogers makes plain, involves the freedom to care, the freedom to love, which again—if David Brazier (1993) is right in his revision of Rogers' thought—is also the re-finding on a higher level of the loving way of being of the infant. It is significant, therefore, that Rogers employs the Christian term for love, *agape*, in describing the way of being of the effective therapist in relation to her client (Rogers & Stevens, 1967: 94). Involving as it does a fully functioning awareness and childlike letting go, Rogers hypothesizes that intrinsic to such a therapeutic *modus operandi* is the communication to the other of the 'core' attitudinal conditions of empathic understanding, prizing or unconditional positive regard, and congruence or authenticity.

Whether for 'therapeutic' we should here read 'spiritual' is a moot point in the light of *The Spiritual Exercises* of Ignatius Loyola (1990) that aim at the development of empathy towards others; not to mention Alfred Adler's assertion that empathy is a form of 'a social feeling' originating in 'a cosmic feeling and a reflection of the connectedness of the whole cosmos which lives in us' (in May, 1967: 79).

Confirming this cosmic-cum-spiritual connection vis-à-vis the fully functioning person, Rogers posits that through becoming 'more free from introjects', and thereby more aware of 'whatever is organismically present', this person is more likely to make conscious choices that are 'in tune with the evolutionary flow' (1980: 127–8).

> Moving in the direction of wholeness, integration, a unified life', he or she, says Rogers, 'more surely ... will float in a direction consonant with the directional evolutionary flow' and so serve 'as a fit vanguard of evolution' (1980: 127–8, 1983: 292).

According to Rogers, therefore, this 'more complete development of awareness' represents the level at which 'new forms are invented' and 'perhaps even new directions for the human species' (1980: 127). With the farthest advance of consciousness involving 'a transcendent awareness of the harmony and unity of the cosmic system, including humankind', it is perhaps here, he suggests, that 'we are touching the cutting edge of our ability to transcend ourselves, to create new and more spiritual directions in human evolution' (1980: 133-4).

So we see that Rogers' revering of the 'mystical, spiritual dimension' relates to his explicitly connecting mystical/spiritual experiencing with the further evolution of the cosmos; to him, the form of consciousness possessed by the fully functioning person represents the spearhead of evolutionary advance.

In drawing such a connection, Rogers' account closely accords once again with that found in spiritual literature. 'In the great mystics', declares Evelyn Underhill, 'we see the highest and widest development of that [spiritual] consciousness to which the human race has yet attained' (1912/1955: 444–5). Whereas F. Happold hypothesizes that if the advance of evolution is to be identified with 'the growth of an ever wider form of consciousness ... which will result in an ability to see aspects of the universe as yet only faintly glimpsed ... may we not see in the mystics the forerunners of a type of consciousness, which will become more and more common as mankind [*sic*] ascends higher and higher up the ladder of evolution?' (1970: 34).

Happold acknowledges that his hypothesis is essentially that of Teilhard de Chardin. Rogers was familiar with Teilhard's work and when interviewed late in life confessed to being open to the notion that Jesus, Buddha and Krishna, and other 'Spiritual Masters' were 'Adepts' involved in evolving 'new forms of spiritual existence', an evolution he associates with Teilhard's notion of 'the *noosphere*' as a new form of consciousness (Rogers, 1984).

THE PRACTICE OF SCIENCE

Another area of Rogers' life pertaining to the mystical, spiritual dimension is his engagement with science, both as a scientific researcher into the nature of psychotherapy and as a writer on the nature of science. 'Like most people who are consumed by a scientific passion', posits Maureen O'Hara, 'Rogers could also be seen as a mystic' for 'like the mystic, the scientist is fired by a desire to come ever closer to a direct experience of this [the universe's] lawfulness or harmony' (1995: 41). 'I don't believe that this is a chance universe', declares Rogers (1984), thereby confirming O'Hara's affirmation that 'at the heart of the scientific vocation is a basic metaphysical belief that must be taken on faith if science is to continue: the fundamental faith that the universe is not random, capricious, or arbitrary but is in fact lawful, orderly, and understandable' (1995: 41).

In theorizing upon the nature of science, Rogers was much influenced by the ideas of Michael Polanyi. In tune with Polanyi, Rogers emphasizes the notion that 'science exists only in people' (1967: 216); that at root it is based upon the sense-making capabilities of individual persons. 'All science, and each individual scientific project, has its origin', Rogers proclaims, 'in the matrix of immediate, personal, subjective experience' (1967: 217). At the outset, he says, 'a good scientist ... immerses himself [*sic*] in the relevant experience, whether that be the physics laboratory, the world of plant or animal life, the hospital, the psychological laboratory or clinic, or whatever' (1967: 216). 'It means', Rogers elaborates, 'soaking up experience like a sponge, so that it is taken in in all its complexity, with my total organism freely participating in the experiencing of the phenomena; not simply my conscious mind' (1968/1990: 269).

For Rogers, then, not only is 'this immersion ... similar to the immersion of the therapist in therapy' (1967: 216), but like the effective therapist, like the fully functioning person, 'the discoverer of knowledge [e.g. Kepler, Einstein] feels a trust in *all* his avenues of knowing: unconscious, intuitive, and conscious' (1968/1990: 270, original emphasis). That is to say, 'the more nearly the individual [scientist] comes to being a fully functioning person ... the more trustworthy he is as a discoverer of truth' (1968/1990: 274).

On the basis of the discoverer's trustworthy sensing or 'indwelling', recounts Rogers, there can come to the individual 'a recognition—usually prelogical, intuitive, involving all the capacities of the organism—of a dimly sensed gestalt: a hidden reality' (1968/1990: 271). He says:

> This gestalt or pattern appears to give meaning to disconnected phenomena. The more that this total apprehension is free from cultural values and is free from past scientific values, the more adequate it is likely to be. (Rogers, 1968/1990: 271–2)

That such a sensing of a pattern is a form of mystical apprehension is implicit in Rogers' affirmation 'that when a pattern is sensed, it must be perceived in its *own* terms; whether those terms are internal, ineffable, subjective, and invisible; or whether they are external, tangible, and visible' (Rogers, 1968/1990: 271, original emphasis). This implicit mystical connection is made explicit, though, when Rogers endorses the claim of Polanyi mentioned earlier: that the discovery of objective truth in science involves 'embracing the vision of a reality beyond the impression of our senses' (Rogers, 1968/1990: 273). For Rogers, Polanyi's 'vision of a reality' is no different from his own 'sensing of a pattern', with both phrases in his view referring to the same thing as the term 'hypothesis'.

ROGERS' COSMIC HYPOTHESIS

Having overviewed Rogers' 'person-centred' conception of science, I move on now to elaborate upon the personal hypothesis/sensed pattern/vision of reality that Rogers sets forth—allied to acknowledging the importance of the mystical, spiritual dimension—in his article 'The foundations of a person-centered approach' (Rogers, 1980).

Rogers' vision is a vision of cosmic unity couched in terms of 'a formative tendency at work in the universe, which can be observed at every level' (1980: 124). Rogers identifies this formative tendency with Smuts' 'whole-making, holistic tendency' and dubs it a 'holistic force' (1980: 113), thereby revealing a close concordance with views found in spiritual literature—with for instance, Underhill's assertion that the mystic experiences 'inundations' of the 'transcendent life-force' (1915/2000: 134); that it is, in White's words, illumination of a 'unifying principle at work' (1972: x).

Elsewhere (Ellingham, 2002) I have elaborated at length upon the character of the workings of the formative tendency as conceived by Rogers, an elaboration that buttresses Rogers' exposition with ideas drawn from thinkers sharing the same fundamental worldview—Michael Polanyi and Lancelot Whyte, especially, both of whom directly influenced Rogers' thinking. Here, having little space, I concentrate on reprising key aspects of my earlier discussion in order to highlight how the formative tendency may serve as conceptual cornerstone for a scientific explanation of mysticism.

To understand how this is possible, consider the nature of scientific concepts, Newton's concept of gravity in particular.

Scientists employ symbols and symbolic devices (words, mathematical formulae, pictorial images) to characterize a pattern present in a wide range of phenomena. The abstract formulation of such a pattern is termed 'a concept' and the more precisely it is formulated and the wider the range of phenomena to which it applies, the more powerful such a concept will be. So, for instance, Newton's mathematically formulated concept of gravity identifies an abstract pattern common to events in the heavens and events on earth. Having apprehended, 'mystically' intuited, a single order/unitary pattern to earthly and heavenly events, Newton symbolized the oneness that he had sensed in terms of his mathematically expressed concept of gravity.

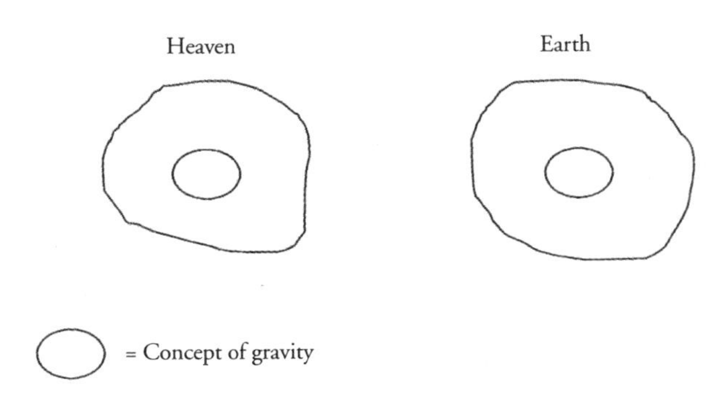

Figure 1: Newton's concept of gravity

By comparison with Newton's interrelating the events of earth and heaven, Rogers

1. speaks of 'aspects of the same order we find in the universe as a whole' being manifested in the in-depth psychological order within the person (1980: 8);
2. identifies a hypothetical concept, the formative tendency, as a 'directional tendency in the universe, which can be traced and observed in stellar space, in crystals, in micro-organisms, in more complex organic life, and in human beings' (1980: 133);
3. characterizes this order, the activity or 'workings' of this universal formative tendency, in terms of verbal description rather than mathematical formula.

Which is to say that Rogers' notion of the formative tendency is first, more all-encompassing than Newton's concept of gravity, embracing all 'levels' in the universe, including the subjective experiencing of the person; second, less precisely formulated insofar as it is characterized verbally rather than mathematically.

Note, then, how Rogers' characterization of the formative tendency can be given greater specificity and so help develop greater conceptual understanding of mysticism.

Describing the pattern to its workings, Rogers speaks of the formative tendency as 'the evolutionary tendency toward greater order, greater complexity, greater interrelatedness' (1980: 133). It is, he amplifies, 'a creative and not a destructive process' whereby 'every form that we see or know emerged from a simpler less complex form' (1980: 125).

Rogers acknowledges the strong influence of Lancelot Whyte's ideas in his developing the notion of the formative tendency, especially Whyte's equivalent concept, the morphic tendency. This influence is clearly evidenced when Whyte speaks of the morphic tendency being 'life-enhancing, not merely adaptive but formative and creative', of its constituting 'the principle that well-formed terminal states can arise from less-formed initial ones' (1974: 43, 83). Beyond Rogers, though, Whyte makes explicit the fact that the ongoing creative emergence of greater forms/wholes from simpler forebears gives rise to a hierarchical structure to the universe. So conceived, says Whyte,

> [T]he universe is arranged in a series of discrete 'levels', which for precision we call a hierarchy of wholes and parts. The first fact about the universe is its organization as a system of systems, from larger to smaller, and so is every individual. (Whyte, 1974: 43)

Specifically, this means that 'the known universe as a whole, and every organism, including man [*sic*] contains a graded sequence of units in each of which a formative tendency has been, or still is, present' (Whyte, 1974: 58).

Further explication of the hierarchical pattern that represents the ubiquitous working of the formative tendency is provided by Michael Polanyi. As depicted by Figure 2, Polanyi posits that when a larger form creatively emerges from a simpler forebear, the simpler forebear continues to have a 'tacit' or 'subsidiary' presence within the structure of the later, more comprehensive form, even as 'focal' manifestations of the simpler form remain present. For example, having emerged from animal form, human form has animal form subsidiarily present within its structure even as animal form continues to be focally manifested by today's non-human animals.

Rogers speaks of nature being 'clearly process' (1963: 19), i.e. patterned activity; but whether such process exhibits itself to us as phenomena that are animal, vegetable, mineral, psychological, or spiritual, etc., in every domain the same hierarchical pattern to the creation and continuing existence of those phenomena is discernible: the ubiquitous pattern represented by Figure 2. If the mystical vision consists in the direct apprehension of a 'transcendent life-force' (Underhill, 1915/2000: 134), 'a unifying principle at work' (White, 1972: x), or as Rogers puts it, 'the formative tendency', then Figure 2 provides us with a conceptual, or formal, representation of that force/principle/tendency.

On such a basis, a modified version of Figure 2, Figure 3 helps explicate the mystical experience of our being one with the world in the sense of what is outside us is the same as within. From an evolutionary perspective, Figure 3 represents the creative emergence of the various forms of existence preceding and including human form.

Depicting the 'ladder' or 'chain' of evolution from inorganic to human form, Figure 3 specifies how

1. the major forms, or levels, of evolution have emerged from simpler forebears, forebears that continue to have an ongoing ('focal') existence in their own right;
2. each more elaborate form possesses a structure in which its simpler forebears have a subsidiary/tacit presence.

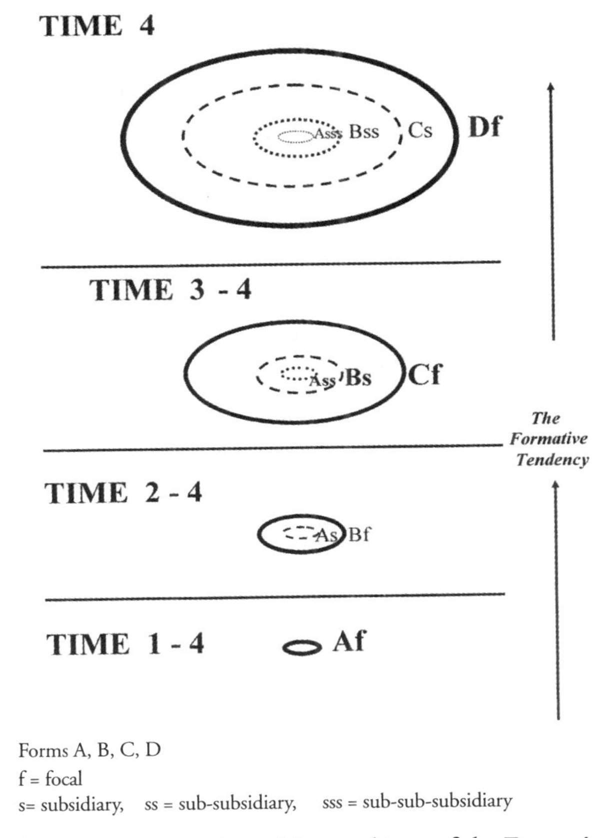

Figure 2: Abstract representation of the workings of the Formative Tendency

Regarding the pattern of processes comprising the human being (i.e. human form, Hf), Figure 3 depicts the tacit presence within the structure of human form of the major evolutionary forms from which human form emerged: namely, inorganic, organic and animal. Such a representation clarifies Polanyi's assertion that in 'the hierarchy of levels' making up each human being 'we can see all the levels of evolution at a glance' (1966: 36).

Viewing the structure of human form in this way highlights the 'sameness' between the patterns of process that comprise a person and those that make up the surrounding world. Apropos human experiencing of this sameness, Alfred North Whitehead posits that not only is 'the human mind … conscious of its body inheritance' (1929/1969: 129), but that all patterns of process have a qualitative 'feel' to them, the same patterns having the same 'feel'.

So understood, the mystic is a person who enjoys states of mind whereby he or she empathically senses that the qualitative feel to the patterns of process that comprise rocks, plants, animals, other humans, is the same as that arising from equivalent patterns comprising their own organism. The mystic, in other words, senses that the 'without' of the world and the 'within' of their own organism are one, in the same fashion as a

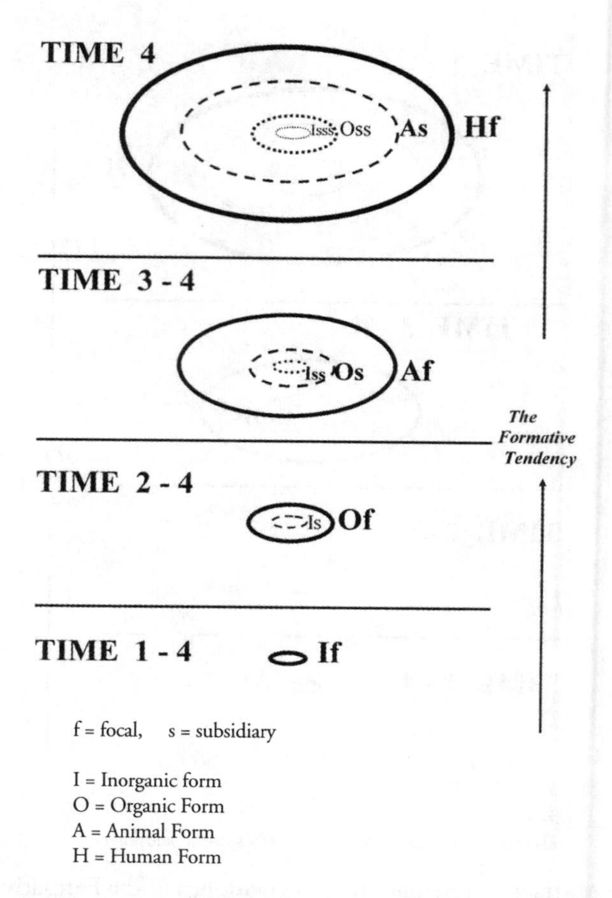

Figure 3: The evolutionary workings of the Formative Tendency

person in a choir perceives that the musical note sung by others is the same that they themselves are singing.

Further, in the same way that with a choir we speak of a unified field of sound waves with centres on self and others, so, in general terms, we might think of a unified field of processes (patterns of activity) with specific nodes centred in ourselves and the surrounding world. Early in the twentieth century Whitehead realized that such a 'process' or field worldview—one in which we view ourselves as 'process immersed in process beyond ourselves' (Whitehead, 1938/1968: 8)—is a general version of the worldview intrinsic to modern physics; which makes it significant that Fritjof Capra (1975) finds a close similarity between characterizations of the world by modern physicists and those of Eastern mystics. 'In modern physics', says Capra, 'the universe is thus experienced as a dynamic, inseparable whole which always includes the observer in an essential way. ... Such an experience, however, is closely similar to that of Eastern mystics' (Capra, 1975: 81). It is significant, too, that Rogers adduces Capra's views to support his own concerning the formative tendency.

Although here it is not possible to go into detail, Figure 2 can also be used to explicate the mode of feeling/knowing intrinsic to mystical experience. Insofar as simpler (e.g. infantile) patterns of sense-making are tacitly present in adult patterns, one can conceive of such modes becoming focal to the adult through a relaxation, 'letting go', of the operation of more developed higher levels. Thereby, a more global, less differentiated sensing of that which lies beyond adult discursive awareness makes itself available for integration into that awareness. New patterns of process become formed as consciousness itself expands and advances. In such a fashion, the mystic, as Rogers expresses, is able 'to create new and more spiritual directions in human evolution' (1980: 134)—he or she being, in Underhill's words, 'a creative artist of the highest kind' (1980: 400).

REFERENCES

Bonhoeffer, D (1959) *The Cost of Discipleship.* London: SCM Press.

Brazier, D (1993) The necessary condition is love. In D Brazier (ed) *Beyond Carl Rogers* (pp. 72–91). London: Constable.

Buber, M (1958) (2nd edn) *I and Thou.* New York: Charles Scribner's Sons.

Capra, F (1975) *The Tao of Physics.* Boulder: Shambala.

Committee on Psychiatry and Religion (1976) *Mysticism: Spiritual quest or psychic disorder.* New York: Group for the Advancement of Psychiatry.

Coxhead, N (1985) *The Relevance of Bliss.* London: Wildwood House.

Ellingham, I (2002) Foundation for a person-centred humanistic psychology: The nature and logic of Carl Rogers' formative tendency. In J Watson, R Goldman, and M Warner, M (eds) *Client-Centered and Experiential Psychotherapy in the 21st Century* (pp. 16–35). Ross-on-Wye: PCCS Books.

Foreman, R (1990) *The Problem of Pure Consciousness.* New York: Oxford University Press.

Gilbert, R (1991) *The Elements of Mysticism.* Longmead: Element Books.

Happold, F (1970) *Mysticism: A study and an anthology.* Harmondsworth: Penguin.

Huxley, A (1946/1958) *The Perennial Philosophy.* London: Fontana.

Inge, W (1899/1956) *Christian Mysticism.* Meridian: New York.

James, W (1902/1982) *The Varieties of Religious Experience.* Harmondsworth: Penguin.

Malcolm, J (1982) *Psychoanalysis: The impossible profession.* London: Pan Books.

May, R (1967) *The Art of Counseling.* Nashville: Abingdon Press.

Morgan, D (2004) The process of transformation within Buddhism. Paper presented at the conference 'The Spiritual Dimension in Therapy and Experiential Exploration'. Norwich: University of East Anglia. Also reproduced in this volume as Chapter 2, pp. 26–34.

O'Hara, M (1995) Carl Rogers: Scientist and mystic. *Journal of Humanistic Psychology, 35* (4), 40–53.

Polanyi, M (1964) *Personal Knowledge.* New York: Harper & Row.

Polanyi, M (1966) *The Tacit Dimension.* New York: Doubleday.

Robinson, E (1977a) *The Original Vision.* Oxford: Religious Experience Unit.

Robinson, E (ed) (1977b) *This Time-Bound Ladder.* Oxford: Religious Experience Unit.

Rogers, CR (1963) The actualizing tendency in relation to 'motives' and to consciousness. In

MR Jones (ed) *Nebraska Symposium on Motivation, Vol 11* (pp. 1–24). Lincoln: University of Nebraska Press.
Rogers, CR (1967) *On Becoming a Person.* London: Constable.
Rogers, CR (1968) Some thoughts regarding the current presuppositions of the behavioral sciences. In H Kirschenbaum & V Henderson (1990) (eds) *The Carl Rogers Reader* (pp. 263–78). London: Constable.
Rogers, CR (1980) *A Way of Being.* Boston: Houghton Mifflin.
Rogers, CR (1983) *Freedom to Learn for the 80's.* Columbus: Merrill.
Rogers, CR (1984) A way of meeting life. *The Laughing Man, 5* (2), 22–3.
Rogers, CR & Stevens, B (1967) *Person to Person.* Moab: Real People Press.
St Ignatius of Loyola (1990) *The Spiritual Exercises.* New York: Bantam.
Smith, M (1980) The nature and meaning of mysticism. In R Woods (ed) *Understanding Mysticism* (pp. 19–25). London: The Athlone Press.
Staal, F (1975) *Exploring Mysticism.* Harmondsworth: Penguin.
Suzuki, D (1957) *Mysticism: Christian and Buddhist.* London: Allen & Unwin.
Teilhard de Chardin, P (1976) *The Phenomenon of Man.* London: Perennial.
Thorne, B (2002) *The Mystical Power of Person-Centred Therapy.* London: Whurr.
Underhill, E (1912/1955) *Mysticism: A study in the nature and development of man's spiritual consciousness.* New York: Meridian.
Underhill, E (1915/2000) *Practical Mysticism.* Mineola: Dover.
Underhill, E (1980) The mystic as creative artist. In R Woods (ed) *Understanding Mysticism* (pp. 400–14). New York: Doubleday.
Westcott, R (1972) States of consciousness. In J White (ed) *The Highest State of Consciousness* (pp. 17–33). Garden City: Anchor Books.
White, J (ed) (1972) *The Highest State of Consciousness.* Garden City: Anchor Books.
Whitehead, A (1929/1969) *Process and Reality.* New York: Free Press.
Whitehead, A (1938/1968) *Modes of Thought.* New York: Free Press.
Whyte, L (1974) *The Universe of Experience.* New York: Harper & Row.
Zaehner, R (1957/1961) *Mysticism: Sacred and profane.* Oxford: Oxford University Press.

CHAPTER 7

OPEN-CENTRED ECOSOPHY
OR HOW TO DO ENVIRONMENTALLY INTERESTING THINGS WITH DR ROGERS' THERAPEUTIC CONDITIONS[1]

CLIVE PERRATON MOUNTFORD

This paper is the record of an enquiry that is probably still ongoing. It is also, in a way that its author does not quite understand as he writes this, product and exemplar of the circumstances that bore its subject. Not disparate, but different voices carry the burden because they do not, they cannot, integrate. Therefore, they will speak for themselves and separately.

1. The Wind in the Sycamore Trees

I pause—the first opening paragraph discarded—and I watch as the wind rolls across the garden and booms against the brickwork of my room. I watch the sycamore trees reflected in the mirror by my desk. The booming intensifies; the sycamores are dancing. Love moves inside me, and it seems—even mediated by a mirror—that my love is reciprocated. It has been like that as long as I remember, and really, there's nothing to be said about it. I love Earth; it feels that Earth loves me: that's just how it is. But working as a therapist, I know that I am not alone in my experience. And working as a philosophy teacher, I know too well that I am not alone in my concern for what humankind may be doing to Earth. I became a philosophy teacher on the back of my concern, and the same impetus led me to counselling. Those threads that root in love, and in Earth, and stretch across my lifetime, and some of the conclusions they seem to reach towards, are what I want to speak about.

In a nutshell, **nutshell number one**:

A consensus grows that human activity is causing huge changes on Earth. The weather is shifting; an extinction of species to rival geological disasters seems underway; molecules found in water, food, breast milk, and living tissue originate in human technology, and those molecules are not benign. Like many others, I am concerned.

Change itself is nothing new; Earth is a dynamic system. Weather, species, chemistry vary across time. Like all living organisms, humankind is part of

1. This chapter has been typeset according to the author's specific requirements.

this process of change. Are people only now noticing that? Is the real issue just that some of us don't relish change?

> Perhaps we want to age beneath the trees we cavorted under as children, hear the same birdsongs in the morning, walk the same trails, and for increasing numbers of us that cannot be. Social and technological change plus population growth equals childhood landscapes obliterated faster than children grow.

Is this why, in the industrialized nations of the north, there is so much agitation about 'the environment': change is just too much and too fast for us?

Well, suppose you and I belong to a large, extended family which has inherited a beautiful old house. I get busy remodelling it, but you don't like that. You protest; you have grounds for protest, it is your house too, but you cannot say I am destroying the house. It is just that I want it modernized, and you like things the way they were. Now suppose you find me up on the roof one morning, chopping a great hole, and the next day I'm hammering down an outside wall. Our family will be in trouble if I am not stopped.

Which scenario best represents human activity on Earth?

The jury is out; we don't know for sure. The changes humankind has initiated may not cause long-term physical harm to our species. On the other hand, publications like *New Scientist* routinely report on models that are the stuff of environmental nightmares.

And there is a detail to consider: if our beautiful old house is located in Yukon, and I am making some summer-time changes, we really are courting disaster come winter.

> Ours is a delicate species. The weather doesn't have to get very cold or very warm before humans cease to function; we need a particular blend of gases in the atmosphere; we need sunlight, but it has to be filtered, and so on. Humankind fits a particular Earth environment; we are in big trouble if that environment changes very much.

Playing it safe in terms of environmental change would seem the wiser course, and my guess is that most people want that security for themselves and their children. But what can they say in support of their concerns?

Let's go back to that first scenario: you don't *like* the changes I am making. More literally, perhaps you don't want to live in a land where the megafauna are extinct and even the little guys fast disappearing. You don't want the night sky obliterated by orange haze and your sleep disturbed by traffic. You don't think that Earth needs six and a half billion people and growing.

> Most people's homes and many of their choices suggest they want to live amongst a diverse and flourishing flora and fauna, to be able to watch trees dancing in a summer wind, and to see the stars at night.

What can those people say about the changes which are happening?

The *What can people say?* question is the subject of this paper. Or, more accurately perhaps, this paper is an expression and taking forward of my relationship with the *What can people say?* question. The language and history of philosophy dominate the first half because it was philosophy that matured the relationship and gave the question shape. In the second half, attention shifts to counselling practice and theory; they offer what is needed for a fuller answer than once seemed possible.

2. My Young Self Asks Some Questions

Circa 1985, I fetched up on the intellectual shore sketched in section one propelled by a very personal quest. Like some clients I have subsequently worked with, my childhood experiences of love and acceptance mostly involved dogs, and cats, and wandering where I would find grass, and trees, and an open sky. In consequence, I had a longstanding, deep, and loving relationship with the non-human world, the *created order*. I had also learned what environmental destruction meant as I moved from an English industrial city to what I thought of as 'countryside', then to Western Canada just before the last of the great old-growth forests were assigned for telephone directories. Back to England, on to the Himalayas—where paradise was only partially ravaged—and over to Western Canada again, where I was trying to develop a radical environmental ethic against the background radiation of analytic philosophy.

The pain, the hope, the experiences that drove me are not material. What matters here is that above everything else I loved Earth, its non-human inhabitants, and its ultimately transient ecology. I didn't want these things destroyed or interfered with, and I figured that if human morality and philosophy were worth much, then they should be able to explain why my beloved should not be harmed. After all, there was a long tradition of trying to establish the sanctity of human beings, now what about the rest?

I asked the question and went looking for answers. What I learned and what I resisted ate a decade, provided an approach to Deep Ecology which—although it has aged well and pleases students—seems to have been designed to offend professional philosophers, and finally led me to train as a person-centred therapist. My hunch was that, amongst its other blessings, the training might provide what I needed to complete the task.

And now I remember how the quest began: I was in the lower sixth form of an English grammar school, and I wanted to know why it was okay to kill a cow for dinner, but it was wrong to kill a human being. Or maybe it all began much earlier when I first learned about 'heaven'. The dog had died, and heaven sounded wonderful until I was told that dogs didn't go there. My four-year-old response was brief, the Christian Church lost another soul to scepticism, and I began to be aware there were things which I needed to understand.

3. A Brief, Tendentious, History of Ethics

I didn't know it in the sixth form, but Jeremy Bentham beat me to that cow question by well over a century. Reasoning from Utilitarian principles enunciated by David Hume, Bentham famously announced that, regarding the way humans treated 'the rest of animal creation', 'The question is not, Can they *reason*? nor Can they *talk*? but Can they *suffer*?'

Contrary to notions of morality revered since Aristotle's day, Bentham loudly asserted that any creature capable of suffering had to be taken into account when human actions might affect it. No longer could one kick the cat with impunity: because it suffered when it was kicked, the cat was a moral person, and it deserved what later philosophers called *moral consideration*.

Bentham's advocacy was a radical move. Traditional systems of morality and most moral philosophy never ask who the moral persons are. It is *assumed* that human beings are both moral agents *and* the proper recipients of consideration. Bentham asked *why* that should be so, and he found against tradition. In the process, Bentham exposed a fundamental question central to moral practice and thought. I think of it as *the moral umbrella question* because morality is like an umbrella which shelters some things from arbitrary usage—traditionally they are human beings—and it leaves the rest out in the rain exposed to human whim. The question is, *What things belong beneath the moral umbrella*?

Whether the Zeitgeist was in an ironic and playful mood, or whether there is some more serious explanation, I do not know, but it wasn't until the 1970s that Bentham's legacy began to bear fruit, and by then even more radical moves were afoot. The non-specialist press was just noticing that there was a case to be put on behalf of non-human animals, and philosophy itself was starting to make the moral umbrella question explicit, when Arne Naess introduced the concept of Deep Ecology and a moral umbrella so large that pretty much everything is sheltered by it: cats, amoebae, trees, mosses, rocks ... the lot, the ecosphere at a minimum.

> That's where I came in; I think it is where I first began to be aware that I had different voices. Some people just find Deep Ecology intuitively obvious, and I was one of them. Arne had it right; traditional morality had things terribly wrong. But when I began arguing for this, I met incredulity and near total incomprehension. Sure, I could speak the language of the academic culture, but I could not speak what looked to me like truth in that language. Yet it *was* my language. I began to try to build a conceptual bridge between the world and language of my love for Earth and the world and language of academic philosophy.

Was the attempt to build the bridge futile? I still don't know; perhaps this paper is the attempt ongoing. I still cannot blend the two languages, and I still do not fully understand what that means. Of late, I have allowed myself the luxury of writing in two or three different voices, like a conversation, and found it easier. Trying to write this paper was initially a nightmare until I realized that the attempt to speak univocally was strangling me.

But the bridge ...

The bridge has heuristic value—my students like it—and with hindsight I do think it helped me achieve a degree of personal integration, the kind of integration you get when members of a family recognize and accept each other's existence and start talking. In **nutshell number two**, here is the beginning of that bridge:

> Any system of moral practice and theory must answer or assume an answer to the moral umbrella question. Traditional moral systems assume an answer—*All and only human beings*—and they can be thought of as *moral humanism*. Jeremy Bentham and his Utilitarian heirs come next, answering roughly: *All and only sentient creatures, that is, creatures capable of suffering or having 'interests'*. This is known as *sentientism*. After that there are brave and radical attempts to answer on behalf of all living things: *All and only individual living organisms whether sentient or vegetative*. I call this *vitalism*. And finally, there are attempts like Arne Naess' which seek to morally enfranchise all living organisms, plus the natural infrastructure they depend upon, and in some cases simply whatever else the universe might hold. This is *ecosophy*.

So far, then, I've identified that there is a moral umbrella question out there and roughly four kinds of potential answer: moral humanism, sentientism, vitalism, and ecosophy. But there is a problem out there, too, and for a time I made myself quite unpopular banging on about it: most if not all answers to the moral umbrella question founder on explanatory difficulties.

There is always a sceptic around who asks *So what*? or *Why*? *So what if non-human creatures suffer*? *Why are the vital interests of organisms lacking experience of any importance to me*? *So what if the new road cuts through ecologically unique chalk downs and woodland*? A lot of work has gone into the answers, but my own conclusion is that there are enough undefended commitments and axiology lurking behind the various ramparts to give a sceptic sufficient reason to remain aloof.

> For me, this problem bites. The moral umbrella question is not theoretical; it is part of the attempt to live a mindful, moral life. As Socrates said, *We are discussing no small matter, but how we ought to live.*
> What to do?

For a long time, I really thought Arne had the right idea. He junks traditional moral philosophy, abandons all pretence to a rigorous, knock-down proof of his position, and says: *Try it and see; I think you will find that what I am advocating will work and will satisfy you*. But amongst the things Arne and his colleagues advocate is a return to Stone Age population levels. You won't sell that in the Forum without a good argument upfront; and there *is* a serious, hard-nosed alternative.

4. Captain Sensible and Friends

I got into these difficulties by asking what one might say to someone who is remodelling humankind's family home. If it was a literal house, like the one in Yukon, and someone *was* chopping holes in the roof and knocking down walls, we could appeal to self-interest: you are going to die come winter. This is precisely the argument most environmental advocacy deploys: *Earth is a complex ecosystem and human beings one small and fragile part of it. We need to protect and maintain the ecosystem for our own well-being.* I call this the voice of *Captain Sensible.*

The good Captain is a very attractive figure, utilizing 'objective' criteria and speaking with the voice of 'reason'. Even better, walking beside Captain S. doesn't entail much moral or philosophical exertion because he offers compatibility with moral humanism and a small moral umbrella.

Unfortunately, the Captain suffers from ailments which his friends prefer not to talk about. First, there is no evidence that humans are capable of acting in their own long-term best interests environmentally speaking. We want wealth, economic growth, knowledge, as many toys as possible; we want them now. We sail as close to the wind as we think we can; we take risks. My hunch is that humans are wired that way. Speaking for myself, I delight in risks which make no rational sense. Second, the calculations that Captain Sensible must make are beyond human competence in practice and probably in theory. We don't know what consequences small environmental changes might eventually have, and that is not just a matter of remediable ignorance. Complex, chaotic systems are involved, and it may be that they cannot be accurately modelled. Third, for those of us who do love Earth, prudence is a cheap and shabby substitute for moral status.

So back to that family home again—the Earth-shaped one this time—and there are now two options on the table, neither of them good ones: there's a series of flawed attempts to open up the moral umbrella, and there's an alliance with Captain Sensible.

For simplicity and symmetry, I characterized all those umbrella opening attempts as the work of *Agent Sage*. Then I floundered with a Captain Sensible-Agent Sage dichotomy for a year or two—and initiated one of my periodic petitions for divorce from philosophy—before I saw a way to appropriate an idea from the academic grapevine. I called the refurbished strategy *Deep Humanism*. In **nutshell number three**, and forming the final part of that bridge I spoke of earlier, it is built like this:

- Step one, for the sake of argument, accept moral humanism and its claim that all and only humans are morally considerable.
- Step two, recognize that we *do* depend upon a quite particular environment; we *are* fragile; there *is good enough reason* to believe we are endangering that environment; and we are *not Sensible*.
- At step three, moral theory is tailor-made to deal with this situation because we can now stand back from all moral beliefs and commitments and ask what human morality would *need to be like to best promote human welfare.* This is taking what the trade calls a *meta-ethical* view of morality, and it is consistent with the usual moral humanist claim that morality's *raison d'être* is human welfare.
- Step four, descend from these dizzy heights and conscientiously set about following the morality now reconstructed.

In other words—and I am leaving most of the detail out of account—moral humanism and its traditional anthropocentric self-interest, plus a realistic assessment of humankind's predicament and our needs as a species, furnish a powerful argument for *renouncing* moral humanism and moving in the direction of Deep Ecology. As a bonus, and with an eye to the ancient practice of brokering a marriage with which to end longstanding dispute, this argument weds Captain Sensible (who is concerned with human welfare, and guides our meta-ethical deliberations) to Agent Sage (who is the bearer of that generously opened moral umbrella the argument delivers).

> It is a clever move, and it does work. Technically, Deep Humanism is a meta-ethical argument about the kind of morality which best serves human interests plus the entirely reasonable requirement to put the argument's conclusion into practice. Logically, philosophically, Deep Humanism is sound, and it has been recognized by Deep Ecologists as an alternative point of entry to the Deep Ecology programme.

However—and in moral philosophy there is usually 'however'—there is a rather large and embarrassing question outstanding: *How does one develop a particular kind of moral commitment? How does one learn to relate to the non-human world as something worthy of moral consideration?* Well, I know what happened to me, but it probably isn't replicable, and it certainly wouldn't be kind to try experimenting. So, in 1995, I concluded work on Deep Humanism by making a few noises about education and the benefits of getting young children involved in gardening, and I began to think about training as a person-centred therapist.

5. Process Reflection

> There was close to just one voice throughout that last section. I don't know what that means, but there it is, and it feels important.

And now, starting from that very here-and-now and personal reflection, I want to step back from the details of what I've been discussing and take a more contextual look at it all. Stepping back initially from my own contribution, it is probably more idiosyncratic than I realized.

For one thing, traditional moral philosophy involves either *ethics* or *meta-ethics*; it doesn't mix and match. Ethics is the kind of deliberation a moral agent engages in once committed to certain principles or a particular outlook: for example, *I am committed to acting rationally; how should I behave*? Meta-ethics holds this kind of question in abeyance and treats morality and moral reasoning themselves to critical investigation. I think people who worry about these matters for a living probably mistrust the mix-and-match approach.

A second oddity is the idea of seeking to become something one isn't at present. This is not at all odd in the context of religious practice, but it is when transposed to analytic philosophy. The name of the game there is to seek truth—capital letters and flashing lights—and truth, as all undergraduate philosophers know, is to be had by diligent reasoning from principles which ... well, isn't that the problem? *Where do they come from*? What I've suggested is that we can obtain the ones needed for an environmental ethic from a proper appraisal of our own predicament plus concern for our skins.

> Is this approach cynical? Does that give offence?
>
> These are the rules of the game (logic etc.); these are the unquestionable values (human welfare etc.); and oh look at that: they support the conclusions I wanted. I guess that's how I understand academic philosophy in the Anglo-Saxon tradition.
>
> And maybe I was also up to something less cynical but more sub-textual. And maybe *that* gives offence.

Traditionally, answers to the Socratic question, *How ought we to live*? grow from one of two cultural sources—religion and philosophy—and those two sources have grown increasingly apart since ... when? The Reformation? Erasmus Darwin? I'm not sure, but they have. And without any clear sense of what I was up to, I was tugging them closer again.

That may seem novel, but it is consistent with what the Zeitgeist has been up to. There are many signs of change in ethics, and environmental philosophy hosts its share. That is because humanist assumptions are so woven into mainstream moral thought and practice that anyone wishing to seriously expand the moral umbrella has to reach outside tradition. What's more, I'm not the first to reach in a direction now more associated with religion. Arne Naess' work is informed by the apprehension of connectedness and others have taken that further.

But back to that humanist commitment entrenched in traditional moral philosophy. I allied myself with it as I cleared the ground for Deep Humanism. I pointed out that *nobody* had a really good argument for moral expansion. They couldn't have because the materials available denied it to them. Arne Naess and most others who seek radical expansion offer *no more* than an alternate *moral option to try* because nothing stronger is left to them.

> That can sound such a sad little whimper beside the traditional cry of *Reason requires this; resist on pain of irrationality!* And in my anger, and in my pain, I used that seeming weakness to establish the need to work with the assumptions of the moral humanists.

Don't let me give the impression that Deep Ecology and other brands of ecosophy are hopeless causes. Far from it; they are fascinating, challenging, ground-breaking, paradigm-busting works. The trouble is that they cannot answer the sceptic who won't even give them a try. It is essential to get people to give them a try because they are built around personal and cultural change on a scale and of a kind which only makes sense when attempted. To put this in other words, most ecosophy proffers a different *way of being* and says, *Suck it and see*. The way of being in question can be characterized by saying roughly ...

> ... what?
>
> Whatever is, is of value; whatever is, is in a sense, myself; whatever is, is not there simply for my use or comfort or amusement, it self-subsists, deserves respect, has goals, directions of its own.
>
> That kind of thing?

That kind of thing.

I don't know whether anyone except me feels the resonance with person-centred counselling practice and theory, but I get a lump in the throat and maybe goose bumps about now. Here is why, in **nutshell number four**:

> Answers to the Socratic question traditionally have one of two sources: religion or secular philosophy. Answers rooted in religious tradition often invoke personal change and ways of being; answers rooted in secular philosophy major in logic and reason. In the latter half of the twentieth century at least two secular responses to the Socratic question have leaned heavily on notions of personal change and ways of being. One is the client/person-centred tradition of counselling and human relationship. The other is the newly emerging ecosophist tradition of environmental sanity and relationship to non-humans.

The former, the client/person-centred tradition, is the more developed, and I believe it has a great deal to offer ecosophy. Therefore, what I shall do with the rest of this paper is expand upon that claim.

> First, there is something more to note. My own reaction to the possibility that the person-centred tradition and ecosophy may be travelling convergent roads is strong and physical, and that is surely because it promises an integration in which I have a large personal stake.

6. A Short Critique of Certainty

There is a sentiment amongst practitioners that *person-centred* goes hand-in-hand with Carl Rogers' statement of the *necessary and sufficient conditions of therapeutic personality change*. For example, in its requirements for entry to the list of person-centred counsellors, the British Association for the Person-Centred Approach has come close to making them an article of faith. But without intending any disrespect to Carl, taken at face value, the statement is absurd. *Necessary and sufficient* means *if and only if*, and even hard science is not often given to claims that strong. It all dates to the sunset of a dream of certainty our intellectual culture has renounced.

I am not the first to think this, and I am not the first to make public noises. Campbell Purton has argued powerfully and elegantly that the necessity and sufficiency statement is a step too far. As Campbell points out, it rests on the hypothesis that all psychic distress is rooted in introjections of conditional acceptance usually experienced in childhood. The conditions posited as necessary and sufficient for healing are the unique antidote to this wounding experience.

However, it really doesn't seem to be the case that conditional acceptance *is* the aetiology of everything that brings clients to therapy. Campbell cites other common factors such as post-traumatic stress, lose-lose choices, bereavement, and childhood *deprivation* rather than *conditionality* ... just two days ago a student was telling me how their experience of therapy fits Campbell's argument.

I feel sure Campbell is onto something. My sense is that what he is onto is no less than a need to re-vision the client/person-centred tradition for the twenty-first century. I say *re-vision* not replace, or lose, or throw out with a little old-fashioned bath water. What is more, re-visioning is integral to the spirit of that tradition. In the theoretical paper offering the most succinct and powerful delineation of person-centred theory, Carl Rogers writes of 'the network of gossamer threads' which comprise it, and of the damage caused by Freud's students when they turned gossamer into 'iron chains of dogma'.

So let me map out a little re-visioning which converges with my environmental agenda:

- First—as Campbell notes— the therapeutic way of being which characterizes client/person-centred practice predates the theory. Client-centred therapy was around long before those gossamer threads woven to explain its efficacy, and it is *that therapy's way of being*, not any particular theorization, which is the heart of the tradition. Although interesting and important, theory is an inescapably flawed attempt to enunciate—and provide a doorway into—a logically and existentially prior body of practice.
- Second, if we will hold the theory lightly enough, it becomes possible and reasonable to ask whether the way of being is *necessarily* anthropocentric in its focus. Client-centred and person-centred therapies are anthropocentric because they seek to help wounded human beings, but *What about the way of being itself*?
- Third, once shorn of their claim to absolute sovereignty, the therapeutic conditions enunciated by Carl Rogers still remain an insightful way to conceptualize the client/person-centred way of being, and their practice remains a useful way to begin acquiring it. In consequence, the *What about the way of being*? question can be approached by asking, *Do the conditions map onto a non-human locus of attention*?

7. Opening the Locus of Attention

Six conditions were described by Carl, and some possible later additions were suggested by others. I shall just pay attention to the six originals here, and I won't be discussing them in their original order.

The unconditional positive regard, or UPR, the prizing which a therapist offers their client, maps onto trees, cats, mountains ... without difficulty. It is easy to love a tree; sometimes, it is easier than loving human beings, I find.

Empathy, too, is not that difficult to extend to most living things. Cats have feelings, purposes, furry cat-shoes to step into. And I don't think we need be put off by disparaging comments about anthropomorphizing so long as we don't get too soft-headed; anthropomorphizing is a respectable ethological tactic these days. Trees may seem a bit harder, but I think most gardeners know empathy for their floral friends. Mountains? Speaking personally, I feel things for mountains that are sometimes overwhelming, and the well-being of a loved mountain is of great importance to me. I'm not alone.

UPR, empathy ... that's two out of the three *core* or *counsellor* conditions, the oft-cited keystone of person-centred being. The other condition is that the therapist be congruent, or genuine and authentic, within the counselling relationship. Can genuineness and authenticity be offered to a non-human? I think the answer is, *Of course it can,* but this probably only applies to creatures enjoying a high degree of sentience.

However, there are two stages to congruence. First, there is openness to one's own experiencing, a kind of inner honesty and acceptance. Second, there is congruent relating and being in the world. The first stage is about how one relates to one's self, and the second stage is about relating to others. Even if one cannot easily be said to be in congruent relationship with a mountain, one can be congruently oneself upon the mountain and act towards the mountain from a place of personal congruence. Furthermore, the counsellor conditions go together; they are one ball of wax: I cannot be empathic and acceptant while holding back on congruence.

I now want to turn the traditional story on its head for a short while. The counsellor conditions are intended to contribute to the right environment for growth and psychic healing in human beings. They are there for the sake of the client. However, they affect the counsellor as well. Routinely seeking to offer the counsellor conditions to others changes the person who is making that offer. At least, that is my experience, and I think I see the same thing in my colleagues and students. Speaking personally, I find that the changes run in two directions. I am more acceptant, fractionally less ego-laden, gentler, more perceptive, more empathic, more desirous that whatever is gets its moment in the sun, its chance to flourish. And I am often more angry, more enraged by the suffering and damage which humankind causes. It begins to seem that offering non-anthropocentric, counsellor conditions to the non-human world is not only possible, but doing so will tend to promote personal changes which will help safeguard Earth from human depredation and foolishness.

What about the other three original therapeutic conditions?

Contact, psychological contact, was the first of them. The therapist needs to work at that. And I see no harm and much good in a genuine attempt to be in contact with the non-human. I don't mean that we should get silly; we just need to notice the way the leaves move, the paws go down; put ourselves in the way of experiencing rain against the cheek; be open to the other, the non-human other, in a way analogous to the openness of a counsellor to their client.

Condition number two was that the client be anxious, vulnerable, incongruent. Does it map at all? In a way, I think it does. Earth and everything on it is vulnerable, much more vulnerable than humans ever imagined until recently. We need to be aware of that, I think, and hold it in awareness.

The really tough condition is the last one: 'the client *perceives*, at least to a minimal degree ... the *unconditional positive regard* ... and the *empathic* understanding of the therapist.' With highly sentient creatures again, both are possible, and I don't mean only those which have evolved alongside us as dogs and cats have. Try walking in the Canadian bush, in moose country, without a gun and without any ill intent towards moose. They abound. Take a gun and go look for dinner. Where are the moose? It may be said that moose just know what guns are. But I remember meeting a mother moose with her young when I was lost and on a very narrow lakeside trail. Mother moose with young are dangerous. I forgot that in my delight at meeting Mistress Moose that afternoon. We stopped, and gazed, and I felt her lack of ill intent towards me as she felt mine. We both moved aside a little, and we passed on that narrow trail.

Can vegetative lives somehow experience or otherwise be affected by our intent, our feelings towards them? There is some positive evidence; science is interested in this question. As for the rest of creation, how much do we really know?

In **nutshell number five** then:

> I am suggesting that Carl Rogers' therapeutic conditions can be read as a recipe for a way of being with the non-human world, with Earth's other creatures and living things, with her bones and substance. That will serve the cause of environmental sanity in two ways. It will tend to change how humans relate to and behave towards the non-human. It will tend to change humans in ways which will make us better suited to live as citizens of an ecological community.

Now what about the moral umbrella I once so badly wanted to expand and the Deep Humanist programme of personal and moral change?

If I step back from a precise statement of the therapeutic conditions, it seems to me that, as a therapist, what I offer to a new client is genuineness, acceptance, absence of judgement, and a willingness to try to understand what it is like being them. Over time, and as I give my close attention to the client, I find warmth, tenderness, and a deep desire for their well-being has grown within me. I am inclined to think that is just how it is to be human. If we offer this stuff, and if we attend, a kind of love takes root within us. And I can find no reason why the offering, and the attending, should not be to the whole of what some call *the created order*. In time, a kind of love will take root inside one if it is not there already, and then there will be no doubt that it all belongs beneath the moral umbrella and warrants our consideration.

> In a way, that writes *finis* to a story that started roughly fifty years ago. If we will only *notice* and remain relatively open and non-judgemental, what we will then experience answers or even obviates the moral umbrella question. By force of circumstances, I guess, noticing and being open was where I started.

To conclude this section, I want to venture onto a branch which feels even thinner and newer than those I've climbed so far. I spoke earlier of Campbell Purton's thoughts on necessary and sufficient conditions, and the clients who do not seem to fit person-centred orthodoxy. My hunch is that every client who benefits from client/person-centred therapy arrives impaired in their ability to accept and to relate. The aetiology of impairment may vary, but what hurts us does not. We fail to accept our own experiencing; we fail to accept ourselves; we fail to accept others. Therefore relationship fails. At the heart of current environmental problems, I think I perceive similar failure. We really are stardust; we really are children of a planet that is fecund, beautiful, and mostly well-disposed towards us. We really are amazing creatures. We really cannot accept any of it. Therefore, we need therapy, and we need to change our way of relating to ourselves, each other, and the world about us. We need both therapy and an ethic much like that offered by the client/person-centred tradition but with an open locus of attention.

8. A Feminist Influence?

> My usual practice is to leave feminism, and feminist discussion, to women. (Is that sexist? I hope not, but untangling what it *is* would take too long.) However, usual practice has now entailed an omission which must be rectified. Reading a draft of this paper, a colleague noted that there were no women in it. Yet where I have now taken what was once Deep Humanism *must* have been influenced by reading, and teaching, the work of ecofeminists. I need to speak to that.

Deep Ecology offers a vision of relationship with Earth which, in my experience, appeals more to men than to women. Female philosophers can be quite critical of its assertion that each of us is really just a part of a much bigger entity. Using the terminology of small-s 'self' and Capital-S 'Self', Arne Naess encourages us to experience the loss of small-s *self* in Capital-S *Self*. Feminist critics respond that this *self-in-Self* stuff misses the point, is arrogant, and even dangerous. I perceive two main reasons for thinking that.

One reason—developed by Val Plumwood—has to do with how our sense of self comes into being. As the colleague who took me to task pointed out: there isn't simply a 'Charlie' or a 'Clive'. There is 'Charlie in relationship to ...' 'Clive in relationship to ... ', and, out of the many relationships we both enjoy, we gather a dynamic sense of who we are. In other words, *self* is not prior to *relationship*; self comes into being *with* relationship.

A second reason—and I recommend Karen J. Warren as its exponent—has to do with the *consequences* of *self-in-Self* perception. She finds that this encourages us to ignore the important *boundary* between self and other, splurging them together, and making it impossible to hold the other in a 'loving perception'. Instead, perception becomes 'arrogant', conquering rather than prizing difference. That loving perception is precious and needs reclaiming because it brings warmth and caring back into a traditional ethics overly focused on dry, faceless principles.

For me, both claims hold water, while Deep Ecology may not be guilty as charged. I see no reason why there cannot be a kind or level of experiencing such that you and I are entirely separate beings, recognition that this sense of our selves as separate persons is dynamic and grounded in relationship, *and* a kind of experiencing such that we sometimes feel we merge.

It also seems to me that my suggested re-visioning of the client/person-centred tradition is consistent with—and is probably informed by—these two insights. There may be other feminist objections which I cannot take on board, but from what I know of eco-feminist literature, I think we are moving in a broadly similar direction. For example, Karen J. Warren also objects to what she calls *value dualisms* such that, for example, Charlie and Clive are hierarchically ordered and one of us has greater worth than the other. Human–human value dualisms are anathema to the client/person-centred tradition, and a human–non-human value dualism would be equally repugnant to its new and 'open-centred' cousin.

9. Voices, Introjects, and Glittering Prizes

My voices ... What are they, these different voices I must speak with? Are they just an expression of my own lack of integration, perhaps my lack of literary skill, or something more interesting?

Roughly speaking, I need a minimum of three voices. There is a cerebral, educated voice: the voice of argument and reason. There is a more passionate, inward, and personal voice: the voice of feeling, of experiencing, and sometimes need. And there is a kind of commentary voice that breaks in occasionally and notices things the other voices are close to and may not quite have in focus. The first two voices are the really important ones; without access to both of them, I lose my fluidity. What's going on?

As I have been writing, I have formed a hypothesis: the division represented by my voices is not innately *mine*; it is an introject from a culture grounded in dissociation.

My professional life and my personal search for understanding have involved exploring at length and in depth aspects of being which are routinely separated, and from whose vantage points people view each other with suspicion. On the one hand, to 'do philosophy'—or engage in most academically respectable tasks—one must set aside and even deny whatever is not resolutely cerebral. But on the other hand, to offer a healing, therapeutic relationship to clients; to engage in spiritual practice; and—I would argue—to enjoy relationship of any kind, one must engage with the inward and the personal.

Academic, professional, and personal credibility attach to skilful and consistent denial of personal experiencing, and honour and financial reward usually accrue to the most cerebral voices. In this way, integration is discouraged, and the paradigm 'rational person' becomes a study in dissociation. In some quarters, however, the valuing system is reversed. Logic and reason are viewed with mistrust, and emoting is celebrated. I think counselling and counsellor-training sometimes offer examples of this.

If I am right, then our culture is sick: we tend either to lead with our heads, which is surely not what heads evolved for; or we lead with our hearts, which is usually a disaster. The client/person-centred tradition—with its emphasis on the wholeness of being and on personal integration—can be seen as partly a response to this sickness, and it has evolved at least two ways of working specifically with the dichotomy. Carl Rogers' colleague Eugene Gendlin continues to develop a means of bringing what he calls the *felt sense* into awareness. It is a source of knowing grounded in experiencing and in the body rather than in our cranial vapours or evanescent emotions. To a similar end, but using different means, there is André Rochais' *Personality and Human Relations* (PRH).

Therefore, these days, when I teach philosophy, I encourage my students to work from their felt sense of the issues. The idea is not to ignore their cerebral talents and emotional responses, but to let those things serve rather than lead. As students get the hang of what I am proposing, they write more fluently and more creatively, and many seem to grow in ways which surprise them. At the University of East Anglia, Campbell Purton is teaching focusing to trainee counsellors, and I am doing the same at Buckinghamshire Chilterns University College. We find that many students gain a way of knowing their experience—and therefore the world around them—which profoundly changes their lives and therapeutic practice. My hunch is that if and when enough people are living in awareness of their felt sense—whether conceptualized that way or not—then environmental issues, too, will take on a whole new aspect.

> There is a voice not yet spoken of or written. I'm not sure it is my voice in the same sense as the others. I don't really know what to do except let it guide me, but it is part of the story.
>
> I love Earth; it feels that Earth loves me. Is that it? Or is there something more than Clive and Earth involved in this relationship?
>
> It seems to me, sometimes, that there is more, but I don't pretend to understand or be able to theorize that seeming. My *experience* is that just as offering a person-centred kind of relationship to Earth is a doorway leading to a different way of experiencing Earth, so that different way of experiencing Earth becomes a doorway ...
>
> If so, then any person or tradition serious about spiritual experience and the spiritual dimension of human life must tend *all* relationships with care, not just human or divine relationships.

NOTES

Section 3

The Bentham quotation is from (1948) p. 311. Hume's thoughts on ethics are presented in Hume (1752).

In April 1973, both Peter Singer's article 'Animal Liberation' and Arne Naess' 'The Shallow And The Deep, Long-Range Ecology Movement: A Summary' were published. Singer's article should not be confused with his later (1977) book of the same name. A translation of Naess' book-length exposition was eventually published under the editorship of Rothenburg (1989).

Section 4
Deep Humanism was formally introduced in Mountford (1995) but it may have appeared in some earlier talks. Who first suggested the idea? I don't know; it came via Professor Earl Winkler, but I doubt either of us can lay claim to it.

Section 5
Socrates asks his famous question in Plato's *The Republic* (circa 390 BCE).
Signs of change in ethics? Alasdair MacIntyre caused some serious rethinking beginning with MacIntyre (1984). In the same year, Nel Noddings (1984) gave impetus to a more feminist and less cerebral approach. Personally, I have always found Richard Rorty's (2003) critiques of great interest. And within environmental ethics, Warwick Fox (1990) developed the 'apprehension of connectedness' and beat a first track from environmental ethics to counselling.
When I say, 'humanist assumptions are … woven into mainstream moral thought and practice' I do not exaggerate. Moral humanism remains the norm in related academic disciplines like economics, and philosophers still argue that language itself prevents attributions of moral status to anything which is not sentient. This last position is probably best represented by Joel Feinberg (1974).

Section 6
Carl Rogers' necessary and sufficient conditions first appeared in Rogers (1957) reprinted in Kirschenbaum and Henderson (1990). They re-appear in Rogers (1959) which is now out of print and hard to obtain. Kirschenbaum and Henderson (1990) contains an edited version, but personally I think it is worth the effort to secure a copy of the larger and more elegant original. The comments about 'gossamer threads' appear on p. 191 of Rogers (1959).
Campbell Purton's ideas first appear as 'Person-centred therapy without the core conditions' in Purton (2002), and are now more fully explicated in Purton (2004); see particularly pp. 39–41.

Section 7
Anthropomorphizing is recommended by no less an ethologist than Frans de Waal (1996). Current scientific thought about the possible analogues of sentience and intelligence in plants can be tracked through the pages of *New Scientist*. The most recent article I have found is 'Not just a pretty face' in vol 175 issue 2353, 27 July 2002, p. 40.

Section 8
That this section exists at all is due to the intervention of Charlotte MacGregor; thank you, Charlie. Val Plumwood's ideas are contained in Plumwood (1991), and the material I cite from Karen J. Warren is in Warren (1990). Judging by what I find in recent anthologies intended for environmental ethics classes, these papers remain current.

Section 9
The most accessible book on Focusing is Eugene Gendlin (1981). More depth and detail is to be found in Gendlin (1996). Campbell Purton (2004) is also a good place to start particularly for anyone interested in how focusing fits into the development of client/person-centred therapy.
A new and accessible introduction to PRH has recently been published (2004) although I think it fair to say that PRH must be experienced to be understood.

REFERENCES

Bentham, J (1948) *Principles of Morals and Legislation.* New York: Haftner.
Feinberg, J (1974) The rights of animals and unborn generations. In WT Blackstone, (ed)

Philosophy and Environmental Crisis (pp. 43–68). Athens, Georgia: University of Georgia Press.

Fox, W (1990) *Towards a Transpersonal Ecology.* Boston and London: Shambhala Publications Inc.

Gendlin, ET (1981) *Focusing* (2nd ed). New York: Bantam.

Gendlin, ET (1996) *Focusing Oriented Psychotherapy.* London: Guilford Press.

Hume, D (1752) *An Inquiry Concerning the Principles of Morals.* Available in various anthologies and editions.

MacIntyre, A (1984) *After Virtue.* Notre Dame, Indiana: University of Notre Dame Press.

Mountford, P (1995) *How Big is the Moral Umbrella.* Vancouver, University of British Columbia: Doctoral Dissertation.

Naess, A (1973) The shallow and the deep, long-range ecology movement: A summary. *Inquiry, 16,* 95–100.

Noddings, N (1984) *Caring: A feminine approach to ethics and moral education.* Berkeley: University of California Press.

Plato, *The Republic* (circa 390 BCE). Available in numerous editions.

Plumwood, V (1991) Nature, self, and gender feminism, environmental philosophy, and the critique of rationalism. *Hypatia, 6* (1), 3–27.

PRH-International (2004) *When Life Breaks Through.* Poitiers, France: Personality and Human Relations International.

Purton, C (2002) Person-centred therapy without the core conditions. *Counselling and Psychotherapy Journal, 13* (2), 6–9.

Purton, C (2004) *Person-Centred Therapy: The focusing-oriented approach.* Basingstoke and New York: Palgrave Macmillan.

Rogers, CR (1957) The necessary and sufficient conditions of therapeutic personality change. In H Kirschenbaum and VL Henderson (eds) (1990) *The Carl Rogers Reader* (pp. 219–35). London: Constable.

Rogers, CR (1959) A theory of therapy, personality, and interpersonal relationships as developed in the client-centred framework. In S Koch (ed) *Psychology: A study of a science vol. 3* (pp. 184–256). New York: McGraw-Hill Book Company.

Rorty, R (2003) http://www.stanford.edu/~rrorty/.

Rothenburg, D (1989) (ed) *Ecology, Community and Lifestyle.* Cambridge: Cambridge University Press.

Singer, P (1973) Animal liberation. *The New York Review of Books,* Vol 20, No 5, April 5, 1973.

Singer, P (1977) *Animal Liberation.* New York: Avon Books.

de Waal, F (1996) *Good Natured: The origins of right and wrong in humans and other animals.* Cambridge, MA: Harvard University Press.

Warren, KJ (1990) The power and the promise of ecological feminism. *Environmental Ethics, 12* (2), 125–46.

SECTION 3

PRESENCE AND THE CORE CONDITIONS

INTRODUCTION

This section develops some of the themes introduced in the preceding sections, most notably the centrality of presence—an indefinable source of energy and truth—to the person-centred approach. The first two papers extend recent research and reflection on the quality of presence within person-centred and experiential psychotherapy (e.g. Geller & Greenberg, 2002). The third considers the place within us from which words may spring in pure form—'naked saying'—to express emergent truth. The fourth presents qualitative research that endeavours to capture the texture of the core condition of acceptance or unconditional positive regard. The fifth suggests that person-centred therapy may be seen primarily as a spiritual discipline.

The section begins with **Veronika Prüller-Jagenteufel's** presentation of presence as a Christian virtue that may also be regarded as a deep realization of the core conditions. Writing as Christian theologian who has also trained in the person-centred approach, and acknowledging the influence of her countryman, Peter Schmid, and the German theologian, Hermann Stenger, on her thinking, Prüller-Jagenteufel argues that developing the art of being present may be regarded as the foundation for the person-centred approach as well as for a spiritual life. The starting point for her investigation was a recognition that her own capacity for being present was deepened by her experience of going on retreat but also by participating in an extended encounter group. Although the nature of the experience of an encounter group may be very different from that of a retreat, they may both be regarded as 'schools of becoming more present' where we can overcome blocks that get in the way of our capacity to be open to 'the sources of a life-giving power'. For Prüller-Jagenteufel presence is essentially relational and she suggests that it is in this respect that therapy and Christian spirituality come together. She proposes that 'to live a spiritual life' may be regarded as 'an ongoing exercise in being present oneself and to recognize the divine presence around us, within ourselves and others and to give in to its liberating and healing power'.

Prüller-Jagenteufel suggests that raising the normal level of our presence involves making conscious and honest effort in relationship, both to others and to the divine. For **Dora Iseli Schudel** there is also an aspect of presence that can be deliberately cultivated by such means as reflection, reading, and the meditative contemplation of nature. These deliberate attempts to bring oneself into the present moment prior to meeting with a client can lead to the deepening of what she terms 'professional presence' and thus to an enhanced quality of relating and process within the session. 'Professional presence' is, however, intrinsically related to what she terms 'presence' or 'presence proper', a quality or state that she recalls very powerfully through her own experience of giving birth to her two children. This experience represented 'a condensed chance to be continuously present' and to participate in an exchange that involved not only the unborn child but also a 'unique energy' or 'life itself beyond or before it takes any material form'. Iseli Schudel proposes that the cultivation of presence is a lifelong task that enhances her quality of being with others, but also opens the way to the profound energy and life-giving quality that informed her experience of giving birth. In person-centred terminology this life-giving quality may be defined as the actualizing tendency in relation to the individual or as the formative tendency in relation to the universe, but the experience itself defied both time ('in my experiencing all was happening at once') and words: 'what actually happened did so without, or prior to, language'.

This points to the central difficulty that we, as human beings, encounter in terms of giving expression to what is most truly powerful and meaningful in our lives. **Sarah Luczaj** takes exploration of the indefinable and emergent and their fragile relationship to language a step further. As an Englishwoman living and working in Poland she is acutely aware of the difficulties and frustrations that come of striving to make oneself understood in a language that is not one's native language. However, this striving and the necessary 'making strange' of the process of expressing herself has opened up the possibility of 'new access' to her experience. Drawing on Eugene Gendlin's work, she explains that we can never fully capture experience in words. At times, however, words spring direct from bodily experiencing, as in the process of focusing. These words 'fit' exactly for the person whose experiencing finds sudden expression. Certain words are instrumental in bringing about a felt shift, but they are likely to make no sense to the listener. This pure expression—or 'naked saying'—is so accurately expressive for the speaker that if it is then 'taken by another and packaged into a certain form of logic, thought or language, it hurts the body'. While, at one extreme, working in a foreign language can get in the way of expressing understanding, at other times the forms can so break down that counsellor and client can be released into a deeply trustworthy state of *not* knowing, identifying neither with the forms of language nor with a fixed 'self' that is seeking to find expression.

The starting point of **Matis Nimetz's** research as presented here was a wish to understand better the quality—or, in person-centred terminology, the core condition—that she sees as underpinning both her professional work and her most nourishing personal relationships, that of acceptance. By interviewing individuals from different cultures, races, nationalities, gender and age, who had in common only the experience of having been at some point in their lives in the role of both counsellor and client, she sought to draw out the common threads in their understanding and experiencing of both giving and receiving acceptance. These threads are presented from the interviews and drawn together as they began to appear to her: as the warp and weft of 'a vast cloth', the image that lies behind her title, 'The Fabric of Acceptance'. This in-depth exploration of the quality of acceptance ends with both interviewees and researcher finding themselves in a space beyond words and Nimetz's conclusion that the encounter of self and other lived in acceptance leads, at times, to a dissolution of the 'I', to a discovery of 'that dimension for which it is difficult to find the words [where] change and healing can take place'.

Martin van Kalmthout addresses the question of whether we can identify something spiritual in the essence of the person-centred approach. He suggests that while Rogers' early views on therapeutic change include a move from 'self-concept' to 'true self', his later writings emphasize rather the move from fixity to changingness. There is a discarding of the self-structure, which van Kalmthout suggests is analogous to views found in spiritual literature concerning the transcendence of self. He then suggests that each of the 'core conditions' of person-centred therapy can take on a spiritual aspect. This can be seen in the emphasis on *unconditional* positive regard, in the transcendence of the therapist's own needs and perspectives which is involved in empathy, and in the dimensions of truth and love which are involved in deep authenticity. He then discusses the 'actualizing tendency' which Rogers sees as central to therapeutic change, and the 'formative tendency' which he discerns in the universe as a whole. The actualizing tendency can be seen as the manifestation of the formative tendency in the human world, so that when people are enabled to follow their actualizing tendency they are tapping into a cosmic force which pervades all things. All of this suggests to van Kalmthout that person-centred therapy can reasonably be construed as a spiritual discipline, though one without the traditional trappings of dogma and ritual. He suggests, finally, that given that the person-centred approach increasingly fails to fit with current trends in mental health care, it may be that ultimately the approach will find its fulfilment in the field of spiritual development rather than in that of psychotherapy.

CHAPTER 8

THE POWER OF PRESENCE

VERONIKA PRÜLLER-JAGENTEUFEL

BEING PRESENT AS A KEY VIRTUE IN (CHRISTIAN) SPIRITUALITY AND (PERSON-CENTRED) COUNSELLING

This article reflects on the concept of presence as one of the areas where Rogers' own reflections, the principles of the person-centred approach, and spirituality, specifically some forms of Christian spirituality, overlap and intertwine.[1] As a Christian theologian I will investigate the concept of presence from a spiritual and theological point of view. Perhaps that will bring an interesting perspective into the person-centred discussion about presence that started with Rogers' own reflections. Rogers names this area rather hesitantly and cautiously. Theologians speak of it much more openly. Perhaps—*prima vista*—a clearly theological approach seems a bit alien to the discussions in person-centred theory, but I hope it will also be interesting for those who do not share my Christian and theological framework of thinking.

Are you all present here? In my country, in Austria, this is the question which starts a common form of theatre for children, a kind of Punch and Judy show. Mr Punch is asking: 'Children, are you all present here?'—and all the children cry: 'Yes!' Maybe for children, very keen on watching theatre—featuring a clown, often a crocodile that has to be overcome, and sometimes a witch—this is really true: they are indeed present as they watch. Present in a specific sense, meaning fully dedicated, fully aware, concentrated on and focused on what is going on.

As grown-ups we are rather seldom present in this specific way; more often we are distracted, as we live in a time of overflowing sensations offered to us by media, internet, by crowded cities, by loud music in almost every shop, by lots of small talk, by long to-do lists on our desks, etc., etc. And even if we want to leave all that behind and be present—in a theatre, a music hall, an encounter, with a friend or a client, or in a church or a meditation, even sometimes when we long for that very special form of presence in erotic situations—we experience that it is not at all easy. There can be a multitude of distracting thoughts and feelings within us, there can be inner blocks of different sorts, and the person who wants to be present in a deeper sense has to sort through them. To become really present seems to be a life-long process.

1. See also Brian Thorne's keynote lecture, (Chapter 3, pp. 35–47) in which this intertwining and overlapping was very obvious and discussed.

Carl Rogers, as well as numerous spiritual advisers, appreciates presence as a key to becoming connected to the healing powers of life. Learning and exercising the art of being present can be seen as foundational for a spiritual life as well as for the person-centred approach.

I. ROGERS' EXPERIENCES

Carl Rogers talks about presence when he is remembering situations in therapy or in encounter groups in which he felt himself in an altered state of consciousness which seemed to be highly helpful for his clients. When he was really present he had the impression that big shifts, not imaginable before, were possible. His presence somehow opened up the possibility for the others to transcend their own inner boundaries and become more present themselves. In these moments there was the feeling of belonging to a wider dimension. Rogers uses words like 'transcendent', 'spiritual', and even 'mystical' to describe these experiences (Schmid, 1994).

The way Carl Rogers talks about being present as a highly helpful attitude of the therapist and about presence as a special state of consciousness in encounters has led to an ongoing discussion amongst person-centred theoreticians about the significance of these experiences of presence. For example, it has been questioned whether presence should be counted as another quality beside or alongside empathy, congruence and acceptance. Whereas some have opted for this, others have warned that to go deeper into this area could mislead the person-centred approach into mysticism. Together with Peter Schmid I prefer to understand presence as a deep realization of acceptance, empathy and congruence. To name and explore this phenomenon of presence may help to deepen our understanding of personal relationships (Schmid, 1994: 244).

EXCURSUS: SOME SIMILARITIES

When I read Rogers' descriptions of his experiences of presence I remembered some of my own experiences in encounter groups (for example in the eight-day Austria Program, which is designed like the La Jolla Encounter Groups). In these groups I shared with others moments of deep connection with one other, of feeling connected to a beyond, to a reality greater than our group. And it seemed to me that these encounters have helped most of the participants to develop further their own ability to be present. After some intensive days we had a higher level of presence in the group. I recognized this by the way it became easier to concentrate on the process of the group as well as on the person that was actually speaking; by more freedom of expression in the group; by the raised awareness for each others' feelings; by the way the group started to act in common.

I realized I had known such a state of consciousness before. In certain ways I had somewhat similar experiences on retreats, in which I used to take part as a way of deepening my Christian faith. On a good retreat, when I go to a monastery, for example, and for some days lead a simple life of prayer and reflection, I also learn and exercise the art of being present—for example by meditating on certain biblical readings or by silent meditation as a form of presenting myself to the presence of the divine. In retreats, spiritual directors advise the participants to try to be aware, to be sensitive, to relate oneself to God and also to others.

After those retreats I often had a very similar feeling of somehow having touched a higher level of being present in the same way as I felt it after those encounter groups—and both times I experienced that at least for some time this state of consciousness somehow lingered and gave more clearness and more friendliness to my work with other people as well as to my day-to-day relationships. Encounter groups and retreats are in my view both schools for becoming more present. They provide a source of power for us which radiates helpfully into our relationships with one another. This is, I think, because they serve in a certain way as door-openers, which help us to get through our distractions and our inner blockades to the sources of a life-giving power: the personal relationship with others and the personal relationship to the divine.

My own experience of similarities between retreats and encounter groups[2] was the starting point of my investigation into the meaning of presence in spirituality and in the person-centred approach. My thesis is: becoming present with others and before God connects us to the foundational source of life, which is a relationship that offers the possibility for personal development.

II. RELATION AS A FOUNDATIONAL CATEGORY[3]

In my Christian theology *relation*[4] is the foundational category. All beings *are* because and insofar as they are related to each other. Therefore being present for one another is rooted in the original relatedness which characterizes all beings. In a Christian view we are not monads, existing for oneself and only secondarily relating to others; we are beings in relation and we exist because we are related. We are ourselves because we are in relationships. Relatedness is the foundational reality. Christian theology tries to find words for that by speaking about the divine as a triune God. The Christian belief pictures God, the foundation of foundations, not as a monolith, a lonely potentate, nor as an impersonal flow of energy, but as personal relationship, as a community, so to speak. Therefore relatedness is the way of being a person.

Presence I see rooted in this foundational relatedness. When a person is present, she/he is aware of this relatedness and gives space and strength to it. Some theologians

2. I am not saying the two are the same and it is very clear to me that neither all encounter groups nor all retreats have positive effects on every participant. I am only talking about my experience as a starting point for my further investigations.

3. I share my approach and many thoughts in this area with Peter F. Schmid, to whom I am grateful for a lot of enriching discussions. In his paper in this book (Chapter 19: 227–46), he gives a thorough foundation for this relational approach.

4. In German we have only one word, *Beziehung*, for both, relation and relationship. In this article I decided to use the term *relation* when I speak about philosophical issues, and the term *relationship* when I speak more specifically of persons, but sometimes there is no clear distinction.

presume that a person becomes present for another person by recognizing and loving the other (Darlapp, 1960). This involves being aware of how the other actually is and accepting him or her in that. It also involves acknowledging the other in her/his wholeness, taking into account not only what can be perceived of her/him 'here and now', but everything which makes her/him herself/himself—including past and future.

So presence seems to be a really universal category. To be present therefore means more than to be in the 'here and now', it includes giving attention to everything which wants to be acknowledged and giving space to all that has been and that is longed for. The more a person is really present, the more of her/his whole personality can emerge and unfold and can consciously become part of the actual relationship.

The theological foundation for that lies in the belief that personal presence is taking part in the presence of God. All relatedness is embedded in this foundational and original relationship which is God. Being present as a spiritual virtue is rooted in that divine relatedness as the source of all—all that is.

III. SPIRITUALITY AS LIVING IN THE PRESENCE OF THE DIVINE

To live your life consciously in the presence of God, in other words to be conscious that God is present and to try to live according to that, is one possible definition of what spirituality is all about. Spirituality is more than prayers and rituals; it is a way of living, it covers all realms of life. According to a theology that describes God as relationship and all human relatedness embedded in God's universal presence, living one's life in the presence of God means living in relatedness: to others, to the world, to oneself. Spirituality therefore can be defined as a life designed to be lived in relationship, to relate to, to be connected—and all that not merely as a fate, but as a dynamic power, which a spiritual person allows to shape her/his whole life.

Spiritual practices in a stricter sense—prayers, meditations, liturgies, rituals—are classical ways of relating oneself to God, of getting in touch with the divine. In all religions there are such practices, which are forms of becoming aware of the powerful divine presence. In the spiritual traditions of the world (as well as in Christianity) we find different variations. Most forms of prayer are ways to present oneself to the divine—although on the surface this can look as if the praying person is trying to draw God's attention to his/her present situation, praying can more deeply be seen as a form of drawing our own attention to the given presence of the divine.

Most forms of meditation are explicitly trying to deepen the connection to God, to become present in the presence of the divine. There are, for example, forms of meditation where you focus on a biblical story and try to picture yourself in that story. Others concentrate on an icon, seen in itself as a form of divine presence. In silent meditation participants try to clear themselves of all thoughts and feelings, to let go of everything which may come into their minds—even to let go of letting go—to become open to God's presence. In a secular frame of thinking meditation is used to become more quiet and centred and less distracted.

Religious rituals and liturgies can be seen as interactions with the divine power and again this is based on the trust that there is this power present and reachable. Another form is the mystical experience of the presence of God. This is, in most cases, a deep feeling of connectedness with the divine, which leaves the mystic astounded and speechless. Those experiences are not any more mediated by words or acts, prayers or rituals, but they can be prepared by those practices.

Nevertheless, most religions believe in mediatory practices and in mediators or priests who are capable of opening the doors to the divine powers. In its origins Christianity abandoned the idea of priestly mediation between God and humans, with Christ as the only mediator, there being no need of any other mediation because every person is directly related to God. However, a strong tradition of priesthood developed within Christianity, which, for example, continues to be practised in the Roman Catholic church today. Perhaps this is due to the fact that most humans have the feeling they do not know how to become present and how to realize the presence of God and that they need somebody to do it for them. I think this is also true for many clients in counselling and therapy; they sometimes would like the therapist to do the work for them. In Christian spirituality, as most Christian theologians of today would see it, the role of a spiritual adviser or priest is not to mediate the power of presence as if their own 'superior' presence would somehow shine divine light on the other person. The task is to facilitate the becoming present of them both, priest and believer, because the divine presence is there for everyone.

That God is present, present for His/Her people and for all humans, is an old conviction of the biblical religions. In the biblical book of Exodus God introduces Him/Herself with a name which is a term that can be translated as 'I who am present'. God is doing this, when She/He talks to Moses, sending Moses to set the Israelites free because God has seen their suffering and has heard their cries for freedom. Moses asks God, 'Who are you? What shall I tell the others about who is sending me?' And God says: 'I am Yahwe'. This translates as: 'the one who is present to you or with you' (Exodus 3: 1–15).

This biblical tradition is foundational for Jewish and Christian spirituality: to believe in a God who is present and whose presence is powerful and liberating. God is not far beyond us, unreachable to humans, but close, with us, present in our midst, sharing our ways, feeling our sorrows and delighting in our joys. God is interested in we humans: *inter esse,* which means to be within, to mingle into, to be dedicated to—to be present.

According to Christian belief the presence of the divine within the human and, vice versa, the human within the divine is what signifies Jesus Christ. By the incarnation, by becoming human, God has definitely turned Him/Herself towards humanity and this is 'because of us and for our salvation'—as expressed in the Creed. So I see it as a deep conviction of the Christian faith and spirituality that the presence of God is powerful and healing.

To live a spiritual life is an ongoing exercise in being present oneself and to recognize the divine presence around us, within ourselves and others and to give in to its liberating and healing power. To become present with others and before God connects us to the foundational source of life, which is a relationship that offers the possibility for personal development.

IV. THE ART OF BEING PRESENT

What might all this mean for therapists and counsellors? I think that the way of spiritual growth (in a Christian framework) and the way of becoming a good therapist (in the person-centred framework) have much in common. Both believe in relationship as foundational. Both require the art of actively relating to others as well the art of being present. This converges, in my opinion, as I see relatedness as the underlying reality of all being, and becoming present as going deeper into this reality.

Theological ethics speak about certain basic values or options by calling them virtues. Justice, mercy, love, or solidarity, or truthfulness, for example, are virtues in this theological sense of the word. In a similar way the art of being present can be described as a virtue. Regardless of whether it is meant as a way of relating to a divine presence or as a way of relating to other people, being present implies the same attitudes: to be as fully aware as possible; to be open to everything that may come into your field of sensibility; to be acknowledging and loving; to be concentrated and clear, not distracted; to be whole but at the same time directed towards the other; open for her or him and all that is with him or her; consciously and actively connected in a relationship meant to be helpful, meant to facilitate life in its fullness.

Describing this attitude of being present as 'a virtue', I am consciously employing this term with its specific theological meaning. A virtue is more than a particular activity or deed, it underlies single acts in which it shows and realizes itself. It is a *habitus*, a habit, an overall attitude. It can be exercised in single acts, but it goes beyond them. To establish this virtue is not only a question of doing certain things, it requires something like dedication, commitment, determination.

To talk about virtue in a theological sense implies that it is something you are gifted with, which is given to you, as a present, a gift. In theological terms we talk about grace. So perhaps, as all virtues, the virtue of being present is also closely linked with an attitude of thankfulness.

Clearly we are not present in the same way in every moment. Rogers has talked about rare occasions in which he experienced that the state of being present was possible for him and he was able to reach the other. Even when I am viewing the virtue of presence as an underlying attitude and as something we can exercise by training our awareness and concentration, I am convinced that the experience of being drawn deeply into powerful presence will never be an everyday experience. However I do think that the normal level of our presence can be raised by honestly trying to actively relate ourselves to others as well as to the divine. Presence is not only there in exceptional situations. Peak experiences are only deep recognitions of it in very intense moments. These exceptionally intense moments arise out of the broader stream of presence which is constant in all personal relations, even though it may not be in conscious awareness.

V. THE POWER OF PRESENCE

Hermann Stenger, a German theologian who specializes in pastoral counselling, speaks about three different forms of power which spiritual advisers (and I think therapists as well) have to cultivate: the integrating power of leadership, which works vertically; the inspiring power of guidance, which works horizontally; and the inducing power of presence, which works radiantly (Stenger, 2000). All these powers are ambivalent. A leader can use his/her authority to oppress others or to empower others. Guidance can be offered in a way which cuts off the potential of others or in a way which encourages the creativity of all who participate. To cultivate and discipline these ambivalent powers, Hermann Stenger suggests, in a pragmatic approach is to get a state-of-the-art training in leadership and guidance and, in a spiritual approach, to recognize these powers as rooted in the power of a loving God and to be aware that each power is God's gift meant to be used for the benefit of all.

In the same way Stenger deals with the power of presence. It too is a power which everybody has to a certain extent and it too is ambivalent. When any person enters a room the atmosphere changes. The vibrations he or she gives off can be vitalizing for the others or destructive. Prior to verbal and even nonverbal communication everyone influences his/her surroundings with a radiant power. Its transmissions can be described as a 'third language' which is communicating inner psychic processes as well as processes in the unconscious (Stadter, 1992). The way a person is present is full of information and of messages. Hermann Stenger says that this power is not controllable and hardly trainable. What we are radiating is only changed by our efforts to grow into a fully functioning personality. But we can also embed this power of our presence in the life-giving presence of the divine. We can accept this power from God's hands.

Hermann Stenger gives the example of Moses who has encountered God, the God who named Her/Himself as 'I who am present for you'. To be able to lead the people of Israel into freedom Moses has to learn to be a leader and to give guidance and to do this he gets in touch with the radiant power of the divine presence. For forty days he gives himself into that presence and when he comes back to his people his face is shining—as the book of Exodus tells the story (Exodus 34). The personal power of Moses as an adviser for his people appears here embedded in a power that goes far beyond (Stenger, 2000: 217).

VI. HEALING PRESENCE

What then is the effect of this power? Can it be used? How does presence work? How can it be helpful to others? I try to describe it as follows: being actively present is to realize foundational relatedness as a healing power. To be present can open up a space for that power, which is never *my* power, but the power of relatedness, or—as I name it according to my theology: the loving power of God.

In an encounter, when one person is consciously longing to be present on a higher level and she/he is trying to be fully aware and open and at the same time is serenely awaiting the gift of presence I trust that this offers the possibility to the other to be more present him/herself. It opens up a space in which there can be what is. And only what is allowed to be can change. In this space of presence the past can arise and the future can be anticipated; there can be a higher awareness of what is felt now and a better ability to express this; there is openness for development. The one who is trying to be consciously present is inviting the other to be present as well, to be who she/he really is—and that again is much more than what he/she is 'here and now'. I believe this is what God is doing for each and every one of us: being present as an invitation to us to become present as well. This is an ongoing process of relationship.

I think all who try to learn the art of presence—in a spiritual way or in the framework of counselling or therapy—are driven by a deep respect for the person and for everything that exists. I see presence as the quality of being which embeds empathy, acknowledgement/acceptance and congruence/authenticity deeply within an understanding of the person as a being of relatedness. The virtue of being present lies in the decision to trust in that power of relatedness, which is the source of the healing power of presence.

Children are certainly present in a theatre—dedicated to what is presented to them. Those who are really present in the theatre of life are open to whatever life may present to them—maybe trusting that, in the end, what life presents to them will be a caring relationship.

I give thanks to Suzanne Keys who helped me a lot by improving my use of English grammar and vocabulary in this article!

REFERENCES

Darlapp, A (1960) Art. Gegenwarts(weisen). In *Lexikon für Theologie und Kirche* Bd. 4 (pp. 588–92). Freiburg: Herder.

Schmid, PF (1994) *Personzentrierte Gruppenpsychotherapie.* Ein Handbuch. Bd. 1 Solidarität und Autonomie (pp. 201–70). Köln: Editon Humanistische Psychologie.

Stadter, EA (1992) *Wenn du wüßtest, was ich fühle . . . Einführung in die Beziehungstherapie.* Freiburg: Herder.

Stenger, HM (2000) *Im Zeichen des Hirten und des Lammes* (pp. 205–21). Mitgift und Gift biblischer Bilder, Innsbruck: Tyrolia.

CHAPTER 9

A PERSON-CENTRED THERAPIST'S QUEST FOR PRESENCE

DORA ISELI SCHUDEL

WHAT IS PRESENCE?

According to his famous passage, Carl Rogers (1986: 198) experienced 'presence' when he was 'at his best', when he was 'close to the transcendental core of his being', when he was 'perhaps in a slightly altered state of consciousness' when 'strange, impulsive behaviors turned out to be right' and his 'inner spirit touched the inner spirit of the other'. It could not be forced and had 'nothing to do with his thought process'. It was an exceptional state, not consciously aimed at or prepared for.

Brian Thorne (1985: 9)—in a strikingly similar description—equates his experience of what he calls 'tenderness' to Rogers' 'presence'. Maureen O'Hara (2000: 16) is convinced that 'moments of eternity are reachable through relationships of unconditional love'.

Geller and Greenberg (2002: 71–86) produced an outstanding qualitative study, condensing the reports of seven experienced, not exclusively person-centred, therapists. Without reference to transcendence or inner spirit they see presence as the foundation of the core conditions and as a result of conscious efforts, careful pre-session and in-life preparation of the ground for it.

Peter Schmid, cited by Rud (2003: 166), combines the spiritual and the 'down-to-earth' understanding of the term: 'Presence is not only to be regarded as an altered transcending state of consciousness but a way of being in encounter.' 'A way of being in encounter' is a main characteristic of presence in all its shadings, similar to the Buddhist concept of mindfulness.

Whoever tackles the elusive subject of presence seems to encounter a painful gap between the part which is verbally expressible on the one hand and the inexhaustible part that is inexpressible on the other. The experienced realities behind the word obviously differ to some extent from one person to the next, if not for the same person from one incidence to the next. Using one term for two distinctly different experiential states, as does Schmid, could cause confusion. I will thus be using the term 'presence' alone whenever an experienced spiritual or transcendental quality is included. Conversely, I shall be referring to 'professional presence' for a psychologically understandable state which can be reproduced by and large.

In my view, these two states represent extremes or two poles of what may in fact be a continuum of shadings or intensities: on the one hand (i.e. in spiritual presence or presence proper) we have the connectedness with what could be called a process-directing spiritual life energy, an overall formative tendency in tune with both the therapist and the client or, as Rogers has put it, both therapist and client being 'part of something larger'. On the other hand (i.e. professional presence) there is the holistic embodiment of the core conditions.

It is my vision, conviction and rare experience that the two poles do coincide as a *conjunctio oppositorum*, that they can meet, but they do not necessarily have to.

'Presence' always points me to the only axiom of person-centred therapy: the actualizing tendency, the innate tendency of the organism to develop all of its potential. I consider 'spiritual presence' to be the therapist's exceptional experience of her self—the actualizing tendency unfolding as it should and as it is meant to by its innate potential, when it is in connection and harmony with the client's self-actualizing tendency and when both are in touch with the fundamental formative tendency in the universe.

So what about 'professional presence'? Unlike spiritual presence, professional presence with all its nuances and intensities stands for the experience of *being* the core conditions, resulting from being deeply in touch with the client's as well as one's own core. I can favour being present in this way by taking preparatory measures. I succeed to varying degrees and I fail time and again.

Personally I have a deep longing for *all* manifestations of presence. The longing for spiritual presence in particular is rooted in my experience of existential borderline situations. I experienced spiritual presence in my childhood, as a lover, as a client, as a companion of beloved persons during their final hours. I also experienced it when I was close to death myself, and especially when giving birth to two children.

In all those existential situations my 'I', my 'Self' was, however briefly, in strong and safe empathic contact with the core of the other person or persons involved and in tune with what I experienced as a storm-like 'energy' filling the space around me and physically reverberating in me. This unique energy felt like the source of my essential aliveness, or as life itself beyond or before it takes any material form.

The result of these exceptional perceptions and experiences was a fearless affirmation of life and its finiteness, a state of calm, peace and safety, basic trust in life and death. I have some clues that the other person or persons involved had similar feelings. Up to now my body and memory stores spiritual presence as a basically reliable source of orientation, strength and reassurance. The source feels sometimes closer, often far off, remote.

I would like to make a plea for 'non-presence' before exploring spiritual presence the way I experienced it twice when giving birth to my two children. In the demanding complexity of everyday life, I often find myself in the probably common state of non-presence: only part of my awareness is in the here and now, let alone open and available for others. The rest of me is distracted in all directions. Distraction from the present moment and from being present in it is too often a means of coping, to let go of it easily. Often in my life the state of not being present may still be a necessity which I may regret but do accept.

SPIRITUAL PRESENCE IN THE PROCESS OF GIVING BIRTH

Carl Rogers' frequently quoted statement that the most personal is at the same time the most universal helps me to explore tentatively the essence of my two childbirths, both of them more than 20 years back in time. More than any training in psychotherapy, the two childbirths have taught me literally through every fibre of my whole being where body and mind are undivided, how the universal formative tendency manifesting itself in individual living beings actually feels. Moreover the two births have taught me how unnecessarily painful it can be when my conscious thoughts, my willpower, my verbal communication are *not* in tune with the overall formative tendency.

What was the process of giving birth like? I am no mathematician—but a Markoff process seems to be a good metaphor for it. A Markoff process—as I was told—is the somewhat paradoxical fact that, contrary to our habitual way of thinking, the past course of events does not allow us to anticipate, or indeed predict, the present state, but only the latter—the present—can influence future states. Thus, giving birth to a child was a condensed chance to be continuously present, moment by moment, by making full use of all my physical and mental abilities.

The child had grown within me over nine months as an invisible, mysterious part of myself and yet already as a living entity in its own right. He or she 'decided' at a specific moment to set out for his or her journey into the world. All I had to do was to be fully available for that journey: a dancing exchange between an irresistible 'guiding energy', the child and the mother with ever-changing rhythmic variations. It was a process of mutual attuning, changing from one moment to the next, sometimes subtle and pleasant, often violent and painful, a dramatic powerful exchange beyond or perhaps before words. At times the process of giving birth was an almost playful exchange of pressure: there was pushing and pulling, then suddenly rest and peace, soon followed by a new pulsating tempest, full of surprises—mainly univocal messages to adapt, to move, to breathe, to let go, to listen, to actively make an effort, to relax. I was permanently in a position of having to respond in ever new unplanned organismic ways in a dance of going towards various qualities of pain, touching them, deliberately going deeper into them, having no choice but to go deeper, receding again and letting go when appropriate.

In short: with my whole being I had to be fully aware of, and genuinely and attentively embody all my respect, my sensitivity and the utmost of my empathy to the invisible unborn child. I really had no choice but to be present.

The process, which is by definition a *sequence* of events, had a paradoxical quality of not happening in the usual dimension of time. This quality seemed to be linked to the unpredictability of events. In my experiencing all was happening at once. Only reluctantly I call it 'being in a different layer or dimension of reality' or 'in an altered state of consciousness'. This choice of words is just one possible attempt to symbolize and communicate my experience. What actually happened did so without, or prior to, language.

On the journeys of giving birth with their ever-changing new territories, I was carefully assisted by my partner, the father of the children. Both of us felt part of what was clearly self-organizing, yet not exclusively biologically determined. Being part of it left both of us, and me as mother in particular, with the responsibility of being aware, active, cooperative, willing and most attentive to what was my share in any given moment: the responsibility of being present.

Occasionally I lost touch with my children's pace of finding their tedious way out into the world. Sometimes I was disconnected from what I call metaphorically 'the directing wisdom'. Then there was fear or hesitation which impeded confidence in the 'bodily sense as … navigational tool' (Geller & Greenberg, 2002: 84). Being dropped out of the appropriate rhythm was immediately followed by additional pain of a distinct, sharp quality: a pain which—no doubt—was not an inevitable part of the process but rather the result of my failures in being sufficiently present.

Quite often I did not get distracted by fear and relied on the safe energy of 'life' in the child, in me and encompassing both of us. I went through moments of both pleasure and pain of various, even extreme, intensities. This pain, however strong, felt fair, transient, inevitable, bearable and a natural, intrinsic part of the process.

In those 'timeless times' when the three of us—the process-directing energy in the child, his father and myself—were in harmonious coordination, it felt like simultaneously composing, playing and letting go of a never heard, never repeatable, unique piece of music.

Here I would like to leave the parents sharing their joy and gratitude to Life (with a capital 'L') for the newborn human beings radiating with white light, a light which faded away after a while. The vivid and encouraging memory of having felt part and instrument of life itself does not fade away, whether it is called an experience of spiritual presence or not. It certainly deepened our understanding of life and love far beyond any rationality.

PROFESSIONAL PRESENCE IN THERAPY

Let us now have a look at therapy: our clients' suffering could be seen as their own want of being present to themselves and lack of presence of significant others in various decisive moments of their life history. Our task as person-centred therapists would be to just be present—a seemingly simple and yet most demanding task.

As a therapist, I sometimes long for the quality of spiritual presence as a kind of god out of the blue, a *deus ex machina*, when in my daily work a client's despair seems endless—and my own hope that therapy would ever be of use to her has temporarily disappeared. But in a therapy session no functional laws come to my aid as they did when I was giving birth. No self-organizing process unfolds using me as instrument, nor does it do most of the laborious work for me provided I am willing to cooperate.

So, in my daily work as a person-centred therapist, I appreciate being able to rely on a reasonable human level of what I call 'professional presence': being more or less aware of myself and my own process *and* open and in contact with the other person or persons who often do not require more—or less—than to be deeply understood and acknowledged in what seems clear, and even more so in what is still hiding in chaos, perhaps hardly accessible in a felt sense at the edge of awareness (Gendlin, 1996). That's why I like to amend Winnicott's well-known 'good enough mother' to a 'good enough therapist'. And as a therapist, whose professional presence is often good enough I have, of course, the commitment to continuously improve it.

Beyond the integration of new insights, knowledge, techniques etc., becoming a better therapist in the person-centred tradition always means to expand one's awareness and sensitivity in all directions. Personally I am most interested in learning more about my bodily physical reactions. What else then if not a permanent, life-long 'quest for presence' is the ongoing task of improving professional competence, of learning from failures, of having resources at hand when needed, of becoming more centred and yet open?

My tools are very common: reflecting on my work, alone, in supervision and with others, reading, taking courses, attending a conference, brushing up—if needed—my own therapy by being a client again, and most important in recent years, taking care of myself in various and changing ways, whenever possible, even sometimes briefly between sessions. One of my favourite instances of this care, which I discovered long ago (and before knowing its medieval roots) is the meditative contemplation of various entities of nature including the sky outside the window. Another tool of mine is to play the occasional little tune on my flute—the clarity of the sound giving me feedback about my breath. Gentle physical exercises or just consciously relaxing or being aware of my breathing activity or switching for a while to a non-professional activity are other examples. I often find Gendlin's focusing technique in my personal adaptation useful too.

It seems that all these and other ways of caring for myself and giving presence to myself reduce fantasies *about* my client and promote presence *with* him. Momentary incongruences are important markers of lacking presence. Currently my favourite way of becoming aware of them retrospectively is taking personal notes as well as the usual report after sessions. Had I been aware of the incongruence on the spot—in the given present moment—I could have handled it for better or worse. In fact my congruence would have been re-established on the spot. To identify it only after the session is in itself evidence of poor handling. Of course I never know how it did affect the client's process, but it certainly disturbs my own. It feels like falling out of the rhythm and pace at birth.

To re-read my notes before the next session helps to avoid getting caught in the same trap again, to put fantasies and judgements apart—or make better use of them. Let me illustrate how far away from professional presence I can be and how complex and difficult the task is from there to being open, non-judgemental, warm, accepting and genuine. And if you call my impediments just countertransferences—so be it.

Here are a few examples of personal notes:

CLIENT A: 5TH SESSION

I was unable to clearly feel on the spot, let alone to name, what I felt was between us: a vacuum irritating me vaguely, a space without conductibility—while out there she was with her desperate need for authority, orientation, support. I had this image of a little girl who wanted to be an adult, a person who fiercely decided not to allow anybody to hurt or even touch her. She hardly looked at me—until I realized that if I did not look at her, she would be able to have a slightly longer look at me as she was speaking continuously. I hardly got a chance to say a word, if I did not want to run the risk of being a threat to her. I repressed my strong motherly impulse to soothe her. She was probably as far away from trusting me as she was from trusting herself. With a smile she kept repeating how great she felt today—I did not believe a word; yet I found myself nodding. Only now do I clearly see my double-bind message—she may have had by far too many of those in her life already.

CLIENT B: 45TH SESSION

(Sessions spread over 2 years in winter only because of B's seasonal depression.)
Relaxed, almost familiar atmosphere. B enjoys talking about incidences of risk-taking and assertiveness she is proud of. Long silence, then she wanted to tell me that her therapy had not really dissolved the constantly critical, nagging clot in her chest; only now and then did she feel better. No difficulty for me in empathizing with her feelings that all her efforts ultimately were in vain as long as not everything was perfect. But I felt a sudden fit of tiredness and resignation: was it hers or was it my own? I was so concerned with sorting out instead of asking her that I disconnected from her for quite a while. I did not even hear what she said—which resulted in additional difficulties mirroring hers: being annoyed at my own imperfection!

CLIENT C: 11TH SESSION

He makes it easy for me by exploring deeply. I am swift, accurate, warm, intense, vaguely perceiving a danger of being too close on his heels, in some way almost eager to keep up with him—some sort of competitiveness obstructing my way—the point of gravity in my body by far too high up to be centred—an almost elegant session—and I ahead of myself and him—listening more to contents, caught by words—and completely exhausted at the end. What did I do to him—and to myself?

I hope these examples may illustrate my shortcomings in even a good enough professional presence when temporarily being either absorbed by or alienated from my own process. However I hope that in my daily practice I am frequently in a state or process of a good enough professional presence.

So what happens when I feel personally and professionally in tune and close to my client and her phenomenological world as well as to myself? What happens when I am without my notorious over-reflecting hesitations? What happens when what I am and what I want to be become one? Sometimes there is a remote repercussion in my body and my mind of my birth-giving experiences, fortunately enough without any physical pain being involved. Then I am clearly aware of myself and at the same time close to and open for my client. The two of us being together in this way represents a quality of unquestionable necessity and self-evidence.

The client's verbal and non-verbal expressions as well as my own come from what I suspect is close to her core, her undistorted, unique, often seemingly simple 'truth'. Whatever the contents, whatever the emotional shading, there is a quality around of simple nakedness: 'that is how I am, how I feel, how I think and by sharing it with you I discover and own it for the first time myself. I enjoy your resonance with who I am. I feel encouraged to go on and risk more.' Sometimes the client is up to something basically new, beyond an appropriate handle for a felt sense. I tend to think of these events as of the actual happening of an ever so tiny yet creative part of the reorganizing process. It might bear fruit now or in a more or less distant future.

An immediate effect is that I often see clients breathe more deeply. Their most frequently reported feeling is some 'sense of freedom' as if physically and mentally the space around them had become less constricted, less determined, less pressured. Later on they often start expanding in what they dare to think, say, feel and do as if to make use of their larger space in this world. There is a tendency to less fear and more determination, less anger and more acceptance of being hurt, less complaint and more courage to act. There is an often slow and gradual awareness and relief of being freed from some self-made constraints and restrictions and a growing hope of living a better life with more personal risks and new choices.

In short: in my experience, times of professional presence seem to deepen and clarify the therapeutic relationship, favouring depth as well as clarity in the client's relating to herself. I cannot present figures—but clients who report a gain of freedom turn out to be successful ones, both in their own evaluation as well as in mine.

Some clients, however, do not perceptibly react to sessions that felt full of professional presence and relational depth to me. I am actually not sure whether I succumb to wishful thinking when I see even some of these clients' subsequent struggles pointing in a slightly more assertive direction. But I also remember clients with various kinds of troubles whose process evolved hardly beyond stagnation, although I would have rated my professional presence high. Furthermore, a few clients left my practice with reasonable satisfaction about the outcome of our joint venture, despite the fact that during the sessions I hardly ever felt like a convincingly present person-centred therapist.

As a therapist I have been—although on rare occasions only—in the realm of spiritual presence or 'presence' proper with its characteristic of being in a qualitatively different state of consciousness. What happens then between the client and myself may deserve to be called with Schmid (2002) 'a Thou–I' meeting, reversing Martin Buber's 'I–Thou'. My experience is of an absence of the sense of time and gravity, the client and myself in a bonding of almost unshakable safety and trustworthiness. The qualities of safety and trustworthiness come out of the nearly palpable presence of the same 'energy' which guided the creative process of giving birth. This energy is everywhere: I perceive it in the client, in me and both of us encompassed by it. I conceive it—if any concept is adequate at all—as the source or principle of life, or in Rogerian terms, as the formative tendency manifesting itself.

Let me stress one amazing and paradoxical fact: the usual empathic understanding of the client—often quite an effort—has no importance in spiritual presence. There is no need to look for it because it is already available, most complex *and* yet extremely simple, probably close to the core and essence of the client, meaningful and surprisingly beautiful. Experiencing spiritual presence reinforces my trust tremendously in the client's ability to find their way out of inflicted sufferings.

Professional presence at its best, and particularly spiritual presence, are not a matter of my conscious intention or willpower. I cannot make presence happen nor deliberately decide to be in a state of experiencing it. But I might contribute to being more or less open, more or less prepared, more or less willing and centred enough for it to happen or not to happen. 'I' am precisely not its source or cause, but its temporary part. At times I am simply not prepared for, or even afraid of it, and prefer, or need, to work in more shallow waters.

CONCLUSION

In order to improve my readiness for presence, I need sufficient time and space for contemplation and reflection. Being better prepared for 'professional presence' comes back to being better prepared for fully and 'really' living the core conditional attitudes in an integrated way.

One way of describing the rare experience of 'spiritual presence' is that the essence, the principle or mystery of life, the formative tendency, is manifest in the situation, in the other person, in me and in the relationship. In therapy defensiveness and resistance in both persons dissolve and give way to an emotional state of unconditional trust and fearlessness without the two denying their separate and different individualities. Both persons seem to meet in such a holistic way that the undistorted parts of their self-actualizing tendencies determine the process in each of them as well as between them.

The older I grow the more I seem to appreciate presence in all its shadings. I wish and hope to be able to work and live ever more often in a state of loving presence—and hopefully one day to die in it. This is the reason why I keep up my attentive and receptive quest for it.

REFERENCES

Geller, S & Greenberg, L (2002) Therapeutic presence: A therapist's experience of presence in the psychotherapy encounter. *Person-Centered and Experiential Psychotherapies 1* (1&2), 71–86.

Gendlin, E (1996) *Focusing-Oriented Psychotherapy*. New York: Guilford.

O'Hara, M (2000) Moments of eternity. *Person 1*/2000, 4. Jg., 5–17. Wien: Facultas.

Rogers, C (1986) A client-centered/person-centered approach to therapy. In LL Kutash and A Wolf (eds) *Psychotherapist's Casebook* (pp. 197–208). San Francisco: Jossey-Bass.

Rud, C (2003) Empathy: The adventure of being present. *Person-Centered and Experiential Psychotherapies, 2* (3), 162–71.

Schmid, P (2002) Die Person im Zentrum der Therapie. Zu den Identitätskriterien personzentrierter Therapie und zur bleibenden Herausforderung von Carl Rogers an die Psychotherapie, in *Z. Person 1*/2002 6. Jg., (pp. 16–33).Wien: Facultas.

Thorne, B (1985) *The Quality of Tenderness*. Norwich: Norwich Centre Publications.

Winnicott, D (1987/4) *Vom Spiel zur Kreativität*. Stuttgart: Klett-Cotta.

CHAPTER 10

'NAKED SAYING' — LANGUAGES, SELVES AND 'NO-SELF' IN THERAPY

SARAH LUCZAJ

For Mariusz Tchorek (1939–2004)

As I live and work using a different language, as a therapist, language and creative writing teacher, I am particularly sensitive to the difficulties and possibilities inherent in attempting to 'express myself' in another tongue. The frustration caused can sometimes be immense as I attempt to shape a thought into another framework, into a shape that could not exist in my 'own' language. I am also aware, however, that this 'making strange' of the process of expressing myself opens up the possibility of a new access to my experience. It also makes clear to me that the very idea of expressing 'yourself' in words is a bit of a myth. This is a starting point for a questioning of the very notions of expression, of self, of the ways in which client and counsellor communicate, whether or not they share a language and cultural background, and most importantly, how change occurs.

As person-centred therapists we attempt to take each person as a fresh, new being, we are used to taking the client's words as ways into a unique experience, using particular words as markers on the journey, with their own cluster of meanings. Often the client and counsellor create a vocabulary all their own, with a richness that would not be accessible to an outsider listening to their conversation. Metaphors, often very extended ones, open up a special access, a way of linking the personal change process to a creative one, often allowing experience to be shared in a freer way, because there is not the pretence, or oversimplification, that the client is directly representing their experience. The counsellor can feel freer to move around inside a metaphor, more able to play, less concerned about trampling the client's meaning. The creation of metaphors, however, seems to me to be intimately linked to culturally shared meanings. They can be hard to follow on a visceral level in another language in which each element carries a different set of associations.

When the client and counsellor do not share the same language and culture a great deal of subtle communication, covered by assumptions of shared meanings, is absent. It may be replaced by a subtle communication of assumptions about the other based on ideas which we have about the other culture, and reactions we have to it. The danger of identification is removed, but replaced by the danger not only of prejudice and power imbalance, but of an accumulation of so many unsaid and maybe unthought communications that the relationship is weighed down, and may move less creatively and freshly.

When the counsellor belongs to the 'native' culture, and is speaking his/her own language and the client is not, s/he is in a privileged position over the client, in a sense, however proficient the client may be in their second language. The therapist can sit back in a position of comfort familiar to native English-speakers. Able to take their own linguistic store for granted, they run the risk of operating from a 'neutral' position, concentrating on the difference of the other while leaving their own linguistic process unexamined.

One might say that the challenge of putting experience into words is always a matter of translation, particularly where feelings are concerned, that translating a feeling into words is to change into the thought-register, and almost inevitably to simplify and maybe drain the feeling of its lifeblood.

The experience of focusing shows us that this is not always the case, that when we are in touch with the felt sense, which is neither thought nor feeling but experience at, maybe, its most elusive and yet concrete, words can arise straight from experience, and be undeniably, absolutely right. The *words* are instrumental in producing the felt shift, the experience of 'rightness' that occurs when they fit. The facilitator cannot experience the true quality of the 'handle' word, the word that 'comes', by itself, when we direct our attention to the felt sense. It remains private to the focuser. Hence at the level at which change occurs, shared meanings are not even possible. Yet the presence of the other, not their verbal understanding, is facilitative. I will return to this point later.

But, outside the special situation of focusing, we are constantly engaged in attempts to communicate our experience to others. Do we ever actually say what we experience? I find Gendlin's theory illuminating here. He takes on the argument that we can never capture experience in words without distorting it, and proposes that language is structured in exactly the same way as experiencing.

The experienced, linguistic and body situations are all forms in which an 'implicit intricacy' functions. This implicit intricacy consists of steps, each holding the next step inside itself, as hunger holds the image of food, makes no sense without it, and leads to the action of getting the food. This intricacy is the movement in the forms of thought, language and physical feelings, which gives meaning in its very moving forward into the next situation. The intricacy prevents language from being experienced purely as a form imposed from the outside. The trust that this moving forward is always in some sense constructive is shared with Rogers, who expressed it firstly in his concept of the actualizing tendency (Rogers, 1951), and later in that of the formative tendency working in the whole universe towards growth (Rogers, 1980).

In the case of language the 'form' consists of a number of different 'thought ways' which are all implied by each word simultaneously. When different thought ways cross, and when the language situation crosses with our body situation and our whole living, communicative situation, there is a space that asks to be filled. Notice the activity here, the space is not passive material waiting for a form to come and explain it, or make it into a communicable shape, the space itself can and does ask for the next step. The intricacy has been touched. It could even be defined as that in us which answers back.

This theory of language is crucially different from the notion of there being a single or dominant truth held in one place and then 'expressed', brought out of the self and into the world. The world and the self in this model are aspects of the same process, inextricable, moving in the same way, interrelating.

Bringing this into a personal context I have found in my work in a foreign language that my use of language functions as a kind of barometer of my own state. A noticeable difficulty in accessing my technical linguistic abilities is often the first sign that I am giving too much space to my own 'external examiner', or inner critic, judging myself or panicking about some perceived inadequacy. Language difficulties are thus a sign of being outward or ego-orientated. However it is not as simple as being unable to express something I know I want to say, it rather becomes difficult to think at all, firstly because of too much attention being channelled outwards, and secondly due to attention being concentrated on the language itself, the form. The interrelations in the systems of thoughts, emotions, language, body, etc. are such that there must be a balance of the attention flowing in each for me to function well.

The same effect occurs in the reverse situation—when I feel strong intimacy I find myself once more linguistically handicapped. This can happen even in my native language: I can become almost pre-verbal in the presence of people with whom I share a deep understanding. My contact with what is more than the forms, the creative place from which the next steps come, is so intense that I can lose contact with the forms themselves. I wonder if this holds the key to my constant wanderings away from my native linguistic environment. By doing this, I fulfil a need for intensity and escape from 'the imposed order' in the form of my own culture and language. It is also, however, an uncomfortable situation in which I have no access to at least half of my resources and am placed, whether I like it or not, in 'child' position.

This special, not to mention stressful, act of speaking in another language, not as social currency but in a therapeutic relationship, as client or counsellor, also offers a unique opportunity. As the words come, from a known place inside, they gather meanings that I cannot entirely know or control. I cannot identify with them in the same way. And when I do not identify-with, change can occur, as when the self-concept is not clung to, the actualizing tendency can break through, or, in later Rogers, with his concept of the fully functioning person, the structure of a person breaks up into an experiencing process, a flow.

It is as if the idea of having an essential, true, in this case English-speaking self becomes an element in my self-concept, another partial interpretation of reality that must be maintained. I have to get past the painful feeling of 'that's not what I meant!' and accept that perhaps I am never going to say exactly what I 'meant', I am going to say something else, from that place, which will lead on somewhere unknown.

Getting past that feeling may be extraordinarily difficult for clients with fragile processes, who need the experience of getting to exactly what they mean, rather than the explanation of what they mean, first. Margaret Warner describes how such clients have an inability to hold, or to name certain experiences, and how, during therapy, they may feel that misunderstandings of what they say threaten their very existence (Warner, 2000: 144–71).

In my experience as a creative writing facilitator, I see that attempts at accurate 'self-expression' have cathartic value for the writer, but do not tend to open out for others, and create new meanings. This on the surface contradicts Rogers' contention that what is most personal is most universal. The kind of poetry I refer to, however, relies on the assumption of a fixed, authentic self with feelings which are similarly authentic and, at the moment of writing, fixed. The range of possible reactions to such work is also limited. I would argue that there is further to dig into 'the personal' before we reach that which everyone can recognize.

The writer of poems that are aimed at expression of 'my real', fixed self is in the same situation as the client who remains stuck, for example, in one emotion—who expresses it repeatedly but does not move on. This is a situation as worthy of respect and acceptance as any other, and may be an essential part of a long process, but this is not the place where change occurs. The kind of poem that is truly personal and universal is one that moves both writer and reader on into unexplored territory.

When I first entered counselling, as a client, I saw a therapist who used English as a second language. His making new of my every word was invigorating, as was the feeling that I was creating, rather than explaining, my world with him. This did not preclude moments of 'that's not what I meant!' although that inner cry often had more to do with my inability to contact my felt sense, to have a starting point from which to speak, than his perceived misunderstanding of me. These 'that's not what I meant!' moments often led to creative discomfort:

> We defend what we said by claiming that we 'really' meant those clear categories. If we cannot say we meant *them*, if they don't *cover* what we said, then we are *uncovered-naked* in what we said. (Gendlin, 1991; original emphasis)

Fragility of process (Warner 1991) may be this—a clinging to what we meant to avoid the discomfort, embarrassment or pain of being uncovered-naked in what we say. 'Maybe I meant something I don't even understand! In that case I can't exist as the person I think I am!' It may also be the intense need to say it nakedly and to have it received exactly—even if not understood—received, and not necessarily through linguistic understanding. 'This is how I am now—but if no-one can hear it, if they think I'm something else, something simpler, then I don't really exist in the world.'

When something that has been nakedly said is taken by another and packaged into a certain form of logic, thought or language, it hurts the body. The body knows the words that fit and those which don't. It knows the difference between that rush of hot shakiness and 'anger', that sudden wave of sweet sadness and 'regret', even if anger and regret fit the story perfectly.

At the point of naked saying there is maximum potential for two people in any kind of relationship, therapeutic or otherwise, to connect, or for the one who has dared to speak nakedly to feel irretrievably isolated and shut down. The counsellor must be sensitive to hearing something that is not covered by previously used categories, and careful not to translate the client's words into more 'understandable' terms.

The accurate understanding I required was usually conveyed either non-verbally or through idiosyncratic empathic responses. Even when my counsellor used words, it was not the words themselves that conveyed understanding. Hence the 'something', which seemed to escape linguistic forms, or an order imposed from the outside—and when working in a foreign language, how we feel that imposition—was received by responses which also in some way escaped the order. Deconstructionists may call this 'something' an excess, a surplus, what is left when old and inadequate structures which cannot describe reality cross each other out. Gendlin points out that where deconstructionists claim subversion, they 'actually ... retain the traditional assumption that only an imposed order is possible', and promises, 'We will soon turn the tragic view over: What is more than forms is not tragic or ephemeral. It is not a fleeting moment between successive forms. If anything is ephemeral, it is the forms' (Gendlin, 1991).

'More than the forms' was what I needed to say, and also the receiving I needed to hear, and this saying and hearing worked in carrying forward my life situation. The secret to change lies in the fact that the implicit intricacy in the situation, language and body, always carries in it the next step, and can always talk back. It is always available, always trustworthy.

'If anything is ephemeral, it is the forms.' Yet the forms require attention, and effort to maintain, and they are needed in order for us to be able to think.

Sometimes maintaining the form of a foreign language is an effort that seems to get in the way of contact with the intricacy, with those points that change when you touch them. Or the form simply breaks down and it seems that communication cannot function. Sometimes, also, maintaining the form of the language crosses with maintaining the form of the different culture, which can produce a sense of either incongruence, or resistance.

However, in moments approaching mutuality with clients I have been able to accept the fact that I am making atrocious technical mistakes, while communicating the essential as well as I could in any language. When we are aware of being a part of the same experience, despite our mangled attempts to say it in words, there is a 'making strange' of the whole process of verbalization. We cannot take it for granted anymore. At the same time, it feels irrelevant.

In such moments it seems tempting but simplistic to claim that we are meeting on a universal human level 'beyond' language. The 'universal human nature of cross-understanding' (Gendlin, 1991) however, is not a state beyond language. It refers to the fact that the implicit intricacy of the world works the same way everywhere, is behind, within, working in all languages, bodies, situations and thoughts. It is the force that carries them forward.

And this Union is not like monism, is not like a big cosmic ONE where there is no more duality at all, no more difference at all, no more individual existence at all. It is just the realization that all individualities are interdependent, relative, empty of inherent existence (Shen Yeng, 1987).

Gendlin sees the implicit intricacy in body, language and situations as a self-organizing force, and emptiness as a construct produced by the imposition of patterns onto reality. If reality comes in the form of patterns, what is not the patterns must be nothing, according to conventional discourse. What is not the forms, however, can also be seen, in Buddhist terms, as emptiness. The individualities Shen Yeng speaks of here are patterns, forms, the imposed order, selves, languages and situations; they do not exist by themselves, they are not content, they are 'empty of inherent existence'. And this emptiness is not a lack, but the true nature of things, from which all forms and human possibilities emerge, and into which they all recede.

Paradoxically, when I do *not* know what I mean (e.g. when engaging with a felt sense, or when trying to grasp something that escapes the form of thought or the language I am using) I may say something that corresponds exactly to my experience. This reminds me of the client quoted by Judy Moore (2003) as saying, 'I only trust you when I don't know who you are'. Letting go of the illusion of knowing—a truth to be expressed, self, or another—puts us in a place in which suddenly our words show us that we do know, we can trust.

REFERENCES

Gendlin, E (1981) *Focusing*. New York: Bantam Books.

Gendlin, E (1991) Thinking beyond patterns: Body, language, and situations. In B den Ouden & M Moen (eds) *The Presence of Feeling in Thought* (pp. 25–51). New York: Peter Lang. Also available at <www.focusing.org>.

Gendlin, E (1995) Crossing and dipping: Some terms for approaching the interface between natural understanding and logical formulation. *Mind and Machines 5*, 547–60. Chicago: University of Chicago Press. Also available at <www.focusing.org>.

Moore, J (2003) Letting go of who I think I am: The importance of becoming nothing? Paper given at 6th World Conference for Person-Centered and Experiential Psychotherapy and Counseling, The Netherlands.

Moore, J (2004) Letting go of who I think I am: Listening to the unconditioned self. *Journal of the World Association for Person-Centred and Experiential Therapies 3* (2), 117–28.

Rogers, C (1951) *Client-Centered Therapy*. London: Constable.

Rogers, C (1980) *A Way of Being*. Boston, MA: Houghton Mifflin.

Shen Yeng (1987) *Faith in Mind: A guide to Ch'an practice*. Elmhurst, New York: Dharma Drum Publications, also available at <www.dharmanet>.

Warner, M (1991) Fragile process. In Lois Fusek (ed) *New Directions in Client-Centered Therapy: Practice with difficult client populations, Monograph Series 1*, Chicago Counseling and Psychotherapy Center, also available at <www.focusingresources.com>.

Warner, M (2000). Person-centred therapy at the difficult edge: A developmentally based model of fragile and dissociated process. In D Mearns and B Thorne (eds) *Person-Centred Therapy Today: New frontiers in theory and practice* (pp. 144–71). London: Sage.

CHAPTER 11

THE FABRIC OF ACCEPTANCE

MATIS NIMETZ

INTRODUCTION

Acceptance: a word used again and again, but yet how can I simply name what it is, how can I simply state its essence? What is it made of? What is its very fabric?

If, professionally, my therapeutic work rests on the offering of acceptance, personally I also have come to recognize that it is the quality of my relating with others that nourishes me. Without this quality of relating, I have come to know that a part of myself dies and that this quality of relating is dependant on acceptance. Carl Rogers uses alternatively terms such as 'acceptance', 'caring' and 'prizing' to describe what he also calls 'unconditional positive regard' (Rogers, 1961: 283, 1980: 116). Since then, many authors have looked at and reflected upon all the meanings which could be contained within those words, and have at times differentiated them. But acceptance has always been a recurring and important theme in relation to the change its offering can bring both within and from the therapeutic endeavour (e.g. Lietaer, 1984: 42–5; Bozarth, 1998: 47, 84; Purton, 1998: 23–36).

Acceptance has been named as the cornerstone of personal and spiritual development (e.g. Freke & Gandy, 1998), as the cornerstone for therapeutic change (e.g. Bozarth & Wilkins, 2001). But yet, through all the discourses I have read, my questions remained unanswered. I needed to know, in some more pragmatic way, I needed to touch the reality of acceptance, as a way to access it and, maybe, to try to become it. In order to explore such a vast subject, but yet to contain it, I decided to gather material from others' experiences and perspectives to try to represent acceptance within both the therapeutic context and the human experience at large. This meant interviewing people who were counsellors, but who had also been or were clients, and who were of different culture, race, nationality, gender and age.

This writing presents, for reasons of space, only a portion of the final research. It is *not* a discourse, but a testimony of people's experiences which took me and can perhaps take the reader deeper into acceptance, touching back and forth the many strands that form the weft and the warp of its fabric, its existence.

Their words are given below in inverted commas and no individual speaker is identified. The main strands to emerge are presented in italics (e.g. 'both counsellors and clients talk about *a space*'). As a last point, I have chosen to represent both genders as s/he and his/her or her/him in the text.

THE UNDULATING FABRIC: SPACE AND MOVEMENT

Reading all the themes that belonged to experiences of acceptance and non-acceptance, I started to feel as if I were on a vast cloth that was undulating in an ample and relentless movement, back and forth, while at the same time weaving a multitude of other movements that were like rising and falling tides that echoed from one another, singular facets but yet part of each other and part of the whole.

In their interviews, both counsellors and clients talk about *a space*. The counsellor is *making a space* for the other, but also in order to offer it, is making a space within him/herself: 'The more space I can clear within myself, which feels then the more space I can be with the client.' It is a space that is based on self-awareness, and is also the consequence of it.

It is very tangible for the client, who can then start to inhabit it, dwell within it: 'I very much felt that space just for me'; 'I feel safe when I feel accepted and it gives me courage to go deeper in myself.'

It is a space where also 'there seems to be *a fundamental truth*' while at the same time 'the feeling of total acceptance *doesn't really have a centre*'. This sense of acceptance as being everywhere calls upon a recurring theme of *wholeness.* The counsellor sees acceptance as 'a holistic thing that comes from the whole of the person', something 'complete in itself and complete from within'. As one interviewee sees it, to be accepted 'is the experience of knowing something fundamental that is the totality of one's own being'. The counsellor receives the wholeness of the other as well as being with her/his whole self: 'For me acceptance is about really welcoming the whole of the person and that might be the bits I have difficulties with.' This resonates with a client's experience: 'I am totally whole, to be whatever, whoever I am.' It is interesting to note that in the literature, the word 'wholeness' has been used interchangeably with 'congruence' (Bozarth, 1998: 71). This is not surprising if we consider that one's own truth comes from within and is in itself complete.

This experience of wholeness contains the lived experience of *freedom*: 'It feels that now I have the opportunity to be free. And whatever that might be, I have the freedom to be. And that, it seems to me, is truly acceptance.' This becomes expansive as in: 'To be totally accepted would be that kind of freedom, just to give everything ... just to throw myself.'

And when the sense of freedom from the counsellor is missing, the freedom is missing for the client: 'There wasn't a sense I could really say what I wanted to say.' It is lived as a freeing process where the sense of *letting be and being let* reinstates a movement, a flow: 'To feel accepted ... to let things move again.' The client is 'being let' to lead, let to choose her/his own way. The counsellor follows, lets go of control and of wanting to control; s/he lets go of his/her own thoughts, reactions and judgements. It is also an inner freeing process of letting a life within be: 'But it is like ... to let it have its own way, to let it live, to let it be, not to block.'

Acceptance is a *living energy*, and again words such as 'stream', 'flow', 'flowing' describe movements that are going through both counsellor and client: 'It does feel very much like a stream running through me.' 'It is an ongoing thing, energizing because of that process of in and out, in and out, not stopping.' As I see it, there is a larger continuous movement that goes forward and within it, two opposite movements of in and out taking place. The whole of those movements are described as *a growing process* as well as being experienced as a process of growth: 'It grows within the process of the relationship.' It takes time and is found to be 'a growth for both', dependant on the sense of trust between the persons. It is the 'trust I will not get hurt', the trust in 'the growing acceptance of myself' as well as the trust in the process. Acceptance as the free movement of self-awareness is and creates a space, is and creates energy, a free movement that is complete in itself.

It gets manifested through a way of being which also contains movement, an act of *doing but without doing*. The act is in the *intention*, in the process of *(self)-awareness*, in the *engagement* of the self with the self and with the other. It is in the *reflecting*: 'Well, what do I make of these feelings of mine that I don't act on them, as it were, but that I try to process them?' It is in the *waiting*, as in waiting for the client, to see what emerges and 'not wanting an answer'. It is in the *observing*: 'And if I allow myself to just ... observe, then I really learn what acceptance is all about.' It is in the *listening* which contains a focused attention, a witnessing, a conveying, a staying. It is being in the moment, with 'a presence in the fullness of each moment' (Freke & Gandy, 1998: 59).

> It is as though he listened
> and such listening as his enfolds us in a silence
> in which at last we begin to hear
> what we are meant to be.
> Lao Tsu (in Rogers, 1980: 40)

THAT WHICH IS THE SUM OF ME

Although the experience of acceptance is offered as one of wholeness, some of the language used to describe it invites the idea of separation. The experience has been described in terms of 'levels'. There will be 'a new level of relating and communicating', which can also 'be sensed without any words at all', as it is sensed as just 'the way one is'. Levels might take the form of a differentiation between 'all that lives in the person that is different from what the person does'. It would be of some interest to explore the use of language further as it can be noted that separation and differentiation bring with them fragmentation, division, withdrawal from the self and from others (Krishnamurti, 1972; Griffiths, 1989). Acceptance is experienced partly at a mental level, concerning cognition, thinking and rationality: 'That is the intellectual exercise then maybe— to understand how I look at somebody else's world.' It is understanding that *this is how it is*, putting *no doubt* on the experiencing, on the presented reality: 'You become very acceptant because you understand that's how it is'; 'there is no question that it is there ... it is real, it is your reality'.

The cognition is without any judgement, imposition, disapproval or criticism: 'If there was the sense of judgement, or even interruption in a sense, in the counsellor trying to impose extraneous thinking, I might back off and close down.' Judgement brings its own personal conflict energy: 'When I am judging, it feels like a battle inside me.' It is also interesting to note that the presence of acceptance within one enables the person to see themselves as their own judge: 'To me that was indeed true acceptance, beyond the skin, regardless of the colour, without judgement. It even removed from myself my own judgement of inferiority upon me, so I am also good.' 'So yes, it lessens the strength of the internal critic that is giving me a hard time.' Making no judgements leaves the space for the client to sense when the counsellor really wants to understand what s/he is saying, what his/her experience is, and this seems inseparable from the counsellor communicating, acknowledging and conveying that understanding. As a client: 'To have someone along who talks in there with me, who doesn't have any doubt about what I feel, that is when I feel accepted as I am.' As a counsellor: 'For me acceptance is conveying ... a recognition, an understanding.' It is the *empathy* that is part of acceptance (Bozarth, 1998: 58). It translates in (or through) a communication that is received as an acknowledgement, fostering self-acknowledgement, self-acceptance and self-esteem (Schmid, 2001: 51). The *offering* cannot be separated from the *receiving* (for both the self and the other) in the way that they will both determine each other as they are determined by a degree of self-awareness.

The cognition addresses a decision, the decision to be acceptant. It involves, in the words of interviewees, 'a preparedness to be acceptant, a readiness to actually do it'. From there comes the decision to clear a space and, for example, to meditate: 'That is the conscious decision.' Again the decision is based on the awareness that acceptance involves both an attention to one's inner life as well as to the client's.

Together with the intention comes *the will.* The counsellor recognizes his/her will to be and stay with the client, her/his will of *wanting* to let go of control. The client wants them to follow her/his lead. With the will comes *a willingness*. This can translate for the counsellor as the determination to follow the client, to seek to understand and follow the client, and to recognize that it is as it is at the moment. It is a determination that can be much challenged by the person's inner world: 'Sometimes it is nice ... to be alone.' There has to be a willingness to recognize one's own feelings such as, for example, recognizing one's own non-acceptance: 'I was trying to find why I was finding it hard to accept. You could say that my acceptance was my willingness to do that, to acknowledge that I have a difficulty with this client.'

There is too the willingness to be oneself, to be true to oneself, that involves also the willingness of *wanting to stay with one's own physical sensations*: 'Like willing to stay with that [underneath] ... to stay with the sheer physical sensations ... which was really helpful.' What is interesting again, is that this theme of willingness is also part of the client's experience in his/her ability to feel accepted: 'I am more willing to be acceptant [as a client].'

In fact counsellor and client's willingness seem to feed each other. As a client: 'It is almost as if I am asking for the acceptance in order to further explore and be further accepted.' As a counsellor: 'With others [clients] there is clearly a willingness on their part to be giving you [the counsellor], part of themselves that you then can accept.'

Allowing manifests the will and willingness, the choice, the decision. Like those elements, it appears to take place towards oneself and towards the other. Again, an in and out movement is happening for each person but also between them. As a counsellor: 'The more I can allow myself and sit back ... then I start to understand.' As a client: 'I have allowed myself to be myself.' 'It [acknowledgement] allows me to go on opening up.'

The *intention,* such as 'the action of straining and directing the mind or attention to something' (Onions, 1973: 2550), is a theme that seems to underlie all the above-mentioned mental processes. There is intention on the part of the counsellor 'to be present and open and accepting', and the intention of 'putting my body in a state of readiness and openness'. There is the intention to show the client that they are welcome. There is 'the active intention to put aside my own state of reference and to dwell with that client in what is there'. There is the intention 'to be present and open and accepting', 'the intention to empty myself of thoughts, worries, preconceptions, pre-judgements', and 'to let go of my feelings [as the listener]'.

On her/his side the client becomes aware of and receives the intention of the counsellor: 'There is the sense that the other person really wants to understand what I am saying.'

Because the intention of the counsellor is an element which conditions one's ability to offer acceptance (Lietaer, 2001: 88) and which can shift the process of therapy (Bozarth, 1998: 85), it seems important for me to look at *what drives an intention.* Within the interviews, the intention has been seen as coming from 'a humanitarian love for other human beings', or as a curiosity: 'There is a world over there with the person I need to come to know.' Or as being rooted in beliefs such as: 'I am pretty certain I have an absolutely deeply ingrained belief that people's worlds are as they think they are.' 'If I actually believe as I do, that a human being, by virtue of being a human being, is of infinite value, in a way I have no choice but to accept them.'

Intention has also been seen as coming from a principle, a desire, *an ideal.* And as such seen as keeping the person away from any awareness and any active part s/he would have in offering, or not offering, acceptance: 'I think it is better when the ... high ideal is not too strong, because then there is a danger that you will not fully own that acceptance.' Acceptance has to be alive in order to exist. Solely as a mental exercise, ideals would expose a delusion; they would keep the person in a state of unreality where acceptance is missing its own presence and the person is not with his/her own truth at that moment. Acceptance in order to manifest needs something else: 'Gradually it comes from the inside, it becomes a real thing, not just a mental thing.'

The *emotional dimension* has been recognized as influencing one's ability to accept: 'When I am unable to be acceptant, then it is likely that I shall feel the discordance not only in my mind, but in my feelings.' A state of acceptance gives a sense of *ease and harmony* with the emotions: 'When I am fully accepting of the other, there is a great sense of calm, of attunement, of ease with myself.' There can be disharmony due to anxiety and fears. There is the fear of getting hurt: 'I think that behind a great deal of anxiety and terror of one sort or another is actually a sense of being wounded or damaged.' I would say here that awareness is the light that helps the wounded to move into a state of acceptance. Acceptance is self-healing.

There are *fears* that extend themselves into *beliefs*: 'At some level I fear that the other will actually do me harm and the extension of that is that in the last analysis, they could annihilate me. Then I lose any capacity to regard them as a person of infinite value.' 'If I am frightened that the other person is going to annihilate me, I am frightened of dying.' This fear of death is understood in the Buddhist tradition as a desire to postpone the inevitable, to avoid facing it and suffering the constant anguish of our mortality. But maybe, most of all, the fear of death ultimately is there because we do not know who we are (Sogyal Rinpoche, 1992: 16). There are fears that come as a consequence of being separated from the self (Nimetz, 2003), and as one interviewee takes it further, a separation from the divine: 'I no longer experience within myself my own acceptability, my own sense of infinite value. I am no longer in relationship with God, with the source of all infinite value. I am not in contact with the source of my own being.' There are fears that are as a result of one's own judgements: 'That fear in front of something bad, when the counsellor doesn't recoil from it, I can feel less anxious about it. That part of me is acceptable.' Stretching this, I could say that one's sense of acceptability, sense of valuing, is in the ability to stay with oneself. 'When there is freedom from fears and wounds, there is freedom from the past at that moment. There is a break from old patterns and that in itself gives access to an immense energy' (Krishnamurti, 1970: 21).

For many interviewees, acceptance manifests itself not only cognitively and emotionally, but also within their *physical* realm: 'It is a bodily feeling of being accepted in my being.'

The emotional expansiveness is felt as a *physical kind of expansion:* 'I have to use words like melting, like my body kind of ... melts. It is like I don't have any bones, it all becomes soft, I feel very warm. I can feel my face soften ... it is like the feelings are diffused throughout the whole body.' Or: 'It is almost like having a solid pillar inside. Yes, I feel it physically, physically solid and I can feel it to the tips of my shoulders, of my fingers. It is a sense of filling every cell of what I am.' Or: 'The feeling can express itself as tearfulness. It may feel like hot flushes in the chest or across the shoulders, or top of my arms.'

Non-acceptance also manifests physically: 'The feeling of non-acceptance is very much in the head, it is very focused.' And it is within that physical frame that a specific place is experienced as the place where acceptance springs from, 'a *holding* within me, which was underneath'. Many traditions and teachings, in and out of the therapeutic arena, have talked about the physical dimension of being and how through listening to our body, we can encounter who and what we are (Moore, 2001: 204–9). Within my body I will meet in PRH terminology[1] 'the pivotal centres of my person' (Moore 2001:

1. PRH stands for Personnalité et Relations Humaines (Personality and Human Relationships), an education program developed by André Rochais (1921–1990), to deepen the understanding of human growth. See also Chapter 16, this volume, pp. 196–200.

204–6), or in eastern terminology 'the Hara' and the 'Chakras' (Kapleau, 1980: 14) or again in Focusing terms 'the Felt Sense' (Gendlin, [1978] revised 1981: 32). There is a recognition that our body, with its endless and changing layers of reactions, emotions, thoughts, sensations as experienced in meditation practices such as the practice of Mindfulness (Thich Nhat Hanh, 1988), of Vipassana (Fleishman, 1991: 6, 7), of Sōtō Zen (Moore, 2001: 205) and others, our body can give us insight into the nature of our reality (Sogyal Rinpoche, 1992: 57). The fact that it is through the body that one understands the other has also been discussed in more recent Western philosophy (Merleau Ponty, 1962: 186). It is by 'contemplating and following fully those sensations etc. … that their energy becomes available to us, enlarging our sense of what life is about' (Welwood, 1983: 89). As well as talking about acceptance as the first law of the physical body, Roger (1997: 11) is also defining acceptance as the first law of the spirit. This also appears through quantum physics terminology, as spirit is defined as matter and energy or again as the lightest form of matter (Northup, 1999: 25). Acceptance *is* and *is of* body and spirit.

BECOMES MORE THAN ME

This sense of spirit is experienced by the participants through a sense of *depth*, 'accepting at a deeper level', and being able 'to say somehow what is deepest in me'. Together with the awareness and exploration of that 'inner world which I perceive as a vast dimension', an expansiveness is experienced as in 'one can feel bigger and fuller', impacting on one's social behaviour: 'I saw myself as more important and it helped me to fit in society well.' As the person inhabits her/himself and becomes more open to him/herself and to others (Kirschenbaum & Henderson, 1990: 27), s/he can 'move towards really social goals' (ibid.: 27, 68).

This two-way movement has been experienced as 'actually more than me' because 'it enables me to be more than I can be'. It is also experienced as enabling access to a transcendent reality that is seen as existing both within and without, as: 'That which is more than me … the eternal, the unborn, the divine … is within, in me.' Through the experience of depth as inner and outer, participants brought with them a sense of a spiritual reality that has also been experienced as a state of grace. In the words of one interviewee, not only does acceptance give access to a spiritual dimension, but it is what constitutes the very relationship with the spiritual dimension: 'When I cannot accept the other, I am not properly in relationship with God.' I will leave this point without comment at the moment, as the analysis, through bringing out more aspects of acceptance, goes back, as in a loop, to the spiritual dimension of acceptance. At present I will just say that the experience of acceptance manifests itself through different expressions, forms, that have been called levels (mental, emotional, physical and spiritual), but which could be called 'dimensions' to reflect in a more encompassing way the different aspects of experiencing that are the oneness of one's being.

Acceptance is the lived principle that *unifies* all dimensions so I am living at one with myself and with the other. Acceptance is also found to be addressing all that we are and more.

In the words of the interviewees, it is being very *close to the other* person, being at one with the other and the self: 'I think there are some signals of unacceptance ... during the session I am not so close.' 'You feel you are at one with that person ... that closeness ...'

It is being in touch with the other, feeling *a connection,* '[When I] accept somebody, it's like being able to openly connect and ... be in touch with as another human being.' This sense of connectedness is experienced as being personally in total harmony, as well as *experiencing something larger than the person,* a connection with humanity, 'a sense of in touchness with the source of creative energy', as well as 'being in contact with the source of one's own being'. In the words of Krishnamurti it is 'this light in one's self' (1999), and it is being at one with and living from one's own true centre, living with the truth of one's own being, expressing one's own truth, being integrated, which is also to rest in God (Thorne, 1998: 25–6). This resonates with the words of the Indian mystic Meher Baba: 'To come to one's own self, is to find God' (1995: 127).

Considering the interviewees' comments, I could also say that the source of creative energy is acceptance itself, because its own movement *is* and *creates* energy. In other words one is one's own source of creative energy as one is in contact with the other in acceptance, and also that creative energy exists in the transcendence of the pre-existing duality that can be posed by the presence of another (Schmid, 2001: 59). 'I am because you are. We are because I am' (Thorne 1991: 186) becomes a synergy that takes the 'I' into a dimension where the notion of the 'I' melts with the other, with the communal, into what seems to be beyond human words and rationality. One of the interviewees did experience that dimension in such words: 'We seem to come to that space ... and then we both become completely inarticulate.'

It is there that I see the meeting point of the East and the West. Through the Buddhist teachings, the concept of the dissolution of the 'I' (Ricard & Xuan Thuan, 2000) comes alive and it is through the encounter of the other—and therefore of the self—lived in acceptance, that the same dimension can be reached. The 'I' transforms itself into something beyond itself which is its non-existence as I know it when I live within duality/separation. It is in the beyond that we touch into a spiritual space that many traditions have tried to define and access through different terminologies and forms (Freke & Gandy, 1998). It is interesting to note that the language used by some interviewees does reflect some of those traditions and beliefs, but in the end, comes to the same place of recognition through a deep self-awareness.

That sense of connectedness carries with it the experience of being *reached and impacted*: 'It is easy to say "I accept what you say" without it touching you. But if it is going to be felt, you have to let it impact on you.' The impact resonates with both persons, as the acceptance of being reached brings in the other the experience of: 'Really being in touch with myself', of feeling it physically. This brings me to ask a question which I see as being at the core of the encounter with another, and I would say with the self: 'How am I with touching or being touched, physically and/or metaphorically?' It is a very tender area, as tender as the wound or the joy it might awaken.

The connectedness implies for interviewees a process of *openness.* It is opening oneself through a process of self-awareness, observing: 'Being aware of what the reaction is', 'accepting one's own limitations', being congruent and transparent: 'The more I am congruent in myself, the more I am able to be open to client's experience.' This congruence and clarity from the counsellor brings in the client a parallel movement of clarity, exploration of one's own reality and truth: 'Yes, that he could help me begin to make sense of things.' As with empathy, congruence is said to be part of acceptance. Bozarth develops that theme further in saying that 'the three conditions are really, ultimately and functionally one condition' (1998: 80). As one is in touch with the self through congruence, acceptance will also mean being reunified with one's own self, which in Bozarth's terms means being reunified with one's 'actualizing tendency' (Bozarth, 1998: 4), with one's movement and potential.

It is an openness to whatever is there, rather than what ought to be, and is felt as *a giving and a receiving for both persons.* As a counsellor: 'As the tangible result of my acceptance, it is important to show, to give something, to care'; 'the work is to surrender, to give myself'. As a client: 'And to be totally accepted would be ... just to give everything.' Carl Rogers emphasizes the fact that acceptance has to be experienced by the counsellor and received by the client (Bozarth, 1998: 76). But there seems to also be another dynamic where the counsellor's degree of openness: 'will depend in part on the openness of the other [the client] gradually showing themselves more to me'. Openness results from a two-way engagement with another as well as with the self. Opening is a movement that requires and furthers self-awareness and each person's level of self-awareness will influence and further self-acceptance and acceptance of the other. Welwood notes: 'Self-acceptance is the naked quality of my life, which contains openness and tenderness, which is healing and from which I can develop compassion for others' (Welwood, 1983: 83).

This *tenderness* (Thorne, 1985) experienced by participants is lived 'as a soft kind of quality'; a feeling of *irrelevance and humbleness* may be part of that experience of self-effacement mentioned by Lietaer (2001: 91). I like to understand this as a place where there isn't a shadow of the operation of the will, where there is no control, and according to Krishnamurti (1999: 55), a place where there is no conditioning and where time, as it is known within our human limits, comes to an end. This would pose the question: 'Can I function without time?' But also, in terms of acceptance, it seems to me that the irrelevance and humbleness are symptoms of the loss of the 'I' as it touches a dimension that is timeless.

There is a feeling of *love and compassion,* from the counsellor as well as from the client: 'If I am feeling accepting ... what I am likely to be feeling, is a kind of love; and similarly when I am being accepted.' 'It is a compassion ... but it goes much deeper than that ...'; '... that kind of love and compassion is actually more than me'. Love here is understood as *agape* and not as romantic and possessive love (Schmid, 2001: 59). Rogers made this very clear when he said: 'Love has here perhaps its deepest and most general meaning, that of being deeply understood and deeply accepted' (Rogers, 1951: 160).

Schmid notes that it is in the space and the openness of the relationship that the source of freedom resides (2001: 59). Acceptance is the openness, the space and the freedom that form the void within which the elements of love and compassion are felt and come alive. As we saw, it has been experienced as transcending the division(s) between selves and the divisions between self and the other. Sri Nisargatta, the Indian mystic, also proposes that acceptance is the element that unifies matter and spirit (Freke & Gandy, 1998: 139). It is also the bridge between matter and spirit. From that point of view, I see acceptance as the very tool that can enable me to step beyond my human limitations, as a gift, if I want it, to enlarge my being.

Having seen how much self-awareness is part of (self-) acceptance, it can be said that love and humility are rooted in self-awareness. One of the interviewees saw a danger in that movement to self-acceptance, as 'the person can get caught in self-inflation'. Dōgen[2] gives a clear direction in relation to that concern: 'When one studies oneself, one forgets oneself' (Moore, 2001: 208), therefore creating more space, openness and freedom not only for oneself, but for others. Here the term 'study' means being attentive to the *whole* of the individual in her/his physical, emotional, cognitive and spiritual existence. Only this process brings true humility.

From that place of self-acceptance, love and humility becomes endless (Freke & Gandy, 1998: 91). Acceptance links the secular and the spiritual dimensions within which we exist. In my and others' experiences, it is that which takes me in the flesh of my humanity as well as to the edge of my awareness, to the limits of my humanness and beyond. Carl Rogers recognized that our experiences involved the spiritual dimension and that he has underestimated its importance (Rogers, 1980: 130). '[P]erhaps we are touching the cutting edge of our ability to transcend ourselves to create new and more spiritual directions in human evolution' (Rogers, 1980: 134). I would say that acceptance is the cutting edge that allows us to transcend ourselves and to evolve on a path that is one of reunification with our own nature and beyond. At the same time it is also that connection, engagement and relationship in and with the presence of the other and in and with the presence of the beyond, a beyond that is also held within … in whatever words one finds himself/herself reflected.

CONCLUSION

Many threads are constantly weaving the fabric and texture of acceptance, many shades and meanings which this enquiry has made more accessible, highlighting a process that is both personal and in relation to others.

Through the research, acceptance has been found as being movements, processes that happen within time and space as that space is created within in order to be offered

2. Great Master Dōgen (1200–1253) was the founder of Sōtō Zen Buddhism.

without. In that space which has no centre, there is a continuous two-fold movement that is and gives energy, a flow and a growth of each person and between them. There is an inner movement that depends on and is the expansion of the awareness and acceptance of self, intertwined with an outward movement that takes me beyond the self and the other.

In the words of Griffiths it is like 'a symphony in which all the notes are heard in a single perfect harmony, but in which each retains its own distinctive character, has its own particular time and place' (1976: 38). All through the analysis we've heard the different notes, and my question here is about what will start the symphony. Is there anything to be addressed before I can take the path of acceptance? My answer is yes, because without a certain consciousness, I might be deluding myself. There will be questions about my understanding and willingness to embrace acceptance. Do I really know what self-awareness involves, where it is going to take me? What about freedom? Do I know what it means to put myself aside but yet to be fully present? Can I hold the difference while holding the togetherness? Am I willing to touch upon a world I can only apprehend in spiritual terms? How do I understand spiritual? Can I be in this world and yet not of this world at the same time? Can I remain both in my humanness and be beyond it? Because it seems to me that this is what the development of a state of acceptance demands: to be with paradoxes and to live them. It demands that I develop a consciousness at a cognitive, emotional, physical and spiritual level that just gives way to a dimension where that consciousness loses the very words by which it defined itself and grew. And in that dimension for which it is difficult to find the words, change and healing can take place.

But is it a necessity to reach that space in order for healing, change, to happen? If acceptance can be seen as the white light of the sun in which all the colours of the rainbow are present (Griffiths, 1976: 38), like the white light of the sun, it is not always *fully* present, but present enough for movements to take place. Acceptance can never be perfect because of the conditionalities contained within us. But yet, just as pale sun rays give daylight, Rogers recognizes that 'even imperfect attempts to create a climate of acceptance ... seems to liberate the person' (Kirschenbaum & Henderson, 1990: 68).

I realize through the research, that in acceptance I see myself, in acceptance I see the other, I heal myself and others can be healed; in acceptance I am with my own mirror as well as in the texture of that mirror. Acceptance takes me beyond the mirror to apprehend another reality that is at the same time always part of me. Coming to the end of the research, I have also gained an understanding of the meeting point and of the commonalities between Eastern/Western spiritual paths and therapies which are based on the offering of acceptance. In this I have found a long awaited freedom that would enable me to develop and be myself spiritually, without the structures of different religions that have created and do create separations and conflicts. For me, this freedom will only be lived through the embodying of acceptance, of everything it contains.

I would like to finish this research on acceptance with an image that encapsulates my learning. It is the image of a tree, the tree that is poised on the earth at a balancing point. In opposite and complementary movements, it develops its roots deeper and deeper, reaching and feeding from matter, anchoring and asserting its own nature of tree, while at the same time reaching outwards, feeding from and reaching for the light, towards the infinite. Developing its own potential of tree also includes participating in its surroundings, such as for example, offering shade, fruits, etc. Acceptance appears to be that process in itself as well as at the same time, creating that process, being the cause of it and being a consequence of it. It is the doing and the being. It is the balancing point. It is complete in itself.

REFERENCES

Bozarth, J (1998) *Person-Centred Therapy: A revolutionary paradigm.* Ross-on-Wye, UK: PCCS Books.

Bozarth, J & Wilkins, P (2001) (eds) *Rogers' Therapeutic Conditions: Evolution, theory and practice, Vol 3: Unconditional positive regard.* Ross-on-Wye, UK: PCCS Books.

Fleishman, P (1991) *Vipassana Meditation: Healing the healer; the experience of impermanence.* India: Vipassana Research Institute.

Freke, T & Gandy, P (1998) *The Complete Guide to World Mystics.* UK: Piatkus.

Gendlin, E (Revised ed 1981) *Focusing.* New York: Bantam Books.

Griffiths, B (1976) *Return to the Centre.* London: Collins.

Griffiths, B (1989) *A New Vision of Reality.* USA: Templegate.

Kapleau, R (1980) *The Three Pillars of Zen.* London: Anchor Books, Doubleday.

Kirschenbaum, H & Henderson, V (eds) (1990) *Carl Rogers Dialogues.* London: Constable.

Krishnamurti, J (1970) *Freedom from the Known.* France: Stock.

Krishnamurti, J (1972) *The Impossible Question.* London: Gollancz.

Krishnamurti, J (1999) *This Light in Oneself.* Boston: Shambala Press.

Lietaer, G (1984) Unconditional positive regard: A controversial basic attitude in client-centred therapy. In FR Levant & JM Shlien (eds) *Client-Centred Therapy and the Person-Centred Approach* (pp. 41–58). New York: Praeger.

Lietaer, G (2001) Unconditional acceptance and positive regard. In J Bozarth & P Wilkins (eds) *Rogers' Therapeutic Conditions: Evolution, theory and practice, Vol 3: Unconditional positive regard.* (pp. 88–108) Ross-on-Wye, UK: PCCS Books.

Meher Baba (1995) *Discourses.* USA: Sheriar Press.

Merleau Ponty, M (1962) *The Phenomenology of Perception.* London: Routledge & Kegan Paul.

Moore, J (2001) Acceptance as the truth of the present moment, as a trustworthy foundation for unconditional positive regard. In JD Bozarth & P Wilkins (eds) *Rogers' Therapeutic Conditions: Evolution, theory and practice, Vol 3: Unconditional positive regard.* (pp. 198–209). Ross-on-Wye UK: PCCS Book.

Nimetz, M (2003) The Fabric of Acceptance. MA in Counselling Research. Norwich: University of East Anglia.

Northup, C (1999) *Women's Bodies and Women's Wisdom: The complete guide to women's health and well-being.* London: Piatkus.

Onions C (ed) (1973) *The Shorter Oxford English Dictionary.* Oxford: Clarendon Press.

Purton, C (1998) Unconditional positive regard and its spiritual implications. In B Thorne & E Lambers (eds) *Person-Centred Therapy: A European perspective* (pp. 23–37). London: Sage.

Ricard, M & Xuan Thuan, T (2000) *L'Infini dans la Pomme de la Main*. Paris: Fayard.
Rinpoche, S(1992) *The Tibetan Book of Living and Dying*. London: Rider Publications.
Roger, J (1997) *Sex, Spirit and YOU*. New York: Baraka Press.
Rogers, CR (1951) *Client-Centred Therapy*. London: Constable.
Rogers, CR (1961) *On Becoming a Person: A therapist's view of psychotherapy*. London: Constable.
Rogers, CR (1980) *A Way of Being*. Boston: Houghton Mifflin.
Schmid, P (1998) Face to face : The art of encounter. In B Thorne & E Lambers (eds) *Person-Centred Therapy: A European perspective* (pp. 74–90). London: Sage.
Schmid, P (2001) Acknowledgement: The art of responding. Dialogical and ethical perspectives on the challenge of unconditional relationships in therapy and beyond. In J Bozarth & P Wilkins (eds) *Rogers' Therapeutic Conditions: Evolution, theory and practice, Vol 3: Unconditional positive regard.* (pp. 49–64). Ross-on-Wye, UK: PCCS Books.
Thich Nhat Hanh (1988) *The Sutra on the Full Awareness of Breathing*. Berkeley, CA: Parallax Press.
Thorne, B (1985) *The Quality of Tenderness*. Norwich, UK: Norwich Centre Publications.
Thorne, B (1991) *Person-Centred Counselling: Therapeutic and spiritual dimensions*. London: Whurr.
Thorne, B (1998) *Person-Centred Counselling and Christian Spirituality: The secular and the holy*. London: Whurr.
Welwood, J (1983) *Awakening the Heart: East/West approaches to psychotherapy and the healing relationship*. Boston: Shambala Press.

CHAPTER 12

PERSON-CENTRED PSYCHOTHERAPY AS A SPIRITUAL DISCIPLINE

MARTIN VAN KALMTHOUT

> I am too religious to be religious ... I have my own definition of spirituality. I would put it that the best of therapy sometimes leads to a dimension that is spiritual, rather than saying that the spiritual is having an impact on therapy. (Rogers, in Baldwin, 1987: 35)

INTRODUCTION

For most person-centred psychotherapists, person-centred therapy is a therapeutic method that has nothing to do with spirituality or religion. When the two are brought into connection with each other, as Brian Thorne has done (1991, 1992, 1998, 2002, 2003), this can give rise to very strong emotions—rejection, and even denunciation and banishment within the person-centred world. Personally, I have found the idea that person-centred psychotherapy can also be viewed as a spiritual discipline particularly fascinating. In keeping with this, I developed the idea that person-centred psychotherapy has the characteristics of a modern system of meaning rather than a psychotherapeutic technique (van Kalmthout, 2004). This is also in keeping with the opinion of Rogers, namely that person-centred psychotherapy is a practical philosophy of life rather than merely a psychotherapeutic method.

Nevertheless, the conceptualization of person-centred psychotherapy as a spiritual discipline goes one step further. Such a vision elicits not only enthusiasm in me, but also a number of questions. I have therefore never gone so far as Brian Thorne, even though I published an article some ten years ago titled 'The religious dimension of Rogers' work' (van Kalmthout, 1995). In the present chapter I would like to take the opportunity to critically examine the proposition that person-centred psychotherapy is primarily a spiritual discipline.

There are numerous ways to do so. One can summarize and weigh the pros and cons associated with such a position, for example. I have opted for a different approach, namely to simply pose the following question: Is it possible to point to something that can be considered religious or spiritual within the essence of the person-centred approach? Should this be the case, then we can speak together with the sociologist Luckmann (1967) of 'invisible religion' or the 'invisibly religious'. What Luckmann means by this is that the religious in the broadest sense of the word can be detected in many systems that are typically not considered religious in the organized sense of the word. Person-centered psychotherapy may be a clear example of this. Should we succeed in pointing out the implicitly religious or spiritual in person-centred psychotherapy, we will have more concrete arguments for the conceptualization of person-centred psychotherapy as indeed a spiritual discipline. Should we come to the conclusion that the religious or spiritual in person-centred psychotherapy is completely absent, we have little or no reason to conceptualize person-centred psychotherapy as a spiritual discipline. In the following, I will explore the religious and spiritual dimension of person-centred psychotherapy using a number of the fundamental concepts from the theory of Rogers, namely: the true self, unconditional positive regard, empathic understanding, authenticity, and the formative tendency.

THE TRUE SELF

In Rogers' theory regarding the origin of problems, the term 'incongruence' stands central. Rogers means by this concept that a dissociation or discrepancy has evolved between what the person feels and what the person says or does. When one honestly says what one feels, one runs—after all—the risk of things not turning out well, which usually means missing the appreciation of others or of forfeiting any relation whatsoever with others. Rogers speaks in this connection of the conditions of worth or prerequisites to be valued and—in contrast—the organismic valuing process or one's own inner appreciation of one's self. In the eyes of Rogers, all psychic problems have their origin in the aforementioned discrepancy between the organismic or true self and the conditioned self. And the aim of therapy is, of course, to do away with this discrepancy. This means that people must learn to take themselves seriously, value themselves, listen to themselves, and become autonomous as opposed to emotionally dependent on others.

Up until this point, very few people will see a reason to attribute a religious or spiritual quality to the concept of the true self. But this might well change when we ask ourselves about our identity or who we are at the very core. The true self points to an inner, unconditioned dimension of existence that stands in opposition to an outer, conditioned dimension that is sometimes referred to as the false self. When someone has contact with this inner dimension, he or she embodies a special quality that can be characterized as the unconditioned. This person or client has broken a conditioned pattern and entered into a deeper dimension. This dimension can also be referred to, following Tillich, as the lost dimension because many people have lost contact with it during the course of their lives, as perhaps has our society as a whole (Tillich, 1962). Another label could be the 'other', which means: that which is of a different nature than a conditioned pattern. The question, now, is whether a religious or spiritual quality can or should be attributed to this lost, other dimension. What is the real quality of this inner source of truth that we should be able to trust and look to for guidance? It can certainly be asserted that this source is different from the conditioned pattern that we automatically follow—and that we have largely lost contact with this inner source. But how can we describe this inner source in more positive terms? Many have attempted to find the right tone and the right language to do this, but the task has proved very difficult.

Rogers wrestled intensely with the question of what, exactly, the quality of this inner source of truth is and came up with a remarkable conclusion (van Belle, 1980). In earlier works, Rogers describes the self largely in terms of the self-concept: the image that people have of themselves. This image is often negative due to conditions of worth. And people must, according to Rogers, abandon this image to make contact with their own organismic valuing process. This was Rogers' first formulation of the inner source of truth, and we spoke above in this connection of the conditioned self in contrast to the organismic self. According to Rogers, the organismic self is a source of knowledge that is larger than the intellect, a form of knowledge that is more physical and experiential than intellectual knowledge, and thus knowledge that transcends the limitations of cognitive knowing. In this stage of Rogers' development, the role of the therapist was to help the client focus on this inner source. But the role of the therapist was not limited to a focus on emotion; the role of the therapist was also to help the client find the words for his or her feelings and thereby a new structure for experiences and thoughts to thus provide a new basis for action. In his later work, Rogers abandons this standpoint to pursue a much more ambitious goal which Van Belle formulates as follows:

> The end result of therapy is now no longer seen as congruency with experience. It is not the increased awareness of, or openness to experience. It does not mean the enlargement of the self so as to include all of one's experience. It is not a matter of basing your self-concept on experience. Nor is it a matter of owning that experience as yours. It does not even mean accepting that experience for what it is. Rather, the end result is that you become the experience that you are. ... This leads to the description of one final aspect of becoming a person which receives the predominant emphasis in Rogers' later publications. It is this, that as a result of therapy the client becomes a process. That is to say, according to Rogers' most mature formulation the experience of therapy does not involve a change from an old, inadequate personality structure, through a process of dis- and re-organization, to a new more adequate personality structure. Rather, it involves a change from fixity to changingness, from rigid structure to flow, from stasis to process, as the major characteristic of the client's existence. (Van Belle, 1980: 49–50)

While the self-concept was viewed by the earlier Rogers as a means for actualization of the self, the later Rogers increasingly viewed the self-concept as an obstacle. In the opinion of Rogers, the self-concept stems from the conditioned self and thus has the constraint of the rigid and fixed nature of the conditioned. The inner source, in contrast, is exclusively characterized by change and process and thus transcends the constrained.

And what holds for the intrapersonal also holds for the interpersonal. That is, the conditioned nature of interpersonal images can be transcended by the interpersonal process. Fixed images no longer determine interpersonal communication but, rather, the fluidity and changeability of the interpersonal contact. It is this type of contact that Rogers begins to refer to in his later work as presence or a contact in which the usual boundaries between two individuals blur.

For Van Belle and other students or followers of Rogers, all of this goes much too far. In a later publication, Van Belle (1990) writes that, by taking this course, Rogers ends up in the realm of mysticism and thereby returns to the fundamental beliefs of his parents. His position as champion of the individual is also—in the opinion of Van Belle—forfeited because of this. I do not share this conclusion at all.

Could it be possible that the 'religious' quality of Rogers' thinking became apparent at this point? The explicit development towards a self that is only characterized by change and fluidity indeed brings Rogers' conception of the self outside the psychological and into the religious and spiritual. The self-concept provides structure and a grip on things and is therefore referred to as 'self-structure' by Rogers. When we discard this self-structure, we indeed enter a deeper layer of experiencing where fixed images of ourselves, others and the world are abandoned in order to penetrate reality further. And this is characteristic of not so much the average psychotherapy but the spiritual quest, involving the abandonment of familiar structures to better experience reality as it is. The discarding of the self-structure is described in some religious or spiritual circles by 'the transcendence of the self' or 'the dissolution of the ego'. And such transcendence is typically considered a necessary component of the spiritual or religious path. Such transcendence does not imply a pleasant undertaking. In fact, the path of transcendence is often described as a lonely journey full of uncertainties, completely unpredictable, and as 'the dark night of the soul'. There is nothing to hold onto, and the journey can thus be brutal. One can rather speak of an 'empty self'—as the Buddhists have called it—than a clear self-image providing a grip on things. But the empty self is not exclusively negative. The hidden possibilities of the self, which have remained inaccessible via the self-structure, are given a chance. But in order to draw upon new and unsuspected potentials, the painful and difficult discarding of the old structures is a necessary evil. Paradoxically enough, we enter the emptiness only to achieve a new fullness.

All of this shows the true self to reflect a complex phenomenon. From a person-centred point of view, such a term as the 'true self' is nothing more than a pointer or an initial indication. It is certainly not a description of a fixed entity, a definitive state, or a final phase. What holds here is what the starting point for person-centred psychotherapy has been all along: words are never equal to reality because reality is always larger than our words, our experiences, and our perceptions. The search and exploration go deeper and deeper and, in principle, never end. The search is a process, the continual approach or battle of the reality referred to as the true self. From this starting point, one can go so far that even the concept of the true self becomes a barrier to further exploration and should therefore better be discarded altogether. This is particularly the case when the true self is found to point to a fixed substance (for example the higher self). Rogers' last definition of the self as a continuously changing and non-fixed process provides all the space for the humanistic notion of potentiality or unsuspected possibilities. At the same time, it clearly fits into the spiritual or religious disciplines in search of our deepest identity and singularity (e.g. Moore, 2004).

UNCONDITIONAL POSITIVE REGARD

Rogers has described the fundamental attitudes that are 'necessary and sufficient' on the part of the therapist for personality change to take place. For these so-called core conditions, he used terms that are—upon further reflection—nothing more and nothing less than highly religious or spiritual. This is the case because what is asked of the therapist stems directly from what I have referred to above as the lost, other dimension of our existence. It is what traditionally within the religious or spiritual domain is referred to as love and truth. It should be noted directly in this connection—that the word 'love' is possibly even more tainted than the word 'truth' or the word 'God'. Perhaps Rogers opted, for this reason, to never use these words in the official formulations of his theory and opted for such neutral terms as respect, empathy, and congruence. However, appearances can be deceptive and further consideration shows these neutral and science-like terms to hide an unfathomably deep dimension of human experience and longing. Positive regard, for example, might well sound as rather neutral, but Rogers speaks of nothing less than unconditional positive regard and the 'unconditional' contains an unquestionably spiritual dimension.

In the modern psychotherapeutic world, everyone has recognized the importance of the therapeutic relationship but not the existential depth. That is the reason why it often is spoken of as a good working relationship or a therapeutic alliance as opposed to a therapeutic relationship. The difference is between useful client-centredness (in order to sell the product better) and a relationship at an existential level. In the latter case, we again enter the spiritual dimension where it is not good working relations that stand central, but the existential meeting—or person-to-person contact. In this contact, both the therapist and the client transcend their usual patterns and roles to meet each other at a deeper level. This deeper level allows us to see and experience each other as we actually are and not as images, patterns, and façades. And such transcendence can certainly be referred to as spiritual or religious.

But what, exactly, does unconditional positive regard involve? Unconditional positive regard does *not* mean that the therapist positively values everything that the client does, thinks, and feels. This would be an overly simple depiction of things and quickly leads to the familiar caricature of a boundless, permissive relationship in which anything is tolerated, every request is responded to, and confrontation is avoided, which is completely in conflict with the fundamental attitude of congruence for the therapist. Unconditional positive regard means that despite everything that the client does, says, feels, or thinks, the therapist continues to value the client as a person. This means in practice that no matter how much we abhor someone, we must continue to search for the true core, which can—in contrast to many of the client's actions—be positively valued. For the client, this is critical because clients all too easily translate feedback regarding patterns and behaviour into personal rejection and confirmation of what they already think deep in their hearts, namely, that they are worthless.

Numerous examples can be thought of in which the demand for unconditional positive regard goes beyond our normal capacities. Social service providers who work with rapists and murderers will confirm this. But even among our average neurotic clients, we sometimes encounter people who repel us to such an extent that we simply cannot discover anything positive. With others, we may find ourselves feeling so powerless that we simply cannot bring forth the effort to continue the search for overlooked possibilities—also because everything seems to suggest that there are none. We must transcend ourselves in such cases and appeal to an almost religious conviction to motivate ourselves to continue, as in the following example from my practice.

She had a very severe psychiatric disorder and had been in therapy with me for years. Prior to that, she had had all kinds of therapy including different admissions, outpatient treatments, all sorts of medication, psychiatric treatment, psychological help, and more extensive psychotherapy. All of this was of no avail. We had worked through her life history and the trauma that had definitely destroyed her life. We had also worked very hard in the here and now to get her life somewhat back on track. All of this appeared to be in vain despite the fact that much had occurred. At many moments during our contact, I decided that continuation of the therapy was of no more use and that we should, in keeping with all the usual criteria, taper off the therapy. The desired results had failed to occur. It appeared that the client was doomed to remain locked up in her trauma and pathological survival strategies until the end of her days. All hope was also gone on the part of the client who often saw but one solution, namely to put an end to her life, which she had regularly, but unsuccessfully attempted to do. Striking was the client's stubborn opposition to the termination of the therapy. At a certain point, I resigned myself to this and we agreed that she could continue to visit me from time to time. For myself, I defined the aim of this therapy as support for a very lonely client who could not turn to anyone else with her misery. Regularly accusing me in an aggressive manner of the therapy not producing results but simultaneously refusing to terminate the therapy was also part of the client's pattern.

At a later point in this therapy, I was surprised to see a side of the client that was not completely new but had not manifested itself as strongly as now. She told me that she had had enough of the type of superficial life that she and her husband were leading and that she was in search of greater inner depth, stillness, and a significant existence. What stood out is that she had no supernatural or esoteric objectives in mind but very everyday things. She wanted, for example, to stop watching television every evening and wanted to listen to music and calmly read a book instead. She also mentioned that she was developing more personal contacts with people and finding this to be increasingly important. She mentioned that she had become interested in spirituality. And at the same time, her complaints and her disorders remained present to the same extent.

What began to intrigue me was that a healthy core appeared to be present in this client—a core that became increasingly more important for her without it as yet allowing her to achieve some sort of order in her life. I wondered if my patience would be rewarded and my client possibly had something that would allow her to recover from the misfortune that had overwhelmed her.

Continuing to hope and trust against all the odds that a potential that has been suppressed until now will still emerge belongs to the core of the person-centred approach and, for that matter, many spiritual or religious traditions. Care and love—which are good translations for unconditional positive regard—are necessary for this to happen. Love has a soft undertone in our culture, and many people will therefore react in a dismissive manner. In the concrete treatment situation, however, love takes a very practical and tangible form. On one of the few occasions that Rogers used the word he described love in the following manner:

> What the client experiences during therapy is the feeling that someone loves him ... not with a love that claims him but with a love that affirms that he has his own personality and own individual feelings ... (Rogers & Kinget, 1959: 75)

So love can be described in person-centred terms as the client having the experience of being deeply accepted and understood, which Rogers called unconditional positive regard and empathic understanding. To the latter of these we turn now.

EMPATHIC UNDERSTANDING

Not only respect is necessary for a client to feel accepted and understood; empathic understanding is also needed. Within the person-centred tradition, considerable attention has therefore been paid to the empathic capacity of the therapist and some people have even gone so far as to aspire to the almost religious ideal of complete devotion to the client. The extremely high value attributed to empathic understanding and the intensity with which it is pursued clearly places it within the domain of the humanistic-religious and not the technological-scientific. It is striking in this connection, however, that relatively little attention has been paid to the development of the empathic capacities of the clients themselves. Person-centred psychotherapy discovered that many people did not receive the respect and empathy that they needed as children. Person-centred psychotherapists thus provided what was missing and taught people to take better care of themselves and not just others. But in some cases this led to the stimulation of what has been called the 'narcissistic personality of our time', which is something that person-centred psychotherapists can be reproached for. In an attempt to compensate for the one-sided focus on others, person-centred psychotherapy has encouraged people to take themselves seriously and to treat themselves with respect. In the justifiable fervour with which this has been done, however, person-centred psychotherapy swung to other extreme and forgot that the giving of love is not only important for therapists but for clients as well. It is now time to establish a suitable balance between the Christian exclusive focus on the other and the person-centred exclusive focus on self. Along these lines, important and extensive work has been conducted by Peter Schmid who has reinterpreted the therapy and practices of Rogers in terms of the philosophers Buber and Levinas (e.g. Schmid, 2002, 2004). These philosophers of the dialogue and the encounter appear to be particularly suited to help us ameliorate the aforementioned one-sidedness of person-centred thinking without damaging the basic assumptions underlying the approach. To the contrary, in fact, a deeper dimension that was always present but not sufficiently developed in the basic philosophy of Rogers appears to be explicated. Within the present context, it does not seem to be a coincidence that two religiously oriented philosophers appeared to be necessary. Schmid points out that Levinas sees the entire Western philosophy—including Western psychology and the humanistic direction within this—as *egology*. That is, the other is consistently reduced to 'what he or she can mean for me'. What is missing is the transcendence of the neurotic 'I' and the narcissism in which I am the middle point and everything and everyone is approached from my needs and my limited perspective. According to Levinas, the encounter involves a call to us from the other—a scream for help—and that we not evade answering this and thus take responsibility. This is completely in keeping with the basic philosophy of Rogers as formulated with regard to the fundamental attitudes of the therapist. We have simply not succeeded, however, in the communication of our basic philosophy and have all too often contributed, whether consciously or unconsciously, to some lopsided narcissistic excesses. In emphasizing the dialogical nature of person-centred therapy, a possibility presents itself for person-centred practices to enter, when desired and justified, a deeper spiritual dimension than was usual up until now. This is also related to authenticity or congruence, to which we turn now.

AUTHENTICITY

In stereotypes, the person-centred approach is often identified with listening attentively and respectfully to someone. It is striking that what Rogers considers most important in his later work, namely congruence, is never mentioned. And it is exactly this that has led to a caricature of person-centred psychotherapy. Rogers repeatedly discovered that the attentive and listening psychotherapist is not enough and may even work counteractively at times. For change on the part of the client, the therapist must—in Rogers' view—be clearly present as a flesh and blood person and thereby allow the client to experience what it is to enter into a real relationship. In addition, Rogers considered the therapist to be listening attentively to not only the client but also to him or herself to be critical. The therapist must take not only the client but also him or herself seriously and share with the client what he or she has heard. Should the therapist not do this, then he or she is not authentic. The therapist can listen respectfully, for example, but also be annoyed by the client without conveying this. The therapist can close him or herself off to intense emotions or painful stories—that is, suppress what such stories evoke. As a person, the therapist must share what is happening in him or herself with the client; otherwise, the contact is dishonest, unauthentic, and incongruent. Rogers considered the latter to be so important that he eventually declared it to constitute the core of his theory.

These useful effects of the therapeutic contact are not the result of some therapeutic tricks intended to attain something from the client, but the result of authenticity or the main value of the person-centred philosophy. Rogers refers to this value in terms of the fully functioning person, which the person-centred psychotherapist is expected to embody, but is something other than being perfect. In the contact with the therapist, the client should be able to feel his or her authenticity and be 'infected' by it. That is, the therapist exudes what is being aspired to in the therapy and thereby transfers this—whether intentionally or unintentionally—to the client. Paradoxically enough, the effect is greatest when the therapist is *not* out to influence the client. That is, steering someone in a particular direction is fundamentally in conflict with an attitude of authenticity. But the pure presence of the psychotherapist, in contrast, does not leave the client unaffected. That is, the client will be confronted via the presence of the therapist with an unfamiliar dimension of existence and then in a very concrete, personal, and direct manner. Different than in the daily social life of the client, there is someone who tells the truth and is trustworthy; there is someone who does not—for the sake of peace—soften the truth, and someone who dares to enter into the confrontation out of love for the client as a person and not to air his or her own frustrations.

In so far as the confrontation is aimed at the provision of useful feedback for the client, there is little reason to speak of a spiritual or religious dimension. But as soon as we search for what being authentic really means, things change. When people in psychotherapy search for authenticity, they quickly enter into the domain of the spiritual or religious quest. Could it be that it is exactly this that people mean by the term God: that which is real, not conditioned, not affected by human touch? In such a manner, we transcend the everyday meaning of authenticity or honesty and enter the lost, other dimension of our existence. The therapist who helps the client in this quest becomes more or less a representative of the other dimension. The therapist 'knows' what the other dimension involves because he or she lives more or less in that dimension. The therapist knows from his or her own experiences the obstacles, pitfalls, and beauty of this way of being.

Naturally, authenticity also has to do with truth and love. In fact, authenticity and love are inseparably intertwined with each other. That is, the person who lives in truth and love is authentic. And perhaps we can construe this description of authenticity as a 'modern' description of what the essence of the religious or spiritual is, that is: a description which is acceptable to people of our times. The religious without frills, without God, without the hereafter, without rituals, and without the pretence of certainty provided by religious dogma. The authentic is not fixed. The authentic is a dimension of existence to be continually explored with pleasant and sometimes unpleasant surprises and unprecedented demands. The completely unique manner in which person-centred psychotherapy explores this dimension consists of the personal contact with the psychotherapist who helps the client explore the authentic in a personal, experiential, truthful, and respectful manner. This exciting and risky quest does not have a certain end and is full of potential pitfalls. And it is possible that this form of self-exploration constitutes the most concrete and modern form of the ancient religious quest: namely, its secular counterpart.

COSMIC FORCES

It is a fact that Rogers devoted serious attention to our relation to the cosmos in his later work and never left it open to doubt that his ideas along these lines were to be taken quite seriously. The title of his chapter on this topic in his book *A Way of Being*, for example, is entitled 'The foundations of a person-centered approach'. In other words, man's relation to the cosmos is not a sidetrack or a specific application but nothing more and nothing less than the foundation of Rogers' philosophy.

> I wish to point to two related tendencies which have acquired more and more importance in my thinking as the years have gone by. One of these is an actualizing tendency, a characteristic of organic life. One is a formative tendency in the universe as a whole. Taken together, they are the foundation blocks of the person-centered approach. (Rogers, 1980: 114)

As already known, Rogers presupposes a tendency towards development, growth, and constructive fulfilment of one's possibilities within every person no matter how malformed, traumatized, or disturbed. Rogers speaks of this tendency in almost biological terms, and any form of mysticism is clearly absent. Rogers considers this tendency towards self-fulfilment or actualization to be a fundamental characteristic of life itself and to provide the basis for trust in the process of life. Given that growth is a characteristic of life itself, it is also therefore not exclusive to man but part of every living organism.

> Whether we are speaking of a flower or an oak tree, of an earthworm or a beautiful bird, of an ape or a person, we will do well, I believe, to recognize that life is an active process, not a passive one. Whether the stimulus arises from within or without, whether the environment is favorable or unfavorable, the behaviors of an organism can be counted on to be in the direction of maintaining, enhancing, and reproducing itself. This is the very nature of the process we call life. (Rogers, 1980: 118)

In light of Rogers' almost biological formulation of the tendency towards growth and self-actualization, the step towards the complete cosmos is not so curious. The most surprising element is that the step is taken at all. Do we not leave the domain of psychology or the study of the human individual and social relations in such a manner? One can observe, however, that Rogers' formulations become more spiritual at the same time. The tendency towards self-actualization is an individual manifestation of a creative force operative throughout the cosmos, according to Rogers. If someone attempts to realize his or her own possibilities in the direction of wholeness, integration, and oneness, then this person participates in the cosmic flow moving in that same direction. Rogers actually puts something that is at the core of the religious or spiritual into his own words here: that the individual can make contact with cosmic forces (Thorne, 2002). For Rogers, it is striking that we are governed by the same laws as the entire cosmos, that we are made of the same matter, and that everything is thus connected to everything. And every individual can experience how connected he or she feels with everything. Awareness of cosmic connectedness nevertheless appears, in the opinion of Rogers, to be unique to human consciousness. It appears that Rogers, in contrast to the average modern natural scientist, has discovered a positive direction in the evolution. And this perspective resembles that of the French scientist and priest Teilhard de Chardin who speculates, analogous to Christian doctrine, that the creation develops in the direction of an ideal end point, the so-called omega point.

All of the preceding appears to be quite far from the concrete practice of person-centred psychotherapy. For Rogers, however, this is clearly not the case. To the contrary, in fact. The climate created by the person-centred psychotherapist is also the climate that helps us come into contact with cosmic forces:

> Thus, when we provide a psychological climate that permits persons to be—whether they are clients, students, workers, or persons in a group—we are not involved in a chance event. We are tapping into a tendency which permeates all of organic life—a tendency to become all the complexity of which the organism is capable. And on an even larger scale, I believe we are tuning in to a potent creative tendency which has formed our universe, from the smallest snowflake to the largest galaxy, from the lowly amoeba to the most sensitive and gifted of persons. And perhaps we are touching the cutting edge of our ability to transcend ourselves, to create new and more spiritual directions in human evolution. (Rogers, 1980: 134)

Such a powerful formulation calls for much more serious treatment of Rogers' concept of the formative tendency by person-centred psychotherapists than has been the case up until now. (See the work of the British person-centred researcher Ivan Ellingham, 2002, for an exception to an otherwise dismissive attitude.) What should we person-centred psychotherapists do with this theory, and what is its significance for the explication of the implicitly religious within the person-centred approach? What we should *not* do is adopt the above as a sort of doctrine and proclaim it as part of person-centred ideology. We should, rather, pay attention to this part of Rogers' philosophy and further develop it in a personal and experiential way. We need not be afraid of leaving our own domain in such a manner. In fact, the exploration of not only the self and our relations with others but also our relations to the cosmos belongs to the domain of person-centred psychotherapy.

CONCLUSIONS AND DISCUSSION

The preceding has been an attempt to explicate the implicitly religious and spiritual in the person-centred approach. The enterprise could certainly be undertaken with respect to a number of other themes—for example, the theme of personality change and the concept of the fully functioning person. The implicitly religious in person-centred psychotherapy can be summarized as follows: it has to do with an inner source of truth, transcendence of our conditioned (neurotic) ego, authenticity, and connectedness with everything that exists. The universal that is present in all living beings is also the most 'personal' for each individual. And in such a manner, every individual is connected to every other organism in the cosmos. Each individual can perceive the fundamental processes of growth and development in every other organism and thereby possibly detect the same processes operative in themselves.

This is a fundamental vision of life—a philosophy of living in which it is assumed that there is but one reality. The deeper dimensions of our existence can thus be found in only this one, undivided reality. Whether these dimensions should be referred to as the religious or spiritual depends on what one means by these words. Rogers, when asked about the relation between psychotherapy and spirituality, provided the following beautiful answer:

> I am too religious to be religious ... I have my own definition of spirituality. I would put it that the best of therapy sometimes leads to a dimension that is spiritual, rather than saying that the spiritual is having an impact on therapy. (Rogers, in Baldwin, 1987: 35)

What Rogers seems to point out here is that the religious or spiritual dimension of life is not to be found in organized religions, nor in religious belief or dogma, but in living life to the full. That is why he did not want to use the term 'religious' in the traditional sense of that word and also hesitated even to use the word 'spiritual', although this changed later in his development. His approach to life might therefore well be characterized as a form of humanistic or secular spirituality, or even atheistic spirituality (Apostel, 1998). To develop this type of spirituality within person-centred psychotherapy seems to me to be one of the greatest challenges for person-centred psychotherapists interested in the relation between psychotherapy and religion or spirituality.

At this point, we can question what the preceding implies with respect to whether it is useful to construe person-centred psychotherapy as a spiritual discipline. My conclusion is that a substantive and sufficient foundation exists to justify the inclusion of the spiritual or religious dimension (as described in this chapter) within the theory and practice of person-centred psychotherapy. This does not imply automatically, however, that person-centred psychotherapy becomes a spiritual discipline in the same way as other religious or spiritual paths like Zen Buddhism or others. Although the latter would be justifiable and imaginable from what was explored and concluded in the foregoing pages, this would imply a break with the organizational context of the field of mental health in which person-centred psychotherapy is rooted. Such a break is not likely to happen at this moment. It might happen, however, in the future, for example at the time when person-centred psychotherapy possibly disappears from the regular mental health care system. Brian Thorne predicted this when he stated:

> Fifty years from now it is likely that Rogers will be remembered not so much as the founder of a new school of psychotherapy but as a psychologist whose work made it possible for man and woman to apprehend spiritual reality at a time when conventional religion had lost its power to capture the minds and imaginations of the vast majority. (Thorne, 1992: 105–6)

Only time will tell whether this comes to pass. In the meantime, it is an exciting enterprise to develop person-centred psychotherapy as a spiritual discipline more fully (see Thorne, 1998, chapter 15 for more concrete examples of this). Independently, individuals, whether they are clients, therapists or whatever, might explore and live person-centred philosophy as a spiritual discipline in their own personal way.

One advantage of including the spiritual dimension more explicitly in our theory and practice certainly is that we as person-centred therapists broaden our perspective and act more according to our essential identity. We will no longer have to frantically manoeuvre in order to sustain ourselves within a context where we increasingly do not fit and attempt to apply our approach in a much wider field than we do now (van Kalmthout, 2002). We can thus devote ourselves to such questions as: What is the lasting essence of the person-centred approach? What is the significance of the person-centred approach and the value of it in the present day? In which areas can the person-centred approach fruitfully be applied and in which areas is the person-centred approach better not applied and in which direction should the person-centred approach be further developed?

The undertaking of these developments is clearly risky and exciting. However, the approach as it now exists is in need of a new vitality, inspiration, or renewal. After Rogers passed away, few major renewals to his approach can be seen to have occurred. This is, of course, inherent in movements brought into life by such brilliant leadership. Perhaps the most impressive innovation in the work of Rogers to date is that of Gendlin, who explored the experiential cornerstone of Rogers' work in such a manner that a real contribution has been made to the development of the person-centred approach. The interpersonal or relational approach to psychotherapy can also be seen as a major addition to Rogers' work, although it has flourished especially within psychodynamic psychotherapy (e.g. Teyber, 2000). For both innovations, however, the essence can be seen to have been already present in the work of Rogers. In closing, it will not come as a surprise to me if the work started by Brian Thorne provides the impulse for a third major renewal of the work of Rogers, again along a dimension already implicitly present in his work.

REFERENCES

Apostel, L (1998) *Atheïstische Spiritualiteit.* Brussel: VUBPress.

Baldwin, M (1987) Interview with Carl Rogers on the use of self in therapy. In M Baldwin and V Satir (eds), *The Use of Self in Therapy* (pp. 45–52). New York: Haworth.

Ellingham, I (2002) Foundation for a person-centred, humanistic psychology and beyond: The nature and logic of Carl Rogers' 'Formative Tendency'. In J Watson, R Goldman and M Warner (eds), *Client-Centered and Experiential Psychotherapy in the 21st Century: Advances in theory, research and practice* (pp. 16–35). Ross-on-Wye: PCCS Books.

Luckmann, T (1967) *The Invisible Religion: The problem of religion in modern society.* New York: MacMillan.

Moore, J (2004) Letting go of who I think I am: Listening to the unconditioned self. *Person-Centered and Experiential Psychotherapies, 3* (2), 117–28.

Rogers, CR (1980) *A Way of Being.* Boston: Houghton Mifflin.

Rogers, CR & Kinget, M (1959) *Psychotherapie en menselijke verhoudingen.* Utrecht: Het Spectrum.

Schmid, PF (2002) Knowledge or acknowledgement? Psychotherapy as 'the art of not-knowing'. Prospects on further developments of a radical paradigm. *Person-Centered and Experiential Psychotherapies, 1* (1&2), 56–70.

Schmid, PF (2004) Back to the client: A phenomenological approach to the process of understanding and diagnosis. *Person-Centered and Experiential Psychotherapies, 3* (1), 36–51.

Teyber, E (2000) *Interpersonal Process in Psychotherapy: A relational approach* (4th ed). London: Brooks/Cole.

Thorne, B (1991) *Person-Centred Counselling. Therapeutic and spiritual dimensions.* London: Whurr.

Thorne, B (1992) *Carl Rogers.* London: Sage.

Thorne, B (1998) *Person-Centred Counselling and Christian Spirituality: The secular and the holy.* London: Whurr.

Thorne, B (2002) *The Mystical Power of Person-Centred Therapy: Hope beyond despair.* London: Whurr.

Thorne, B (2003) *Infinitely Beloved: The challenge of divine intimacy.* London: Darton, Longman and Todd.

Tillich, P (1962) *Die verlorene Dimension.* Hamburg: Furche.

Van Belle, H (1980) *Basic Intent and Therapeutic Approach of Carl Rogers.* Toronto: Wedge.

Van Belle, H (1990) Rogers' later move towards mysticism. Implications for client-centered therapy. In G Lietaer, J Rombouts & R Van Balen (eds), *Client-Centered and Experiential Psychotherapy in the Nineties* (pp. 47–57). Leuven: University of Leuven Press.

Van Kalmthout, M (1995) The religious dimension of Rogers' work. *Journal of Humanistic Psychology, 35,* 22–39.

Van Kalmthout, M (2002) The future of person-centered therapy: Crisis and possibility. *Person-Centered and Experiential Psychotherapies, 1* (1&2), 132–43.

Van Kalmthout, M (2004) Person-centered psychotherapy as a modern system of meaning. *Person-Centered and Experiential Psychotherapies, 3* (3), 193–206.

SECTION 4

PERSONAL REFLECTIONS AND WORKSHOPS

INTRODUCTION

One of the greatest challenges in terms of putting this book together has been how to represent the many experiential sessions of the conference, how to capture something of the feel of the artwork, the music, the dance, the conversation and the silent meditation through which individuals were able to find a place of stillness and nourishment or give expression to the creative life within them. The decision to include colour and some illustrations was prompted by Tess Sturrock, who facilitated two Expressive Arts workshops. She wrote to us as follows:

> I have struggled with writing some left-brain reflection on the two workshops in Expressive Arts that I facilitated. These were both wonderful experiences, each in very different ways. However, writing up something on them led to me being very stuck. Exhausted, I found myself envisaging a white book, with a single pink page at its centre. This was the inspiration for what I wrote. The Expressive Arts are so much a part of spiritual experience for me; I notice that I didn't want a book on our conference to go forth without some contribution from this area. Helping readers to have some experience of Expressive Arts via a pink page (or golden or turquoise, etc.) just felt more right. (email, 4 November 2004)

What Tess wrote appears as the first item of this section. The illustrations from different workshops we have been able to include appear elsewhere, representing only a small taste of a rich variety of experiential sessions—Hawaiian Flying Dance, Godly Play, Japanese doodling—that ran throughout the conference in parallel with the more academic presentations.

On the final evening of the conference we all participated in a period of silent meditation in Norwich Cathedral, a vast edifice rich in Norman vaulting and colourful roof bosses, with a peaceful cloister that once formed part of the monastic buildings for the Benedictine community that dwelt adjacent to the cathedral until the Reformation. The second piece in this section, 'Cathedrals: Places of Discovery', reflects on what cathedrals may inspire in our inner lives. **Mary Green** writes as a member of the cathedral community in which her own spiritual path is grounded. Open to the richness not only of the 'unobtrusive, but engaging' community, but of the awe-inspiring cathedral building itself and all that it can offer, she concludes her reflections by describing how vividly she experienced it impacting on a six-year-old child. The child she was accompanying on his first visit to the cathedral passed from rushing around in the cloister labyrinth to silent wonder on entering the main building, 'dropping down into something within himself', and, as he took in the immensity of all that was there, 'brimming over in awe, curiosity and wonder'. **Stephen Platten** meanwhile reflects on what it means to lead a cathedral community, an indefinable gathering of people who have no parish and no defined locality. He suggests that cathedrals offer a 'transcendent anonymity' which can open up for individuals their own particular 'path to God'. A cathedral, both writers suggest, can be open to what each person brings and offer what each may need, containing within its vast spaces, rich in centuries of spiritual presence, the potential of being alive to what Peter Berger terms their own individual 'signals of transcendence', of which the awe and wonder of the six-year-old child is one clear manifestation.

Just as a cathedral opens up space but does not impose meaning, so **Mary Hill** and **Suzanne Keys** sought in their workshop, 'Longing in practice: prayer and therapy', to open up a space for participants to explore the themes of longing and prayer and what these might mean for their professional practice. Through the playing of music, the sharing of prayers, poems and artwork, they sought to bring the flavour of their individual religious traditions—Sufi and Christian—to their reflections on longing and prayer and how these inform their work as therapists. In their account of the workshop they include feedback from participants, given two months after the conference, which helps create a more vivid sense of the experience, which was indeed so powerful that they were immediately asked to repeat the workshop for those who could not attend the first. We cannot hear the playing of the harmonium, the sounds of the musical Zikr from the Sufi Way or the Islamic 'call to prayer'; we cannot see the artwork, be present for the prayers that were offered or participate in the reading of Psalm 42, but we can understand something of their effect on the workshop participants. The facilitators' introductions are presented as they were in the workshop, individual testimony of their own faith and practice. Both make clear their view of the importance of prayer in developing a quality of 'presence', which is argued in the previous section to lie at the heart of the core conditions and of any healing relationship.

In their dialogue **William West** and **Chris Jenkins** discussed the theme of 'honouring spirituality in counselling'. They draw attention to the painful experiences of clients who are unfortunate enough to encounter counsellors who impose their own spiritual (or anti-spiritual) views on the client. They note that there is an important educational and self-development need here, and that there are already research findings which suggest the positive impact of religion and spirituality on mental health. However, for those who are impressed by this point, there is the issue of to what extent spiritual companionship can find a place in counselling, and what the boundaries are between counselling and spiritual direction. There is also the issue of to what extent a counsellor may draw on their own spiritual awareness in responding to the client. These issues are important ones, both theoretically and clinically, and the authors hope that through their discussion they have at least raised the questions in connection with counselling practice, training and supervision.

The final piece in this section is **Robina Scott's** account of the PRH workshop she presented, entitled 'Towards a deeper experience of who I am'. PRH (Personnalité et Relations Humaines), a methodical programme of self-discovery, founded by André Rochais, is notoriously difficult to describe in any way that captures the power and the impact of the life-changing courses it offers. In this 'taster' workshop Robina Scott, currently the only qualified PRH educator in Britain, invited participants to respond, silently and in writing, to a series of questions designed to take them more deeply into their experiencing of their own spirituality. Participants then shared as much or as little as they wished of what they had written with the rest of the group, their experiencing deepening through the act of self-expression and through being silently open to the experiencing of others. Scott draws attention, in her brief introduction to the PRH model of the person, to the importance of what is termed in PRH 'the being'. The concept of the being has much to offer in terms of our understanding of the deeply spiritual nature of every person. It is described as constituting 'our intact, essential self' and is presented as 'a concrete reality that we can access in ourselves'. The being can be accessed through awareness of bodily sensations, a living, physical reality that connects us with the Transcendent. Much of what is written throughout this book may be described as relating directly to the growth and life of the being, presented through a range of individual experiences and through apparently divergent spiritual traditions. PRH offers a universal language that speaks both of and to our common humanity.

Imagine that this page is pink

or yellow or turquoise or red
or black or blue or ochre
or gold or silver.
Imagine it is whatever colour comes
to you in this minute.

Now imagine the colour of your page
is music—deep or loud
or soft or tinkling
or whatever is your music
in this moment.
And imagine that this sound,
whatever it is, is emanating
from you.

And now imagine the dancer
to that sound. Perhaps a whole shoal
of fish gliding and darting.
Perhaps a whale. Perhaps a clan
of morris dancers. Perhaps Nureyev.
Perhaps a single solitary figure
standing in a field of corn. Imagine
your dancer and let your body
be the dance.

And now imagine
that you are soft chalk or paint—
a chosen colour upon the page.
You are the colour that moves
the dance to the music
upon the page. Imagine
the movement on paper
without thought—
sweeping, wheeling—
silent now but for the noise
of paint, of chalk on paper,
soft swish express glide
concentrate sweep be.

And now imagine
that you are the pen
that makes words on paper,
even as the body dances
and the voice sings
and the colour moves.

And now imagine others, moving
with you, colour on paper, colour in
dance, dance and sound, music
and colour, words and movement

And now stillness
with colour around
you, with singing
in your veins and movement
in your bones. And you are holding
the hand that is next to you, that joins
you to the circle on each side. The warmth
of your blood and colour and dance goes
from your hand to
others—and others flow
to you.

Tess Sturrock

Chapter 13

CATHEDRALS: PLACES OF DISCOVERY

Mary Green and Stephen Platten

1. ROUTES TO GOD: FINDING A WAY FORWARD

Mary Green

About ten years ago the Church and I parted company. My experience of God felt unacceptable, my spiritual discernment unorthodox and my attempting to take the spirit of a child seriously was laughed at. I felt powerless to express my yearning soul, which needed validation, engagement, and respect. Stillness, presence and the grace of humanity has opened my heart to a greater personal conviction in striving to be me within the body of the Church. Profoundly important for me has been facing the intimacy of fear through the I–Thou relationship, spoken of originally by Martin Buber and used extensively within the theory of Carl Rogers. My definition of this relationship is: coming to honour the unfolding mystery of the sacredness and truth of oneself, towards the heightening of self-knowledge, and thereby acknowledging and reaching out towards that in another person. Of parallel importance for enabling me to move on has been the Cathedral as a place in which to be present. Here I discovered God in my own stillness and space, within an unobtrusive, but engaging community. Worship has had an awesome sense of God's abundance and glory, enticing me towards the greater mystery of the connectedness of love. It was a place where those coming into it could engage with it in whatever way they chose; a place where the creative arts were exhibited and experienced as powerful routes to God; and a place where exhibitions on social injustice and inequality were given raised platforms from which to speak.

My lack of trust in God had stemmed from the experience of numerous human relationships of being loved and accepted but only 'conditionally'. Thus, equally important has been the intimate relationship that can be uniquely afforded by counselling. The more intimately acceptable I am to myself, the more open I am to an intimately acceptable relationship with God—and consequently more able to offer and risk the honesty of such a relationship with others. The awareness of a new courage to speak with someone of the shame and the guilt of feeling unacceptable—which has often rendered me frozen with fear, and quite incapable of finding words—leaves me powerfully touched by acceptance and deeply moved by unconditional love. At a time when a person is unguarded or open, God reaches out—in my experience of transcendental moments—and offers a glimpse of the truth of an intimate relationship.

Kindling, rekindling and sometimes igniting the sacredness of self, therefore, feel vital to me in my survival as an individual within a spiritual community.

This route to God, combining the Cathedral and its community with the deeper discovery of what it means to be fully human, enabled me to seek my own spiritual education. It allowed me to follow and trust the curiosity and increasing desire to find ways of nourishing my soul. The personal challenge of self-discovery, learning, and living from a greater truth and vulnerability was significantly empowered by the example of leadership which engaged with the reality of asking questions, acknowledging uncertainties, and taking risks.

Coming to acknowledge and trust this emerging and unique sacredness, and meeting it in others, led me towards an ever-growing need to be aware of the personal responsibility towards spiritual discernment. Perhaps it is in the hope and vision of its paradoxically anchored freedom, within the hopelessness and chaos of the present world, that there feels a necessity to nurture and prize the 'I' alongside the 'Thou', knowing that 'we' are part of a deeply wounded but deeply loved and connected community. In those rare and fleeting moments of absolute trust in this divine mysticism—where suffering and love seem intricately entwined—the sanctity and diversity of 'we' feels all the more precious for not needing to be spoken.

2. CATHEDRAL COMMUNITIES

STEPHEN PLATTEN

> Knock and the door shall be opened unto you,
> Seek and ye shall find.

These familiar words, in this case sung as a hymn, took on a new resonance as students and staff from the theological college processed across Castle Square and through Exchequer Gate into Lincoln Cathedral some twenty years ago. It was just as they passed in through the Great West Door that they sang, 'Knock and the door shall be opened'. The effect of this moment on so many of those people will be remembered throughout their lifetimes. Entering into that great 'womb-like' nave was breathtaking. In German, the word for a cathedral nave is *Schiff*, which is ship; Lincoln's nave really is like the upturned hull of a great sea-going vessel. Not just adults, but children too, are daily amazed into wonder standing in that great transcendent space. So there was the four-year-old who would insist on passing through the cathedral on his way to the nursery—'look at the *baffedral*' he would say in dazzled wonder.

Such buildings can often touch the hearts of even the most hard-headed adult. Those leading such communities, responsible for such inspirational spaces, have therefore, literally, an awesome task. How do these spaces speak to the different moods and conditions of the myriad people who pass through them? What of the person aching to open her heart to another human being? What of the soul troubled and needing a priest? What of the person profoundly moved by the building, but wishing to treasure and ponder things in his or her own mind and soul? Each of these will pass into the warm heart of these buildings and somehow must be given the freedom to respond, and to be responded to, as their desires take them.

But it is not only the building and its effect upon solitary souls. There is also something about the communities that have formed these places over the centuries. Uniquely in England, before the Reformation, certain cathedrals were also the homes of religious communities—mainly Benedictine, but some Augustinian. This continues to give a particular feeling and depth to these great churches. Elsewhere these vast buildings were owned by the whole community, sacred and secular. They were a focus for the city and the region in which they were set; indeed this was also true of cathedrals with a monastic foundation, but there was also a resident community.

In our world, cathedrals perform a diverse role. Multitudes of people make occasional visits; within the locality hosts of different communities know the cathedral to belong to them. Even football clubs and universities call cathedrals their own. It is this universality and multivariety that lends the 'difference' to cathedrals. They belong to everyone and yet they belong to no one. Cathedrals offer a transcendent anonymity. Even the dioceses of which the cathedrals are the focus are not quite sure how to relate to these extraordinary places. But cathedrals do have their own 'native communities'. How does this transcendent anonymity affect the regular worshipping congregation coming Sunday-by-Sunday—or even more frequently? Cathedrals generally have no parish; they serve no defined locality. Indeed, many worshippers come to avoid some of the more constraining characteristics of parish life; they may be avoiding certain types of involvement. They positively relish both transcendence and anonymity. This all gives life to a very distinctive sort of community.

All these factors outlined, relating both to the building and to the associated communities, mean that the way in which those who are called to lead cathedrals—in every aspect—will be called to handle the local congregation in a unique way. It will not directly parallel parish or other sorts of community life. Most richly of all, the myriad ways in which these buildings affect both individuals and the multitude of communities which gather around them can help people to find their own paths towards meaning and transcendent reality in very different ways. There are almost as many paths to God as there are different personalities and human characteristics. Cathedrals are blessed with opportunities to open up these different pathways in a manner which is unique within our contemporary world.

3. PATHS TO GOD

Stephen Platten

'... [S]how hospitality to strangers, for thereby some have entertained angels unawares'. So writes the unknown author of the 'Letter to the Hebrews', in the *New Testament.* About a generation ago, the celebrated sociologist, Peter Berger, wrote a seminal essay that he entitled simply *A Rumour of Angels* (1970). He gave it a tentative subtitle *Modern Society and the Rediscovery of the Supernatural.*

It is a book that still repays careful reading. It starts from the place wherein Berger himself then stood, that is the burgeoning world of the human sciences. One of the disturbing effects of the study of anthropology, psychology or sociology is the tendency towards relativization. The study of human behaviour, either individually or in groups, can lead to the assumption that all human activity is subjective and open to change and decay. Humanity becomes the measure of all things, to misquote Protagoras. The critical study of history has similar effects. To use an analogy, once one has been backstage one comprehends the realities of a dramatic production—the rain is not real, and the nymphs and fairies fly only with the help of the invisible silken strands attached to their torsos. Objectivity dissolves like the morning mist. There is no longer such a thing as human nature or a common culture; religious belief, and the alleged transcendence behind it, also are illusions, social constructs. Berger, a seminal thinker in the realm of the sociology of knowledge, was amongst the earliest to press home this case. In a way, the shift towards so-called *postmodernism* is the natural extension of this process; each person or community decides on his or her own truth.

As Berger began to reflect, however, he realized that the very process of relativization is subject to a similar critique. We cannot stand outside our own critical world. Even the analysts are analysed; the critics are criticized; the relativizers are relativized; they cannot push the same bus inside which they are sitting! Berger looks to mathematics for an analogy. Mathematics is undoubtedly a human construct, but, despite this, the deepest aspects of nature display these same mathematical patterns, and humanity also includes them. Does not this point to something deeper, even objective? If so, why not investigate humanity and see if religious pointers are there too?

This Berger does, and he identifies what he calls *signals of transcendence*, what we might call *paths to God.* These cannot be characterized as direct revelation, but they are steps towards a world of ultimate reality. Berger identified five sets of *signals of transcendence*, but there is no empirical reason why there cannot be more. There is not space here to look at all these, but let us focus on one of his examples, the argument from *ordering*. A child wakes up at night, perhaps feverish, perhaps from a bad dream. The mother takes the child and cradles him and reflects: 'Don't be afraid—everything will be all right'. In saying this, the mother is not operating cynically. She is relaying a real sense of order in the universe.

Remembering these different signals of transcendence, these varied routes to God, let us return to cathedrals. Imagine the child with her eyes caught in the glorious kaleidoscope of light from a sunny day through stained glass; the rays themselves induce wonder. Or there is the visitor looking up into Lincoln's vaulting; some sense of the deeper order in creation is stimulated in the soul. Then perhaps it is sacred music; music takes us deeper into our own soul, there to discover a reality that transcends our own soul. Or there is a sermon, touching the mind and heart as never before. It may even be arriving in this great building on a day of profound sorrow. Or it may be being caught up into the mystery of redemption itself; the Easter Vigil and 'new fire', and the Mass of the Last Supper in Holy Week are particularly pregnant in meaning here.

In his book, *Part of a Journey*, Philip Toynbee (1981) describes an experience which captured both he and his wife, at Evensong, in Peterborough Cathedral. Here, it appeared to be a combination of the liturgy, the music and the building that mattered. But it could be something else caught up in the relationships within the Cathedral community, affecting basic human instincts of pride or humility, sexuality, fear or hope, anger and hate. Cathedrals, for reasons already explored, have a unique opportunity of awakening in both children and adults a path to God that may speak only to them.

4. REDISCOVERING WONDER: A TRANSCENDENT JOURNEY

MARY GREEN

Amidst the chaos of the world, it seems there is one thing of which we can be certain: a baby knows who it is, and what it wants. Engaging and prizing this unique and fearless intimacy they have with themselves should not be confused with giving them whatever they want. Perhaps this is best summed up with a sense of irony in the girl I noticed recently who was walking down the road. She was about nine years old, wearing designer clothes and accessories, and a T-shirt covered with large lettering, which said: 'Do you know what my name is?' I have a sense of a missed opportunity, for not stopping and saying: 'No, but I would really like to'.

Carl Rogers wrote of the infant: 'What happens to this highly efficient soundly based valuing process? By what sequence of events do we exchange it for the more rigid, uncertain, inefficient approach to values that characterizes most of us adults?' (Kirschenbaum & Henderson, 1990: 172).

Perhaps R. S. Thomas hints at something similar in his poem, 'Children's Song':

We live in our own world
A world that is too small
For you to stoop and enter
Even on hands and knees,
The adult subterfuge.
And though you probe and pry
With analytic eye
And eavesdrop all our talk
With an amused look,
You cannot find the centre
Where we dance, where we play,
Where life is still asleep
Under the closed flower,
Under the smooth shell
Of eggs in the cupped nest
That mock the faded blue
Of your remoter heaven.

Children have a wonderful ability to hold on to their own knowing, until they are made to feel stupid, humiliated, fearful or wrong. This certainty, however, is not for the detriment or humiliation of another—indeed quite the opposite. It would seem to me the more confidently they hold on to their belief, the less threatened they are by another. I was walking my six-year-old son to school with a child of a similar age. He looked into the window of a shop: 'That is absolutely disgusting', he said of a dress. Rebecca looked and turned towards us and said: 'That is the most beautiful dress I have ever seen'.

Within seconds, the two children ran along the pavement skipping, laughing and talking together—they had a dialogue where they could not have disagreed more strongly, but that did not weaken their relationship. Indeed it appeared to strengthen it. There was no adult intervention, no undermining of each other or of either person by some other party. Strengthening, accepting and trusting the personal spirit of discernment seems paramount—paramount to the child in their dialogue, paramount to the adult in their spiritual search.

I left school, convincingly assured that in the most part I had failed, but that, apparently, (I quote) 'one day I would make a very good mother'. I have made a good job of being a mother and I say that unashamedly. Ironically, it is in fact through my children that I have also learnt that the greatest wisdom is not taught—it is inherent.

Recently I went with a six-year-old friend into the Cathedral. He had never been there before. He was slightly fearful of the noise of the clock as he rushed around with a paper sword defending himself against his friend in the cloister labyrinth. Entering the building, I had an almost tangible experience of him dropping down into something within himself as we stood looking towards the light coming through the west window at one end and then looking the other way uplifted into the space and glory of the east. It seemed that he was in a space, both outside himself and within, that was both real and awesome. I followed his curiosity:

'Why does everyone have a book? What is in them? Why do you sing? What is that noise that sounds like a piano? What is that stick in the middle of that table and why are there candles? What is the spirit of Jesus? Who is God?'

It was a real experience, brimming over with awe, curiosity and wonder. I was filled with an enormous joy and a sense of profound responsibility *towards* this child—that I could share my experience of a God of love who wants nothing more than that we express all that we are created to be. Beside me was a little boy who had the vulnerability of an open unwritten book—more in touch than any adult with the real experience of God.

REFERENCES

Berger, P (1970) *A Rumour of Angels.* London: Allen Lane/Penguin Press.

Buber, M (1937 and 1958). *I and Thou.* New York: Charles Scribner's Sons.

Kirschenbaum, H & Henderson, V (1990) *The Carl Rogers Reader.* London: Constable.

Thomas, RS (1993) *Collected Poems.* London: JM Dent.

Toynbee, P (1981) *Part of a Journey.* London: Collins.

Chapter 14

LONGING IN PRACTICE: PRAYER AND THERAPY

Mary Hill and Suzanne Keys

INTRODUCTION

In this chapter we want to convey something of the flavour of the workshop we co-facilitated by offering, as in the workshop, our individual thoughts on the subject, some of the subjects we covered in the discussion, and the prayers and music we shared. We hope that you, the reader, will find something to connect with that might lead to learning and exploration about your own longings in prayer and therapy. We asked participants for feedback two months after the conference and that is included in italics[1] throughout.

> *I clearly remember the powerful sense of peace and in depth connection that I experienced throughout and that for me was facilitated by the atmosphere that you both created. That speaks to me of prayerfulness that flows as a result of the preparation and willingness to be open at a spiritual level which you gifted to us in that shared space.*

MARY: LONGING AND INTIMACY

I searched
But I could not find thee.
I called thee aloud
Standing on the minaret.

I rang the temple bell
With the rising and setting of the sun.
I bathed in the Ganges in vain.
I came back from Kaaba disappointed.
I looked for thee on the earth.

---

1. Many thanks to David McCormack, Mitsuyo Takeda, Mary Wishart, Mairin Breathnach, Tess Sturrock, Jonathan Smith, Caroline Kitcatt and Ian Carty for their responses.

> I searched for thee in the heaven, my beloved.
> And at last I have found thee,
> Hidden as a pearl in the shell of my heart.
> (Sufi Inayat Khan, 1923)

My work as a counsellor is often intimate: beautifully and preciously intimate. I believe a human experience of God is through intimacy.

My experience of prayer is also about intimacy, with God and with myself. For me it is both a process of opening myself to glimpses of this intimacy and a longing to deepen my capacity to relate to this inner self, the pearl in the shell of my heart. Prayer is a way of nourishing this process of invoking intimacy and, paradoxically, seems to journey outwards and inwards at the same time.

I ask myself: what is prayer? I love the phrase 'prayer is doing the beautiful'. I was fortunate to join an interfaith pilgrimage to Syria a few years ago. This experience opened up a joyful learning of different types of prayer. I experienced difference and connectedness at the same time. I prayed in a mosque, in an Orthodox church and I prayed in a Jesuit monastery. In all these places I heard prayers spoken in the same language, Arabic. I did not understand the language but heard beautiful sounds and vibrations, experiencing a peaceful feeling of connectedness.

I was touched by the beautiful word 'Allah' used in the Call to Prayer by the Muezzins from the minarets, like angels' voices in the night; in the communal prayer Salat in the mosque; the gentle voices of the nuns in the monastery and the impressive ritual in the Orthodox church.

It seems there is so much to learn and experience, so many different and connected ways to pray. Not in a universal pick-and-mix way, but in an authentic honouring and appreciating of difference.

In this workshop I shared a practice of musical Zikr from the Sufi Way.[2] Zikr means remembering or mentioning God. It is the process of repeating sacred words with concentration, that it may impress the meaning of the words on the entire self of the one who repeats them. The value of repetition has been known and realized by the ancient mystics of various religions. The Brahmins repeat their mantra which they call Japa, the Parsis their Gathas, Jews repeat the names and verses from the Kabala. Sufis have always understood the importance of repetition of the sacred word which they have named Zikr.

In 'Developing a Spiritual Discipline', Brian Thorne, writing of Carl Rogers' description of presence, states:

> I believe that, as a person-centred counsellor, I have a responsibility to attend to my own being and to the relationship with clients in such a way that this quality of presence with its remarkable capacity for promoting growth, healing and energy is more likely to be experienced ... it is my belief that a commitment to such a discipline on the part of the counsellor greatly increases the likelihood

2. The Sufi Way is an inner school in the lineage of the Indian mystic, Sufi Inayat Khan.

> of therapeutic relationships where the transcendental core of client and counsellor can be brought together with a resulting release of healing energy. (Thorne, 1994: 44–5)

For me the relationship between the practice of prayer and therapy is a continuing process, towards valuing, evoking and developing a quality of presence with myself and with others.

> *I loved your playing,*[3] *Mary, that opened the workshop, and your clear words which included the word 'longing'. I felt my tears rising up—a deep well of longing in myself to have this experience of being open and moved more often. I loved your own personal sharing, the space for each of us to share if we wished, and then the chanting and silence together. I said then and afterwards, 'If church was like this I would go!' I do go, of course, but mostly don't feel nourished in this way.*
>
> *I notice that I'm looking for ways to have this experience more often ... The ingredients are: a chance to draw and sound and move and sing, a chance for personal sharing, some sense of connectedness with our world religion roots and each other, and silence.*
>
> *I found particularly powerful the prayers/calls to prayer that you played us or we sang at the end of the workshop—and, of these, the complete version of the 'an Islamic call to prayer from the minaret' was deeply haunting and moving. Indeed, for me, it created a kind of longing.*
>
> *This is a little reflection inspired by your Workshop. ... Learning to hear the voice of my inner being ... I feel the more I am able to do this ... and to enter into the gentleness of my own inner being or 'soul' that it changes the tone and quality of my life. I am in touch with the invitation to step onto the path of creative change ... 'less in need of the trappings'. Out of the music and song beauty appeared to me ... there is profound belonging in music it is as though the music instinctively knows where I dwell and what I need.*
>
> *There is no standard translation of 'presence' in Japanese, both in counseling books and even in the Bible. I noticed this after I read Psalm 42 at the workshop ('When shall I come before the presence of God?') and tried to find out how it would be translated into Japanese. ... Now I feel, for me as a counselor, 'presence' means the integration of Rogers' ideas. And, as a woman in middle age, 'presence' is a key word, helping my journey of seeking and my prayer.*

3. Mary was playing her harmonium as people arrived for the workshop and settled.

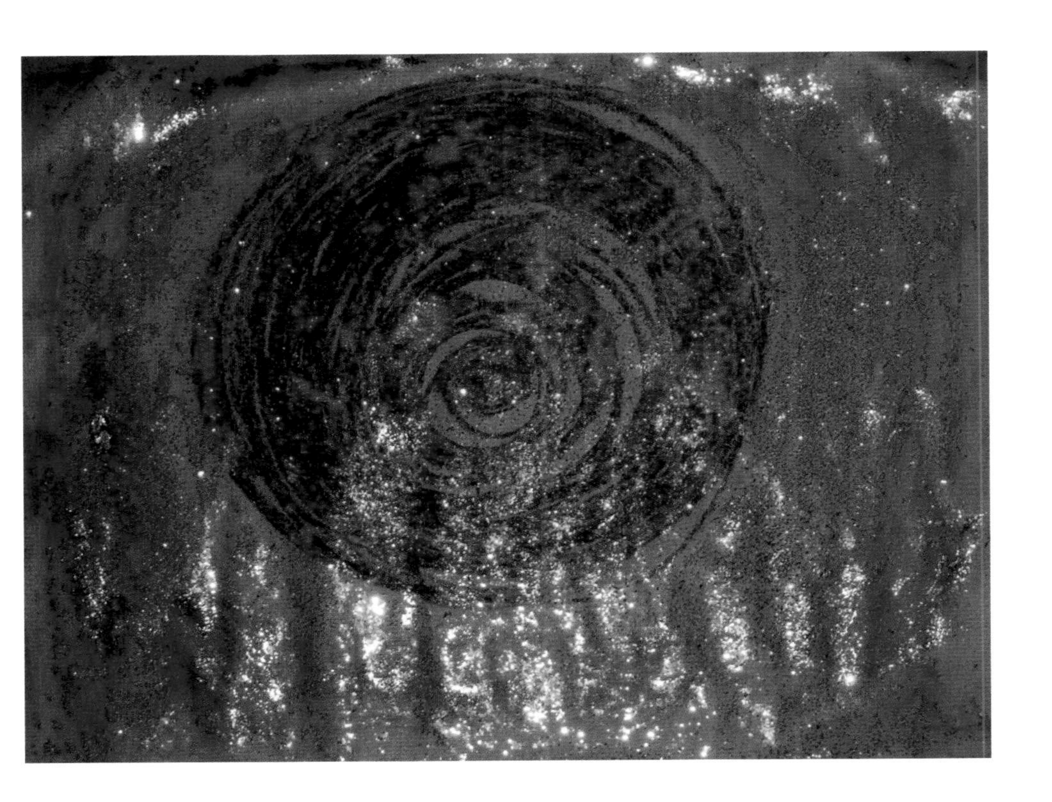

Suzanne Keys
Orgasm: sexual and spiritual. Irradiating, timeless, fragmentary moment where there is both focus and diffuseness, connection and disconnection, meeting and coming apart, joy and sorrow, gift and loss. (See page 185.)

Mikio Shimizu
'These are from the Japanese Doodling Workshop. The results are not so important as the doodling process itself and what happens after the session from having expressed inner experiences in this way.'

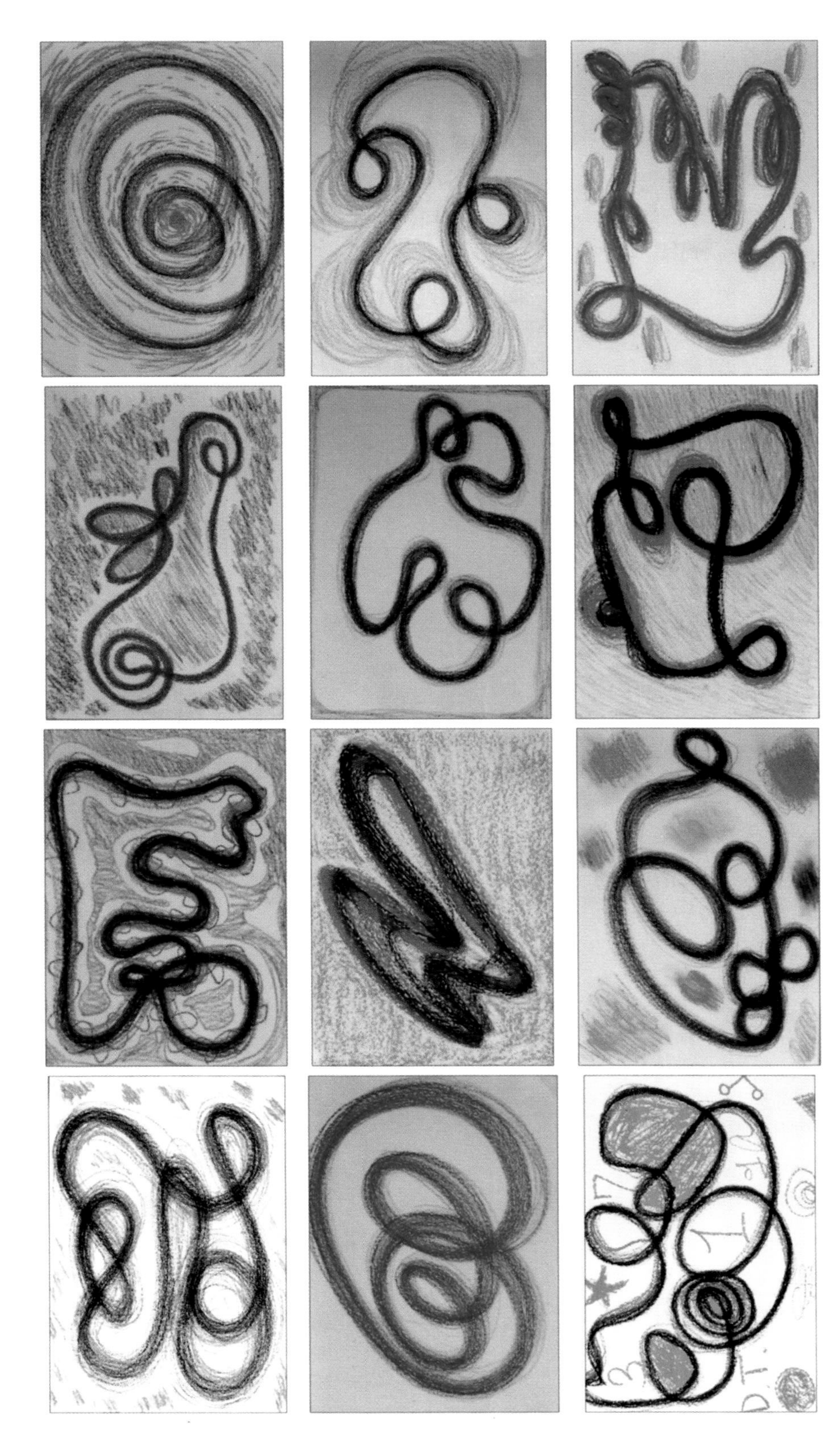

Alison Woods
'This was done in response (to the conference) and was a real breakthrough shedding of an old way of being.'

SUZANNE: LONGING IN PRACTICE

> The night has passed, and the day lies open before us;
> Let us pray with one heart and mind.
> (Silence)
> As we rejoice in the gift of this new day,
> So may the light of your presence, O God,
> Set our hearts on fire with love for you;
> Now and for ever.
> Amen.
> (*Common Worship*, 2002: 100)

This prayer is meaningful for me because it is one that I say every weekday morning at Morning Prayer with people at my local church. It is about the discipline of prayer and the collective power of prayer. It is also about taking time to recognise and acknowledge new beginnings and to come together. It is about a drawing together and focusing 'with one heart and mind'. There are words spoken together and there is shared silence. There is also thanksgiving which I have increasingly found important in my spiritual life in terms of a path to openness and loving. When I can acknowledge and appreciate the gifts of life then I am also able to be open to whatever lies ahead. It renews my hope and faith. It opens my heart and then I can relax into the moment and the unexpected.

RELATIONSHIP: LONGING FOR/RESPONDING TO

This prayer also encapsulates a central question about longing for me. I long for God, but does that longing come from within me or is it sparked by God's longing for me? Am I longing for or in response to? The answer has to be that it is both. This longing comes from deep within me as well as in response to a calling from without. In prayer I reach out to God in response to God and in my work I reach out towards another person in response to them. I am both subject and object but, beyond that, longing and responding lead me in to relationship, what is in-between and beyond me and the other. Without relationship I cannot exist. This is the central tenet of my faith as well as my work. I feel a desire as well as an obligation to respond—my existence depends on my ability to respond, it is my response-ability (Schmid, 2001a: 57). This response is from my whole being—it involves all of me, it is drawn out of me, it is bodily, it is not cognitive, it is a matter of faith. I cannot help but respond, it is part of my human nature. I long to understand and to be understood, to accept and to be accepted and to see and be fully seen by the other. I long for relationship, connection, meeting, encounter, dialogue, intimacy, love. I long to be changed and to learn and to grow. I grow long with my desire to be in contact with the other.

My longing in response to the other is both about the need and desire to be loved as well as to love. David Brazier critiques Rogers' focus on the need for positive regard as the driving force in our lives and emphasises instead the need to love: 'a primary altruism rather than a primary narcissism, at the root of human nature' (Brazier, 1993: 90). Brian Thorne underlines the importance of having one's loving accepted:

> As I think of some of the most challenging clients I have encountered during my lengthy career as a therapist, I know that most of them have required that I accept their love. Not to do so ... would be to condemn them to continuing alienation and to a sense of their unworthiness to be a part of the human family. (Thorne, 2002: 16)

So as a human being I long to love and to be loved, to give and to receive. Furthermore I receive in being received by the other. But love moves beyond the I and Thou to what is 'between I and Thou'. 'Love occurs' (Buber, 1970: 66). This is what I long for: to be in love, to know God in, through and by relationship.

UNION: TO BE ONE AND TO BE TWO

> For by nature our will wants God, and the good will of God wants us. We shall never cease wanting and longing until we possess Him in fullness and joy. Then we shall have no further wants. (Julian of Norwich, 1966: 71)

I wonder whether I share, with the Christian mystics, a longing and a thirst to be in union with God, with the other—to be one? Am I prepared to surrender to God, to relationship, to the unknown? To be prepared to lose myself to find myself (Matthew, 10: 39)?[4] Is this language inappropriate in terms of thinking about what I do as a therapist? Can I surrender myself in therapy the same way I would in prayer: be open to what will happen, be open to be changed by the relationship? Do I want to transcend our being two to share in a moment of relational depth or to encounter each other in a way that we are both changed? I want to remember the power differential inherent in a client–therapist relationship and that I am necessarily different to the client because I am their therapist. I want to attune myself to the client's world 'as if' it were my own (Rogers, 1957: 99) but there is a deeper attunement happening which changes both those present. Evidence even suggests that this can be seen on a physiological level in 'limbic resonance' (Lewis, Amini and Lannon, 2000: 63–65). Are attunement and meeting the same as union? The paradox is that it is in our difference that we meet. It is the fact that the other is different to me that draws me into encounter. But is that driven by a curiosity about difference and a desire to be in relationship or by a wanting to know the other and be known and to transcend our difference? Can union allow for difference? Perhaps the religious word 'comm-union' is more like what I long for in my meetings, where brokenness, fragmentation and diversity can be made whole without being denied. To meet beyond difference, to be one in our meeting as well as two individuals—that is what encounter can mean. As a word it can hold the paradox of being both one and two simultaneously.

---

4. Biblical references are from New Revised Standard Version, Anglicized Edition, Oxford: OUP.

ORGASM: SATISFACTION AND LOSS

Orgasm too is a word that holds both being one and being separate. One with an other or one with something beyond myself as I transcend time and physical body. It is about a peak moment as well as a process: the pleasurable build up, the anticipation, the excitement mixed with the fear of disappointment, the ultimate meeting or coming together, the being lost in a timeless moment, being at one with the universe but in that moment there is also the loss or the *petite mort* (the 'little death', which is the French for orgasm). It cannot be held on to, it cannot last; it is momentary and fragmentary in its fullness. It is an irradiating moment where there is both focus and diffuseness.[5] The word orgasm holds in it simultaneously connection and disconnection, meeting and coming apart, joy and sorrow, gift and loss.

Longing can lead to orgasm, to glimpses of satisfaction and fulfilment, to momentary union but it is always tinged with the knowledge of its transience. When I drink in a supremely beautiful landscape or when I catch a wave on a surf board and the energy is harnessed, I am in the divine slipstream and there is harmony but there is also the knowing that the wave is coming in to land, the moment is always lost and that more time is spent in trying to get the next wave than in riding it.

TENSION: LONGING AND ACCEPTANCE

The tension inherent in longing is to feel it and be drawn by it whilst at the same time accepting the unsustainability of what I long for. This is a central tension for me in my life and my work as a person-centred therapist. I have gradually come to admit to myself that I do want healing for the people I work with, I therefore want it to be different, but that comes from accepting things as they are. This acceptance is like an alchemical process.

> [T]he curious paradox is that when I accept myself as I am, then I change. I believe that I have learned this from my clients as well as within my own experience—that we cannot change, we cannot move away from what we are, until we thoroughly accept what we are. (Rogers, 1961: 17)

This does not stop my longing for things to be different—for myself, others and the world. My prayers are full of these longings. This motivates and energizes me and yet I also accept that we are where we are and that, although change is inevitable, I cannot tell what that change will be. I know that my experience of life is of contradictions, not knowing and imperfection and yet that is not what I long for. I long to know, for clarity and for some kind of harmony or ideal. Is it, as Yalom suggests, that we appear to be 'meaning-seeking creatures who have had the misfortune of being thrown into a world

---

5. At the workshop I showed a picture I had done of what sexuality/spirituality meant for me. It is included in the Illustrations section of this volume.

devoid of intrinsic meaning' (Yalom, 2001: 133). Am I wanting to understand the un-understandable? Is empathy 'the art of not knowing' (Schmid, 2001b: 53)? It is the mystical paradox of knowing through unknowing (Backhouse, 1985: 23).

In *Indiana Jones and the Last Crusade*, the last in the trilogy, Indiana has the Holy Grail within his grasp as he dangles over the precipice of death, hanging on to his father by his fingertips. His father urges him to save himself and thus lose the chalice. The process of searching, the illumination along the way, the relationships formed have been what was important, not the prize. The prize has driven the searching but, in the end, is let go of in favour of life.

Deye mon ge mon is a Haitian proverb meaning 'behind the mountain there is another mountain'. Living is about the process of longing, not about staying at the top of the longed-for mountain.

CONCLUSION: PARALLELS BETWEEN THERAPY AND PRAYER

Prayer is the manifestation of my longing to be in relationship with God and therapy is the manifestation of my longing to be in relationship with another person. Both are responses to a calling. Both involve discipline. There are many times when I feel that my prayers are a meaningless routine.

> So he (our Lord) says, 'Pray inwardly, even if you do not enjoy it. It does good, though you feel nothing, see nothing. Yes, even though you think you are doing nothing. For when you are dry, empty, sick, or weak, at such a time is your prayer most pleasing to me though you find little enough to enjoy in it. This is true of all believing prayer. (Julian of Norwich, 1966: 125)

Likewise there are times when I feel that nothing is happening in my work as a therapist, I question and doubt my effectiveness, my ability to be empathic, accepting and congruent. I wonder about my capacity to love. Mostly I carry on in faith, hope and trust. It is the discipline at this point that keeps me going and the fact that I am part of a bigger framework and that one prayer, or one therapy meeting, is part of an ongoing relationship.

The ancient songs of the psalms, covering a vast range of emotions and feelings, are said or sung together as part of the daily discipline of Christian communities. In the workshop we read Psalm 42 together which begins: 'As the deer longs for the water brooks, So longs my soul for you, O God' (Psalm 42).

My approach to therapy is about a way of being, a value system in the same way that prayer is part of my whole life, involving all of me. It is a sensory experience, a bodily experience. I cannot pray or be in a therapeutic relationship in a disembodied way. All of me is in relationship.

Prayer and therapy are also both about openness and attentiveness. They can involve trance-like states or altered states of consciousness. I am totally focused on what is happening in the present moment within a particular relationship. I am open and present to myself and to the other. I am aware of 'subtle contact' (Cameron, 2003: 103).

Prayer is also part of my therapy in that I often pray as I meet someone for therapy: pray for God to be with us. I sometimes clear the room and ask for blessing on the space, sprinkling water in the corners. If I feel stuck or useless I sometimes pray in desperation to have an open heart and trust the process. In a 2002 survey of therapists Peter Gubi discovered that fifty-nine per cent of respondents had used prayer covertly with clients and twelve per cent overtly with Christian clients and only twenty-four per cent had discussed it in supervision (West, 2004: 51). This highlights how hard it can be to talk about prayer and yet how it is part of the practice of many therapists.

I sometimes pray about my client in an intercessory way, asking God to hold them. I am struck by Brian Thorne's spiritual discipline in his prayerful 'holding' of his clients with 'double vision'.

> There is about this discipline the cultivation of a profound faith both in the nature of personhood and in the transformational power of relationships. In pursuit of such faith the therapist will hold clients in his or her thoughts each day for a brief period—probably no more than a couple of minutes for each client—and the focus will be on both their current state of being and on their essential natures. This 'in-seeing' of clients will hold the visual image of their actual appearance in mind as a reference point while the eyes of faith will dwell on their inner beauty and resourcefulness, their sacredness and infinite worth. At the same time the therapist, while yearning for the client's good, imposes no direction upon the process and no pre-determined goal. This is a silent and passionate accompaniment without expectation but with absolute commitment to the client's evolution towards the fullness of being. (Thorne, 2002: 42)

What I long for in therapy and prayer reflects my values. I long for peace, justice, growth, healing, transformation, the fulfilment of the potential of the individual through relationship to the other and the world. Dare I come out and live my life according to these values? Can I bear the tension between my longing and the reality of the world I live in?

Words from a recent poetry reading with the Uruguayan writer Eduardo Galeano have stayed with me describing this tension as being like walking towards an ever receeding horizon. He asks: Para que sirve la Utopia? Para eso sirve: para caminar. The point of the horizon and of utopia is to keep me walking. My longing in both my prayer and my therapy work is what keeps me going even though it often seems like groping and stumbling in the dark with a very dim, occasional awareness of the light of God's presence.

> *The conviction I have that the shape and texture and inner experience of need and longing for a meaningful universe with some pattern and shape in the face of evil, suffering and the apparent randomness of experience, for me is so intensely felt everyday that to*

imagine there not being a God to answer that call is the height of absurdity. That was the energy that brought me to your workshop and that felt met by you and the other participants.

The area I am working on in my own faith at the moment about wanting this big flash of light to direct me when I know there are a million small messages every day that offer me insights and direction that I'm simply ignoring and 'putting out of the door'.

I think my abiding thought then and since has been 'what is not prayer?' Prayer for me is about intention, waiting, yearning, reflection, connection, relationship.

I came away somehow deeply comforted, connected, stimulated, singing. This is what I want on a regular basis—nourishment for my heart and mind, connection deeply with others and a sense of understanding and confirmation about me and others in the world—'We are all connected—there is hope'.

REFERENCES

Backhouse, H (ed) (1985) *The Cloud of Unknowing.* London: Hodder & Stoughton.

Brazier, D (1993) The necessary condition is love: Going beyond self in the person-centred approach. In D Brazier (ed), *Beyond Carl Rogers* (pp. 72–91). London: Constable.

Buber, M (1970) *I and Thou* (Trans. W Kaufman). Edinburgh: T&T Clarke (original work published 1923).

Cameron, R (2003) Psychological contact. In J Tolan, *Skills in Person-Centred Counselling and Psychotherapy* (pp. 87–109). London: Sage.

Church House (2002) *Common Worship Services and Prayers for the Church of England: Daily Prayer.* London: Church House Publishing.

Gubi, P (2002) Practice behind closed doors: challenging the taboo of prayer in mainstream counselling culture. *Journal of Critical Psychology, Counselling and Psychotherapy, 2* (2), 97–104.

Julian of Norwich (1966) *Revelations of Divine Love* (Trans. C Wolters). London: Penguin (original work written c. 1393).

Lewis, T, Amini, F and Lannon, R (2000) *A General Theory of Love.* New York: Random House.

Rogers, CR (1957) The necessary and sufficient conditions of therapeutic personality change. In *Journal of Consulting Psychology, 21* (2), 95–103.

Rogers, CR (1961) *On Becoming a Person.* Boston: Houghton Mifflin.

Schmid, PF (2001a) Acknowledgement: the art of responding. Dialogical and ethical perspectives on the challenge of unconditional relationships in therapy and beyond. In J Bozarth and P Wilkins (eds) *Rogers' Therapeutic Conditions: Evolution, theory and practice. Vol 3: Unconditional positive regard* (pp. 49–64). Ross-on-Wye: PCCS Books.

Schmid, PF (2001b) Comprehension: The art of not knowing. Dialogical and ethical perspectives on empathy as dialogue in personal and person-centred relationships. In S Haugh and T Merry (eds) *Rogers' Therapeutic Conditions: Evolution, theory and practice. Vol 2: Empathy* (pp. 53–71). Ross-on-Wye: PCCS Books.

Sufi Inayat Khan (1923) *Gayan.* London: Sufi Publishing Company Ltd.

Thorne, B (1994) Developing a spiritual discipline. In D Mearns *Developing Person-Centred Counselling* (pp. 44–47). London: Sage.

Thorne, B (2002) *The Mystical Power of Person-Centred Therapy. Hope beyond despair.* London: Whurr Publishers.

West, W (2004) *Spiritual Issues in Therapy. Relating experience to practice.* Houndmills: Palgrave Macmillan.

Yalom, I (2001) *The Gift of Therapy: Reflections on being a therapist.* London: Piatkus.

CHAPTER 15

HONOURING SPIRITUALITY IN THERAPY: A DIALOGUE

CHRIS JENKINS AND WILLIAM WEST

CJ: I want to begin by saying why I am doing research in the interface between counselling and spirituality.

I began this research thinking it was about improving things for clients—and I hope it still is. I had heard many stories of people who had either come to me or to other colleagues for counselling because they had been elsewhere and their spirituality/ faith had been excluded. They felt as if they had to split themselves. Hence the title of my research 'A Voice Denied'. I'm focusing on what happens when the counsellor excludes the spirituality of the client because of the counsellor's issues. (Counter-transferentially, if you want to speak that language, Lannert (1991).)

I said above that that was why I started the research—to help give clients a voice. However as the research has proceeded I've had to acknowledge just how much of this is about me. About what it means to be a counsellor who is also a priest, to work in the space between the mainstreams of both therapy and spirituality/religion (not that I am equating them!).

The people who have participated in the research so far do tell dreadful stories of having their spirituality excluded and pathologized—and these stories do need to be heard. And I am challenged—of course—with regard to my own practice, especially when I am working with people whose own spiritual tradition is close to mine but also sharply different. I recognize for myself at least some of the religious and spiritual positions I find it hard to accept in my own work, the things that push buttons for me and that I find it much easier to work with atheists than with fundamentalist Christians!

This reminds me of what Jonathan Wyatt said in his excellent article (Wyatt, 2002), that when he is aware of where he stands—wherever that is—with regard to spirituality he is able to allow his clients to be where they are.

Which has brought us back to the counsellors' experience—so, over to William.

WW: I want to begin with reflecting on the values that underpin our work as counsellors. I don't think we talk about this often enough. If we insist that we are client-centred in our work then that is a value. For instance, it is different to working with the client in the context of their family. Our view of the good life—see Gordon Lynch's latest book (Lynch, 2002) which explores this—will impact in many ways on the way we work with our clients. Sollod (1978) has written about how much Freud owes to Judaism, and Rogers' early Protestant upbringing is apparently evident in the person-centred approach, likewise Gerry Egan's Catholic and Jesuit upbringing can be found in his skilled helper model (Egan, 1990). In fact much of Western therapy is implicitly Christian in values.

There is also a strong pseudo-scientific professionalized evidence-based approach, which scorns that which cannot be measured and which seems trapped in a nineteenth-century modernist anti-religious viewpoint, endlessly re-fighting the science versus religion debate. And of course many in the churches are caught up in this.

The point I am seeking to make is that our values are not neutral and have a profound impact on our work and the more we understand and are explicit about this the better. And we communicate, consciously or unconsciously, verbally or non-verbally, these values. Many counsellors and therapists are in my experience 'un-worked-out' around spiritually and especially religion. Many counsellors are over forty-five and many had a religious upbringing explicitly or implicitly and the damage done at times leads people to reject the whole idea of religion. Consequently there is a powerful anti-religious streak among counsellors (not anti-spirituality) that reflects this unresolved and largely unprocessed hurt.

CJ: A good example of what William is talking about is the story of the lady I call 'Third time lucky'. What is particularly interesting in her experience was that she was hit from both sides, the 'religious' and the 'anti-religious'.

When the sexual abuse of children began to be publicized and spoken of more openly she became aware of her own experience of abuse. She thought, 'They're getting help so why don't I?' She went to a local counselling agency and asked to see a Christian counsellor. However, in the first session, after hearing only a little of her story, the counsellor asked her if she had ever been involved with the occult. When she said that she had once messed with a ouija board as a child the counsellor said: 'I thought so, you've let Satan in' and proceeded to try and 'deliver' her. The client sat there thinking 'I don't know what this is about but it has nothing to do with me.' Not surprisingly the relationship quickly broke down. However when, a while later, she tried again, this time with a therapy group, she encountered a facilitator whose own anger against religion spilled out. 'If I talked about God, or the Church she'd say, "They're the problem, can't you see!"' She found herself more and more censoring what she wanted to say or turning to the other facilitator who listened to her. Again she felt that the anger of the first facilitator had nothing to do with her and was an obstacle to her getting what she needed. Thankfully in the end she found a space, with some inner-child therapists, to do the work she had always needed to do—a space where, as she put it, 'I was allowed to be me.'

In my research so far such a tale is far from unusual. Particularly extreme are the stories of people who have been in mental health settings and found that, because the therapists pathologized their religious/spiritual experience, the only way to 'get out' was to split themselves and not speak about these issues. As one new patient was told by members of a therapy group, after speaking about his faith, 'Don't talk about that stuff here, they'll never let you out.' The research sponsored by the Mental Health Foundation, *Taken Seriously* (Nicholls, 2002) also echoes these experiences. (See also Macmin & Foskett, 2004.)

One more example is of a young woman really struggling to keep going for whom meditation was 'a calm place amidst all the chaos'. Her therapist, who had already told her she was an atheist, forbade her to meditate and would not listen to her dismay at this. As she said to me, this caused damage that she feels she is only now recovering from.

Clients put up with this kind of treatment, when they do, because in other ways the therapy is being helpful or because they accept the therapist's role as 'doctor' to their passive 'patient'. David Rennie's research on client deference (Rennie, 1994) highlights the ways in which clients 'go along' with therapist behaviour, even though they disagree with what is being said or done. This rings true to the experience of a number of my interviewees.

What can the profession do about this?

WW: First of all, the profession can wake up to the research findings (discussed in West, 2000) that having an active religious or spiritual life is associated with health and well-being. Secondly, to consider the evidence of the value of working with the client's spirituality as explored in Richards and Bergin's excellent book, *A Spiritual Strategy for Counselling and Psychotherapy* (1997). Thirdly, to be honest about their own countertransference issues. Many therapists, especially of my generation who grew up in the 1950s and 1960s, were damaged by a very Victorian and remote version of Christianity that pervaded our culture and did not 'spare the rod'. (Incidentally I find it hard to accept that some Christian schools in Britain still want to retain corporal punishment. Is this Christian? Can you imagine Jesus beating a child?) So therapists need to connect with the healthy aspects of religion and spirituality today. To be humble enough to learn about it and in the process drop their own prejudices and, who knows, maybe reclaim their own spirituality in the process. Even if a particular therapist remains an atheist or agnostic they could still value and respect (a pretty basic requirement in a therapist!) spirituality in the life of their clients.

In conclusion, there is a self-development need and an education and training need so that therapists can truly be present to their clients' spiritual natures. This need extends to supervisors who need to be willing to value spiritual interventions as used by their supervisees. I am not suggesting that all spiritual and spiritual interventions are healthy—as therapist and supervisors we need to use our therapeutic common sense. A blanket rejection of religion and spirituality is no longer tenable and clearly a sign of prejudice. If the profession accepts this then there are some profound changes, especially in training and in therapeutic practice, that will follow.

There will remain some difficult and tense areas, for instance around the use of prayer (again, well discussed in the Richards and Bergin book), but the solution, I suspect, is for us to live with this tension rather than ignore it or pretend it does not exist. As David Hay's research shows we are more spiritual in Britain than we might think. There is an enduring interest in spirituality that is perhaps less focused on traditional religion but no less powerful nonetheless. It is this group, largely untouched now by organized religion that often finds its way into the counselling room. But then what reception does this spirituality get?

CJ: Sometimes when I have discussed these issues with therapeutic colleagues the response I have had has been along the lines of, 'We're not qualified as spiritual directors; we can't work with those issues.' But, in fact, that is not what our clients require of us. They need us to be good counsellors—as long as 'counsellor' is understood in a generous sense. They need us to listen carefully, to explore, not to assume, to hold uncertainty, to be open to what comes. If we have some knowledge of different spiritual and religious traditions that can be helpful—as long as we don't assume that our clients use words like 'sin' or 'hope' necessarily in the same way we do.

To give a concrete example from an interview I did two days ago. The client had a recurring image of a 'new house'. The house was full of light. At first the client thought this was about her desire to move from where she was living, indeed she did move. However, as the work went on, she realized that the meaning was deeper: this light represented spiritual awareness and awakening. Her counsellor explored this with her, looked at what such a process would mean for her, and supported her. When, in fact, she chose to follow the path of her own religious tradition this too was explored, gently, empathically, without the counsellor imposing her views. Indeed the former client still has no real idea what the counsellor's spiritual views were, just a hunch of 'Buddhist leanings', but she did know she was supported in the spiritual exploration she needed to make. The client finally recognized that it was time to move on and seek more 'specialist' accompaniment within her religious tradition but the counselling work, begun in order to look at family issues, had become a true spiritual journey that she continues to draw on.

Of course some colleagues still feel uncomfortable with this kind of work—as counsellors might with many kinds of work. It seems to me that the ethical response is to recognize our own limitations (BACP, 2001), not claim that our comfort zone is the proper sphere of counselling and anything beyond is not! At the same time there is a question around whether 'counselling' represents an adequate name/frame for work of this spiritual depth?

WW: You have hit a particular nail on the head there. I have been struggling with this boundary between counselling and spiritual direction/friendship for some time now. There is an extra boundary issue for me, which is that some of my most intuitive/advanced empathic responses come from what I believe is a spiritual source. (It is not necessary to view it this way, but it is how I make sense of it.) My dilemma is: when I am working spiritually–intuitively with my clients, accompanying them on their spiritual unfolding process, can I legitimately say, 'This is counselling as other counsellors and our various professional bodies would agree'? You might say, 'so what?', but of course my research has shown how problematic this issue of spirituality is for counsellors and that the conflict is played out in supervision or, worst of all, hidden away. Peter Gubi (2004) has discovered in his researches into counselling and prayer how much prayer goes on in and around counselling and how little of it gets explored in supervision. I want to bring spirituality out of the closet for counsellors! Also, to debate these issues out in the open. It does not make me popular, nor is it a good career move but at least we can talk about it now.

Hopefully clients are now getting a better experience, your researches notwithstanding, and maybe counsellors are that bit better informed, but we still have a long way to go. I think it is part of a wider debate about just what the limits of counselling are, who sets them and why, and how some of the growth points happen at edges or boundaries where courageous counsellors creatively draw on what is available to them to help their clients move on. Of course there are ethical issues here, especially around the openness and intermingling that can be part of altered spiritual states, but we should operate from ethical common sense and not a rigid adherence to working in a particular way.

CJ: I think this raises a very specific area for me, William. It seems we are talking about almost two levels of 'working with the spiritual'. One is working with the spirituality of the client, as described above. This, it seems to me, should be within the ability and necessary openness of all counsellors. At the least, if someone can't work with this kind of material because of their own blocks, they should seek to refer rather than exclude the client's spirituality.

What you are now talking about seems to me to be more around the counsellor using their 'spiritual' awareness. Presumably something seen as beyond simply advanced empathy or heightened reactive countertransference (to use those two psycho-languages). This area is clearly more problematic as many (most?) counsellors don't experience (allow/recognize?) such spiritual insight. Indeed, I know counsellors who would say, 'It's you who need the therapist if you are experiencing such things!' At the same time the growing literature around transpersonal therapy (e.g. Boorstein, 1996; Cortwright, 1997) or on the transpersonal facet of the therapeutic relationship (Clarkson 1995, 2002) puts these issues firmly on the agenda. As does the comparative study of Frank and Frank (1993), which suggests we need to see the whole therapeutic enterprise against a much richer backcloth.

I hope this dialogue will at least raise questions for colleagues around their own experience, practice, training and supervision.

REFERENCES

BACP (2001) *Ethical Framework for Good Practice in Counselling and Psychotherapy*. Rugby: British Assocation for Counselling and Psychotherapy.
Boorstein, S (1996) *Transpersonal Psychotherapy.* New York: SUNY Press.
Clarkson, P (1995) *The Therapeutic Relationship*. London: Whurr.

Clarkson, P (2002) *The Transpersonal Relationship in Counselling and Psychotherapy*. London: Whurr.

Cortwright, B (1997) *Psychotherapy and Spirit: Theory and practice in transpersonal psychotherapy.* New York: SUNY Press.

Egan, G (1990) *The Skilled Helper*. Pacific Grove CA: Brooks/Cole.

Frank, J & Frank, J (1993) *Persuasion and Healing: A comparative study of psychotherapy.* Baltimore: Johns Hopkins.

Gubi, P (2004) Practice behind closed doors: Challenging the taboo of prayer in mainstream counselling culture. *Journal of Critical Psychology, Counselling and Psychotherapy, 2* (2), 97–104.

Lannert, J (1991) Resistance and countertransference issues with spiritual and religious clients. *Journal of Humanistic Psychology, 41* (4), 68–76.

Lynch, G (2002) *Pastoral Care and Counselling*. London: Sage.

Macmin, L & Foskett, J (2004) Don't be afraid to tell. *Mental Health, Religion & Culture, 7* (1), 23–40.

Nicholls, V (2002) *Taken Seriously: The Somerset spirituality project.* London: Mental Health Foundation.

Rennie, D (1994) Clients' deference in psychotherapy. *Journal of Counselling Psychology, 41* (4), 427–37.

Richards, D and Bergin, A (1997) *A Spiritual Strategy for Counseling and Psychotherapy.* Washington: APA.

Sollod, R (1978) Carl Rogers and the origins of client-centered therapy. *Professional Psychology 9*, 93–104.

West, W (2000) *Psychotherapy and Spirituality*. London: Sage.

West, W (2002) Being present to our clients' spirituality. *Journal of Critical Psychology, Counselling and Psychotherapy, 2* (2), 86–93.

Wyatt, J (2002) 'Confronting the almighty God'? A study of how psychodynamic counsellors respond to clients' expressions of religious faith. *Counselling and Psychotherapy Research, 2* (3), 177–84.

CHAPTER 16

PRH: TOWARDS A DEEPER EXPERIENCE OF WHO I AM

ROBINA SCOTT

INTRODUCTION TO PRH AND TO THE WORKSHOP

The only prerequisite for following the PRH method of personal and spiritual growth is to have a desire to grow.

PRH (Personnalité et Relations Humaines/Personality and Human Relations) is a school of training and research in human growth. It offers an auto-pedagogical or self-teaching method of self-discovery, with emphasis on the discovery, emergence and consolidation of our essential essence which is where we experience, amongst other unique truths, our relationship with the Transcendent. It is based on observation of one's own lived reality through sensations in the body.

Influenced by Carl Rogers, the Frenchman, André Rochais—the initiator of this method—began to offer courses in the 1970s which he had developed through his structured and meticulous observation of the human person. It is now an international organization with educators on all continents who also offer transformative personal accompaniment using the PRH helping relationship method.

In the workshop we allowed ourselves to connect with our inner reality through simple questions designed to lead to a deeper understanding of our truth.

WHAT DO WE MEAN BY GROWTH IN PRH?

In PRH we make the following assumptions:

Growth *is not*:

- Discovering, developing and ordering ideas, principles, theories at a cerebral level, although this can, up to a point, be satisfying for those with a propensity for this.
- Feeling better, gaining more of an emotional equilibrium.
- Being able to achieve more in our physical environment.

Growth, however, *is*:

- The *experience* of the emergence and consolidation of our deep qualities. We gain a greater sense of who we are internally in order to manifest it externally in our activities and in our relationships. Our identity grows, as does our relational ability.
- Progressively discovering what our essential activity is in this life—that which feels unique to us and for which we were made and which gives us deep fulfilment. Our purpose grows.
- Discovering and being consistent with the deep bonds that connect us to others with the same path and purpose. Our community dimension and our commitment to humanity grow.
- Opening up and committing to what Transcends us—what is in us, yet greater than us. Finding ever greater substance, nourishment, meaning and direction through this deepening *relationship*. For some of us this is the pinnacle and priority of growth.

HOW CAN WE GROW?

In PRH terms this is not a question of thinking, feeling or doing (all of which are vital and have their place) but rather about being.

PRH starts from the Rogerian premise that in our depths all is positive. And that this constitutes our intact, essential self, our *being* which is a concrete reality that we can access in ourselves and which is an autonomous centre.

Our *being* is made up of the four dimensions outlined above—our identity, our essential course of action, our deep bonds and our openness to a Transcendency.

In order to connect with our *being*, we need to listen to those sensations in the body with a psychological content which, as we decipher them, take us to ever deeper levels of ourselves.

In PRH we prioritize the being but the other *pivotal centres* have to be taken into account at all times:

The 'I': the pivotal centre where the intellect, freedom—the capacity to make choices—and the will function. Its role is to govern persons in the growth of their being and toward an overall harmony. It is also an autonomous centre. It is the 'thinking' centre.

The sensibility: the pivotal centre which acts as a conductor of messages that come from the other centres within us as well as externally. It is the 'feeling' centre.

The body: our biological and physiological reality with its own laws and which inevitably conditions our whole person.

We are also immersed in our *human* and *material environments* and these heavily influence us. As with our internal centres we can learn to take them into account but not be led by them.

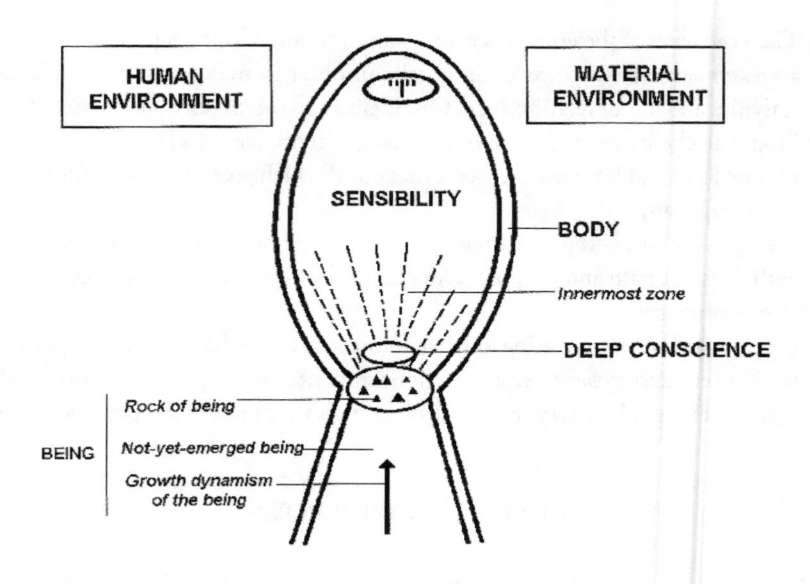

Diagram of the Pivotal Centres of the Person—the PRH model[1]

This is the role of *the deep conscience*—a 'locus' of synthesis in our very depths close to the *being*. It serves as an internal reference to help us discern what is in line with the inner *being* and its fulfilment. It also functions in assessing the actions taken in relation to the overall growth of the person in any given situation (i.e. in relation to their inner world and to their external environment). It is the place of the person in the process of growth and guides us to true autonomy.

Learning to discern from our deep conscience is a fundamental part of the PRH methodical tool and leads to growth and a deeper sense of self far more fulfilling than the satisfactions gained at other levels as mentioned earlier—the development and re-education of the 'I' and the healing and harmonious functioning of the sensibility and the body.

THE STRUCTURE OF THE WORKSHOP

Each one of us has the answers within us if we stop to listen to the richness of our bodily sensations.

An important part of the PRH method is learning how to do this by staying fully in the present, tracking and expressing the content of each sensation without attenuating it.

1. Reprinted with permission from PRH International. In *Persons and Their Growth: The anthropological and psychological foundations of PRH education,* (1997: 53).

The questions used in the workshop were as follows and participants were invited, having spent time endeavouring to access their inner sensations, to write down their responses to each:

WHY HAVE I COME TO THIS WORKSHOP?

As we allow ourselves to go beyond our immediate cerebral reaction—what we already know or can categorize—we connect with the deepest physical sensation, which has psychological content within the body and is awakened by this question, before noting down its content. We might surprise ourselves. We certainly give ourselves the opportunity to connect with our deepest motivations and with the energy of intention.

WHAT DO I ASPIRE TO LIVE IN MY LIFE THAT WILL BRING ME THE DEEPEST SPIRITUAL FULFILMENT?

This question gives us the opportunity to connect with our deep aspirations and potentialities and express them simply in full sentences. It allows us to connect with the essential nature of our humanity in its search for meaning.

WHAT DIFFICULTIES DO I FACE IN TRYING TO LIVE THIS ASPIRATION?

After connecting with our deep truth in the last question we are here awakened to all that is present at other levels (cerebrally, emotionally or physically) that is not functioning harmoniously and causes a lack of unity, a distorted perspective, suffering and/or most importantly, impedes our spiritual growth—*what we may be* (Ferrucci, 1983).

WHAT SENSATION AM I LEFT WITH AT THE END?

We return to our present sensation, checking in with our reality of the here and now, so as to avoid ascending into our cerebral functioning. In this way we stay close to our desire for the truth and allow it to manifest through our experiencing in the present.

DO I FEEL INVITED FROM DEEP WITHIN TO DO ANYTHING? IF SO, WHAT?

Mobilized by the life dynamism (Rogers' 'actualizing tendency'), the nature of our being is to want to 'be' more. We would be wise, therefore, if we want to collaborate in our growth, to listen to its impulses, its intuitions and invitations and to take them seriously. This question recognizes the nature of the never-ending process of growth and by listening to what it opens us up to we give ourselves the opportunity to progress.

Each response to the above questions will be unique to each participant, reflecting their individuality. When individuals share their responses to the questions, many of these responses will awaken resonance in others as a part of their own truths not yet, or not yet fully, in their awareness when they answered the question. The effect after the sharing is very often a sensation of individual uniqueness and universality at the same time, which reinforces Rogers' observation that what is most personal is most universal.

We aim to live the sharing of our discoveries from our *being*. Reading out what we have discovered we can connect with our aspiration to exist with our truth, connect with our self-dignity and solidity. When we listen we try to do so from unconditional acceptance and positive regard and wonder at the life within the other. This provides the nurturing environment so badly needed to stimulate authenticity (Rogers' 'congruence') and self-expression, which are a fundamental part of the phenomenon of growth and human actualization.

Sometimes the questions awaken suffering that either comes from past wounds in our sensibility, from not having our needs met or from not being able to be fully ourselves. What pains us most is not to be able to live what we are fully capable of and for what we have been created—namely, in the spiritual dimension which is being explored here, a fully life-enhancing relationship with our deepest self and with what transcends us.

The PRH vision and approach is to provide an environment with optimum conditions for growth and to facilitate an auto-pedagogical process so that persons can awaken to the life that wants to emerge and manifest in them. Its simple method, lived both individually in a one-to-one growth relationship and/or in group environments, is effective in deciphering experience so as to increase awareness, self-fulfilment and a richer and more substantial incarnation of our spiritual selves.

It does indeed lead me to a definable deeper experience of who I am, both in my uniqueness and in my universality, in my humanness and in my transcendental dimension.

REFERENCES

Ferrucci, P (1983) *What We May Be: Techniques for psychological and spiritual growth through psychosynthesis.* New York: Jeremy P Tarcher.

PRH International (1997) *Persons and Their Growth: The anthropological and psychological foundations of PRH education.* Poitiers: Personnalité et Relations Humaines-International.

PRH International (2004) *When Life Breaks Through: The dynamics of PRH helping relationships.* Poitiers: Personnalité et Relations Humaines-International.

Rogers, CR (1980) *A Way of Being.* Boston: Houghton and Mifflin.

SECTION 5

CHRISTIAN PERSPECTIVES

INTRODUCTION

In this section three therapists address issues of spirituality in relation to counselling from an explicitly Christian perspective. The fourth writer, Jan van Blarikom, considers the influence on the theory of the client-centred approach of Carl Rogers' Protestant upbringing in the Chicago suburb of Oak Park.

Stephen Hitchcock sees counselling as a spiritual activity, and offers three biblically based metaphors for the role of the therapist. Each of these roughly corresponds with one of the three conditions which, according to Carl Rogers, it is necessary for the counsellor to embody if the client is to be helped. There is first the metaphor of *seeing*: the seeing of God, the way in which Jesus saw Peter at the moment of his betrayal. This kind of seeing can be effectively related to the notion of unconditional positive *regard*. But also the eye can be experienced both as a window and as a mirror. Through eye contact client and therapist open windows into the other's soul, and also each sees something of themself mirrored in the other. Then it has often been suggested that in our secular society counsellors play something of the role that priests played in more traditional societies. Hitchcock suggests that there are counselling analogies for the priestly roles of 'drawing alongside', pastoral care, intercession, reconciliation, absolution and spiritual exploration. Above all, the role of the priest can be seen as involving empathic understanding. Finally, in the notion of the 'living temple' Hitchcock finds a metaphor for 'congruence', a being true to oneself as an embodiment of God himself.

Jeff Leonardi reflects on the theme of self-giving love in Christianity, and explores the relationship between this principle and the concepts of the person-centred approach, especially those of the 'core conditions' and of self-actualization. Self-actualization is a notion which has drawn criticism from a number of Christian writers, to whom it suggests egotism, and part of Leonardi's aim is to show that Christian self-giving and therapeutic self-actualization are not incompatible. He suggests that the conditions of empathy, genuineness and unconditional positive regard all have in them something of the quality of self-giving: empathy requires us to move into the *other* person's world; genuineness often involves a vulnerable openness to the client; unconditional positive regard sets aside one's own conditional regard for the sake of a spiritual and unconditional regard for the client. Leonardi discusses the difficulty that an emphasis on 'self-actualization' sees the individual in isolation from their social relationships, and along with other recent commentators holds that—at least in his theoretical writings—Rogers did not fully acknowledge the human person as intrinsically relational. Nevertheless, in practice the person-centred approach places a strong emphasis on the relational nature of human beings, and Leonardi sees the cultivation of the 'core conditions' as essentially a cultivation of self-giving. He ends with the question of whether self-giving can be taken further in the direction of the self-emptying characteristic of the mystical traditions. He notes the danger in this of colluding with those who see the self in an entirely negative way, and suggests that the person-centred approach has much to offer, in the form of a healthy complement to the self-emptying that is commended in the traditions of Buddhism and mystical Christianity.

Peter Schmid presents a theological analysis of human being as essentially relational, and suggests a possible grounding of person-centred theory in the Trinitarian Christian tradition. In this tradition the image of God and the image of the human being are inherently connected: hence, Schmid argues, we can move from the Christian image of God as a community of three persons to an understanding of human life as essentially communal, or conversely we can move from the communal nature of human life to an understanding of God as a community of persons. On the other hand, as well as the *multum* aspect of human beings and of God there is also the unity—the *unum*—to be taken into account. This has been the dominant view in Western Christianity, but in Schmid's view it needs to be balanced with the *multum* view which is more characteristic of Eastern Christianity. Schmid sees social and political consequences as following from his view: because God is seen as a community of equal persons, so should human beings be seen as a community of equal persons. Along with several other contributors to this volume, Schmid emphasizes the importance of love, but his Trinitarian perspective allows him a distinctive emphasis: that love means not just to love each other but to love together. To bring in a third person creates something new, a *group*. For Schmid, 'God is group', a thesis which he links to the group emphasis found in some strands of the person-centred approach.

Schmid sees a range of implications for person-centred theory, which needs to be re-thought from the point of view of the essentially communal nature of human life. This will involve moving from the current 'I–Thou' emphasis to a 'We' emphasis, and there needs to be a corresponding move in practice from individual psychotherapy to 'sociotherapy'. However Schmid emphasizes at the end of his paper that this movement should not go too far in the other direction: in the person-centred approach individuality is as important as the group. We need the *unum* as well as the *multum*.

Finally, **Jan van Blarikom** considers the positive impact for his later work of Rogers' family life in the thriving and rapidly-expanding Protestant community of Oak Park, Chicago, in the early years of the twentieth century. The Oak Park community was peopled mainly by Protestant families from New England, who in turn were descended from Puritan emigrants who had crossed to America from England to escape religious persecution in the early seventeenth century. These emigrants, steeped in the theology of Luther and Calvin, believed themselves to be a 'chosen people', a 'covenanted community' whose aim was to establish a visible kingdom of God in their new world. Oak Park, in van Blarikom's view, was an example of such a 'covenanted community' and there Rogers became immersed in a reformed Christianity, characterized not only by sobriety and high ideals, but also by an emphasis on realness, presence and visibility. Van Blarikom demonstrates that Rogers was open throughout his life to texts redolent with the language of Christianity, such as Kierkegaard's *Concluding Unscientific Postscript,* which emphasize the notion of the person constantly in the process of becoming more deeply who he or she is. Rogers' later mysticism is seen as unrelated to his early Protestantism, but the Reformed Christian character of his upbringing is regarded as bearing fruit in his call to us to be present to ourselves and to each other, to be who we really are before God.

CHAPTER 17

SELF-GIVING AND SELF-ACTUALIZING: CHRISTIANITY AND THE PERSON-CENTRED APPROACH

JEFF LEONARDI

Self-giving is a central theme in Christianity. Jesus' teaching includes many exhortations to care for others, even at cost to oneself, e.g. the parable of the Good Samaritan (Luke 10: 25–37).[1] In this story a man is robbed and injured and left lying in the road, and while others avoid getting involved, one man—the Samaritan—comes to his aid, dressing his wounds and transporting him to an inn to recover, promising to pay for the expenses he incurs. The 'cost' of this help is therefore multiple: time, energy, money, delay, risk, etc. Jesus taught that love for one's 'neighbour' was one of the most important duties, and explained who one's 'neighbour' might be by telling this story.

Throughout his ministry Jesus cares for those who seek his help, even when inconvenient for him. He takes the care for others a step further by proclaiming that the greatest love a person can show is at the ultimate cost of the giving and loss of life itself. ('No one has greater love than this, to lay down one's life for one's friends', John 15: 13; and 'unless a grain of wheat ... dies, it remains alone; but if it dies it bears much fruit', John 12: 24.) His eventual arrest, trial, torture and execution by crucifixion are then explained in these terms: 'When I am lifted up from the earth I will draw all people to myself' (John 12: 32). Jesus gives his life for the sake of others. He does not want to die, but offers his life in the belief that this will fulfil God's purposes: 'My Father, if it is possible, let this cup pass from me; yet not what I want but what you want' (Matthew 29: 39). Before his death he encourages his followers to practise a life of self-renunciation and service to others: 'If any want to become my followers, let them deny themselves and take up their cross and follow me. For those who want to save their life will lose it, and those who lose their life for my sake will find it' (Matthew 16: 24–25).

The history of Christianity is full of examples of those who have tried to follow these principles, often at great cost to themselves and their families, and even to martyrdom or other early death. This 'glorious' history of Christian discipleship evokes complex responses for many today, not least because there are other, less wholesome associations which can be evoked by the practice of self-renunciation, in the history of Christianity and many other faiths. Asceticism and the 'mortification of the flesh' can seem more expressive of self-hatred than of the love of God and care for others, and

1. All quotations from the Bible are taken from the New Revised Standard Version.

extremes of this kind are frequent in the history of religions and into the present day. But this should not obscure the genuine article, i.e. people in whom the love of God and for others is expressed in ways which are both beneficial to those served and at cost to the 'servant'. The experience of being a recipient of such love is frequently decisive in bringing a person to make a faith commitment of their own, in response to the example of the other.

Self-giving love, then, is a defining principle of the Christian faith. The purpose of this paper is to explore the relationship, if any, between this principle and those of the person-centred approach, as expressed in the core conditions and in the concept of self-actualization.

I believe that at first sight the concepts of self-giving and self-actualizing will be deemed incompatible when viewed from these two viewpoints. From the person-centred perspective many, if not most representatives have a passing or real acquaintance with Christian faith and the concept of self-giving, but may have reservations about institutional religion and may associate self-giving with the tendency towards self-denial in Christian and other faiths, which at its extreme, as we have suggested, can amount to self-hatred, or at least a denigration of aspects of self which might be valued from the person-centred perspective.[2]

From some Christian viewpoints, self-actualization is a troubling concept which suggests egotism or even ego-worship (e.g. Paul Vitz, 1994). It is the aim of this paper to explore these tensions and see whether they are necessary philosophical disagreements, or whether the debate arises from a mistaken understanding of the two concepts concerned. Further, I shall suggest that an enhanced understanding of the concept of Christian self-giving has a deep but largely unrecognized relationship with the core conditions of the person-centred approach, while the person-centred understanding of the authentic self, and of nourishment for this self, has much to offer Christianity in its search for life-enhancing and not life-destructive directions. Finally I will want to argue that self-giving is an essential characteristic of the actualized(ing)[3] person.

A CHRISTIAN CRITIQUE

Paul Vitz's book *Psychology as Religion—The cult of self worship* (Vitz, 1994) epitomizes the capacity of the Christian 'Right'[4] to castigate humanistic psychology in general—and the person-centred approach in particular—for eliminating external constraints on human wilfulness by abandoning God and elevating humanity to the place of deity:

---

2. This touches upon a wider debate between Christianity and the person-centred approach which I address in my current doctoral thesis.

3. In the person-centred approach, the conception of self-actualization denotes a continuing process and not a final outcome or destination or state.

4. Other Christian writers who are troubled by humanistic doctrines include Roger Hurding (1985) and Robert C. Roberts (1993).

hence the accusation of 'Self Worship' or 'Selfism' as Vitz describes it (p. xii): 'psychology has become a religion: a secular cult of the self'. In this polemical work Vitz ascribes many of the hedonistic and licentious behaviours of the Western world to the effects of these dangerous tendencies in psychology: '... the theoretical principles of Rogers, unrestrained by sensible limits and moral responsibility, allow or even encourage the patient to slide into a self-gratifying, narcissistic world' (Vitz, 1994: 33).

Vitz displays a fairly superficial awareness of the theory and practice of the person-centred approach based on Rogers' early writings, and considers only two of the core conditions, empathy and acceptance (which he interestingly claims to be impossible, except for God), without the essential counterbalance of genuineness. His argument is succinctly expressed in Chapter 10, 'A Christian Critique':

> The search for and glorification of the self is at direct cross purposes with the Christian injunction to lose the self. Certainly Jesus Christ neither lived nor advocated a 'self-actualized' life. For the Christian the self is the problem ... [which requires] an awareness of sin, especially the sin of pride; correcting this condition requires the practice of such unself-actualized states as contrition and penitence, humility, obedience and trust in God. (Ibid.: 126)

'For the Christian the self is the problem.' This is a very troubling statement for any number of reasons, but chief among them is the lack of any distinction between self and ego. If we were to substitute 'person' for 'self' in this statement the absurdity of it would be clear: 'For the Christian the *person* is the problem'! There are different senses of the word 'self' ranging from egotistical to personal identity. Vitz does not separate these meanings and much of his argument relies on a conflation of ego with self. His claim that Jesus did not live or teach a self-actualized life is highly questionable, as we shall see, and there is no a priori reason why self-actualizing persons should not embody the Christian qualities Vitz espouses, such as penitence and humility, etc. There is a case to be answered, however, as to whether the essential Christian value of self-giving is compatible with self-actualization.

The first thing to note is that in Rogers' writings, self-actualizing is defined as a *tendency* not as an intention or desire, i.e. that it is not that the person *wishes* to actualize his/her self, but that the developmental principle is 'in-built' as it were. Secondly, the self to be actualized is identified with the inner or true *organismic* self, not the ego-self derived from introjected values.

The evolution of the concept of the self-actualizing or *fully functioning* person owes a great deal to Abraham Maslow. In his *Motivation and Personality* (1970, Ch. 11) he lists the following characteristics of the self-actualized person:

1. efficient perception of reality and comfortableness with it;
2. acceptance of self and others;
3. spontaneity;
4. an autonomous self independent of culture;

5. creativity;
6. having 'peak' experiences, i.e. oceanic or mystic experiences;
7. democratic, egalitarian, and humanitarian character structure and values.

It is item 7 on this list which might most readily suggest a connection with self-giving, but I would think that the tenor of the whole list is more evocative of powerful and creative personhood than of self-giving as such. In an earlier work, *Towards a Psychology of Being* (1968) Maslow writes:

> The achievement of self-actualization ... paradoxically makes *more* possible the transcendence of self, or of self-consciousness and of selfishness. (Original emphasis)

Rogers describes the process of self-actualizing persons in many places in his writings, and there is some evolution of the concept as we shall see. In *On Becoming a Person* (Rogers, 1967) he ascribes great importance to the achievement of accurate organismic awareness by the individual, through therapy: 'the person comes to *be*—in awareness—what he *is*—in experience. He is, in other words, a complete and fully functioning human organism' (ibid.: 104). Rogers suggests that rather than fear what we are 'inside', the truth is that we need only fear what we are *not* truly, that is what our inappropriate conditioning may have made us, but that when we are liberated or restored to this fully functioning state we are

> an organism which is beautifully and constructively realistic ... able to achieve ... a balanced, realistic, self-enhancing, other-enhancing behavior ... he is to be trusted, his behaviour is constructive.[5] (Ibid.: 105)

In a section which resonates with Maslow's statement that the self-actualizing person transcends self-consciousness, Rogers writes (p. 147) 'This is a being in the moment, with little self-conscious awareness ... The self *is*, subjectively, in the existential moment. It is not something one [the subject] perceives' (original emphasis).

At this stage in his writings Rogers' main focus is on the individual's functioning: implications for relationships with others emerge as a consequence or by-product of the individual's growth: 'he moves towards a friendly openness to what is going on within him ... as he moves towards acceptance of the "is-ness" of himself, he accepts others in the same listening, understanding way'.

At another point in the same work Rogers explores the nature of creativity as one of the characteristics of the self-actualizing person, and suggests (p. 351) that creative activity which issues from a person who is well integrated is likely to be socially

5. The debate about the inherent goodness versus 'sinfulness' or aggressivity of the human being is mostly beyond the scope of this paper, but again will be addressed in my wider research.

constructive. More than this, Rogers makes a powerful claim for the social nature of the person who develops therapeutically:

> [A]s the individual becomes more open to, more aware of, all aspects of his experience, he is increasingly likely to act in a manner we would term socialized. If he can be aware of his hostile impulses, but also of his desire for friendship and acceptance; aware of the expectations of his culture, but equally aware of his own purposes; aware of his selfish desires, but also aware of his tender and sensitive concern for another; than he behaves in a manner which is harmonious, integrated, constructive. The more he is open to his experience, the more his behavior makes it evident that the nature of the human species tends in the direction of constructively social living. (Rogers, 1980: 353)

Rogers makes these claims on the basis of his extensive therapeutic experience with individuals and groups, and nothing in his later experience made him change any of them.

In 'The Emerging Person', Chapter 12 of his 1978 work *Carl Rogers On Personal Power*, he writes that those who most embody person-centred qualities,

> ... are caring persons. They have a deep desire to be of help to others and to society ... The help so freely given by emerging persons is a gentle, subtle, nonmoralistic caring ... These persons are seeking new forms of community, of closeness, of intimacy, of shared purpose (Rogers, 1978: 270).

In the concluding section of this chapter Rogers lists in summary some of the directions of the culture espoused by such persons. I have selected those most relevant to the theme of self-giving:

> Towards a non-defensive openness in all interpersonal relationships—within the family, the working task force, the system of leadership.
> Towards the prizing of individuals for what they *are*, regardless of sex, race, status or material possessions.
> Towards a more even distribution of material goods.
> Towards a more genuine and caring concern for those who need help. (Ibid.: 282, original emphasis)

These concepts were reiterated by Rogers in the final chapter of what turned out to be his last book, *A Way of Being* (Rogers, 1980), in a chapter entitled 'The World of Tomorrow and the Person of Tomorrow' (see especially pp. 350–2).

Earlier in this important and concluding work of Rogers' life, he articulates more fully then ever his understanding of the formative tendency in the universe and the self-actualizing tendency in human beings. He claims that the self-actualizing process he has encouraged in himself and others all his working life is actually consistent with the *evolutionary needs and direction* of the human race:

> It seems that the human organism has been moving toward the more complete development of awareness. It is at this level that new forms are invented, perhaps even new directions for the human species ... With greater self-awareness a more informed choice is possible; a choice more free from introjects, a *conscious* choice that is even more in tune with the evolutionary flow. (Ibid.: 127, original emphasis)

In the following section Rogers introduces and describes his experience of the quality of *presence*, where, in a different and heightened state of awareness, achieved or rather entered upon by the disciplined application of the core conditions of the person-centred approach, he finds he can trust his very *being* to respond in creative and helpful ways to another person, ways that prove to be deeply healing for the other:

> ... it seems that my inner spirit has reached out and touched the inner spirit of the other. Our relationship transcends itself and becomes a part of something larger. Profound growth and healing and energy are present. (Ibid: 129)

This experience, or some degree of it, is known to very many person-centred practitioners. Reading Rogers' statement, one can readily compare the quality of awareness and relationship he describes with the Gospel accounts of Jesus' encounters with others, encounters where Jesus displayed a deep insight into the personality and needs of another person and related to them in ways which were richly liberating and healing for them (see for example the healing of the paralytic man, Luke 5: 17–26; the 'sinful' woman, Luke 7: 36–50; the woman at the well, John 4: 5–30; the accused woman brought before him, John 8: 1–11).

It may be thought fanciful by some to compare Rogers' description of the therapeutic power of his 'presence' or being with that of Jesus. The latter was a miracle-working 'Son of God' and Rogers a very human and unassuming professional psychologist and educator. At either extreme we might take exception to the comparison: as a minor 'blasphemy' to the Christian, or an unhelpful 'spiritualizing' of psychotherapy to the secular professional. But at the level of self-giving, and of the simple description of experience, there are undeniable comparisons.

Rogers did become much more acceptant of parapsychological and spiritual dimensions of his work in later years, a development that troubled those with a more secular and/or rationalistic outlook. But the terms and language with which he seems to have entertained these more mystical dimensions of human experience bear all the hallmarks of his life-long commitment to the tentative and honest exploration of all aspects of his experience. It was his personal experience, within himself, with individuals and in groups, in literature and after the death of his wife that almost compelled him to acknowledge a widening of his comprehension of what being human entails and signifies.[6] In *On Personal Power* (Rogers, 1978: 130) he writes: 'Our experiences in

6. See for example Rogers, 1980: 82, 'Opening Up to New Ideas'; also pp. 88, 90–92, 99–101.

therapy and in groups, it is clear, involve the transcendent, the indescribable, the spiritual. I am compelled to believe that I, like many others, have underestimated the importance of this mystical, spiritual dimension.'

But we do not have to extend consideration to these spiritual dimensions of the person-centred approach in order to establish the credibility of self-giving as a perspective on it. In its very nature and process, the person-centred approach has deeply self-giving attributes. The core conditions of empathy, genuineness and unconditional positive regard all partake of this quality. This will be readily seen with regard to empathy: the willingness to enter into another person's world and perceive it as they do on an ongoing basis, sharing in all aspects of their felt experience as well as meanings and difficulties, to 'feel as another feels' without losing the 'as if' quality. This means to share in a person's pain and suffering, anger or outrage, hurts and vulnerabilities, as well as joys and satisfactions. The fact that empathy is quite different from sympathy or identification does not diminish the real cost, emotionally and psychologically of the preparedness to share another's life experience. It is, in this way, the antidote to the fear of isolation and outcasting expressed in Shylock's protest in Shakespeare's *Merchant of Venice*: 'if you prick me do I not bleed?' Empathy crosses the 'safety zone' between people and establishes a 'bridgehead' on the other's shore, a position of outreach and vulnerability.

While empathy has a more obvious reaching-out or self-giving character, genuineness, or congruence, seems more to do with self-expression than self-giving, at first sight. However congruence, like all the core conditions, is to do with the qualities in the therapist which will foster positive development in the client, and in that fundamental sense is 'for' the benefit of the other; it is not gratuitous or self-indulgent self-expression, but alert and disciplined communication of the self to the other. It can (and should) be spontaneous at times, but it is a spontaneity which arises from long practice and exploration, not least in person-centred groups and supervision.

It is also potentially costly and vulnerable 'to be oneself', honestly and openly with another, especially in the context of the person-centred disavowal of the framework of professional expertise and power which are contained in many other helping approaches. The very willingness not to offer 'answers' or diagnoses and prescriptions may in itself expose the person-centred practitioner to anger and criticism from the client or group members. Brian Thorne (1991) explores the language of 'not-knowing', or helplessness and powerlessness, with the client:

> it was difficult to be powerless and perplexed ... the way forward proved to lie in and through stuckness and silence ... to trust [them] as points of departure. ... a patient acceptance of not knowing what to do, an admission of a lack of clarity and expertise, a willingness to rest in a relationship with love but without expectation ... we had both accepted our joint incapacity to find a way forward but were content to wait. (Thorne, 1991: 98, 99)

This vulnerability to not-knowing, this capacity to hold and bear the tensions of a struggle without evasion or easy get-outs, characterize the best aspects of the person-centred approach and simultaneously show its openness to anger and criticism—by the client or by the professional audience. We live in times which require competence and accountability of its professionals, and the person-centred practitioner may evince incompetence or unhelpfulness by her very honesty to the truth of the situation and relationship.

The third member of the trinity of core conditions is acceptance or unconditional positive regard. We have already referred to Paul Vitz's assertion that this extent of acceptance is humanly impossible and the province of God alone. Interestingly I also concluded (Leonardi, 1998: 1) that unconditional positive regard is *impossible*, humanly speaking, because it requires a 'super-human' level of perfection.[7] My conclusion differs from Vitz's—not surprisingly!—that unconditionality must therefore embrace an inescapably *spiritual* dimension. In theological language this is meant to signify that to embody unconditional positive regard the therapist must 'partake of' the divine unconditionality (Leonardi, op. cit.). Not all person-centred therapists hold a theocratic spiritual faith and so this description, of the inescapable spirituality of unconditional positive regard, would not be conducive to them. But however we describe it, unconditional positive regard is a high aspiration. At the human level it is fostered by growing in self-acceptance, usually through the agency of significant others who can offer such depth of acceptance. Its provision for others requires regular developmental work in professional supervision. Every aspect of a therapeutic relationship which regresses to a form of conditionality requires working through with a supervisor or other colleague until the roots of judgement have been untangled and unconditionality restored.

Such discipline and engagement is inherently self-giving. It requires self-honesty, openness and humility on the part of the therapist and it resides in a deep respect for the right of the other to be themselves, with their own values and self-determination, even or especially when these conflict with those of the therapist. The latter is continually prepared to give their own personal standpoint second place, honouring and affirming the selfhood of the client. The value of such self-giving is clear for individuals in therapy, and is even clearer when operating in groups, especially where conflict resolution is an issue, as we shall see.

In summary then, the core conditions of the person-centred approach can be seen to be a discipline and vehicle for self-giving on the part of the practitioner, a 'Path to Holiness' (Thorne, 1998). Two examples for me particularly express the devotion of a therapist to their client's well-being in a way which connotes self-giving. One is Brian Thorne's account (Thorne, 1991, Chapter 6: 'Beyond the Core Conditions') of his work over time with a client. Both in the work itself and also then in exposing his account to public and professional scrutiny, Brian reveals a willingness to give of himself at cost. In the relationship with the client he shows a fidelity and trust in the person-centred process and relationship with his client which is clearly hugely demanding, risky and costly, as well as immeasurably rewarding for both participants (Thorne 1991:

7. Cf. Mearns and Thorne, *Person-Centred Counselling in Action,* 1988: 60 '... it should be noted that in its literal sense it is impossible to achieve "unconditional" positive regard. Every counsellor is limited and fallible and therefore must have some "personal limits" ... the counsellor cannot therefore guarantee unconditionality.'

24): 'It took me to the extreme edge of vulnerability and to the fullest limits of mutual trust'. In publishing the account of the therapy he risked accusations of unprofessional behaviour (acting as 'a beacon for my critics' (Thorne, 1991: 23) and went ahead out of a sense that this relationship, which had so exceeded what are normally accepted as safe boundaries, had huge implications for a true understanding of the spiritual dimension of therapy. It amounted to (Thorne 1998: 84) 'a perilous leap of faith undertaken on behalf of a human soul who had shown me such trust that I could be nothing less for her than my total self'. This is the language of vision, of courage, and of self-giving.

The second example is detailed in Dave Mearns and Brian Thorne's *Person-Centred Therapy Today* (2000). It is the account of Dave Mearns' work with 'Bobby': 'an erstwhile Glasgow gangster' (pp. 57ff). Bobby had learned to protect himself from hurt by frightening others and by hurting them first. Entering upon therapy with such a client was to risk becoming his victim also, especially if he got too close. As he got to know this complex and dangerous person, Dave came to *love* and accept him (p. 59). At one point Bobby tells Dave (p. 68): 'I think I will be able to tell you if I have to kill you'. The word 'kill' is a metaphor for how Bobby would keep someone from getting too close, but is still a scary word and Dave acknowledges that he can be scared at times with Bobby, but that in a strange way he is not afraid of him, as he gets to know him (p. 68). In a decisive episode in the therapy Bobby says that he has lost the use of his previous strategies for controlling the pain of his life, but has no 'new' substitutes (p. 72):

> *Dave: So you might have* no *ways to handle this ... no control at all ...*
> *Bobby: That scares the shit out of me ... no control at all.*
> *Dave: It scares me a bit too ...*

To be with a man who knows his capacity for violence and to hear him confess his helplessness to 'control' himself in this new state could well 'scare (one) a bit'! In the final excerpt Bobby has come through to a genuine facing of his state, one which now offers hope—after first acknowledging just how 'scary' that previous meeting was (p. 72):

> *Bobby: ... I wasn't far from being the 'villain' either—when I realized I didn't have any control.*
> *Dave: Maybe that's why we were both scared.*
> *Bobby: Well maybe I'm just going to have to survive without* having *'control'. Maybe I'm going to have to cry and be desperate like everyone else. I've kept myself away from pain since I was a kid—maybe I just have to face it.*

This may not sound like a triumphant therapeutic resolution, but in the context of Bobby's journey it really is a turning point—in the face of fear and pain—towards an authentic living which does not use threat and violence to avoid one's own pain. It will be clear from these brief extracts, I believe, the depth and intimacy with which Dave encounters Bobby, and the risk and emotional cost of doing so. Again, there seems no other description more appropriate for such an endeavour than self-giving love.

RELATIONALITY AND EXPERIENCE IN GROUPS

In Carl Rogers' body of work a great deal of emphasis is placed on the individual getting in touch with their real selves, 'self-actualizing', and it could be thought that the beneficial consequences for the individual's relationships are just that, a consequence or outcome, but not the core business of therapy. This has been a real cause for concern about the theory of the person-centred approach that to an extent the emphasis is too much on the individual in isolation from and to the neglect of his or her social relationships (see for example Peter Schmid, 2002; 2004). This can be true of the description of desirable therapeutic outcomes however much the content of therapy may include extensive exploration of an individual's relationships. In a vital sense therapy is intrinsically relational, person-centred therapy certainly, but there is an extent to which Carl's writings do not treat the person as *fundamentally and intrinsically relational.* Rogers acknowledges the individualistic, as opposed to communalistic, basis for the person-centred approach in *A Way of Being* (Rogers 1980: 183–4): 'The philosophy of democracy, of human rights, the right of self-determination ... Out of such a soil has developed ... the person-centered approach.' It may be that there is a more balanced presentation of the person-centred approach possible, one which begins from the *person-in-relationship* and not just the person in isolation, one which acknowledges that human beings are fundamentally relational as well as inner- and self-directed.

Whatever the theory, it will be clear from all that has gone before that the person-centred approach is deeply relational—and self-giving—in its expression in one-to-one therapy. In Rogers' own writings, this will be seen even more clearly when we attend to the person-centred group experience. He devoted a whole book to this theme (Rogers 1970), and wrote about it in many places, but it is again in his last work, *A Way of Being* that he distils his long experience of groups in a chapter entitled 'Building Person-Centered Communities'. Here he writes of the compelling regularity with which groups facilitated by the person-centred approach grow uniquely but in similar ways towards community:

> In these communities most of the members feel both a keen sense of their own power and a sense of close and respectful union with all of the other members. The ongoing process includes increasingly open interpersonal communication, a growing sense of unity, and a collective harmonious psyche, almost spiritual in nature. (Rogers, 1980: 182)

If we attend to the methodology with which Rogers encourages or facilitates such groups with others, we find a thoroughgoing consistency with his approach to individuals: he will apply the core conditions, he will seek to *be* there with openness and transparency, he will seek to honour every voice, every person—especially the more timid or unpopular, he will seek to be receptive to the angry, discordant or critical voices. These are deeply caring, giving ways of relating, and are experienced as such. As the climate penetrates the awareness of the participants so each one feels affirmed and able to be themselves, often more fully than before, and the group grows in belonging and acceptance and moves towards celebrating uniqueness and diversity in unity (pp. 187, 190). There is an almost extravagant willingness to cater for each person's contribution and feelings about group decision making, even at cost of holding back the 'majority' from proceeding as they wish, until everyone has been heard and understood—and then the decision may simply emerge 'of itself' because of the foregoing:

> ... does the wish of *everyone* have to be considered? And the silent answer of the group is that, yes, every person is of worth, every person's views and feelings have a right to be considered[8] ... The process seems slow, and participants complain about 'the time we are wasting'. But the larger wisdom of the group recognizes the value of the process, since it is continually knitting together a community in which every soft voice, every subtle feeling has its respected place. (Ibid.: 195 ff, original emphasis)

Here Rogers is referring to the group as having a consciousness of its own—'the larger wisdom of the group'—which is derived from all the individuals which belong to it but which transcends their separateness and takes on a 'transpersonal' life of its own. Again he is compelled by his experience to acknowledge a reality which he would otherwise or hitherto have hesitated to countenance (p. 196):

> ... its transcendence, or spirituality. These are words that in earlier years, I would never have used. But the overarching wisdom of the group, the presence of an almost telepathic communication, the sense of the existence of 'something greater', seems to call for these terms. (Ibid.: 196)

These tendencies of groups of separate individuals to achieve impressive harmony and understanding through respecting the uniqueness and diversity of each member have of course important implications for resolving inter- and intra-communal tensions, and Rogers' later years were dedicated significantly to operating in such contexts: Northern Ireland, the former Soviet Union under communism, South Africa under apartheid, etc., as well as more localized racial and ethnic conflicts. He wrote about these experiments at length, and some of them are available on film. Because it is 'local' to the UK I will refer to just one in particular, a group of mixed Catholics and Protestants which met for a total of just 16 hours in Belfast (and was filmed and made available as *The Steel Shutter*). Rogers wrote about the experience in *Carl Rogers on Personal Power*, in a chapter entitled 'Resolving Intercultural Tensions: A beginning':

---

8. There is a striking comparison here with the Christian theology of the infinite value and worth of each person in God's eyes, and therefore for every other person too. In this way the person-centred approach can be seen as the application of what the Christian means by the love of God.

> During the sessions the hatreds, the suspicions, the mistrusts of the two feuding groups were very evident, sometimes in covert form, gradually becoming more open in their expression. The individuals were speaking not only for themselves but for generations of resentment and prejudice ... yet during that incredibly short period these centuries-old hatreds were not only softened but in some instances deeply changed. (Rogers 1977: 131)

'Blessed are the peacemakers.' The communication and understanding which developed in this group—and it is representative of many other such person-centred 'experiments'—was real at the time and extended beyond the life of the group in continuing relationships and reconciliation work. Some of the breakthroughs which took place in the group were not included in the film for fear of the potentially hostile reactions of the wider, warring communities.

Such facilitation is demanding and risky for all concerned. It is therefore self-giving. There are of course no guarantees of 'success', either at the time or afterwards in terms of the outworking of what has been achieved. Such groups are only small initiatives in a large theatre, but the world is enhanced by each one of them that takes place. Camp David with President Carter, and the Truth and Justice Commission in South Africa, can be seen to emerge at least in part from Carl's dedicated efforts in these ways.

SUMMARY

I think we have seen that there is a great deal which can be justly described as 'self-giving' in the Christian sense, in the activities with individuals and groups by practitioners of the person-centred approach. The person-centred core conditions offer a relationship which requires dedication, discipline, honesty, openness, alertness, compassion and vulnerability on the part of its exponents, and is therefore inherently self-giving. The outcomes for those for whom this focus is provided, whether individuals or groups, in therapy or in organisations, institutions or communities, are likely to be in the direction of greater self-awareness, greater creativity and resourcefulness, healing and integration, and towards enhanced interpersonal relationships and community living. Such individuals are likely to wish to engage in relationships and activities which also are aimed at helping others to grow and thrive in similar ways, i.e. to this extent, lives of service, or self-giving to others. This is not to say that those who work in, or benefit from, the person-centred approach are inevitably or necessarily 'good citizens' or 'do-gooders' as a result! But there is a deep connectedness between the kind of experiences we have described and a grateful, celebratory and creative response. If we become more deeply aware of what it is to be human, then that is likely to mean more loving. As Carl put it (Rogers, 1980: p. 204), there is a movement towards recognizing that 'the strongest force in our universe is not overriding power, but love'. St Paul said something similar: 'So faith, hope and love abide, these three; but the greatest of these is love' (1 Corinthians 13: 13).

CONCLUSION

There is a further step to be taken in this discussion, and that is to ask the question whether, in the self-actualizing process as we understand it, there is for some at least, an instinct to go beyond a more or less 'comfortable' version of self-giving and move towards some kind of self-transcendence. All the mystical traditions have this as the ultimate goal of human development. In Buddhism the self which is attached to desire can be transcended and enlightenment achieved. In Christianity, as we have seen, there is a life to be found which can only become available through the 'death'—literal or metaphorical—of all that binds the human being to a narrow existence. St Paul's letter to the Philippians contains a hymn of praise to Jesus (Philippians 2: 6ff):

> who, though he was in the form of God,
> did not regard equality with God
> as something to be exploited,
> but emptied himself,
> taking the form of a slave,
> being born in human likeness.
> And being found in human form,
> he humbled himself
> and became obedient to the point of death—
> even death on a cross.

This *kenosis* or 'self-emptying' is paralleled in Christianity by the mystical *apophatic* or 'not-knowing' tradition and finds expression in the fourteenth-century treatise *The Cloud of Unknowing.* These have a profound respect for the limitations of words, especially about God, and a corresponding reliance upon the experiential journey, in life and prayer, but without any connotations of self-denial in the form of self-hatred. They cohere with the celebratory view of the relationship between Creator and creature, God and human being, found in Julian of Norwich.

There is a saying: *In order to give oneself, one must first have a self to give.* The danger of Christian self-emptying is of colluding with a distorted and punitive attitude and undernourished approach to the self. The person-centred approach can offer much to the Christian churches about the proper understanding of what it is to be human, marvellous and well-made, and of proper nourishment for the self. It may surprise the person-centred exponent to hear that her vocation has much in common with mystical Christianity or Buddhism, among others. We have referred earlier to the person-centred practitioner's willingness to undergo the vulnerability or helplessness of 'not knowing' with an individual (p. 210 this chapter, and Thorne, 1991: 98–9), or, we might now add, with a group. Peter Schmid has developed this perspective recently in a paper entitled 'Knowledge or Acknowledgement? Psychotherapy as the "art of not-knowing"' (Schmid, 2002).

The committed practitioner of the person-centred approach has taken on a most demanding dedication to the disciplined pursuit of self-knowledge and the kind of self-emptying which enables another to be truly received and responded to in depth, without reliance on a superior 'expertise' or knowledge base and with access to a wider 'energy' or consciousness. Is it fanciful to consider whether in fact the wholehearted practice of such person-centredness might also be a path towards self-transcendence in a truly spiritual sense? There is much in common to these apparently diverse 'paths to holiness'.

To really conclude, some Sanskrit words:

Gate Gate Paragate Parasamgate Bodhi Svaha
(Gone, Gone, Gone beyond, Gone altogether beyond, Awakening, All Hail!)

REFERENCES

Hurding, RF (1986) *Roots and Shoots.* London: Hodder & Stoughton.

Leonardi, J (1998) Christianity and the person-centred approach. Paper presented to the 7th International Forum for the Person-Centered Approach, Johannesburg.

Maslow, A (1968) *Towards a Psychology of Being* (2nd ed). New York: Van Nostrand Reinhold.

Maslow, A (1970) *Motivation and Personality* (2nd ed). New York: Harper.

Mearns, D & Thorne B (1988) *Person-Centred Counselling in Action.* London: Sage.

Mearns, D & Thorne, B (2000) *Person-Centred Therapy Today.* London: Sage.

Roberts, RC (1993) *Taking the Word to Heart.* Grand Rapids, MI: Eerdmans.

Rogers, CR (1967) *On Becoming a Person.* London: Constable.

Rogers, CR (1970) *Carl Rogers on Encounter Groups.* New York: Harper & Row.

Rogers, CR (1978) *Carl Rogers on Personal Power.* London: Constable.

Rogers, CR (1980) *A Way of Being.* Boston: Houghton Mifflin.

Schmid, PF (2002) Knowledge or acknowledgement? Psychotherapy as 'the art of not-knowing'. *Person-Centered & Experiential Psychotherapies, 1* (1&2), 56–70

Schmid, PF (2004) Back to the client: A phenomenological approach to the process of understanding and diagnosis, *Person-Centred & Experiential Psychotherapies, 3* (1), 36–51.

Thorne, B (1991) *Person-Centred Counselling: Therapeutic and spiritual dimensions.* London: Whurr.

Thorne, B (1998) *Person-Centred Counselling and Christian Spirituality.* London: Whurr.

Vitz, PC (1994) *Psychology as Religion—The cult of self worship* (2nd ed). Grand Rapids, MI: Eerdmans.

CHAPTER 18

SEEING EYES, ROYAL PRIESTS AND LIVING TEMPLES: A BIBLICAL PERSPECTIVE ON THE ROLE OF THE COUNSELLOR

STEPHEN HITCHCOCK

In this paper I will be concentrating on three biblical metaphors for the role of the therapist, which I have called 'Seeing Eyes', 'Royal Priests' and 'Living Temples'. It is an overtly Christian and personal reflection. I see counselling as a spiritual activity, and I believe that something transpersonal is going on in the counselling room. I also believe that the Bible has much to teach me about the way of relating to clients. Whether or not you share my Christian faith, or believe in the authority of the Bible, and whether or not you work as a therapist, I hope that you will find it interesting to reflect on your own role, and how it relates to what we will be looking at here.

SEEING EYES

For those who are counsellors or psychotherapists, I wonder how we see our clients. As cases to be worked with? Problems to be solved? Pathetic figures to be pitied? People with worse problems than our own, and therefore making us feel better? Or do we see them as possessing a divine quality?

If ever I'm struggling with acceptance, or I am aware of a lurking prejudice, I try and remind myself that the person in front of me is made in God's image. 'So God created man in his own image, in the image of God he created him; male and female he created them' (Genesis 1: 27).[1] So if they are created by God, to be like God, who am I to reject them, or to judge them? How can I not accept them unconditionally? If I am rejecting the person in front of me, it feels to me that I am rejecting God himself. Conversely, if I am accepting and respecting the person before me, I am honouring God himself.

Empathy can be described as entering the client's frame of reference, setting aside our own, and trying to see our clients as they see themselves. But I would suggest that we might also see them as the Bible says that God sees them, that is to say, as being 'very good'. 'God saw all that he had made, and it was very good' (Genesis 1: 31).

God prized his creation. But that might not be how people see themselves. I believe that we are talking here about *God's* 'frame of reference', how *He* sees them, totally accepting them as they are at this moment in time, but at the same time seeing their true potential—what they are capable of becoming.

1. Bible references are from the New International Version (1988) International Bible Society.

Can we do both: empathizing with our clients' view of themselves, whilst also being true to the way God sees them? Maybe if we seek to see others as made in the likeness of God, the three 'frames of reference'—theirs, ours and God's—will start to coincide.

I'd like us to look at an example of the way that Jesus saw people. Following the arrest of Jesus, the disciple Peter was observing events from a distance. He had already denied twice that he was associated with Jesus, and was now being accused for a third time.

> Peter replied, 'Man, I don't know what you're talking about!' Just as he was speaking, the cock crowed. The Lord turned and looked straight at Peter. Then Peter remembered the word the Lord had spoken to him: 'Before the cock crows today, you will disown me three times.' And he went outside and wept bitterly. (Luke 22: 60–2)

Was that look of Jesus one of condemnation, do you think? Or of hurt betrayal? If so, that's what Peter might have well have expected, and felt he deserved. He was probably not prepared for a look of love, which I believe is the most likely, in the light of the way in which Jesus was later to reinstate Peter. And this was almost too much for Peter to bear. It demanded a radical re-adjustment to his self-concept. He had just disowned his best friend, his hero, the Son of God, and here he was being given a look of love! This was life-transforming for Peter, and I maintain that it can be life-changing for us and for our clients. The self-concept might well fight back, but if our look of acceptance persists, unconditionally, surely our clients have to make some adjustments?

Even if they don't, however, I believe that this story tells me something about unconditional acceptance, acceptance that is not conditional upon the changes that our clients may make. Carl Rogers spoke of the 'as if' quality of empathy (sensing our client's world 'as if' it were our own), but I wonder if we also need to cultivate the '*as is*' quality of unconditional positive regard—accepting our client 'as he or she is', at this moment in time, regardless of whatever changes they might subsequently make.

The expression 'unconditional positive regard' (Kirschenbaum and Henderson, 1989) tends to trip off the tongue and could be in danger of losing its meaning, especially when referred to as 'UPR'. Taken literally, unconditional positive regard has to do with a way of seeing, or of looking. In counselling skills training, we are taught at length about 'active listening', and the difference between hearing and really listening, but what about 'active seeing'—the difference between looking and really seeing?

The eye can be both a window and a mirror. It was Cicero, apparently, who wrote '*oculus animi index*' ('the eye is the index of the mind'), and we are perhaps familiar with the concept of the eyes as the 'windows of the soul'. In the therapeutic setting, giving eye contact helps to make us 'transparent', allowing our clients to see something of us. It lets them in, to some extent, and we risk making ourselves vulnerable. 'Your eye is the lamp of your body. When your eyes are good, your whole body also is full of light' (Luke 11: 34).

Clients often avoid eye contact with us, maybe because it makes them feel transparent and exposed to the light. Therefore I feel that we need to be careful how we look, ensuring that it is not with eyes that are penetrating, or threatening, or voyeuristic, but with eyes of compassion, of tenderness, and of love.

And what about the eyes as mirrors? Do our clients see something of themselves when they look into our eyes? Do we reflect something of our clients' true worth, of their inestimable value, of the love that God has for them?

> When this sad, hurt, self-punishing, angry and lovely young woman leaves me an hour later she gives me a wan smile. I tell myself that perhaps for a moment she has had a fleeting glimpse in the mirror of my eyes of her true countenance. (Thorne, 2003: 18)

> When we look attentively into the face of another person, we may end up seeing something of ourselves through their reaction to us. So in the attempt to see God, we see more clearly who we are: confused, easily distracted, often disappointed but constantly drawn on by the love of God. (Sinton, 2003: 65)

But what about those clients who make it difficult for us to see them at all? Who do not give us eye contact, who dare not take their eyes off the carpet and look up, whose lives are a mess, whose issues seem overwhelming for them (and maybe for us)? It's perhaps easy for us to see God in beauty, in creation, in happiness, in a smiling face. Can we still see God in ugliness, in pain, in brokenness?

At the Last Supper, Jesus took the bread and broke it, and said 'This is my body, given for you', and there are a number of stories in the Bible where it was in the very act of breaking bread that Jesus was recognized. One of his resurrection appearances is described by Luke: 'When he was at the table with them, he took bread, gave thanks, broke it and began to give it to them. Then their eyes were opened and they recognised him' (Luke 24: 30–1). So for me there is a powerful connection between brokenness and restoration. Dare we, I wonder, look intently into the faces of the 'broken', as we are invited, and in so doing recognize God? Whatever the state of our clients, our total acceptance, or unconditional positive regard, is, I believe, the 'royal road' to the consciousness of God's presence, around and within.

I'll end this section with a quote, not from the Bible, but from the musical version of Victor Hugo's *Les Misérables*: 'To love another person is to see the face of God' (Kretzmer, 1985).

ROYAL PRIESTS

> But you are a chosen people, a royal priesthood ... (1 Peter 2: 9)

The role of a counsellor is sometimes likened to that of a priest. Whereas the priest used to occupy a significant place in people's lives, as spiritual leader, personal friend and confidant, sadly they are now more often portrayed by the media as objects of derision or, worse, subjects of perversion. So what were the functions of the priest, some of which we might feel called to take on ourselves? I have identified seven, although I am sure there are many more.

DRAWING ALONGSIDE

—as an utterly trustworthy companion, a Paraclete or advocate, one who is prepared to listen intently.

> Rejoice with those who rejoice; mourn with those who mourn. (Romans 12: 15)

I believe that we can look to the example of Jesus here (who is referred to several times in the Bible as the 'Great High Priest'). Jesus got alongside people, spoke their language, 'walked the talk' as we might say nowadays. He called them his children, his brothers and sisters, his companions. He identified with their humanity, but in the process he showed people that they were more than human—that they also shared in his divine nature. He revealed to them their true worth.

PASTORAL CARE/SERVICE

> Whatever you did for one of the least of these brothers of mine, you did for me. (Matthew 25: 40)

In serving others, ministering to them and treating with honour and respect those who are made in his image, I believe that we are serving God himself.

If God is in others, he is no less in ourselves, so there is also a sense, I believe, in which we are not just serving God in others but also serving him *within* ourselves, honouring him, pleasing him, and allowing his power to flow freely through us, without being impeded or stifled or squandered by us.

INTERCESSION

I do pray for my clients, and my supervisees, before and after each session. In so doing, I believe that I am invoking a power that is greater than my own, submitting myself to a divine, transcendent process, enabling me to 'hold' my clients without them weighing me down. By leaving them in 'higher hands' I am not left to carry them alone.

> Such a resting [in the presence of God] is in no sense a giving up. It is rather a willingness to be open to forces greater than oneself and a readiness to cooperate with them ... a willing participant in the operation of grace. (Thorne, 1991: 16)

Intercession is also possible even when we do not know how or what to pray. You might well recognize the kind of feeling that can arise during, or after, a counselling session, when we feel a real heaviness, like an inner groaning, at the horror of what we're hearing, or the seeming hopelessness or stuckness of the situation. At such times I draw comfort from the words in Paul's letter to the Romans: 'We do not know what we ought to pray for, but the Spirit himself intercedes for us with groans that words cannot express' (Romans 8: 26).

RECONCILIATION

> All this is from God, who reconciled us to himself through Christ and gave us the ministry of reconciliation: that God was reconciling the world to himself in Christ, not counting men's sins against them. (2 Corinthians 5: 18–19)

I see part of our therapeutic role as helping our clients to be reconciled to their 'true selves', as they were created and intended, but from which they may have strayed far, perhaps through guilt or shame. The therapeutic process is sometimes described as the convergence of the self-concept with the 'organismic self'. However, if we perceive God not just as an external reality, but also as the God within—our internal, loving, life-giving power—then I wonder if reconciliation with our true self might go hand-in-hand with reconciliation with God.

ABSOLUTION

This is perhaps even more controversial! I can recall being dismayed to discover that only ordained priests could pronounce the Absolution—'Your sins are forgiven'—at the Eucharist, or service of Holy Communion. I questioned not so much their right to pronounce that we were forgiven, but rather that it was only they who were qualified for this joyful task of liberation. Dare we, I wonder, claim to have priestly authority to forgive sins?

In the words of the Lord's Prayer, we read, 'Forgive us our sins *as we* forgive those who sin against us' (Matthew 6: 12, italics mine). This implies that we can forgive sins, and that somehow as part of the same process our own sins are forgiven. I maintain that as counsellors we do have at least a part to play in the process of releasing others from their sense of guilt and shame; challenging the inappropriate guilt that they may have been carrying for so long, assuming that it belonged to them (perhaps brought on by experiences of abuse or a guilt-ridden upbringing); affirming them in their search for healing and wholeness.

However, for such release to be conceivable, and credible, we have first to offer it to ourselves, in other words to model self-acceptance and self-forgiveness.

SPIRITUAL EXPLORATION

It is important, I feel, for counsellors not to shy away from their spiritual responsibilities and opportunities, but to be willing to accompany clients on their spiritual quest. It may be that no one else is prepared to explore the spiritual landscape with them, without feeling threatened, or without seizing the opportunity to proselytize a captive audience and an already vulnerable client. 'If I recognise only naturalistic values, and explain everything in physical terms, I shall depreciate, hinder or even destroy the spiritual development of my patients' (Jung, 1969: 351).

> The therapeutic devaluation of Christianity is a major factor in the reluctance of black British citizens to pursue counselling. ... It is not unusual for people to come into spiritual paths while their psyches are still so much in need of earthly help. (Clarkson, 2003: 203–4)

VOCATION

In much the same way that priests are ordained and consecrated for their ministry, I consider counselling to be a vocation. We are called to a work that is usually lonely, often thankless and always unseen, and in which the outcomes are unsung. Yet it is an immense privilege. 'Commitment lies at the very heart of the vocation to ministerial priesthood and the religious life ... It is a call to live at depth, whatever the risks, whatever the cost' (Strange, 2004).

I wonder if that is how you see your work. Perhaps we need an awareness of our own 'vocation' in order to accompany our clients, as they, too, search for a sense of purpose and meaning, and follow their 'calling'.

LIVING TEMPLES

My description of ourselves as 'living temples' is taken from Paul's letter to the Corinthians: 'Don't you know that you yourselves are God's temple and that God's spirit lives in you? ... God's temple is sacred, and you are that temple' (1 Corinthians 3: 16).

I will now take a slight detour, to provide some background to the significance of the temple, and also to explain my excitement at the prospect that we can all be 'living temples'.

The temple in Jerusalem, at the time of Jesus, was a place of magnificence, signifying the glory and splendour of God; it represented the presence of God with his people, where they might meet with him; it was a place of prayer; of praise; of pilgrimage; a place of forgiveness, where sacrifices for sins would have been offered up; a place of holiness, with many cleansing rituals; but also, at that time, a place of exclusivity. The outer area was the Court of the Gentiles, accessible to all; next was the Court of Women, and then the Court of Men (Gentiles trying to enter these areas would have faced the death penalty); next came the Court of Priests; then the 'holy place' where a priest might be allowed to go once in his lifetime. Beyond the final curtain was the Holy of Holies, which could be entered only by the High Priest just once per year, on the Day of Atonement.

To the consternation of his disciples, Jesus was to prophesy the temple's destruction. 'I tell you the truth, not one stone here will be left on another; every one will be thrown down' (Matthew 24: 2). However, even more amazingly, Jesus was to take the place of the temple *himself*. After the 'cleansing of the temple' incident, when Jesus overturned the tables of the money-changers, we read:

> Then the Jews demanded of him, 'What miraculous sign can you show us to prove your authority to do all this?' Jesus answered them, 'Destroy this temple, and I will raise it again in three days.' The Jews replied, 'It has taken forty-six years to build this temple, and you are going to raise it in three days?' But the temple he had spoken of was his body. (John 3: 18–21)

Wherever Jesus went, there was God's presence, no longer confined to the temple in Jerusalem. He himself had become the living temple, perfect and holy, giving glory to God. His personality was such that people were drawn to him. Wherever he was, there too was healing, feeding, teaching, restoration, fulfilment. He gave himself as the sacrifice for sins. He provided access to God the Father, taking on the role of the Great High Priest. When he died on the cross, we read, 'At that moment the curtain of the temple was torn in two from top to bottom' (Matthew 27: 51). The barrier separating the people from God's presence (the Holy of Holies) was now superfluous to requirements. In other words, the Jerusalem temple had done its job, and we know from history that just forty years later it was to be destroyed.

But there's a further sequel to this story. 'Do you not know that your body is a temple of the Holy Spirit, who is in you, whom you have received from God?' (1 Corinthians 6: 19). 'For we are the temple of the living God' (2 Corinthians 6: 16). It would appear that the functions of the Jerusalem temple, that became subsumed in the person of Jesus, have been entrusted to *us*!

Philip Yancey, in *Disappointment with God*, writes:

> Three temples appear in the Bible, and together they illustrate a progression: God revealed himself first as Father, then as Son, and finally as Holy Spirit. The first temple was a magnificent structure built by Solomon and rebuilt by Herod. The second was the 'temple' of Jesus' body. And now a third temple has taken shape, fashioned out of individual human beings. The progression—Father, Son, Spirit—represents a profound advance in intimacy. At Sinai the people shrank from God, and begged Moses to approach him on their behalf. But in Jesus' day people could hold a conversation with the Son of God; they could touch him, and even hurt him. And after Pentecost the same flawed

> disciples who had fled from Jesus' trial became carriers of the Living God. In an act of delegation beyond fathom, Jesus turned over the kingdom of God to the likes of his disciples—and to us. (Yancey, 1988: 155–6)

'I tell you the truth, anyone who has faith in me will do what I have been doing. He will do even *greater* things than these, because I am going to the Father' (John 14: 12). Here Jesus seems to be suggesting that because the Spirit—the presence of God—is within us, even greater things can be achieved than by Jesus on his own.

It was St Augustine who said, 'Without God, we cannot. Without us, God will not.' In other words, God seems to choose to delegate responsibility to us, maybe even to depend on us, to carry out his work. 'He seems to do nothing of himself which he can possibly delegate to his creatures' (Yancey, 1988: 156).

Again, I find this extremely inspiring and challenging, but deeply humbling, to think of myself as a 'living temple', and to conceive of my work as a counsellor as fulfilling the function of a temple: a place where God resides, that is holy and consecrated, cleansed and uncluttered, and yet that is accessible and inclusive; where others might recognize God's presence; where God is honoured and glorified. Something bigger is going on, and I am allowed to be a part of that process.

As a child, Jesus went missing for a while and his parents were anxiously looking for him. '"Why were you searching for me?" [Jesus] asked. "Didn't you know I had to be in my Father's house?"' (*New International Version*) or '"about my Father's business?"' (*Authorised Version*, Luke 2: 49), as if the temple was the most natural place for Jesus to be found. Am I prepared to see myself as a temple where divine processes are at work? Where I am 'about my Father's business'?

'"It is written," he [Jesus] said to them, "My house will be a house of prayer [quoting from the prophecy of Isaiah 56: 7], but you have made it a den of robbers"' (Luke 19: 46). Is the 'temple of my body', as a therapist, more like a 'house of prayer' or a place of exploitation? Do I represent a place where others might find acceptance, and freedom from the burden of guilt?

Temples were traditionally built on the acropolis, literally 'above the city'. As a 'living temple', am I shrinking or ashamed, or evidently present? 'The God who made the world and everything in it is the Lord of heaven and earth and does not live in temples built by hands' (Acts 17: 24). His temples today are as diverse, dynamic, and alive as you and me.

To think that God is willing to take up residence in us, to make his home with us! What a risk he has taken, allowing himself to be confined or released, according to our free will. I have the freedom and the responsibility either to make myself available to the flow of his healing power, or to block or to squander it.

'We incarnate God in the world; what happens to us happens to him' (Yancey, 1988: 158). It was not just down to the Virgin Mary to provide a body for Jesus! I believe that we, too, can have that privilege. In *Infinitely Beloved*, one of Brian Thorne's 'clarion calls to the church' is: 'Lead us to the holy city within so that we may find Jesus enthroned in our own hearts' (Thorne, 2003: 87).

CONCLUSION

To sum up, then, these three metaphors help me to define both my identity as a Christian and my role as a person-centred counsellor. To me, they seem to correspond quite naturally to the core conditions of person-centred therapy:

'Seeing eyes', representing acceptance, literally unconditional positive *regard.*

'Royal priests' symbolizing empathic understanding.

'Living temples' that demonstrate congruence—being true not just to our thoughts, feelings and current experiencing, but to our divine calling as the incarnation, the embodiment, of God himself.

REFERENCES

Clarkson, P (2003) *The Therapeutic Relationship* (2nd ed). London: Whurr.
Jung, C (1969) *Collected Works.* London: Routledge & Kegan Paul.
Kirschenbaum, H & Henderson, V (1989) *The Carl Rogers Reader.* London: Constable.
Sinton, V (2003) *Encounter with God.* Milton Keynes: Scripture Union.[2]
Strange, R (2004) Why did you want to be a priest? In 'The Faith Page', *The Times,* 1May 2004.
Thorne, B (1991) *Person-Centred Counselling: Therapeutic and spiritual dimensions.* London: Whurr.
Thorne, B (2003) *Infinitely Beloved.* London: Darton, Longman & Todd.
Yancey, P (1988) *Disappointment with God.* Grand Rapids: Zondervan.

2. Text copyright Vera Sinton from *Encounter with God,* published by Scripture Union and used with permission.

CHAPTER 19

IN THE BEGINNING THERE IS COMMUNITY: IMPLICATIONS AND CHALLENGES OF THE BELIEF IN A TRIUNE GOD AND A PERSON-CENTRED APPROACH

PETER F. SCHMID

INTRODUCTION

Western tradition tends to give preference to the individual and their values of autonomy and authenticity. On the other hand, there have always been traditions favouring the community and esteeming the value of relationship and of thinking in societal categories. Throughout occidental history the unum–multum problem (the question about unity and plurality) has dominated the building of conceptions in theology, philosophy, psychology and psychotherapy. In theology, the conception of and belief in a triune God ('God as communication and community') brought the dialectics of unity and plurality, identity and difference, individuality and community to a hitherto unknown peak of human thinking and understanding of both God and their image, the human being. This leads to tremendous consequences for the understanding of the human being as a person, a being of innate plurality, for example, as man and woman. It is communication, originating in encounter and presence, which builds community.

The foundations of a person-centred comprehension of the human being originate in experiences people understood as experiences with God and initiated by God. In other words: at the early beginning of what we know today as the person-centred approach (PCA) there was spirituality and reflection upon it. I am convinced that we need to go to its roots to really understand what the PCA is about. Some major examples of these roots lie in the Judaeo–Christian tradition and its spiritual, theological and philosophical considerations of what it means to be a human being.

In this chapter I will explore the social and community-centred aspect of Christian belief and its consequences for a *person*-centred image of the human being, both in anthropological theory development and the practice of person-centred work, particularly in groups.[1]

1. Revised and abbreviated version of an invited lecture given at the International Conference 'The Spiritual Dimension in Therapy and Experiential Exploration', Norwich, 20th July 2004. See Schmid, 1998c, chapters 1 & 2, with detailed quotes and description. The full text will be published as a Norwich Centre Occasional Publication. For more references see this publication and Schmid, 1998c.

THE IMAGE OF GOD

WHY AND HOW TO ASK THE QUESTION ABOUT GOD

To talk about God, even to talk about the Trinity—what an enterprise, what presumption! Wouldn't it be much more adequate to fall silent or perhaps restrict oneself to meditation? Of what use should it be to ask such a question, particularly in the context of psychotherapy? Wouldn't it be wise to refrain and remain agnostic?

And yet—from a Christian perspective at the beginning of the question about the human being and their relationships with one another, there has to be the question about God, because the human being is understood to be the image of God. 'God created humankind in his image, in the image of God he created them' (Genesis 1: 26). This basic statement simply means: we cannot talk about God without talking about ourselves and vice versa. Hence we do so in order to understand ourselves better as human beings.

Thus, although it can always be only most temporary, most tentative, in a completely seeking manner to ask the question about God, it does make sense to bring this question forward. To be precise: we cannot think or talk 'about' God; any endeavour to do so can only be an attempt to 'ask and think towards' God, 'in the direction of' God; in other words: to seek God. Any conversation about God is more wrong than right or, it is only analogous, i.e. similar, illustrative, metaphoric, symbolic. We only can stutter and approach the question cautiously and carefully.

Yet—it is profoundly human to ask oneself and others, where we do come from? Where we are going to? What is our life about? Psychotherapists and counsellors are as familiar with this as theologians and pastoral workers. Existential questions are demanding, they need to be uttered, even if we know that we never will have final answers. 'Theo–logy' (i.e. literally 'speaking about God') does the same, only in a systematic, scientific way.

Furthermore, from a Jewish–Christian–Muslim perspective (the religions of revelation) it was God who started the dialogue, who spoke to we humans, who revealed himself. God addressed us and therefore we are invited to respond, to enter into the dialogue. All our speaking, in fact our whole life, is answering God's call. This is what the term 'person' (whence the name of the PCA comes from) refers to in its most profound meaning (see below).

Revelation is one side of the coin, the other side of which is experience. And here the question becomes important to psychotherapists and counsellors: how do we see the human being? How do clients experience themselves? How do we think about them and ourselves as humans?

In summary: the image of God and the image of the human being are intrinsically and inseparably connected. We are permitted to draw conclusions from us to God and from God to us.

What is the relevance of such a statement for practice? In the course of the history of reflection on the experiences with Jesus Christ this led to a breathtaking inspiration:

to the understanding of God not only as the One and Only and thus the origin of our individuality but also as a Trinity, which means as community and communication and thus as the source of our being-in-relationship, being sociable and living gregariously: as the source of our nature as inevitably social beings.

Christians are baptized and begin their prayers 'In the name of the Father, the Son and the Holy Spirit'. What makes the Christian belief different from all other religions is the belief in 'the Father, the Son and the Holy Spirit', theologically called Trinity (as expressed in the Creeds) in God as a Triune. The distinctive Christian image of God is God as a tri–unity.

But what does that mean? Before we investigate this further we need to look at the wider context which will show that this is far more than theological speculation, irrelevant to our everyday life. On the contrary, this leads us into the middle of our existence.

THE UNUM–MULTUM PROBLEM

The question about the nature of God is a special case of what is referred to in the history of philosophy as the unum–multum problem. Traditionally unity, uniformity and uniqueness on the one hand and plurality, pluriformity and variety on the other hand have been seen as being incompatible opposites. The unum–multum problem preoccupied thinkers in Eastern and Western European philosophy and theology, the problem of the 'one' versus the 'many', the singular versus the plural, unity and uniformity versus diversity and pluriformity. The contrast, the opposite of the one and the many, the individual versus community or society, is a basic issue throughout occidental thinking and self-understanding.

Is it *the 'unum'* that is at the beginning, that is the guiding principle? And therefore: is diversity diversification, is multitude something deriving from the original one, deviating from it? Hence something deducted, of less value, power, importance, something inferior? Finally this would mean that the goal of all will have to be regaining the original unity, towards the one and only. In politics this is the question of the understanding of power and leadership: is mon–archy the true state system, given by God and only responsible to him? Is hier–archy the adequate constitution of religious systems, e.g. the church? Is there only one church, realized in many communities? And, much more generally: do we live in a uni–verse (where everything is 'turned' towards the 'one')? Will we find a 'world formula' explaining everything from one principle—in the natural sciences as well as in the humanities? Does spirituality tend towards finding *the* meaning of life? And finally: is there only one God? Is monotheism 'the ultimate religion'?

Or is *the 'multum'* present from the beginning? Does plurality characterize an original principle making unity a second-order category? Is it only unification that leads to unity, based on induction, agreement, negotiation? Is unity only achieved by uniting, the consequence of finding commonalities? Is therefore the further development of individuality and diversity a ruling principle that leads to progress? And shouldn't it be combined with relationship building and the fostering and celebrating of diversity, looking at the differences of the 'multum' and their richness, rather than at the commonalities? Therefore, democracy would be the adequate state system, power equally shared, responsible to all, in political as well as in religious organizations, a synodical principle for the constitution of churches where the many have the say. Are there many communities that are churches in the full meaning of the term, which together form a worldwide church, 'catholic' ('concerning the whole') in the original meaning of the word? Do we live in a 'multi–verse' (Rickert, 1911)? A cosmos the structure of which is interconnection among the many (ideas, human beings, things), without *one* world formula but with many principles and cores, more like a net than a family tree structure? Does spirituality encompass essentially different contents and directions for different people without any pre-set, and thus essentially common, values? Are there as many gods and goddesses as there are peoples or even people? Are different religions and spiritual movements simply an expression of this fundamental, essential diversity? Is polytheism the genuine reflection of this belief?

In the course of time European thinking, originating in Greek culture, has tended to give preference to the 'unum', the individual and their values of autonomy and authenticity. The 'multum' got the reputation of the inferior—which can be seen as an ongoing fear of becoming and transience (Beinert, 1998: 157). If there is not *one* highest principle, one truth, one position from which to determine what is right and what is wrong—won't this lead into chaos? This might well be the strongest psychological motive for the desire for hierarchical structures and clear, pre-determined positions and values and therefore the strongest motive for the traditional preference of the unum, of our individualistic and hence ultimately narcissistic view.

One example might be the idea that wo–men derive from men—an exegesis of the biblical narrative of Adam's rib that does not focus on the message of equality ('bone of my bones and flesh of my flesh' Genesis 2: 23) but on the priority of the man (Hebrew 'איש ['îs]') over the wo–man (Hebrew 'אשה [iššā]') (ibid.), making the woman the second, the one being derived from the original. Consequently, the woman has to obey the man; the man is of higher rank and value. Ultimately it might well be the fear, in both women and men, of losing clear, although discriminating, structures: it is easier to dominate and submit than to negotiate, consult and strive towards agreement—in gender dialogue as everywhere else.

On the other hand, in Western intellectual history there have always been traditions favouring the community, the value of relationship and thinking in societal categories. We have heretic traditions, heretics that became saints; we have the clown at the side of the king; at carnival time the structures of power were turned upside down. In the church for example, there are not only the hierarchical and patriarchal traditions, but also the monastic and synodical structures; tradition knows the prophets alongside the priests. There are ancient democratic traditions in politics, religion and private and public opinion. The issues of Western thinking were not only about power and might but also about sharing and love. In the last century individualism, on the one hand, came to a hitherto unknown predominant paradigm in society, politics, economics and science, also in psychology and psychotherapy. On the other hand, later in the same century, there was the rediscovery of relationship and community. Not only was the group discovered, according to Carl Rogers (1970: 1) 'probably the most potent *social* invention of the [twentieth] century', but philosophy, psychology and psychotherapy realized the importance of relationship and encounter anew: dialogical philosophy, constructivism, systems theory, the encounter movement, group, family and systems therapy and particularly the person-centred approach. Such a development from a more individualistic focus to a balanced conviction, also valuing the fundamental relational categories can, for example, clearly be traced in the life and work of Carl Rogers and the development of the PCA.

THE BELIEF IN A TRIUNE GOD

Christianity with its roots in Jewish thinking and heavily influenced by Hellenistic philosophy, developed an outstanding way of dealing with the unum–multum dialectics. *The* Jewish achievement was monotheism, carefully defended against all temptations from surrounding and occupying powers. Its core was the covenant between God and his people: one God, one chosen people (Exodus 31). Christianity went one step further: it opened up to all people on earth and understood itself as the new covenant between God and humankind, now open to everybody from everywhere (Matthew 26: 28).

But there was more. The experiences with Jesus of Nazareth led to a new understanding of God and of those who decided to live their lives according to his gospel, i.e. his message, and in his spirit, i.e. their experiences as a community. They gradually came to understand that the main mission and message of his life was to show and verbalize: 'The way I relate to you is the way God relates to you' ('Whoever has seen me, has seen the Father' John 14: 1). In encountering and experiencing Jesus, they believed, they encountered and experienced God. Even more: in living their lives according to Jesus' life (in his spirit) they understood themselves as living in God's spirit, his holy spirit becoming present and presence. Thus as a community in Jesus' spirit they realized that they believed in encountering God by encountering each other. Therefore these questions arose: who is this Jesus in relationship to God, whom he calls his 'Father'? What does their most intimate relationship, expressed by the words 'Father' and 'Son', mean? What or who is this 'Spirit' we experience when we, in–'spired' by him, come together? A mental attitude, Jesus himself, God himself, or even God *themselves*?

Hence, quite rapidly, experience pushed and demanded further development of the image of God. Experience made the Fathers of the Church re-think it, leading to a new understanding of God. And this was how after a few generations the idea was born that was coined in the term 'a triune God', in the contemporary language of that time, formulated as 'one God in three persons'—unity and diversity at one and the same time.

GOD IS COMMUNITY—A SOCIAL UNDERSTANDING OF THE TRINITY

Out of all possible ways of understanding the mystery of the Holy Trinity we are interested here in a specific way which is known as the social understanding of the Trinity.

As with the understanding of person (where both dialectically linked meanings are equally important, i.e. the substantial and the relational dimension), so with the understanding of God as a triune: the 'tri' is as important as the 'une'. The substantial aspect of God's being as totally different, the absolute Other, the transcendence and holiness, the original unity and absolute independence is usually stressed and associated with God. Therefore I here shall emphasize the aspect of community, to regain the balance.

During the history of theology we can find two paradigms of interpretation of the Trinity. The more Western one, also called the 'psychological model' (e.g. St Augustine in *De Trinitate*) moves from the unity to the trinity and therefore stresses the unity (and thus the Father); the more Eastern one, also called the 'social approach' or 'the interpersonal, dialogic analogy', focuses on the community of the Three and goes from there to the unity. This second analogy is closer to the experience told in the Bible. In the 'social approach' unity is seen as perfect community. *It is the relationship that makes the unity*. The Father's, Son's and Holy Spirit's beings are totally wrapped up in one another, their mutual penetration by love ('perichoresis'; see below) without giving up their respective characteristics. This shifts the focus from a hierarchical, patriarchal, androcentric idea towards an understanding of the Trinity as a community. *It is relationship and community that is God's nature and intention*:

- God him- or herself is relationship.
- God is relationship to us.
- God is the foundation of our relationship with each other.

The peak of the universe is not isolation and loneliness; it is community and life at its fullest.

In analogy: God is 'society', God is 'group'.

GOD IS 'PERSON' IS 'GROUP'

Usually we say that we believe in a personal God. This term, 'person', refers to our present-day understanding of a person, which is almost identical with 'individual'. We say, for example, 'There are three persons in a car.' However, at the time, when 'persona' was introduced from everyday language into theology and philosophy, it was a role term, a relationship term, used to denote independence in a relational structure (i.e. the judge, the lawyer and the prosecutor at a trial were called 'personae', i.e. 'persons'). This understanding, paralleling the biblical relational thinking, was used at the time of the Fathers of the Church to develop further the image of God. Thus relationality became equally important to the Greek substantial thinking—a balance, which ever has to be gained anew, and is still important for the understanding of the human being as a 'person' today as underlying, for example, the PCA.

Now, if we say: 'God is "person"' and think the way we do in everyday language, there is the danger that we overemphasize the individual aspect. Another term might help to balance this.

Although this might sound unusual, after the above mentioned considerations we might also say: 'God is "group"'. As it is with 'person' (that God is 'person' in a unique, analogous way; God is not only unique but the only one), so it is with 'group': God is 'group' in a unique, analogous way. Relationship is not only an aspect of God's being—God *is* relationship in a unique and fundamental way. God is 'person' is 'group'.

This might sound strange and make you think about God anew, which is fine. I can even refer to Pope John Paul II (1979) as a witness. He used the analogy of the family to talk about God: 'Our God in his deepest mystery is not an individual, but family'. The analogy is far reaching: the members of the family are only through the family what they are (without being mingled) and the family is only through its members what it is.

God is in a unique way 'person' and in a unique way 'group'. Thus to say *'tri–unique God'* would be most adequate. God is originally community, from the very 'beginning'. At the same time this eternal, most intimate community is so perfect that it is a complete unity: community as unity of and in differences without mingling.

Therefore, ultimately, in God 'person' and 'group' coincide, because substantiality and relationality coincide. In God there is no tension between 'being fully from oneself and oneself' and 'being fully towards the Other'. God is unity in distinctiveness. Hence it makes sense to say: *'God is "person" is "group"'.*

The theology of trinity marks the peak in dealing with the unum–multum dialectics. The understanding of God as mutual love and as '*communio et communicatio*' means that God himself is unity *and* diversity, identity and difference, equally original and tantamount, dialectically interrelated. This view is known as the doctrine of perichoretic love. 'περιχωρησις (perichoresis)' originally means 'a dance around each other'—what a charming, expressive and meaningful picture: God as a dancing triad, a dancing group! Perichoresis points to the deepest unity in sharpest distinctiveness. It is because of this perfect being-within-each-other, this perfect interrelation, that this belief does not lead to a tri–theism, to three gods.

Recently in the English language the singular 'they' began to be used again in order to avoid gender-discriminating language. It fits perfectly when talking about God, not only in order to avoid one-sidedly connecting the idea or the image of God with a male notion but also to point to the tri–unity and thus intrinsic community of God. So we can say: God in *their* common play of dancing, God in their interplay of perichoretic dancing and love.

And this God invites us to join their dance.

THE IMAGE OF THE HUMAN BEING

WHAT DOES THE IMAGE OF GOD SAY ABOUT THE IMAGE OF THE HUMAN BEING?

God's being is being-with—'within' God as well as towards the human beings. This is expressed in God's name 'Jahwe' (Exodus 3: 14, literally: 'I am who I am' or: 'I am the I–am'), which, as an answer to Moses' question, as to who he is, means: 'I am who is here for you and will be with you', or simply, 'I am who is present for you'.

The idea that God's relationship to humankind belongs to their essence leads to tremendous consequences for the understanding of the human being as a person, which, among other things, emphasizes that the human being is a being of innate plurality. And it means that it is communication, originating in encounter and presence, which builds community:

- Anthropology: If the nature of God is *community*, being-with, then the nature of the human being is being-with. The human being is a homo socialis. This is one of the essential meanings of being a *person*, a term characteristic of the Judaeo–Christian culture (and a proper description only for this world view).
- Sociology and social psychology: A community whose model is the Trinity, is always open, turning to the others; it is inviting and thus guaranteeing and fostering plurality. Because, if God is *plurality*, then the human beings are essentially plural and pluralistic. The important aspect here is the difference, the other one as really an Other. This is the origin of *encounter.*
- Epistemology: And finally, if God is *communication and dialogue*, then what makes the human being truly human is communication and dialogue. Communication anticipates community, it leads to community, and yet it already needs community to communicate. Both are interrelated. Communication and community require *presence* and a fundamental understanding of the nature of relationship as being touched and surprised by the disclosure, the revelation, of the Other.

COMMUNITY: THE HUMAN BEING AS A PERSON

If God is community and the archetype of community, the human being is only a fully human being in community and when initiating community. Thus, the relationship-focused image of God leads to immense, far-reaching consequences for the understanding of the human being as a person, a being of innate plurality, e.g. as man and woman (see below).

The essence of being human is founded in the relationship of God to us. It was God who initiated this relationship. What makes the human really human is to respond to God's call into the relationship. This is what the profound meaning of the term 'person' is. *To be a person means to be a response to the call and invitation into the relationship with God the Triune.*

As a matter of fact, the notion of 'person' as underlying and characterizing the very essence of the *person*-centred approach, is rooted in the above mentioned theological and philosophical considerations. It springs from the attempt to understand better who God is. As a matter of fact, the understanding of the human being as a person developed out of thinking about God as person and God as persons.

Substantiality and relationality

What it means to be a person and which consequences follow for the PCA, I have described in detail several times (Schmid, 1991, 1994, 1998a, 2001a, 2002a: 58–65). Here we lack space for more than a short summary.

According to two different, yet dialectically linked, traditional strands of meaning, the human being is characterized as a person if he or she is denoted in his or her unique individuality, autonomy, worth and dignity (the substantial notion of being a person) as well as his or her interconnectedness, being-from and being-towards others (the relational conception of becoming a person). Thus, to be a person describes both autonomy and solidarity, and sovereignty and commitment as being equally important.

Rogers combined the two views in a unique way when he built his theory and practice upon the actualizing tendency which is at its best in facilitative relationships of a certain kind. Person-centred personality and relationship theory understands personalization as a process of becoming independent *and* of developing relationships.

Response

Both autonomy and interrelatedness as a person, are responses to God's call into their relationship with them. This is what the profound meaning of the term 'person' is as developed in the aforementioned theological and philosophical considerations: a response to the invitation into the relationship with God the Triune.

Re–sponse (from Latin 'respondere') etymologically means 'answer to an engagement, a promise'. 'Spondere' means 'promise, bind oneself by contract'. (This meaning can still be found in the term 'spouse'.) The original meaning of 'respondere' is 'correspond' in the sense of being compatible and consistent. Thus to be a person means to 'co(r)–respond'.

In a *developmental psychological perspective* the human being is what he or she is out of communication. Their identity is drawn from the relationship with their parents and other significant others. The human being is response to these relationships, corresponding to the relationship offer of those in whose community they were born. It is encounter they stem from in their self-understanding.

In a *philosophical perspective* the human being is response to what was offered to them, to the promise they got. The 'promise' (Latin 'mittere' means 'send, give as a present, dedicate') is what was given to them. Being human means to respond to this promise.

Hence, *in an ethical perspective*, from being a response derives re–sponsibility due to their freedom and being-with one another, i.e. this responsibility is a co(r)–responsibility in the community of the humans. It is through becoming a person as a response to persons and within the community of persons that a person realizes their personhood (Schmid, 2002c).

In a *theological perspective* human beings are persons because they are from God. 'Person' is the corresponding answer to *Jahwe*, the 'God who is present', the free, autonomous and responsible answer to God's promise to be with us. It is an existential, dialogical answer to God who spoke to us, to God as a being-with, from the human being, understood as God's image, as a being-with in respect to God and their fellow humans.

The specific of being human is being addressed by God: God is the one saying 'I am' making the human being a 'Thou'. The human being is a 'Thou' before becoming an 'I'. They are addressed (also by their parents and fellow humans) as 'Thou' and become 'I' through their corresponding existential answer. A person is, who is addressed by God. As a person the human being is addressed by God to be God's image, in Trinitarian language, to be included in God's community.

In such a theological perspective the substantial notion of 'person' is to be found in the fact that the human being is loved by God as he or she is (see Galatians 2: 20). The human being is an autonomous counterpart of God, free, sovereign and responsible—the image of God's autonomy and sovereignty. The relational notion of 'person', the more original one, as can easily be seen now, derives from being God's creature, originating in the relationship God offers. The human's fundamental being is a relational being, interrelated from the very beginning. This orientation towards relationality and community stems from a being that is relationality and community in themselves: God the Triune is where we come from and where we go to. So, ultimately, in the light of Trinitarian reflections, this means that the person is a response to a We.

Person means to co(r)–respond to and have community with God the Triune.

PLURALITY: BECOMING ONESELF THROUGH THE ENCOUNTER WITH THE OTHER

Understanding what a person is leads us to the plural nature of the human being. In a historical and cultural perspective the Trinitarian formula can be seen as a dialectical overcoming of both positions. On the one hand the dichotomy of classical antiquity between 'own' and 'foreign', the strict and barbarous distinction between 'Us' and 'Them'. And on the other hand the totalitarian claim of monotheistic cultures, i.e. to see oneself as the only one having the truth, the ultimate one, representing the demand that anything else has to become part of it. Trinitarian thinking is the demanding and ambitious work to find a way beyond exclusion and monopolization. It is the foundation for tolerance, acceptance, dialogue and love.

Societal and political consequences

Among others, the theology of liberation (e.g. Boff, 1986) underlines the political consequences of the Trinity as a model for human living together that is based on equality and respect for difference. Because of their belief in God as a community the Christians demand a society that reflects the Trinity. This means participation, equality, plurality. It challenges the traditional idea of a hierarchical society and implies a model of egalitarian community and communication. In taking the triune image of God seriously we find a sharp contrast to the predominant thinking in traditional authoritative structures ('God in heaven and the king [father, boss] on earth') with their tendencies to turn into authoritarian structures and their anti-emancipatory implications. A rigid, one-sidedly interpreted monotheism is paralleled in and furthers political totalitarianism, religious authoritarianism and social paternalism and machismo in family and professional life. One can see this reflected in expert-oriented psychotherapies. As it used to be in politics and religion, power and knowledge are attributed to the authority without being questioned, as if it came directly from God—a vertical paradigm in belief and social order, usually connected with thinking in classes (priests, clergy, scientists, therapists, etc.). In a word: God at the top and down via the experts to the ordinary people; everything is in a vertical order. Trinitarian thinking questions and raises objection to such traditional expertism. It furthers empowerment.

Sexes and sexualities

In a similar way feminist theologians took up the belief in a triune God as a community and realized that mutual perichoresis is the way of living together that overcomes patriarchal and androcentric images of God and forms the matrix and foundation of men and women without domination in mutual respect and acknowledgement. In the human being as the image of God the original plurality is reflected in the fact that the human being is man and woman. And only in this innate plurality is the human being the image of God. 'In the image of God he created them; male and female he created them' (Genesis 1: 26). Sexes and sexualities refer to the human being's innate plurality. The human's fundamental providence renders two most important consequences: it equally forms the foundation for the pride in one's own individuality and identity as it forbids the devaluation of other individualities and identities.

The Other

In talking about plurality, the important aspect is difference. Human community is not supposed to be a community of the same, of the like-minded, of those of the same origin, same age, same sex, same education and culture, etc. It is diversity that makes the community of human beings human. This means that the other one really is not another Me, not an alter ego, but truly an Other one as encounter (dialogical) philosophy pointed out. Therefore we have to see other persons not as copies of ourselves but as truly Others. This also means that we have to overcome any idea that we could heal ourselves and become what we are only by ourselves without others—a monistic, individualistic, a Trinitarian misconception, to be found in some forms of humanistic psychology, which, on the contrary, therefore prove to be inhumane.

Encounter

Before we can have community with the others we need to respect them for their own value. The respectful way to meet is called encounter. The roots of the present-day understanding of encounter also lie in the Judaeo–Christian tradition, particularly in the Jewish commandment of brotherly and sisterly love. Jesus made it even more radical by broadening the understanding of love from charity to love towards enemies. 'Encounter' (from Latin 'contra', i.e. 'against') means 'to meet the unexpected'. To en–counter another person first of all means recognizing that the Other really 'stands counter', because he or she is essentially different from me (Schmid, 1998b). Encounter means an amazing meeting with the reality of the Other, to be touched by the essence of the opposite. In order for this to happen, there must be a non-purpose-oriented openness, as a prerequisite for amazement. 'Being counter', according to Buber (1974: 18) is the foundation for meeting face to face. The I is not constituted until such an encounter relationship: 'The I becomes through the Thou. Becoming an I, I say Thou. All real life is encounter' (ibid). According to Levinas (1983: 120) encounter is always a challenge: 'Encountering a human being means being kept awake by an enigma'. He points to the fact that there is not only one Other; there is also the Other of the Other; there are the Others. This leads right into the very essence of Trinitarian thinking (Schmid, 1991, 1994, 1998c).

The Third One, We, the Group

Love of the one to the other is the principle that overcomes the being different and brings about community. It overcomes the exclusion of the one by the Other, brought about by individuality. This means the transcendence of the being opposite to a We, the overcoming of separation by the Third. 'Three' as a symbol means perfection. The Third One, the Holy Spirit always was understood as God's love. Augustine (*De Trinitate*, VIII 8, 12) hits the point: 'You see the Trinity, if you see love!'

True love is more than to love one another. It means con–dilectio—a term used by Richard of St Victor (*De Trinitate*) who took friendship as a model for the understanding of love—to love together, to co-love a third one. In overcoming the restrictions of 'amor mutuus', the mutual love, to 'communio amoris', the communion of love, Richard pointed out that true love always means more than to love each other, it means to love together; a Trinitarian view. (To understand what this means just think of a loving couple becoming a family and including the child in their love, making their love creative and inclusive.)

Levinas went in the same direction. In his social philosophical approach of encounter philosophy, trying to overcome the typical Western 'egological' understanding of philosophy, he laid the foundations for an understanding of interpersonality in a Trinitarian sense. Love here transcends the loving ones from the couple to the group—'the Third' being a symbol for the transcendence of the couple—towards an understanding beyond 'I–Thou' to 'We'. In such a relationship community nobody is a means but everyone is a mediator.

Therefore, in a theological perspective the group, as far as it is truly a group open for encounter, is *the* place of community. It is a 'sacrament of the Trinity', a sign of the triune God. Such groups have a Trinitarian structure. Here we do not only talk *about* the Third (as it happens in a dyad), we talk in the Third's presence, we talk *with* him or her, including him or her.

COMMUNICATION: PRESENCE THROUGH AND IN DIALOGUE AND DIAKONY

Dialogue

Plurality is the foundation of and for relationality: it is through communication, originating in encounter, that community emerges. The way of communicating which corresponds genuinely to encounter is dialogue. Dialogue means that the Other is not seen as the source of conflict but as a chance for mutual development.

To be the Other is not the last thing that can be said about another one. Hence encounter—after acknowledging the difference—can become the overcoming of being different toward a new community. Fully respecting the difference and the respective characteristics, the one and the other can find 'together' in a new way. This happens through dialogue and is the Trinitarian way of dealing with difference and plurality. Dialogue, therefore, is a fundamental way of human existence. It has its foundation in God's revelation. The community of God explains why love wants to communicate itself. Dialogue, the alternative to dominating power, rests on the power of love, founded in Trinitarian perichoresis.

As it is dialogue that makes it possible to experience God, so it goes for human communication: only dialogue is the adequate form of communication to acknowledge (Schmid, 2001b) and understand (Schmid, 2001c) another human being.

An understanding of empowerment, equality, encounter, clients' expertise and responsibility is a fruit of an overall paradigmatic revolution that is currently being performed in our society. Co-operation, participation, teamwork, democracy, co-understanding and co-developing are the foundations of an alternative view of human living, be it in politics, religious life or therapy after the catastrophes in the twentieth century. The experience that humans can live together well without authoritarian structures might have been similar among the first Christians and in our contemporary life. This corresponds with an image of God which takes its starting point at the Three—Father, Son and Holy Spirit. The unity is not questioned but it is understood in and through their relationships. In this view unity is a pro-social term that can be fully understood only out of a comprehension of the nature of love.

Presence

'I am who is present for you' (Exodus 3: 14), God says to Moses in a dialogue. In God's actions, e.g. in the foot washing by Jesus (John 13:1–20), we can experience God's diakony (i.e., service). Both are signs of God's presence. God's presence means their closeness and their liberating and healing power, a presence that is im–media–te, without any means in between (see Prüller-Jagenteufel, 2004).

Indeed presence, as we understand it in the PCA, has aspects of perichoretic love. Rogers' (1986) description of the therapeutic relationship as being present to the Other is a basic and comprehensive depiction of a therapeutic encounter relationship in an existential way. The challenge is at one and the same time to be oneself and in relationship—the Trinitarian principle par excellence (Schmid, 1994, 2002a, 2002b).

CONSEQUENCES FOR THE UNDERSTANDING OF THE PERSON-CENTRED APPROACH

Our theological considerations shed light upon important foundations of the image of the human being as it can be found in the understanding and practice of the PCA. The uniqueness of its underlying image of the human being and its practice of therapy and counselling can be more profoundly understood if we take into account the impact of the above described image of God and the human being from a Christian perspective.

CHRISTIAN THEOLOGY AND THE PCA: TWO DIFFERENT, YET MUTUALLY CHALLENGING APPROACHES

This does not mean seeing the PCA as a baptized psychology or Christian belief as a prerequisite for a person-centred approach. They are two different systems.

Obviously there are commonalities and differences in their conceptions of the world, their philosophies of life, principles and practice. Both conceptions denote a change of paradigm in many respects, particularly regarding the image of the human being compared with the prevailing images. Concerning anthropology, Christianity and the PCA share the phenomenological conception; both are approaches aiming at 'becoming who you are', they both have the belief in a constructive principle instead of a dichotomy or dualism of 'good' and 'evil', or 'forward' and 'backward' (while a dichotomic principle can be found, for example, in Freudian metapsychology). In terms of the epistemology, both share an original plurality and constructivist foundations ('everything is relative, if only God is absolute; even God is to be understood as relational, as a process of becoming'), together with a fundamental encounter conception. As to the philosophy of science, they have the position in common that the crucial point of one's belief is acting according to one's conviction. In the theory of acting and in praxeology, they correspond regarding the empirical and kairotic (i.e., regarding the right acting in the right time; see below) starting point. In practice they share a scepticism towards methods and techniques and favour a self-understanding of their practice as art. From an ethical point of view both rely on social ethics and from a political viewpoint they share a self-understanding as politically relevant and challenging (see Schmid, 2000).

However, there are serious differences and tensions between the two world views, which constitute a challenge to both sides, particularly the different starting points, the different basic beliefs. A God revealing himself, believed to be the origin of all communication; God's incarnation in the historic Jesus of Nazareth, believed to be the Christ, the Saviour; the belief that humankind already is redeemed by God and does not have to struggle in order to redeem itself, to name a few central points. All of them mark a position of trust and an image of the human being that has its ultimate worth outside of itself. On the other hand experience is the only guideline, valued above anything else (Rogers, 1961: 23–4) and scepticism towards all traditions, e.g., there are different positions towards the phenomenon of evil. And, certainly, there are differences in the tasks: Christianity and pastoral care as a consequent task for every Christian, arising out of their belief, is different from the person-centred task of a counsellor. Both require relationships person-to-person. However, pastoral care, to be understood as mutual support in being a Christian by fellow Christians, is a life-long responsibility and a completely mutual enterprise (once we really have left the hierarchical model behind). PCT is a temporary facilitation, a relationship aiming at making itself superfluous.

So, Christian faith and practice and theological reflection on the one hand and person-centred convictions, practice and theory on the other hand must be seen as mutually challenging ways of acting and thinking, enriching each other and questioning each other. They share common ground and they contradict each other. It is a matter of intellectual honesty to respect their different starting points, axioms, scientific methods and practices. (Incidentally, it can be said that at present theologians are usually much more open to therapy than the other way round. You only need to evaluate the numbers of pastoral psychology studies and papers in comparison to studies and papers dealing with the impact religious convictions have for people's lives—almost a taboo in the realm of psychology and psychotherapy, although such questions definitely occupy people existentially (see Schmid, 2003a).)

THE ESSENCE OF THE PCA

In an earlier work, I formulated three essential statements regarding the nature of the PCA describing the distinguishing characteristics of a truly person-centred approach (Schmid, 2003b), where I emphasized that three short, seemingly simple statements imply a revolutionary change of paradigms:

1. Client and therapist spring from a fundamental 'We'.
2. The client is the expert.
3. The therapist is present.

It does not come as a surprise that these statements are grounded in and developed out of an anthropology with its roots in Judaeo-Christian thinking. Acknowledging this helps us to understand better what these person-centred principles actually mean. I will point to a few important issues only (see Schmid, 2002e).

A fundamental 'We'—The person in the community

Person-centred therapy and each person-centred work starts with a fundamental 'We' (Schmid, 2003b), which can be found in the basic statements of the PCA (Rogers, 1957), rooted in the conviction that we are not merely acontextual individuals, we only exist as part of a 'We'.

This denotes:

- *a political perspective*—the We includes commonality *and* difference as in Trinitarian thinking, valuing both equally, as opposed to a simplistic dichotomy, where sameness is positive and difference is negative;

- *a co-perspective*—client and therapist are co-experiencing, co-responding to what comes up, co-operating, co-creating the relationship, respecting the Other as truly an Other and regarding person-centred work from within this context, which according to our theological and anthropological considerations is not only a context but a foundation;
- *a group perspective*—which is aware that the enclosed, acontextual dyad is an artificial construct and that taking the human seriously as a social being, a person in the group, results in a re-evaluation of the indication for single and group therapy (Schmid, 1996). It was Brian Thorne (1996, 1998) who pointed out the analogy of group life and Trinity and emphasized that the experiences to which encounter groups lead, namely strengthening both the sense of self-esteem and the sense of interconnectedness with others, are paralleled by spiritual and mystic experiences.

The client is the expert—plurality and encounter

The reflections on plurality and diversity clearly show that there is no way to have knowledge about the Other in a traditional sense. We only can ac–knowledge the Other. This is the position of an encounter perspective. According to Rogers' phenomenological approach the therapist responds to a call and the relationship. Thus the respective task is to co(r)–respond as a person (see Schmid, 2003b, 2004a). The client, seen as the expert for both contents and process of therapy, is the one who 'knows' what it is all about and how to communicate, i.e. to choose the means of therapy—a stance only to be found in genuine person-centred therapy. Thus the task is to really foster plurality and diversity with our way of doing therapy: to really encounter our clients and to be open to be surprised instead of suspecting or already knowing.

Furthermore, it is important to be aware that there is no person except as a man or a woman. Thus we need to delve into sex- and gender-specific issues if we really are to acknowledge the nature of the human being. (Fairhurst, 1999; Schmid, 2004b; Proctor & Napier, 2004). The gender-specific aspects in therapeutic and psychosocial relationships need to be genuinely further developed. Consequently, this would stress the social nature of the person (see Schmid, 1996: 497).

The therapist is present—person-centred communication as dialogue

In a personal context to respond existentially means to be present and available as a person to the client. Presence is the fundamental way of 'being together', the existential foundation of the core conditions (Schmid, 1994, 2002a: 62–5, 2002b, 2003b; Brodley 2000; Geller & Greenberg, 2002).

Presence is:

- co-operation arising out of co-existence (person-centred therapy is truly a dialogue);
- co-responding (to given experiencings) out of co-experiencing;
- co-creating out of (in its best moments, mutual) encounter.

Some of the basic dimensions of 'presence' are (see Schmid, 2002b: 190–201):

- *its principled non-directivity*: non-directivity (not at all outdated in the understanding of PCT) is a way of facilitative responsiveness (Schmid, 2005a).
- *its kairoticity*: kairology is the science of the right acting in the right time (see Schmid, 2002b: 183–4). In therapy the question always is: what presents itself in the very moment?
- *its 'im–media–cy'*: presence happens without (preconceived) media or tools, because the only 'tool' is the therapist himself or herself as a person, his or her own 'instrument'. Methods are of second importance, even irrelevant; PCT never acts 'in order to' achieve a certain goal as love never does anything 'in order to'.

In a transferred sense presence also means that creative approaches to theory *development, research and training* are necessary. Instead of classification and an arrangement within traditional medical and social security systems, it is creativity that is demanded in the understanding of the uniqueness of every single person and their particular capabilities (Schmid, 1996, 2004a, 2005b).

Furthermore, presence means that instead of borrowing ideas and techniques from other schools and propagating eclectic or so-called integrative methods, more self-confidence in our own foundations is crucial. This will also lead to a clearer public identity. If we recognize that psychoanalytic, behaviouristic and systemic approaches have recently achieved positions the PCA has held prominently for a long time (e.g., the impact of a personal relationship), then we can be encouraged by our pioneering role again to take up a challenging position in the *dialogue with other orientations* (Schmid, 2000).

A PARADIGM SHIFT WITHIN THE PERSON-CENTRED APPROACH

Our reflection of 2000 years of Christian spiritual experiences has led to a new understanding of the human being through a reconsideration of the image of God: to be a person means to have community with God the Triune, with a God who is community in themselves. The human being is a being unavoidably interconnected with others, a being of innate plurality, having to rely on communication with others, a co(r)–responding being.

If we seriously re-evaluate the anthropological foundations of the PCA in the light of these reflections this may well lead towards a paradigm shift within the PCA. I think we are on the edge of a theoretical and practical reorientation of the approach—faithful to its own tradition. The PCA may well face a turning-point in its self-understanding. In respect to the outlined Trinitarian-founded anthropology, I picture the step from the individual to the person, from relation to encounter as a step from the view of the person-centred relationship as an I–Thou–relationship to a view as a We–relationship and therefore finally towards a 'social therapy'. Sociotherapy, implying the communities that humans live in, will come to be ranked as highly as psychotherapy (see Barrett-Lennard, 2002). Thus, the political significance will become obvious (Schmid, 2003b).

The person-centred relationship is to be regarded as a process of spontaneity and creativity, a process in which both client(s) and therapist(s) develop while aiming at personal encounter, a process which provides a model for understanding mutual responsibility in society, a process of self-understanding for people who are open to new experiences and to the revelations of others, and a means to build a We which rests on the strengths of individuals and supports individuals to develop their strengths from the communities and relationships in which they live.

On the other hand, the PCA must not become one-sided and overlook the individual. It lives through the tension between We and I, group and person, relationality and substantiality, encounter and self-reflection, i.e. from the dialectic connectedness of communicative relatedness and individual development. The connecting link is the understanding of the person in both his or her individuality and his or her relationality. Hence, the PCA will become a truly personal, truly dialogic and anthropological approach, a fully *person*-centred approach.

Christians can understand what they do as a response to a promise they can rely on: '*Where two or three are gathered in my name, I am there among them*' (Matthew 18: 20).

REFERENCES

Barrett-Lennard, G (2002). The helping conditions in their context: Expanding change theory and practice. *Person-Centered and Experiential Psychotherapies 1* (1&2), 144–55.

Beinert, W (1998) Kontextualität als Struktur der Theologie: Der Einzelne in der Gemeinschaft der Kirche. *Pastoraltheolische Informationen, 18,* 151–73.

Boff, L (1986) *A trinidade, a sociedade e a libertação*. Petrópolis: Vozes.

Brodley, B (2000) Personal presence in client-centered therapy. *Person-Centered Journal, 7*, 139–49.

Buber, M (1974) *Ich und Du. In: Dialogisches Leben*. Heidelberg: L Schneider, (8th edn).

Fairhurst, I (ed) (1999) *Women Writing in the Person-Centred Approach.* Ross-on-Wye: PCCS Books.

Geller, S & Greenberg, L (2002) Therapeutic presence: Therapists' experience of presence in the psychotherapy encounter. *Person-Centered and Experiential Psychotherapies 1* (1&2), 71–86.

John Paul II (1979) Sermon in Puebla, January 28.

Levinas, E (1983) *Die Spur des Anderen: Untersuchungen zur Phänomenologie und Sozialpsychologie.* Freiburg i.Br.: Alber.

Proctor, G & Napier, MB (eds) (2004) *Encountering Feminism: Intersections between feminism and the person-centred approach.* Ross-on-Wye: PCCS Books.

Prüller-Jagenteufel, V (2004) The power of presence. Paper presented at the Conference 'The spiritual dimension in therapy and experiential exploration'. Norwich. Also reproduced in this book as Chapter 8, pp. 119–26.

Rickert, H (1911) *Das Eine, die Einheit und die Eins*. Tübingen: Logos II.

Rogers, CR (1957) The necessary and sufficient conditions of therapeutic personality change. *Journal of Consulting Psychology, 21*, 95–103.

Rogers, CR (1961) *On Becoming a Person: A therapist's view of psychotherapy*. Boston: Houghton Mifflin.

Rogers, CR (1970) *On Encounter Groups*. New York: Harper and Row.

Rogers, CR (1986) A client-centered/person-centered approach to therapy. In I Kutash & A Wolf (eds) *Psychotherapist's Casebook* (pp. 197–208). San Francisco: Jossey-Bass.

Schmid, PF (1991) Souveränität und Engagement: Zu einem personzentrierten Verständnis von 'Person'. In: C Rogers & PF Schmid. *Person-zentriert: Grundlagen von Theorie und Praxis* (pp 15–164). Mainz: Grünewald.

Schmid, PF (1994) *Personzentrierte Gruppenpsychotherapie: Ein Handbuch. Vol. 1: Autonomie und Solidarität*. Cologne: Edition Humanistische Psychologie.

Schmid, PF (1996) *Personzentrierte Gruppenpsychotherapie in der Praxis: Ein Handbuch. Vol. 2: Die Kunst der Begegnung*. Paderborn: Junfermann.

Schmid, PF (1998a) 'On becoming a person-centred approach': A person-centred understanding of the person. In B Thorne & E Lambers (eds) *Person-Centred Therapy: A European perspective* (pp. 38–52). London: Sage.

Schmid, PF (1998b) 'Face to face': The art of encounter. In B Thorne & E Lambers (eds) *Person-Centred Therapy: A European perspective* (pp. 74–90). London: Sage.

Schmid, PF (1998c) *Im Anfang ist Gemeinschaft. Personzentrierte Gruppenarbeit in Seelsorge und Praktischer Theologie*. Stuttgart: Kohlhammer.

Schmid, PF (2000) 'Encountering a human being means being kept alive by an enigma': Prospects on further developments in the Person-Centered Approach. In J Marques-Teixeira & S Antunes (eds) *Client-Centered and Experiential Psychotherapy* (pp. 11–33). Linda a Velha: Vale & Vale.

Schmid, PF (2001a) Authenticity: the person as his or her own author: Dialogical and ethical perspectives on therapy as an encounter relationship. And beyond. In G Wyatt (ed) *Rogers' Therapeutic Conditions: Evolution, theory and practice, Vol 1: Congruence* (pp. 217–32). Ross-on-Wye: PCCS Books.

Schmid, PF (2001b) Acknowledgement: the art of responding: Dialogical and ethical perspectives on the challenge of unconditional personal relationships in therapy and beyond. In J Bozarth & P Wilkins (eds) *Rogers' Therapeutic Conditions: Evolution, theory and practice, Vol 2: Unconditional positive regard* (pp. 49–64). Ross-on-Wye: PCCS Books.

Schmid, PF (2001c) Comprehension: the art of not-knowing: Dialogical and ethical perspectives on empathy as dialogue in personal and person-centred relationships. In S Haugh & T Merry (eds) *Rogers' Therapeutic Conditions: Evolution, theory and practice, Vol 3: Empathy* (pp. 53–71). Ross-on-Wye: PCCS Books.

Schmid, PF (2002a) Knowledge or acknowledgement? Psychotherapy as 'the art of not-knowing': Prospects on further developments of a radical paradigm. *Person-Centered and Experiential Psychotherapies 1* (1&2), 56–70.

Schmid, PF (2002b) Presence: Im-media-te co-experiencing and co-responding. Phenomenological, dialogical and ethical perspectives on contact and perception in person-centred therapy and beyond. In G *Wyatt* & P Sanders (eds) *Rogers' Therapeutic Conditions: Evolution, theory and practice, Vol 4: Contact and perception* (pp. 182–203). Ross-on-Wye: PCCS Books.

Schmid, PF (2002c) 'The necessary and sufficient conditions of being person-centered'. On identity, integrity, integration and differentiation of the paradigm. In JC Watson, RN Goldman & MS Warner (eds), *Client-Centered and Experiential Psychotherapy in the 21st Century: Advances in theory, research and practice* (pp. 36–51). Ross-on-Wye: PCCS Books.

Schmid, PF (2002e) Was ist personzentriert? Zur Frage von Identität, Integrität, Integration und Abgrenzung. In C Iseli, W Keil, L Korbei, N Nemeskeri, S Rasch-Owald, PF Schmid, P Wacker (eds) *Identität—Begegnung—Kooperation: Person-/Klientenzentrierte Psychotherapie und Beratung an der Jahrhundertwende* (pp. 219–54). Cologne: GwG.

Schmid, PF (2003a) Menschengerechte Förderung und Herausforderung: Die Bedeutung der Pastoralpsychologie für die Seelsorge, die Theologie und die Psychologie. *Diakonia, 34*, 234–40.

Schmid, PF (2003b) The characteristics of a person-centered approach to therapy and counseling: Criteria for identity and coherence. *Person-Centered and Experiential Psychotherapies, 2* (2), 104–20.

Schmid, PF (2004a) Back to the client: A phenomenological approach to the process of understanding and diagnosis. *Person-Centered and Experiential Psychotherapies 2*, 36–51.

Schmid, PF (2004b) New men?—A new image of man? Person-centred challenges to gender dialogue. In G Proctor & MB Napier (eds) *Encountering Feminism: Intersections between feminism and the person-centred approach* (pp. 179–90). Ross-on-Wye: PCCS Books.

Schmid, PF (2005a) Facilitative responsiveness: Non-directiveness from an anthropological, epistemological and ethical perspective. In B Levitt (ed) *Non-directive Person-Centered Psychotherapy* (pp. 75–95). Ross-on-Wye: PCCS Books.

Schmid, PF (2005b) Authenticity and alienation: Towards an understanding of the person beyond the categories of order and disorder. In S Joseph & R Worsley (eds) *Person-Centred Psychopathology: A positive psychology of mental health* (pp. 75–90). Ross-on-Wye: PCCS Books.

Thorne, B (1996) Person-Centered Therapy: The path to holiness. In R Hutterer, G Pawlowsky, PF Schmid & R Stipsits (eds) *Client-Centered and Experiential Psychotherapy: A paradigm in motion* (pp. 107–16). Frankfurt/M: Peter Lang.

Thorne, B (1998) *Person-Centred Counselling and Christian Spirituality: The secular and the holy.* London: Whurr.

CHAPTER 20

TO BE WHAT YOU REALLY ARE IN REFORMED THEOLOGY

JAN VAN BLARIKOM

We are on delicate ground here. (Bouwsma, 1988: 12)

OAK PARK

Come out from among them, and be ye separate. (2 Corinthians 6:17)[1]

Carl Rogers was born on the 8th of January 1902 in Oak Park, a suburb of Chicago. His parents came to live there around the turn of the century. Some five years after Rogers was born, the family moved again, in Oak Park, to an 'upper-middle-class neighbourhood' (Kirschenbaum, 1980: 3). Rogers went to the Holmes School. In the same period this school was attended by Ernest Hemingway and the children of the famous architect Frank Lloyd Wright.

Rogers was given a religious upbringing. Later he spoke about this on various occasions. 'I was brought up in a home marked by close family ties, a very strict and uncompromising religious and ethical atmosphere, and what amounted to a worship of the virtue of hard work' (Rogers, 1990: 5). Father came from a family of Congregationalists and mother from a family of Baptists. Both parents were typical representatives of a long Protestant tradition in North America. Every day the Bible was read by the family and they prayed. On Sundays the family went to the church of the Congregationalists, at first by horse and wagon, later by car (Kirschenbaum, 1980). There were many prohibitions: drinking, smoking, playing cards, dancing and going to the cinema (Rogers, 1980).

The parents controlled their children in a subtle way. 'They were masters of the art of subtle and loving control' (Kirschenbaum, 1980: 6). Rogers was particularly attached to his mother. She had the greatest influence on him in religious matters:

1. Biblical quotations are from the King James Version, Cambridge University Press.

This chapter is an abridged version of the original paper 'To be what you really are in Reformed theology' presented at the conference. If you are interested in the original with more detailed reference information, you can apply for a copy to the author. Email <janvanblarikom@gmail.com>.

> My Mother was a person with strong religious convictions, whose views became increasingly fundamentalist as she matured. Two of her biblical phrases, often used in family prayers, stick in my mind and give the feeling of her religion: 'Come out from among them and be ye separate'; 'All our righteousness is as filthy rags in Thy sight, oh Lord'.[2] (Kirschenbaum, 1980: 5)

The first phrase seemed to reflect family life. The children learned that they were different from others. In Rogers' words, 'Other persons behave in dubious ways which we do not approve in our family ... So the best thing to do is to be tolerant of them, since they may not know better, but to keep away from any close communication with them and to live your life within the family' (Rogers, 1980: 28). In connection to this Rogers spoke about his 'unconsciously arrogant separateness' in respect of his peers and of 'the distance and the aloofness that I had taken over from my parents' (1980: 28–9).

When Rogers was 12 years old, the family moved from Oak Park to a farm 25 miles outside Chicago, according to him due to his parents' need to keep 'a growing adolescent family' away from 'the temptations of suburban life' (Rogers, 1990: 6). Rogers' biographers, Kirschenbaum (1980) and Thorne (1992) also emphasized that the family felt they were different from others, even 'chosen' and that they had to watch out for bad influences from outside.

However, this vision on the extraordinary family life of Rogers asks for a critical evaluation. With respect to a study *Fall from Grace* by James Bundy, about the development of Oak Park between 1870 and 1917, it has already been remarked in *Carl Rogers: The Quiet Revolutionary* that, 'the lifestyle of the Rogers family was in reality within the mainstream of Oak Park' (Rogers and Russell, 2002: 310). An important aspect of the American Protestant culture, to which most of the families in Oak Park belonged, was the feeling of being part of a special community, different from those in the big city. Bars were prohibited in Oak Park. In this culture the longing to move on to a new world, pure and untouched by the negative influence of modern life, lived on (Bundy, 1991).

The phrase 'Come out from among them and be ye separate' was very popular with a group of Baptists in New England during the *Great Awakening* around 1740. Undoubtedly this phrase expresses a need for isolation, forming a community of believers, separate from the non-believers. But he who uses this phrase also knows the obligation of an exceptional life: living your life whilst being critical of life as commonly lived; always having a feeling of being predestined to something exceptional.

Carl Rogers has carried out exceptional work. He abandoned the dominant traditions of the times of the behaviourist and psychoanalytical psychology. His whole life was filled with a special mission: paying attention to the personal. His opinions are still considered radical, even within the person-centred movement. In the end he did, in his own way, fulfil his mother's biblical words.

The words of Isaiah, 'all our righteousness is as filthy rags' easily give rise to

2. First phrase: 2 Corinthians 2: 17; second phrase: Isaiah 64: 6.

misunderstanding, and Rogers clarified his mother's biblical quotation as 'that at our best we were unspeakably sinful' (Kirschenbaum, 1980: 5). The notion of righteousness will be brought up in the discussion of Protestant theology. For now it is enough to remark that in the Protestant religion it is not man who is pictured as worthless, but his overrated self-importance. Without faith nothing is expected from man. Naturally this opinion stands in sharp contrast with Rogers' person-centred psychology. The contrast that Thorne pictures between Rogers' psychology and his parents' orthodox religion is generally justifiable:

> Rogers' experience as a therapist and psychologist brought him increasingly to the conviction that human beings are essentially forward-moving organisms drawn to the fulfilment of their own creative natures and to the pursuit of truth and social responsiveness. Such a conviction stood in sharp contrast to the negative and guilt-inducing view of human nature enshrined in the severe interpretation of the doctrine of Original Sin which characterized the theology of the Rogers' household. (Thorne, 1992: 21)

However it goes too far to speak of 'the perverse theology of the fundamentalistic evangelicalism of his childhood' (Thorne, 1992: 21). Perhaps Thorne wrote this in the heat of his argument, in which he especially wanted to make clear why Rogers rejected the Christian religion so completely. But in his zeal to give 'Christian spirituality' a place in person-centred psychology, he rejects Rogers' parents' religious opinions in an unnecessarily harsh way. When Thorne reduces the parents' religion to a 'perverse theology' he surely does no justice to the centuries-old Protestant tradition in North America.

GENEVA AND NEW ENGLAND

> Predestination is an excellent example of teaching which ... cannot be grasped unless one has an eye for its social and psychological roots. (Oberman, 2003: 118)

In the spring of 1630 a fleet of eleven ships with 700 passengers left Southampton for New England. Under the leadership of Governor John Winthrop a new colony was founded: Massachusetts Bay. Over the next ten years 20,000 people would leave England, as many as the number of inhabitants of Norwich, England's second largest city in those days (MacCulloch, 2003: 535). The majority of the emigrants settled in the new colony. Winthrop is considered the 'forgotten founding father' of America. In 1636 he founded the University of Harvard in the small town of Cambridge.

Earlier a small group of religious separatists, the Pilgrim Fathers, had left for North America, after trying to form a separate community in Leiden, Holland. This group led a relatively isolated life in the Plymouth Colony in Massachusetts. They had broken completely with the Church of England.

The later group, under the leadership of Governor Winthrop, especially sought a 'purification' of religion. They linked up with the tradition from the last decennia of the sixteenth century where a section of English Protestantism, known as the Puritans, wanted to reshape the Church of England to the model of the Reformed church in Geneva. Purification meant reforming according to the opinions of Calvin.

In the period 1625–40 the Puritans had a very difficult time in England. Because of this, people who felt attracted to the Reformed religion were persuaded to venture across the Atlantic. The idea of emigration was closely connected to the Reformed religion, as preached by Calvin and other reformers and which had been preached from the pulpits in England since 1560 (MacCulloch, 2003).

The emigrants were 'chosen people'. Like the people of Israel they set out for the wilderness. They had a covenant with God. It was not their intention to isolate themselves in a closed community as they sought a 'truer form of established Church' (MacCulloch, 2003: 537). In a sermon before they sailed to New England Winthrop impressed on his fellow travellers that the new community, the 'covenanted community' had to be an example to all, 'For we must consider that we shall be as a city upon a hill'[3] (Bundy, 1991: 9). The eyes of the world were upon them.

To the emigrants the journey to New England meant a continuance of the Reformation. They were the 'chosen people', safe in God's providence. To learn about the origin of these thoughts one has to go back to the two main representatives of the Reformation, Luther and Calvin.

LUTHER (1483–1546)

An important difference between Luther and Calvin was their notion of time. Luther thought the end of time was near, 'This damned Last Time' (Oberman, 2003: 73). Calvin knew he stood at the beginning of a new time. Luther's life was driven by fear. Fear drove him into entering a monastery, after he barely survived a strike of lightning. He says of himself that he was made anxious by his parents. His mother once beat him until he bled for stealing a nut. His father once hit him so hard that Luther avoided him for some time.

Luther was educated to become a priest. He was always afraid of doing something wrong. He was never sure if he had performed a ritual exactly right. He took his doctor's degree in 1512 and he started the so-called '*Bible Vorlesungen*' (*'Bible Lectures'*) to his students in 1513. During the years 1513–19 he came to a new insight—Luther himself mentions a 'breakthrough' (see Lohse, 1997). Probably there was a close relationship between his personal development and the intensive study of a number of biblical texts, which led more than once to the voicing of a new insight (Ebeling, 1985).

A nascent insight is also to be found as a note in the marginal line of the sermons of Johannes Tauler (Ozment, 1969). At first Luther follows the anthropological schema

3. Matthew 5: 14: 'Ye are the light of the world. *A city that is set out on an hill cannot be hid*' (author's emphasis).

of the mystics Tauler and Gerson, about the sensory human founded on senses and the rational human founded on reason, but then there is a deviation: '*homo spiritualis qui nititur fide* (the spiritual man relies upon faith)' (Ozment, 1969: 2). With this statement Luther parts with the medieval mystical anthropology in which the existence of spiritual man is founded on a source within man himself. Luther defines the existence of spiritual man only in relation to God. This insight became famous especially through the following line in Paul's Letter to the Romans: 'The just shall live by faith' (Romans 1: 17).

This understanding became Luther's great certainty. It formed the justification of his existence. He believed that a life cannot be justified by what a man does or does not do. Existence is justified by complete trust in God. We are no more than what is carried by God.

CALVIN (1509–1564)

Contrary to Luther, Calvin was an introverted man. We know little of what was going on in his mind. At the age of four or five, he lost his mother (Bouwsma, 1988). His father soon remarried. Calvin was placed in the house of another family when he was six or seven. Somewhere between the age of 12 and 14 he went to Paris for further studies. Originally his father wanted him to be a priest, but some years later the father changed his mind. Calvin had to end his studies and begin studying law in Orleans. His father died in 1531 and Calvin went back to Paris to study. There was a lot of interest in the new, humanistic, *ad fontes* approach to the Bible. This approach would be the basis of a renewal of the church.

William Bouwsma wonders in *John Calvin: A Sixteenth-Century Portrait* why there is so little attention to the events of his childhood. It is very well possible that, 'the death of his mother when he was a small child and his subsequent exclusion from his father's household may have begun in him a sense of homelessness that would be later deepened by exile; he grieved for his motherland all his life' (Bouwsma, 1988: 11). Bouwsma further states, 'we are on delicate ground here, but I do not see how any account of Calvin as a human being can ignore such basic experiences' (1988: 12).

On 1 November 1533 Calvin had to flee Paris after one of his friends was arrested because of a sermon he had preached. He roamed France for over a year, while the situation for the Protestants hardened. In 1535 he arrived in Basel where he wrote the first version of *Institutes*, originally meant to be a simple book for students, which later grew into his systematic main work (Oberman, 2003). He was asked in 1536 to take on the organization of the Protestant church in Geneva. Calvin did this with such vigour that he was sent away two years later. He was a minister for French refugees in a church in Strasbourg for three years before returning to Geneva in 1541, having married, in the meantime, a refugee's widow and possibly mellowing somewhat. Geneva had become a city of refugees, in 1550 there were 13,000 inhabitants, in 1560, 21,000. This growth was mainly the result of the arrival of Protestant refugees from France and Italy (Selderhuis, 2000). Calvin remained in Geneva until his death in 1564.

In his *Initia Calvini* Oberman (1991) states that we can look at Calvin in two ways: Calvin as a teacher and Calvin as a researcher. As a teacher, Calvin mainly wanted to clearly explain the Protestant religion, as in his *Institutes* in which he explains religion as a system. But Calvin was also a dedicated researcher. This we encounter in his comments on the Bible, in which his own experiences and those of his contemporaries are incorporated. To Calvin it was impossible to comment objectively on texts such as Abraham's trek to the Promised Land. With his history as a refugee, living in a city full of refugees, this text contained a deeper, personal meaning:

> The persecution that drove Calvin from his homeland forced him to seek the meaning of the Christian pilgrimage more deeply. Abraham's trek to the Promised Land (Genesis 12: 1) became for him as much a key narrative as was the certainty of being inscribed in the book of God (*praedestinatio*). (Oberman, 2003: 72)

Calvin's predestination has come to lead a life of its own. The concept was taken out of its original context and became part of a speculative theological system (Oberman, 2003). But to Calvin and his contemporaries, this concept voiced a trust in a better future, which enabled them to face the harsh present. Many people lived in exile, they had lost their motherland and persecution was a part of everyday life. There was a lot of confusion, including in religious matters: 'For those who had no permanent place of residence, not even a fixed stone on which to lay their heads, neither a valid passport nor a residence permit, predestination became their identity card' (Oberman, 2003: 157).

To the first groups of Protestant emigrants to the New World, predestination—safe in God's providence—was a part of their story. Persecutions belonged to a very recent past and the future was insecure. During the following generations, 'when the refugees had become settlers and citizens' (Oberman, 2003: 115) the concept lost its original meaning. It became a element of study in dogmatics. It was even considered a privilege, a 'civil right', which someone had earned because he belonged to a certain community. To follow this history of predestination, we return to the Puritans in America.

A COVENANTED COMMUNITY

The social life of the Puritans in New England took its form from the *covenanted community*. They imagined living their lives as a chosen community. As previously mentioned, the Puritans did not intend to isolate themselves completely. They did however want to lead their lives within their own community, which would find justification in the eyes of God. But the covenanted community should also be an example to the world: 'The Puritans came to New England not merely to save their souls but to establish a 'visible' kingdom of God, a society where … a smooth, honest, civil life would prevail in family, church and state' (Morgan, 1966: 3). The goal to establish a 'visible' kingdom of God entailed a heavy responsibility not only for the community as a whole, but also for each individual. The covenant was developed within strict regulation and offences were severely sanctioned. This promoted the foundation of moralistic communities, in which individual life was severely suppressed. A famous example of the suppression of individual life by a Puritan community is to be found in *The Scarlet Letter* by Nathaniel Hawthorne (1850).

Although a restricting organization of social life based on religious foundations is mostly experienced as a very negative thing by modern society, we need to view this from an historical perspective. As Oberman (2003) stated, Calvinism is not suited to the founding of a state if the Calvinists are the majority. As a minority they make a useful contribution in relation to social responsibility. While the Calvinists were living in foreign countries, in small groups, as refugees or emigrants, they controlled life in their community. Oberman gives an example of a father who was reprimanded for abusing his children, in a community of Protestant refugees in London (Oberman, 2003: 146).

In the same way Puritans in New England during the seventeenth century guarded the social life of the members of the community. What we now look upon as a merely restrictive form of social control was in those days also an important form of protection. The man was head of the family, like everywhere else. But within the marriage, husband and wife were supposed to treat each other in an equal manner, based on mutual love (Morgan, 1966). Beating and scolding were forbidden and were punished. Parents were obliged to raise their children in a responsible manner. Parents that left their children alone at night were reprimanded. Love played an important part in the married life of the Puritans. A tender intercourse was set as an example, as long as the love between husband and wife was not at the expense of the love for God. The well-known historian Edward Shorter even states that: 'References to romantic love as an active force in the life of the couple began with the Puritans and never ceased thereafter' (1975: 65).

The Puritans were always part of society as a whole. Even though they formed their social life in a community of their own, this life was not considered as separated from the existing culture. The first generation of Puritans sailed from England to *New* England. They wanted to bring together, in an ideal and pure form, the values they thought to be important in their own English culture, together with the Protestant religion, in the formation of a new community. In the centuries that followed they regularly returned to the image of a covenanted community. This was not about a restoration of the values of the Puritans' lifestyle in the seventeenth century, but rather the goal was the realization of the 'highest ideals' and 'deepest commitments' that were an implicit part of their own culture (Bundy, 1991: 10).

At the beginning of the twentieth century the image of a covenanted community reappears when Oak Park, a suburb of Chicago, becomes an independent city. Oak Park is at the beginning of a stormy period of growth. The city grew gradually between 1880 and 1900 from 2,000 to 10,000 inhabitants. Between 1900 and 1917 this number increased to 35,000 inhabitants (Bundy, 1991: 90).

Around 1840 Oak Park was a small settlement west of Chicago, with only a church and a small school. Oak Park became important when a number of influential Protestant families, the majority from New England, came to live there and found themselves united in the principle of temperance. In 1873 the last three 'saloons' were bought out and that was the end of the sale of spirits in Oak Park. The place now developed further into a, literally and figuratively, respected suburb.

The phenomena of suburbs came into being in America at the beginning of the nineteenth century. They were described as places where 'all the advantages of the city and the country' had been combined (Bundy, 1991: 151). Around 1900 Oak Park was considered 'Chicago's garden'. It was a modern city with spacious houses, gardens and many parks. The upper middle classes, who mostly worked in Chicago, found a comfortable home there. But Oak Park was more than that. It was a 'refuge' and a 'model' that was described as 'ultra-respectable' (Bundy, 1991: 59, 31).

At the time that Oak Park got its own administration at the beginning of the twentieth century, the inhabitants began to speak of a 'civic ideal' and a 'model village' (Bundy, 1991: 58). Oak Park had to become a 'model community' that would show the world how a community based on Christian values can be founded near a big city. A number of religious principles were considered of great importance. In first place was the prohibition of alcohol, but also included was the limited sale of cigarettes, keeping the Sabbath and encouraging church attendance. Also, there were earnest discussions about the desirability of certain forms of theatre and film:

> The sense of being a model community, the belief in a missionary purpose, the consciousness that religion lay at the foundation of community life ... all these qualities that Oak Park held as a part of its self-image had been integral to Puritan notions of community. (Bundy, 1991: 66)

We can describe the city where Carl Rogers grew up as a modern suburb of America. Although religious ideas put their stamp on life in the city, the inhabitants thought of themselves as progressive. They had created a safe refuge for family life in proximity to a big city. In the creation of this safe refuge they had answered the problems of modern society. The family of Carl Rogers, as far as their ideas were concerned, belonged in this city. If we want to describe Rogers' religious background, we cannot speak of a narrow-minded religious family life. Rogers was raised in a family that is representative of the modern Puritan community in America at the beginning of the twentieth century.

ROGERS, KIERKEGAARD AND LESSING

> I wanted to find a more dynamic way of communicating what happens to the person. (Rogers, 1990: 73)

After the Second World War Rogers leaves for the University of Chicago (1945–57). He is given the opportunity to start a Counseling Center (Rogers and Russell, 2002) and this becomes a very successful period in his career (Kirschenbaum, 1980). He surrounds himself with enthusiastic colleagues. Psychotherapy and research continue to develop together. The book *Client-Centered Therapy*, first published 1951, is the output of the first part of this period. Rogers' fame increases in the early fifties and he is frequently asked to give speeches.

Beginning in 1951, Rogers regularly took leave from the university during the winter. Together with his wife Helen he visited Mexico or the Caribbean for their holidays. He used this annual winter leave as a period for relaxation and to enable him to review his work from a distance. During one of these holidays, probably in the winter of 1952, he became acquainted with the work of Kierkegaard (1813–55) and Buber (1878–1965). He wrote in his introduction to the article, 'Persons or Science? A Philosophical Question': 'I first became acquainted with the work of Søren Kierkegaard and that of Martin Buber at the insistence of some of the theological students at Chicago who were taking work with me' (Rogers, 1990: 199).

We find the result of this acquaintance with Kierkegaard for the first time in his short talk, 'Personal Thoughts on Teaching and Learning' (Rogers, 1990). It was an introduction to a conference on education, at the University of Harvard in April, 1952. Rogers' thesis that a direct form of education is practically useless resulted in tumult. Rogers had become of the same opinion as Kierkegaard.

The Danish philosopher in his turn had been inspired by Lessing (1729–81). He introduced Lessing in his *Concluding and Unscientific Postscript* (Kierkegaard, 1992), first published 1846, as the figure that opened his eyes to an important insight about the relation between man and his religion. Religion is a personal matter. One cannot rely on historical facts. Lessing says, 'contingent truths of history can never become the demonstration of necessary truths of reason' (Kierkegaard, 1992: 97). According to Kierkegaard this statement does not necessarily lead to a critical attitude towards religion. Lessing explains that religion is not a system that can be transmitted by tradition or education alone. The extraordinary thing about Lessing is that:

> He closed himself off in the isolation of subjectivity, did not allow himself to be tricked into becoming world-historical or systematic with regard to the religious, but he understood, and knew how to maintain, that the religious pertained to Lessing and Lessing alone. (Kierkegaard, 1992: 65)

According to Lessing the gap between religion and reason cannot be bridged. 'That is the ugly broad ditch that I cannot cross, however often and however earnestly I have tried to make the leap' (Lessing in Kierkegaard, 1992: 98). Kierkegaard admired Lessing for not trying to solve this contrast with a trick—a philosophical speculation or a so-called historical fact.

Kierkegaard's *Concluding Unscientific Postscript* is about making our relation with religion subjective: 'Every subject is an existing subject, and therefore this must be essentially expressed in all of his knowing' (Kierkegaard, 1992: 81). In his time Kierkegaard was hardly understood. Not until the first decennia of the twentieth century was the significance of the philosopher acknowledged. Kierkegaard's *Concluding Unscientific Postscript* is the predecessor, if not the beginning, of existentialism, and has had an enormous influence on the philosophy and Protestant theology of the twentieth century.

In his *Concluding Unscientific Postscript* the emphasis is on man as existing as subject. This is another aspect of Kierkegaard that appealed to Rogers, who referred to the 1941 edition of *Concluding Unscientific Postscript*. In relation to change occurring in the course of the therapy he writes:

> I cannot help but be reminded of Kierkegaard's description of the individual who really exists. 'An existing individual is constantly in process of becoming ... and translates all his thinking into terms of process. It is with him ... as it is with a writer and his style; for he only has a style who never has anything finished, but "moves the waters of the language" every time he begins, so that the most common expression comes into being for him with the freshness of a new birth.'[4] (Rogers, 1990: 171–2)

It is not about possessing, but striving for the truth. Lessing had already described this in an original way:

> If God held all truth enclosed in his right hand, and in his left hand the one and only ever-striving drive for truth, even with the corollary of erring forever and ever, and if he were to say to me: Choose! I would humbly fall down to him at his left hand and say: Father, give! Pure truth is indeed only for you alone! (Lessing in Kierkegaard, 1992: 106)

In 1953 Rogers wrote an article entitled 'Some Directions and Endpoints in Therapy'. He claimed to have a 'personal fondness' for this piece (Rogers, 1990: 73) which is about a number of important events in the process of therapy. A few years earlier he had written a chapter in *Client-Centered Therapy* (1951) called 'The Process of Therapy' but he became unsatisfied with it. He was looking for, 'a more dynamic way of communicating what happens to the person' (1990: 73). According to Rogers, an essential event in the course of the therapy is that, 'The person comes to *be* what he *is*' (Rogers, 1990: 104, original emphasis).

The person comes to *be* what he *is*. We can consider this a part of the therapy. The person becomes aware of feelings from which he had been estranged. 'The individual comes to be—in awareness—what he is—in experience' (1990: 104–5). But something deeper resounds in this statement: a question that concerns all persons. To be that self

4. In the expression 'moves the waters of the language' there is a reference to John 5: 3–4 to the waters of a pool: 'in these lay a great multitude of impotent folk, of blind, halt, withered, waiting for the moving of the water. For an angel went down at a certain season into the pool, and troubled the water: whosoever then first after the troubling of the water stepped in was made whole of whatsoever disease he had.'

which one truly is: the difference between a life in estrangement and being the person that you truly are. It appears to be a fundamental matter in the life of every human being. Rogers quotes Kierkegaard in relation to this in a lecture for the Oberlin College, 'On Becoming a Person', in 1954:

> In this connection I have been astonished to find how accurately the Danish philosopher, Søren Kierkegaard, pictured the dilemma of the individual more than a century ago, with keen psychological insight. He points out that the most common despair is to be in despair of not choosing, or willing, to be oneself; but that the deepest form of despair is to choose 'to be another than himself.' On the other hand 'to will to be that self which one truly is, is indeed the opposite of despair,' and this choice is the deepest responsibility of man. (Rogers, 1990: 110)

We find this quote from Kierkegaard in *Sygdommen til Døden* or *The Sickness unto Death* (1941b).[5] This book's title is based on Jesus' statement when he receives the tiding that Lazarus is ill, 'This sickness is not unto death' (John 11: 4). For he who believes, death is no longer the end. But despair is. 'Despair is the sickness unto death', according to Kierkegaard (1983: 17).

The longing, 'to be that self which one truly is', has been developed by Rogers through Kierkegaard into a well-known concept. There is however a significant difference between Kierkegaard and Rogers. Becoming yourself, according to Rogers, is a psychological process that comes about within a therapeutic relationship. 'To be that self which one truly is', according to Kierkegaard can only be achieved before God. According to Kierkegaard it is not about a state of psychological well-being. A person has to be able to stand his ground before God.

> There is so much talk about human distress and wretchedness—I try to understand it and have also had some intimate acquaintance with it—there is so much talk about wasting a life, but only that person's life was wasted who went on living so deceived by life's joy or its sorrows that he never ... became aware and in the deepest sense never gained the impression that there is a God and that 'he,' he himself, his self, exists before this God. (Kierkegaard, 1983: 26–7)

Rogers borrows concepts from Kierkegaard's work which are originally religiously charged. This language enables him to describe the process of therapy in 'a more dynamic way'. Rogers must have been aware of the religious charge in Kierkegaard's language but apparently it did not bother him. The question is: how big is the difference between

5. This can be found in Kierkegaard (1983: 20) *The Sickness unto Death*: 'For to will to be the self that he is in truth is the very opposite of despair.' Rogers quoted from an older (1941b: 29) edition: 'For to will to be that self which one truly is, is indeed the opposite of despair.'

Kierkegaard and Rogers in the final analysis? Kierkegaard was looking for an authentic life before God in the first half of the nineteenth century. At the beginning of the second half of the twentieth century Rogers was looking for a description of the authentic person. Taking the two together, we could state: without the subjective there is no access to God.

HEIDEGGER

If Rogers had referred to a philosopher of the twentieth century, Heidegger (1889–1976) would have been a logical choice. Heidegger's work was directed against the thesis that, 'beings are only true in so far as they enter the polarized bond of rational subject and verifiable object' (Steiner: 1978: 69–70). According to Heidegger, Western thinking had been caught in an 'onto-theology'.[6] Philosophy as well as theology tended 'to locate truth and ethical values in some abstract "beyond"'. But, 'there is nowhere else' (Steiner, 1978: 63). Heidegger thought the subjective was very important and he continued Kierkegaard's work. With Kierkegaard it was about the subjective before God; Heidegger gave the subjective simply its place:

> *Das Zuhandene der Umwelt ist ja nicht vorhanden für einem der Dasein enthobenen ewigen Betrachter, sondern begegnet in die umsichtig besorgende Alltäglichkeit des Daseins ... Das ist jedoch eine 'Subjektivität', die vielleicht das Realste der 'Realität' der Welt entdeckt.*
> [The immediacy of the environment is not accessible to the eternal observer elevated above existence but is encountered in the prudent attention to the daily round of existence. That is, however, a 'subjectivity' which perhaps reveals the most real aspect of the world's 'reality'.]
> (Heidegger, 1993: 106)

The world—*das Zuhandene der Umwelt* [the immediacy of the environment]—cannot be seen apart from the concrete existence of man. Man is not a spectator. There is no objective point of view—no *einem der Dasein enthobenen ewigen Betrachter* [no eternal observer elevated above existence]—from which reality acquires its meaning. Being is no objective fact, but realizes its meaning in the existence of man. In George Steiner's words, who wrote an interesting monograph on Martin Heidegger, 'Being does require man, for it is in him that it finds its privileged "clearing"'[7] (Steiner, 1978: 71). The meaning of existence becomes visible in the daily acts of man, in art and in literature. Man 'is' nothing in itself. There is no core or substance which lets itself be determined, apart from concrete existence. Man's essence is existence. '*Die Substanz des Menschen ist*

6. Onto-theology: an attempt to found the meaning and reality of existence in some ultimate principle or divine agent. (Steiner, 1978: 69)

7. 'Clearing' is the translation of *Lichtung*, the light that lingers deep in the woods, without being obvious where the light exactly is coming from (Steiner, 1978: 67).

nicht der Geist als die Synthese von Seele und Leib, sondern die Existenz' [The essence of humanity is not spirit as the synthesis of soul and body, but existence itself] (Heidegger, 1993: 117).

Heidegger was a philosopher. When asked for the religious meaning of being, he kept silent (Safranski, 1994), but his language was religiously charged (Steiner, 1978). In his definition of the essence of man, mentioned above, Luther's echo resounds: spiritual man relies upon faith. Luther defines man in relation to God. Heidegger defines man in relation to being. The similarity between Luther and Heidegger is that both start from a dynamic anthropology. Man is not a fixed fact. He exists in time.

Rogers quoted Kierkegaard's description of the individual who really exists: a person who is continuously in a process of becoming. As Heidegger, Rogers defines man in relation to being, a psychological well-being, wherein the person comes to be in awareness of what he is in experience. A definition of man that the twentieth-century man was longing for; it was a description of an authentic life *in accordance with the times*, a *zeitgemäss* description. Rogers himself was a person who was constantly in a process of becoming. Translating his experience, he moves the waters of language, each time anew. Until the domain of mystical experience …

MASTERS OF SPIRITUAL TRUTHS

> And they all began to make excuses. (Luke 14:18)

In the last ten years of his life Rogers was subject to a striking development that Van Belle (1990) described as 'Rogers' later move towards mysticism'. After the death of his wife Helen in 1979, his interest in experiences concerning life after death increased (Rogers, 1980). He became more attentive to mystical, transcendental experiences, even in person-centred therapy and in his work with groups. In a final report on one of his individual therapeutic sessions, he wrote, 'Our experiences, it is clear, involve the transcendent, the indescribable, the spiritual. I am compelled to believe that, I, like many others, have underestimated the importance of this mystical, spiritual dimension' (Rogers, 1986: 199). A number of people, including Van Belle, consider the step towards the mystical a decline. In Rogers' earlier work there was mention of a 'profound respect for individual persons' (Van Belle, 1990: 47). In his later work a 'mystical universalism' (1990: 56) developed, at which the boundaries of the individual began to fade. Van Belle even wonders whether this 'esoteric' and 'otherworldly' vision, 'differs all that much from the world-avoiding fundamentalistic view of his parents which he abandoned as a youth' (1990: 55).

Other people belonging to the person-centred movement do appreciate Rogers' increasing development towards spirituality. Thorne even takes it as far as to say that, 'Fifty years from now it is likely that Rogers will be remembered … as a psychologist whose work made it possible for men and women to apprehend spiritual reality' (Thorne,

1992: 105–6). Elizabeth Sheerer, one of Rogers' colleagues from his time at the University of Chicago, sees no contradiction between Rogers' work as a person-centred therapist and his Christian background. She claims, 'his work is so profoundly influenced by his background in Christianity. I don't think he could have developed without that background' (Thorne, 1992: 23).

The question is where in Rogers' work the influence of the Christian religion can be found. I think it is nonsense to connect the spiritual experiences in his later life to his Puritan, Christian upbringing. This Protestant tradition cares little for mystical experiences which go towards unification with a comprehensive universe. These experiences belong, if anything, to the New Age mystic, which was the framework for spiritual experiences for many people in the last decades of the twentieth century.

The Reformed-Christian character of Rogers' upbringing is voiced in his work through the emphasis on realness. 'To be who you really are'; that is Rogers' credo: his belief in man as he really is. This emphasis on realness can also be found in the Protestant tradition. Luther looked for a foothold in front of God. He had nothing else to offer but himself. What the traditional, Protestant man fights out with God, modern man seems to fight out with himself. To Rogers, God had become meaningless—but Rogers' language is religiously charged. He recognized himself in Kierkegaard's work—but he left God out of it. God is beyond *Sein und Zeit* [being and time]—but in the language His presence reverberates.

Each epoch knows its 'masters of spiritual truths' (Steiner, 1978). It concerns men who, through personal experiences, acquire the culture of their time and formulate in a unique way what is meaningful to other people. These masters did not rise above their time, but penetrated deeply into it. We do not come to understand the insights of these masters by abstracting them from their own time, but by projecting ourselves into those times and their personal backgrounds. In such a way their insights, the 'spiritual truths' come to life again. This can be applied to Luther and Calvin, who stood, in Oberman's words, at the frontier of the 'last days' and the 'new world'. Luther reconfirmed his life, after an anxious childhood, as an individual before God. Calvin gave his persecuted contemporaries an identity and a sense of security through the concept of predestination. We need the work of a theological–historical scholar such as Oberman to develop an eye for the social and psychological roots of predestination. It is astonishing how difficult it is for person-centred therapists to imagine themselves in the life and times of these and other men. It seems to be a lot easier to settle the case with prejudices like 'world-avoiding fundamentalistic' and 'perverse theology'.

In the twentieth century, man could no longer be a spectator. Rogers adopted the image from Kierkegaard of man who is 'constantly in the process of becoming'. As was Kierkegaard in the nineteenth century (although unrecognized), was Rogers in the twentieth century: a 'master of spiritual truth'. His concept of realness is an appeal for presence: an appeal to be there for the other as you really are.

Man is called in two ways. First there is an 'instrumental' call. It is expected of man that he does what he can; that he works according to his ability. It is a good thing to construct something, to be an example to others, help to build the city on the hill.

Man is free in his answer to this call. He can reflect on it. How will he handle it? He only has to do it if the work seems attractive enough or if he is paid sufficiently for it.

There is also an appeal to man in a second way. But this time the appeal is not about what he can do. There is no time to reflect on it. This is awkward. Because he is not yet ready. When Moses is called by God to lead the people of Israel from Egypt, he answers, no, thank you, find someone else; this is not my cup of tea. He is taken by surprise. It takes quite a fight before Moses returns to his people (Exodus 3, 4).

This calling goes a lot further than a question of doing something. It is a compelling question to be present: where are you? There is no time to reflect. No space for a preposition. Man is invited to come in. But most prefer to stay outside.

> A man prepared a great supper and invited many people. He sent his servant to fetch them all. But they all began to make excuses. The first had to go to his piece of ground that he had just bought. The second had to go and tend his oxen. Yet another had just got married. The master of the house became angry. He told his servant, search all the streets and alleys of the city and force the beggars, the blind, the lame and the maimed to come in. My house has to be full. (Luke 14: 16–24)

The similarity between this story and today's world is of course that nowadays, still, no one has time. We have less time than ever! This also applies to those in the helping professions. An appointment can always be made. But to accept an invitation just like that? No, I am sorry, now is not a good time. The strange thing in this story is that the beggars are forced to go inside. It seems nice to invite them, but to force them? Modern people do not let themselves be forced. They don't like to be taken by surprise.

Predestination is compelling. And fortunately so. The belief in God is the belief in the existence of man in the margin. If man who is free to choose is in charge, then there is no time left for man who has nothing to choose. Yes, there would be time, but only by appointment. Predestination is standing still for a moment, acknowledging that not everything can be made or improved. Being thrown back on an infinite modesty.

Throughout history man could turn to God in his misery. That is the meaning of religion in tradition. But this God has lost nearly all his meaning for man. Man's misery however, is still here. Man is still appealed to in two ways. First we must do what we can to help one another. To those who have made this their profession, that is a beautiful thing. Secondly we are invited. There is no question really. We have no choice. And that is an awkward thing. You are being called. You really are there or you are not. There is no choice. At best you can try not to deny who you are. That is Protestant spirituality. And that is what Rogers brought us in the twentieth century. When you are really there for the other, who has got stuck on his way, you catch a glimpse of man in the image of God. Man as he truly is before God.

REFERENCES

Bundy, J (1991) *Fall from Grace.* Brooklyn: Carlson.

Bouwsma, W (1988) *John Calvin. A sixteenth-century portrait.* Oxford: Oxford University Press.

Ebeling, G (1985) *Lutherstudien. Band III.* Tübingen: Mohr.

Heidegger, M (1993) *Sein und Zeit.* Tübingen: Max Niemeyer.

Kirschenbaum, H (1980) *On Becoming Carl Rogers.* New York: Delta.

Kierkegaard, S (1941a) *Concluding Unscientific Postscript.* Translated by Swenson and Lowrie. Princeton: Princeton University Press.

Kierkegaard, S (1941b) *The Sickness unto Death.* Translated with an introduction by Walter Lowrie. Princeton: Princeton University Press.

Kierkegaard, S (1983) *The Sickness unto Death.* Edited and translated by H Hong and E Hong. Princeton: Princeton University Press.

Kierkegaard, S (1992) *Concluding Unscientific Postscript to Philosophical Fragments.* Volume 1. Edited and translated by H Hong and E Hong. Kierkegaard's Writings, XII.1. Princeton: Princeton University.

Lohse, B (1997) *Martin Luther: Eine Einfurhrung in sein Leben und Werk.* München: Beck.

MacCulloch, D (2003) *Reformation.* London: Allen Lane/Penguin Books.

Morgan, E (1966) *The Puritan Family.* New York: Harper & Row.

Oberman, H (1991) *Initia Calvini: The matrix of Calvin's Reformation.* Amsterdam: Koninklijke Nederlandse Akademie van de wetenschappen.

Oberman, H (2003) *The Two Reformations.* New Haven & London: Yale University Press.

Ozment, S (1969) *Homo Spiritualis.* Leiden: Brill.

Rogers, CR (1951) *Client-Centered Therapy.* Boston: Houghton Mifflin.

Rogers, CR (1953) Some directions and endpoints in therapy. In O Mowrer (ed) *Psychotherapy: Theory and research* (pp. 44–68). New York: Ronald Press.

Rogers, CR (1980) *A Way of Being.* Boston: Houghton Mifflin.

Rogers, CR (1986) Client-Centered Therapy. In: IL Kutash & A Wolf (eds) *Psychotherapist's Casebook* (pp. 197–208). San Francisco: Jossey-Bass.

Rogers, CR (1987) *Client-Centered Therapy.* London: Constable.

Rogers, CR (1990) *On Becoming a Person.* London: Constable.

Rogers, CR, and Russell, D (2002) *Carl Rogers: The quiet revolutionary.* Roseville: Penmarin Books.

Safranski, R (1994) *Ein Meister aus Deutschland. Heidegger und seine Zeit.* München: Carl Hanser.

Selderhuis, H (2000) *God in het Midden: Calvijns theologie van de psalmen.* Kok: Kampen.

Shorter, E (1975) *The Making of the Modern Family.* New York: Basic Books.

Steiner, G (1978) *Martin Heidegger.* New York: Viking.

Thorne, B (1992) *Carl Rogers.* London: Sage Publications.

Van Belle, H (1990) Rogers' later move toward mysticism: Implications for client-centered therapy. In G Lietaer, J Rombauts & R Van Balen (eds) *Client-Centered and Experiential Psychotherapy in the Nineties* (pp. 47–57). Leuven: University of Leuven Press.

SECTION 6

HUMANISM

INTRODUCTION

Suzette van IJssel's paper draws attention to a tradition of counselling that has no exact analogue in Britain. Humanistic counselling developed in the Netherlands as an alternative to pastoral counselling for non-religious people. It is grounded in a secular understanding of the world, and in the principle that it is human beings themselves, rather than any 'higher power', who create the meaning of their lives. It draws strongly on person-centred principles which encourage clients to trust in their own experience, and find their own values. In recent years, however, this tradition has encountered two new developments in Dutch society (which seem indeed to be prominent throughout the Western world). One is the growth of a managerial orientation towards health care, which emphasizes efficiency, target-setting and outcome assessment. This is in many ways inimical to humanistic counselling with its emphasis on counsellor 'presence' in the service of clients finding their own paths and goals. On the other hand there has been a mushrooming of interest in a whole range of 'spiritual' traditions—Hindu, Native American, New Age and so on—which presents a challenge to the essentially secular underpinnings of humanism.

Van IJssel's research is into the role of spirituality in the practice of humanistic counselling. She reviews the literature on the relationship between spirituality and psychotherapy, in which several themes emerge: the importance of raising counsellor awareness of clients' religious beliefs; the importance of differentiating healthy from unhealthy spirituality; and the offering of methods of spiritual intervention as adjuncts to counselling. She then compares these themes with the perceptions of humanistic counsellors, and finds a very different picture. The psychotherapy-spirituality literature seems, from the perspective of the humanist counsellors, to be oriented towards forms of spiritual diagnosis and treatment, which are almost as inimical to humanist counselling as the medical-managerial approach. From the humanist perspective any form of assessment or diagnosis is likely to block spiritual understanding, to set up the therapist inappropriately as an 'authority', and to impose on the client the view that they are required to change. Humanist counsellors hold that spiritual forms of counselling should refrain from any explicit or implicit direction of the client.

However, van IJssel suggests that this humanist view may itself be too extreme. In many traditions of spirituality what is emphasized is the *balance* between 'authority' and 'individual experience', 'acceptance' and 'need for change', or between 'will' and 'surrender'. Further, the humanist counsellors—as much as the 'spiritual directors' or the 'medical managers'—have their own framework of beliefs and values out of which they do what they think will be best for their clients. Van IJssel helps us to see that there is not going to be any quick and easy path through these crucial issues.

Jack Earl's paper, based on a study by his late wife, Anne Earl, explores some of the same issues in the context of a British counselling centre, which, while started by a group of Christians, and in other ways having Christian connections, is committed to a humanistic and person-centred approach. Anne Earl had interviewed both counsellors and ex-clients of the Centre about their expectations in connection with clients coming to a 'Christian centre'. Client feelings were typically those of 'not wanting to be preached at': Christian clients tended to feel safer because they anticipated that in a secular environment their faith might not be valued, while agnostic clients had some anxieties that *their* stance might be attacked in a Christian setting. Regarding the goals of counselling, the Christian and humanist counsellors had very similar views, embodying to a large extent a commitment to person-centred principles. However, interviews with Christian clergy who had an interest in the work of the Centre revealed differences as well as similarities in attitude. Some clergy held views similar to those of the Christian counsellors; others felt that there were significant differences, but welcomed these differences; still others thought that much secular counselling is based on a misunderstanding of what distressed clients really need.

Jack Earl explores the possibility that the differences between Christian and humanist approaches to counselling are largely due to differences in language. Christian terminology can seem alien or 'worked to death', and many clients prefer to find their own forms of expression, or to remain with a sense of things without formulating it in words. On the other hand, the interviews indicate that some of the disagreements involve substantive differences in world-view, although one might add that it is not so easy to separate off language from world-view.

Earl suggests that the principles of person-centred counselling have something important to bring to the encounter between world-views. Empathy and unconditional positive regard encourage new and creative ways of expression which can 'bypass the difficulties we have in understanding one another's language'. Further, there are at least some points at which, in spite of the different world-views, it seems plausible to say that 'the same thing' is being said in 'different languages'. Earl cites the example of the humanist concern for people to reach their full potential, compared with the Christian concern for people to be what they are called to be. Or again, he compares the Christian saying 'If we love one another God lives in us' with the words of the 'humanist' Pliny the Elder, 'A mortal's God lies in helping his fellow-mortal'. Earl quotes Wittgenstein's remark 'Only in the stream of thought and life do words have meaning', and there is here the suggestion that some of the difficulties we feel in connection with conflicting world-views may find their resolution through a better understanding of how religious language works, a theme pursued by Hans Schneider in his chapter in the Philosophy section.

CHAPTER 21

WHOSE HEAVEN? THE SPIRITUAL DIMENSION IN HUMANIST COUNSELLING

SUZETTE VAN IJSSEL

WHAT IS HUMANIST COUNSELLING?

HISTORY

Humanist counselling is a special kind of counselling that has been developed in the Netherlands since World War II. The founders of the Dutch Humanist Association wanted to provide an alternative to pastoral counselling for non-religious people in institutions like the army, prisons, hospitals and homes for the elderly, etc. Dutch humanists after 1945 aspired to present a philosophy of life that could give life direction and meaning and that could prevent the domination of the nihilism amongst non-religious people that they believed threatened Dutch society at that time. As such, humanist counselling should not be confused with humanist psychology or the human potential movement in psychology featuring Rogers and Maslow.

Humanist counselling grew out of the activities of volunteers, who received no special training, into the professional form of counselling we know nowadays. Today, humanist counsellors are trained at an academic level, attending courses in ethics, philosophy, religion, sociology, psychology and more practice-oriented courses like communicative training, existential biographical research and qualitative research. Humanist counsellors are working as colleagues of pastoral counsellors, and sometimes imams and pundits, in the above-mentioned institutions.

HUMANISM

The practise of humanist counselling is based on and inspired by humanist principles and values. The exact content of these principles and values was, is and probably will be for a long time, a point of debate within humanist circles. 'The humanist philosophy of life' is generally understood to be a secular understanding of the world and our existence in it. It acknowledges solely the human ability to give meaning to life and existence, often in contrast to a religious concept of an external, transcendent, non-human almighty and influential p/Presence. It emphasizes human solidarity and individual responsibility.

CONDITIONS

Humanist counselling takes place mainly in institutions and is always entirely on the basis of free choice of the client(s). Humanist counsellors work on a one-to-one basis as well as in groups. The most important feature that humanist counselling has in common with pastoral counselling is the so-called 'sanctuary-function'; all conversations are strictly confidential and not to be shared with others in the institution. A small but significant change has occurred in the last decade. Previously, humanist counsellors used this 'sanctuary-function' to avoid any exchange of information, but today they often choose differently. Not participating in an organization easily leads to a marginal position and little influence of the specific knowledge and perspectives counsellors have to offer. Although this led some humanist counsellors to become more actively involved with their fields of work, they are never part of a 'treatment staff', in the sense that they do not formulate 'treatment plans' they have to account for to others. In fact, there is no 'treatment indication' for humanist counselling at all.

CLIENTELE/CONTENT

As I mentioned above, humanist counselling takes place mainly in institutions where people go through difficult, alienating or frightening situations: a soldier far away in a foreign land under dangerous circumstances; a delinquent facing the consequences of breaking the law; a hospitalized person dealing with a failing body; an elderly person facing death; or a problematic personal biography. These and other profound life-events evoke the need in people of secular orientation to find their own personal perspective to moral and existential concerns like the meaning of life; the relation between freedom and destiny; the meaning of autonomy and responsibility and attitudes towards suffering, unhappiness and death. All these conditions call for a process of readjustment and reorientation, a process humanist counsellors are trained to help people with (van Houten & Mooren, 2002: 115).

METHODOLOGY

The question about what kind of methodology is fitting for humanist counselling is very much alive and to a certain degree open. Theory on humanist counselling is work in progress, resulting in diverse and sometimes even contradictory views. In essence humanist counselling was and to a large extent still is a 'Rogerian' person-centred method, putting the trust in human capabilities central in its methodology. The counsellors basically rely on the same core values though expressed in different contexts. The emphasis on individual responsibility causes humanist counsellors to aim at strengthening the sense of meaning in their clients. The way in which they do this is by supporting and encouraging the clients to explore their emotions, thoughts and actions and to put into words their goals, their desires, their views on life and existence and their moral and emotional dilemmas. Another value humanist counselling shares with Rogerian practices is the symmetrical relationship. This is best expressed in a form of communication that has the character of a dialogue, a conversation in which none of the participants has an authoritative position (van Houten & Mooren, 2002: 113). Together with the counsellor, the client searches for meanings or a reformulation of problems. Not the interpretations of the counsellor, but the experience, the meanings and the valuing process of the client are the centre of attention: they are at the same time a point of departure for and goal of the relationship. In training, it is however not the client-centred communicative technique that receives most attention. The focal point of a humanist counselling methodology is the inner disposition of the counsellor, aimed at congruence and an attitude of genuineness and empathy. This is considered to be an essential condition for the counsellor to be able to counsel clients in a way that guarantees their autonomy and humaneness (van Houten & Mooren, 2002: 113).

But the client-centred approach, with its emphasis on self and autonomy still considered a necessary condition, has turned out to be insufficient for professional expertise. In the last few years, humanist counsellors have been growing towards the development of a strategy to become independent, as a profession on its own with a clear professional and humanist profile. One of the reasons behind this development is the continuous process of reorganization and economizing at the level of government finances that rule the field of humanist counselling. In the Netherlands the government, the institutions of health care and care for the elderly are fascinated by an economic management style, concentrated on efficiency and effectiveness. Seen from this perspective, humanist counselling is a rather 'soft' profession, without clear instrumental outcomes. This conflicts with the tendency of managers to think in economic terms of products and results (van Houten & Mooren, 2002: 117).

In an attempt to describe a professionalization fitting for humanist professionals such as humanist counsellors, the term *normative professionality* has come up. Since humanist counselling is about world-views and values, largely based on personal experience and wisdom, the normative dimension is essential. In the process of counselling the counsellor is present with all his or her own norms and values, hopes and fears, ways of looking at life and existence. The principle of symmetry asks from the counsellor not to deny this behind the mask of the professional, but to acknowledge this, which demands a high degree of self-reflexivity and transparency in this respect to the client. The decisive quality in humanist counselling is the capacity of the counsellor to be *present* as a person of flesh and blood, without ever losing client-centredness (van Houten & Mooren, 2002: 117).

Humanist counselling is often defined in contrast to psychotherapy. Whereas therapists are used to conceptualize a clients' questions and problems in terms of psychological theory, by focusing on the psychological dimensions, humanist counsellors are trained to reflect on a wide variety of questions concerning the way life is, can be, and should be, experienced or perceived. In respect of this, more narrative approaches to counselling have been developed, in which the various aspects of the narrative processes in which people deal with or develop a meaning of life or moral perspectives receive attention. The absence of any kind of treatment plan or indication in humanist counselling is a vital factor in its methodology. In theory, it makes humanist counselling a *presence practice*, as opposed to an intervention practice. The respectful trust in a client's innate capacity to find his or her own solutions to existential problems or moral dilemmas makes the term 'advice' better suited to characterize the relationship between counsellor and client than treatment does.

RESEARCH ON SPIRITUALITY AND HUMANIST COUNSELLING

HISTORY AND CONTEXT

My research on the role and identity of spirituality in humanist counselling has been instigated by a major societal change or development, namely the emergence of the term 'spirituality' in ideas and narratives concerning mostly individual orientations on life. Due to the ongoing processes of secularization, detraditionalization and individualization in our Western societies, people are forced to make more conscious individual decisions about their life than at any time in the past and consequently are desperately in search of an authentic self to justify those choices (Beck, 1992). These developments, which are very demanding on the individual, are often viewed as a cause for the rapidly growing interest in spirituality amongst people with a secular life-stance (Borgman et.al., 2003). This has led to a multiplicity of forms of spirituality that are less and less related to an institutionalized religion or rooted in some religious or philosophical doctrine. The current spiritual landscape shows a proliferation of ideas, practices and intuitions.

In a way this outburst of spiritual ideas and practices in our Western societies has revived an old schism within Dutch humanism. Religion or spirituality has always been a difficult subject that has evoked much tension in humanist circles. In order to position and present humanism within a society that was dominated for centuries by some form of Christianity, most humanists defined their views mainly in opposition to (Christian) religion, especially the concept of an almighty God. Some to such an extent that humanism became atheistic or even anti-religious, focusing on reason or rationality as the highest value and ultimate human capacity in accordance with seventeenth and eighteenth-century 'Enlightenment' philosophy. Yet there has always been a minority of 'religious humanists' who have tried to verbalize a secular form of religion or mysticism, with a more relativistic attitude to human rationality. The 'rational and atheist humanism' seemingly had the upper hand in the 70s, 80s and especially the 90s of the last century, but the zealous attempts to purify humanism from everything remotely religious backfired in the end. It eventually led to a strong criticism from religious, or as we call them nowadays, spiritual humanists. The current call for a re-evaluation of spirituality seems to come especially from the field of humanist counselling. They argue that an exclusive and excluding attitude towards certain reality-transcending inner experiences and ideas (that in our contemporary culture are articulated as spiritual) or their quick rationalization by humanist philosophy undermines the very foundation of humanist counselling. Because in a humanist counselling situation, it is neither the counsellor nor the humanist philosophy of life that is the main source of signification, it is the client him or herself. And the client—as well as the humanist counsellor—is, like most people, searching for answers to questions concerning life, death, truth and ethics in Dutch society today, confronted with a fast-growing offer of diverse views on life from every possible culture on earth, and from every possible era. This leads to situations in which for instance one can find the Christian St Francis of Assisi being considered part of the same source of inspiration as the Hindu Bhagavad Gita, or the practice of zazen being mixed with Teresa of Avila's contemplations on the unconditional love-nature of the Divine, whether or not combined with a visit to a Native American sweat lodge or an Aboriginal didgeridoo concert.

Even if the humanist counsellor him or herself is not sensitive to these current—or any other—forms of spirituality, it is important for humanist counsellors to be able to relate to all of this in an open, dialogical manner. To recapitulate; the societal shift towards secular or non-institutional-religious forms of spirituality and its influence on the way humanist and non-humanist persons reflect on existence, meaning and morals created a need for theory and research on spirituality from a humanist perspective.

THE TERM 'SPIRITUALITY'

The translation of the terms 'spirituality' and 'humanist counselling' from Dutch to English poses interesting problems. The English term 'spiritual' corresponds with two different Dutch words, namely *geestelijk* and *spiritueel*. The term *geestelijk* is used in the traditional Dutch name for humanist counselling, namely *humanistisch geestelijke begeleiding* (humanist spiritual counselling). Gradually, the term *geestelijk* grew beyond a (semi-) religious context and started to refer more and more exclusively to mental or intellectual capacities. For instance, we call a mentally handicapped person *geestelijk gehandicapt* (spiritually handicapped). The Dutch language has no real equivalent for the English term 'mind', so we use *geest* (spirit), and although we know the word *mentaal* (mental), it is not commonly used. Relatively recently, the terms *spiritueel* and *spiritualiteit* (spirituality) have come up, alongside *geestelijk* in order to articulate human capacities and experiences that lie somewhere in between the mental and emotional realms. These terms have come from the Roman Catholic religion, and although the terms are no longer exclusive to this tradition, they are often used in relation to religious phenomena. Particularly this aspect makes some people—some humanists—quite uncomfortable with *spiritueel*, so they prefer *geestelijk*. This little elaboration shows how difficult a phenomenon like spirituality is in relation to language, especially different languages. Both the terms *spiritueel* and *geestelijk* are part of a universal search for words to describe human experiences of depth and connectedness, of something higher, more than the ordinary. These experiences transcend our physical, emotional and mental awareness and are usually—but by no means exclusively—found, shaped and invoked within religious traditions.

RESEARCH METHOD

The largest part of my research on the role and identity of spirituality in the practice of humanist counselling is a qualitative research, based on nine open interviews with humanist counsellors from different fields of work, gender, age and experience. The one thing they have in common is their ability to reflect on spirituality, all but one because of a personal affinity with the subject. Prior to the interviews I formulated a provisional theoretical framework based on literature and exploratory conversations concerning spirituality, humanism and humanist counselling. From this I derived several theses that were tested in the interviews and modified through the corresponding analysis (Maso & Smaling, 1998).

The research and interviews evolved around three questions that were intensively explored. First I asked humanist counsellors how they perceive or define spirituality. The second question concerned the way they see spirituality as an element of their profession, how they see the role of spirituality in their counselling practice. Thirdly, I asked how they relate spirituality to humanism. In this article I will concentrate on the second question: *how do humanist counsellors perceive the role and quality or trait of spirituality in their practice*? But first I will say something more about the way I have theorized and conceptualized both spirituality and humanist counselling.

THEORETICAL FRAMEWORK: SPIRITUALITY

My initial goal was to form a view on spirituality that was as little cultural and denominational-biased as possible, because I didn't want to exclude any kind of spirituality beforehand and therewith claim the concept to suit my own or a humanist view. The vision of spirituality that I articulated was therefore based on the assumption that there are common elements in all kinds of spiritual and religious traditions. This is supported by a growing tendency, both in and outside the academic world, to consider a somewhat universal approach of spirituality as a specific of our current spiritual climate and journey.[1] Distinguished scholars in the field of religious/spiritual studies (Cousins, 1996; Waaijman, 2000) and participants of new spiritual movements (New Age) agree

1. The current spiritual and religious diversity essentially point to one and the same spiritual reality. New forms of spirituality are not concerned with historical traditions themselves but with the like-minded, deep and universal truths they announce. From this perspective there are many roads to the one truth (Hanegraaff, 1996, Aupers, 2004). The spiritual view on religions is that they are expressions of the same cause. As such spirituality is characterized as trans-religious. Religions are often compared to a ladder, an instrument with which one can achieve a certain goal, the rooftop. But once one has reached the rooftop, the ladder is no longer needed and has become irrelevant. The view from the rooftop shows different ladders, different religions all leading to the same goal. The founder of the Theosophical Society, Madame Helena Blavatsky, compared the worldwide variety of religions with different rays of sunshine, all originating from and reflecting the same spiritual source. The spirituality I am speaking of in this paper is based on a commonality of mystical experiences of all religions worldwide. Of course this does not imply that more specific aspects of religions such as attitudes, practices, beliefs, deities, etc. should be regarded as the same or interchangeable.

on the legitimacy of a trans-cultural and trans-denominational perspective on spirituality, especially when direct experience is concerned.[2] Therefore I focused mainly on the experiences of my respondents and less on their beliefs.

In order to start off my research as inclusively as possible, I decided not to begin with a definition of spirituality but to formulate and describe five (sub) sectors of spirituality, which I will very briefly describe below.

First of all, spirituality is a word that most often refers to a *development*, a process of change or transformation. Words, concepts and images that are used to articulate this process are deeply influenced by cultural expectations, which create a variety of representations of such a process. In my opinion these can be roughly divided into two categories. Firstly, it can be envisioned as relational and ontological, for instance as the relationship between God and a person in a theistic setting. Spirituality refers to the transforming influence that this relationship has on the individual. Secondly, a spiritual process can also be perceived as a development of awareness, from a relative reality to an Absolute Reality, '*from the unreal to the real, from darkness to light, from death to immortality*' as the Indian Upanishads say. This 'shift' in awareness, is more often articulated in Eastern philosophies and Western esotericism, and is better suited to non-theistic representations of spirituality. This aspect of spirituality leads to the question of whether counsellors perceive spirituality as a process and how they experience, articulate and represent the changes—both in themselves and in their clients—that such a process brings about.

Second, spirituality has everything to do with *experiences*. These are experiences in which separations between a person and him or herself or the o/Other(s); between a person and nature; between a person and the whole existence; between a person and life-events or destiny, cease to exist in different gradations. There are many different kinds of experiences that are associated with the realm of the spiritual, ranging from transcendental mystical experiences to paranormal or psychic experiences. The question is what humanist counsellors perceive as spiritual experiences and if they have (had) such experiences themselves (and if so, under what conditions or in what context).

A third element that plays an important role in the concept of spirituality is the *philosophical view on life or reality*. Often, spiritual experiences, like mystical experiences of interconnectedness and oneness, are felt and understood as *more real* by the experiencers than so-called 'normal' experiences, which are dominated by a sense of separation. This often results in a philosophy of life that places this oneness as a central denominator and signifier instead of our 'normal' everyday experience of fragmentation and division. The question is what counsellors perceive to be spiritual ideas and convictions and how important these are to them.

---

2. Apart from their eclectic profile, new forms of spirituality distinguish themselves from 'old religion' by putting experience and mysticism in the centre, instead of religious dogma, and emphasizing the commonality of spiritual experiences throughout a diversity of cultures and times. Self-realization, enlightenment, Christ-consciousness, Buddha-awareness; nowadays these are all considered to be different cultural expressions that refer to more or less the same kind of experience of reality, usually called mystical experiences.

Closely connected to the philosophy of life is the fourth element, namely the way that this *life is lived* and the way *someone acts*. Spirituality is often perceived as a certain inner fundamental attitude that is linked with the moral choices an individual makes. In specific spiritual traditions the belief in or the experience of the interconnectedness of life are both cause and result of a certain attitude to life and ways of acting. In this respect one can think of the Buddhist custom to dedicate every action to the well-being of all living things, or Christian charity. This leads to the question, what do counsellors perceive to be a spiritual attitude?, that is, do they connect spirituality and inner attitude at all?

The fifth element is spiritual *praxis*. This is a Latin term that refers to the techniques and methods that have been developed in spiritual traditions in order to either manifest and mediate the spiritual dimension or initiate and stimulate the process of spirituality. This ranges from rituals to meditation, from prayer to spiritual counselling. The question is whether counsellors are acquainted with such practices, if so, which, why and how and what importance these have in their life and practice.

THEORETICAL FRAMEWORK: HUMANIST COUNSELLING

At the same time I have differentiated five—in reality closely interconnected—aspects of a humanist-counselling situation in which spirituality can play a role.

First is the client, who plays a very important role in this primarily client-centred practice. Spirituality can be present in the experiences, meanings and valuing process of the client.

Second is the personal development of the counsellor and the influence spirituality can have on that. In the past, when asked to define their methodology, humanist counsellors used to say: 'The client is the goal, I am the method', which indicates how closely connected the counsellor and the methodology are perceived to be. It is this factor that is explicitly pronounced in the concept of normative professionality.

Another normative aspect of the profession is the content of the advice that humanist counsellors provide. Although the focus is on the client, the counsellor does sometimes offer advice, opinions and interpretations that are closely linked with his or her own life experiences and philosophy, which can contain spiritual ideas and perceptions.

The fourth aspect refers to the forms humanist counsellors use to create a connection with a client. The communication in humanist counselling goes mainly through language, basically in the form of a dialogue. This aspect, however, can include working with symbols, rituals or other (spiritual) practices.

The fifth aspect concerns the inner attitude and inner experience of the counsellor. It raises the question of what counsellors perceive to be spiritual about this.

SPIRITUALITY IN PSYCHOTHERAPY AND HUMANIST COUNSELLING

PSYCHOTHERAPY AND SPIRITUALITY

In the last part of this article I will explore the spiritual dimension in humanist counselling in the context of a variety of literature on spirituality and psychotherapy/counselling. Through a short study of literature that contains the terms spirituality and psychotherapy or spirituality and counselling in the title,[3] three themes in particular caught my attention. These themes not only seemingly dominate this literature;[4] they can also be seen in sharp contrast with what my respondents perceive to be the spiritual dimension in their counselling practice. I will first discuss these themes, and then I will go into what humanist counsellors perceive as spiritual about their practice.

Raising awareness and providing knowledge

The first theme has a person-centred trait in the way that it is based on attention to the clients' beliefs, meanings and valuing process. By far the most literature on spirituality and counselling or psychotherapy is concerned with raising awareness about the importance of religious or spiritual beliefs to counselling sessions. They emphasize the need for a practitioner to consider and explore the religious systems that order their clients' world, for mainly two reasons. First, spirituality is increasingly recognized as vital for growth and essential for dealing with life's trials (Sperry, 2001). Second, because religious beliefs may influence the clients' engagement in counselling or psychotherapy and it is important to know how one, as a counsellor, can respectfully address resulting issues. Often such studies include information to help psychotherapists better understand religious beliefs, cultures, practices and clinical issues of members of specific religious denominations or communities (see Richards & Bergin, 1997; Miller, 2002; Fukuyama & Sevig, 1999; Kelly, 1995). By doing so they often exclude non-traditional/New Age, secular, humanistic, or atheistic forms of spirituality (Buddhism excluded), and confuse spirituality with religion (see Richards & Bergin 1997). In some cases the word spirituality turns out to refer to only one religious tradition, usually Christian (see Schreurs, 2001), or to only theistic forms of belief and practice. The overall theme is that religious competency is stressed as an essential component of effective psychotherapy and the aim is to integrate the religious dimension of clients' lives into the therapeutic process. It is often very closely aligned

3. Chandler, Holden & Kolander, 1992; Kelly, 1995; Richards & Bergin, 1997; Fukuyama & Sevig, 1999; West, 2000; Young-Eisendrath & Miller, 2000; Schreurs, 2001; Sperry, 2001; Miller 2002, Wiggins Frame, 2003.

4. I am fully aware of the fact that I do no justice to the above-mentioned works by reducing them to these three themes. Some of the literature does also include other aspects and approaches to spirituality. See for instance West (2000) who dedicates a whole chapter to how the therapeutic space can be experienced as spiritual (pp. 66–74).

with multiculturalism (Fukuyama & Sevig, 1999), and intends to help therapists acquire the knowledge and skills needed to practise with a diverse client population (Kelly, 1995). It coincides with the dawning awareness amongst psychologists and therapists of the importance of addressing existential and moral concerns as part of psychological health and with views of counselling and psychotherapy as spiritual disciplines on their own (van Kalmthout, 2001, 2002).

Offering views for spiritual assessment and diagnosis

Many of the above-mentioned studies aim at providing knowledge and insights to psychotherapists that can function as a basis for assessment and diagnosis. They focus on the ability of psychotherapists to recognize and evaluate their clients' spiritual experiences and beliefs. Models for spiritual wellness differentiating healthy from unhealthy spirituality (Chandler, Holden & Kolander, 1992) or concepts of mature spirituality (Young-Eisendrath, 2000) are being developed or represented (Wiggins Frame, 2003; Sperry, 2001). Most work in the field of transpersonal psychology, for instance Grof and Grof (1989) and Wilber's integral psychology (2000) coincide with this aspect. As does Assagioli's psychosynthesis and all other kind of psychological maps of human development, human consciousness or stages in a spiritual journey. Some studies explicitly approach this theme from the point of view of a certain life-stance like non-dual (Advaita) philosophy (Tiemersma, 2003) or Buddhism (Young-Eisendrath, 2002).

Offering tools for spiritual treatment

Naturally following from the first two approaches to spirituality and counselling is the focus on how the knowledge that is presented as such can eventually result in a way to treat clients. The aim is to integrate spiritual interventions into one's own counselling style (Fukuyama & Sevig, 1999) or offer treatment techniques and models for intervention (Kelly, 1995; Miller, 2002; Wiggins Frame, 2003; Sperry, 2001). They address the effectiveness of using not only spiritual concepts but also spiritual practices, symbols, techniques, disciplines, exercises and rituals, as useful adjuncts in the practice of spiritually attuned psychotherapy and counselling. The terms treatment, strategy and intervention dominate this discourse.

THE SPIRITUAL DIMENSION IN HUMANIST COUNSELLING

Although all of my respondents struggle to put into words something that often in their opinion belongs to the realm of the inexpressible, something that cannot be articulated, they in a certain way very much agree with each other when it comes to what they see as spiritual in their practice. Below I will present their main views in four steps.

A deep connection

To humanist counsellors spirituality first and foremost refers to inner experiences. Other aspects of spirituality such as beliefs or praxis are found to be more or less related to spirituality, but not essentially to what spirituality is about. A central concept in the way counsellors describe a spiritual experience is the term 'connection'. It refers to a feeling of being part of a movement, a dynamic that is larger than the individual 'I'. It is often accompanied by a sense that the individual 'I' doesn't really matter or becomes overwhelmed with feelings of humility. Being alone in nature or together with another person are two of the situations counsellors mention most as possible environments for these experiences to occur. Sexuality, cultural phenomena like music, art or religious environments like a church are hardly ever mentioned. Although the first kind of setting—alone in nature—can indirectly influence their work, the second one—in relation to another person—is obviously most associated with the counselling practice. It is experienced and articulated as a connection that transcends the two people involved. Some counsellors describe it as a connection that is made with the other person on the level of the heart. These moments are highly valued by the counsellors and are regarded as moments in which they fulfil their own expectations of the work. Counsellors experience that such a connectedness with a client heightens the quality of their own response.

Personal development

The counsellors consider these experiences as a powerful impulse, in both their professional and personal life. It encourages them to become more whole and more authentic human beings. So humanist counsellors also perceive spirituality as a process or development of change or transformation. The process is usually articulated in terms of a development towards a 'fuller' or 'higher humanity', a becoming *more* human, although some of them use terms like enlightened, divinity, god-like. They are learning to become more loving, more real or genuine, more courageous and peaceful people. In relation to counselling the emphasis is not so much on what their own spiritual development has brought them in terms of views, insights or beliefs. The accent is on what it has brought them in terms of skills, like the ability to deal with confusing situations without losing peace of mind, to embrace pain and grief with love and compassion and to keep their minds free from any kind of judgement. One of the counsellors says that a spiritual connection *only* happens when you are able to recognize, accept and embrace yourself, in other words, when there is a deep level of self-acceptance, a being comfortable with everything there is inside yourself, good and bad, brilliant and fallible, powerful and vulnerable.

Inner attitude

Closely connected to personal development and skills, is the inner attitude counsellors associate with spirituality and strive for as professionals. Their aim is to be capable of providing an unconditional space for everything that presents itself in a counselling situation in the moment, inwardly and outwardly, in themselves and the client. As such, humanist counselling is all about being present and not about treatment, about relationship and connection instead of change. The central value that defines both humanist counselling and spirituality according to all humanist counsellors is *unconditional love*, a state of being that enables concentration on the other person to such an extent that their usual 'self-centred' awareness dissolves. But besides love they also mention values like respect for the other person's individuality and autonomy, the importance of openness of mind, and the courage needed to trust themselves and such experiences. To all humanist counsellors these are the conditions for a real, spiritual connection with another person.

But there is a paradox: at the same time that counsellors link the appearance and working of the spiritual dimension to their own abilities and inner conditions, they also experience that such a connection can not be forced or created by willpower or any other kind of method. Often it just seems to 'happen', resulting in the feeling that they have no control whatsoever. What their work basically comes down to is creating a space that invites these kinds of connections to happen, this spiritual dimension to open up.

Ways of communicating and acting

The consequences of this connection and the conditions needed for what is verbally expressed by a counsellor in a counselling setting are twofold. First of all, counsellors are primarily present as listeners, not interpreters. Although they are called advisors, their work is basically about paraphrasing, asking the right questions and consciously using the art of silence in order to help the client to express and clarify his or her story. Some counsellors are overly aware of the danger of 'disowning the story' by their subjective interpretation and stress time and time again that humanist counselling is not about their own personal thoughts, beliefs or concerns. Most humanist counsellors only explicitly articulate their private points of view or interpretations when asked to do so. Otherwise they are mainly concentrated on asking about the significance of things to their clients in order to reveal the thoughts, feelings, and attitudes of their clients.

But at the same time, counsellors find that when they are totally empathically and mentally focused on the client, this 'togetherness' produces certain knowledge and subsequent responses. One counsellor, who goes out of his way not to use spiritual imagery and terms, describes it as being confrontational out of a 'joint knowledge'. Others describe such a situation as a moment in which their attitude and perception are deeply influenced by the spiritual dimension. This often leads to what some of them call—for lack of a more concrete term—'intuition'. Images and questions just pop up in one's consciousness, accompanied by a feeling of their importance and vitality, without counsellors being able to rationally explain the how and why of those images, questions or corresponding feelings. Some of the humanist counsellors speak of inner guidance, to put words to the experience in which ideas and insights seem to just come to you out of nowhere. But however each of them individually describes this experience, they all agree that any kind of action undertaken from this state of being always feels more effective and healing than other actions.

A SPIRITUAL METHODOLOGY

The stories produced by humanist counsellors—however differentiated—show a very dissimilar perception of spirituality from most contemporary literature on spirituality and therapeutic counselling. To some extent spirituality-related thoughts and practices as expressed by humanist counsellors contradict the importance of the previously mentioned three themes (raising awareness, assessment, treatment). This discrepancy can be traced back to the differences in the point of departure for both professions. Since addressing existential, religious and moral concerns is intrinsic to their profession, humanist counsellors are already deeply convinced of the importance of knowledge about different religious and non-religious beliefs, cultures and practices. According to some definitions humanist counselling already counts as a spiritual profession or practice, merely because of this line of approach. The fact that my respondents, contrary to psychological literature, do not consider these aspects to be specifically spiritual should be understood in this context and against the background of the earlier mentioned 'confusion' in the Dutch language concerning the terms *geestelijk* and *spiritueel*, because humanist counselling can also be translated as 'humanist spiritual counselling'. However, humanist counsellors qualify their work as a spiritual practice in so far as they feel called or somehow driven (essentially by love) to act in ways that transcend their personal interests. To them neither spirituality nor counselling is primarily about (intellectual) knowledge, but about relationship, love and presence.

The differences in starting points and/or aspired goals between psychotherapeutic counselling and humanist counselling cause further and more methodological dissimilarities in the way spirituality is perceived in both professions. As the analysis of the interview material shows, the conditions and content of humanist counselling, as well as the core values of its methodology, are largely reflected in the way humanist counsellors perceive the spiritual dimension in their work and could even be seen as creating the necessary conditions for spirituality to play a significant role. The lack of goals, treatment and methods that largely defines the profile of humanist counselling helps counsellors to stay very close to their intention to be of service to the other. Theoretical approaches of humanist counselling are often critical about other methods of mental/spiritual health care or some tendencies towards methodology-development in their own profession, for instance in terms of 'philosophical diagnosis' and related treatment plans (Bouwer, 2002: 81). Working with methods that require assessment, diagnosis or intervention is considered to be objectifying and therefore dehumanizing. Most counsellors I spoke to agree with this. They tend to be very cautious when it comes to defining their work in terms of methods, which in their opinion is very much in conflict with what they perceive to be a spiritual practice.

This resistance amongst humanist counsellors—although not always expressed in terms of spirituality—comes down to the following concerns. If we visualize the spiritual connection between two people as an empty but dynamic space or as a certain flow of energy, then methodological ingredients like assessment, diagnosis, the setting of goals, treatment or intervention, often crowd the empty space or block the flow of energy.

This occurs because such a methodology stimulates or sustains—often unconscious—needs, wants or beliefs amongst counsellors and/or their surrounding environment (society). All caregivers—including humanist counsellors—struggle (or in their opinion should struggle) with the way their own beliefs, feelings of helplessness or fear, or desire for power participate in and potentially influence their practice. Such 'hidden agendas' can lead to all too familiar situations in the field of counselling. Caregivers either want the other person to adapt to what the caregiver has experienced to be beneficial to him- or herself , or they want the other person to live up to certain perceptions of what the caregiver considers good, healthy or normal. Sometimes they just want the other to stop suffering because of their own incapacity to deal with it, or they keep their distance from such a deep emotional investment into the well-being of the other (and have no access to the knowledge and insight this can bring). Because of these 'all-too-human' tendencies, from a spiritual point of view, there is a need for a methodology that counters this. But instead, activities like assessment or intervention only seem to strengthen these cognitive, emotional and one-sided impulses. Analysis of the interview material shows three possible ways in which, according to humanist counsellors, a methodology that relies on assessment, treatment and intervention, makes it impossible to engage in a spiritual connection with each other.

First of all, to humanist counsellors, an openness of mind is vital, which means that a client should never be regarded as understood or known. Methodological acts like assessment and diagnosis though, encourage caregivers to label their clients or his or her behaviour, which bears the risk of not seeing the other person for who he or she is at that given time. Instead, humanist counsellors are focused on the whole person, on his or her 'being human' no matter what the circumstances are. They regard the other as someone with a personal biography, someone who is much more and much larger than the problem or situation he or she is in at the time. Approaches in counselling like assessment or diagnosis are, in the eyes of my respondents, seldom successfully combined with a true, respectful and egalitarian attitude and usually block the way to a spiritual connection and the specific kind of understanding this brings about. Second, on a more emotional level, a professionalism of assessment and intervention can strengthen an attitude of distance and authority. This shields caregivers from the discomfort of owning up to one's own 'not knowing' or being 'lost, helpless and naked'. Particularly one of my respondents, the one who is most critical of spirituality, stresses the importance of being aware of one's own vulnerability as a human being. In his opinion, not only a professionalism of assessment and intervention, but also some spiritual beliefs and practices deny or hide this vulnerability. As such, the client is deprived of the real, deep, spiritual bond with the caretaker that humanist counsellors tend to see as vital to 'healing'. And finally, intervention models implicate an approach to a situation or person with the intention to change. This intention sabotages the acceptance that is needed in the view of humanist counsellors, to form a spiritual connection. A methodology of real love and respect for the ultimate right to one's own self (autonomy) means adjusting your pace, accepting boundaries and remaining non-directive. One of the counsellors told me that she doesn't have the need or desire to change other people; she doesn't think the other should be different than he or she is at that given moment in time. In psychotherapy there is usually a lot of wanting and confronting going on. Another humanist counsellor has a therapeutic background and had to unlearn his tendency to 'treat' during his training as a humanist counsellor. He has come to the conclusion that as a therapist, he can circumvent the awareness of the client and easily pinpoint where it hurts, but in the end, this is often not really helping the other person, because it doesn't get to the root of what is there. According to this respondent it takes much more patience, self-control and self-less space for the other, to both reach the depth where things really matter and transformation can take place.

CONCLUSION: WHOSE HEAVEN?

In humanist counselling, the understanding of spirituality and counselling focuses not on spiritual models, techniques and information, but on awareness, personal development and inner attitude. According to humanist counsellors, spiritual forms of counselling should refrain from explicit and implicit ways of directing the client, as is often stimulated by a methodology of assessment, intervention and treatment. Such approaches to the other person, the relationship and the situation don't allow room for the spiritual dimension to open up, manifest itself or have any influence whatsoever. To the reader of this article this point of view might come across as too rigid. After all, it excludes the possibility of a successful, 'spiritual' combination of knowledge of assessment-models on the one hand and keeping an open mind on the other, or of the desire to change a wrong situation and being able to fully accept the 'here and now'. The multicultural legacy of traditions of wisdom and religion show that spirituality is always found in the combination of opposite 'qualities', such as wilful direction and surrender, holding on and letting go, being and becoming. In actual practice humanist counsellors have to deal with the difficult area of tension between being fully present as a person of flesh and blood and being fully person-centred at the same time. Besides, further analysis of the research material shows that the practice of humanist counsellors also consists of frameworks, goals and personal/societal influences. They too interpret, assess or diagnose, in the sense that they evaluate whatever the client says or how he or she behaves, and they also have intentions, in the sense that they want certain things to happen to their clients, to the relationship or to themselves. Too strong a rejection of methodological elements like assessment or intervention not only hinders the debate on possible 'spiritual' methodological combinations, it also obscures the level of transparency as a main quality of their professionalism.

But seeing their standpoint against the background of a society and field of work that seems to worship instrumentalist approaches, this contribution to the debate is a very important one. Humanist counsellors articulate a perspective that often seems to get lost in the narrow-minded focus on simplified and fragmented cause–result relations devoid of long-term thinking. Their voices remind all in the field of counselling and care-giving of the fact that that which is weak, unknown, complex or difficult to put into words, cannot be reduced, ignored or suppressed without paying a price. Although a spiritual connection seems to flow from certain conditions, at the same time, it cannot be created by calculated 'wanting', in the form of a strategy or a scheme. A spiritual 'method' comes down to a way of being with the other, not acting. It is not something you do, it is who you are, and it is about letting the other be who he or she is. Or, as one of the counsellors has put it: *'it is not my desire that they go to my heaven. It is my job to help them find their own'.*

REFERENCES

Aupers S ((2004) *In de Ban van Moderniteit. De sacralisering van het zerf en computertechnologie.* Amsterdam: Askant.

Beck, U (1992) *Risk Society: Towards a new modernity (Theory, culture and society).* London: Sage.

Borgman, E, van Harskamp, A & Vos M (ed) (2003) *Hunkering naar heelheid: over nieuwe religiositeit in Nederland.* Budel: Damon.

Bouwer, J (2002) De hermeneutisch diagnostische competentie van de geestelijk zorgverlener. *Tijdschrift Geestelijke Verzorging.* 6e jaargang, nummer 28, Zoetermeer: Boekencentrum.

Chandler, C, Holden, J & Kolander, C (1992) Counseling for spiritual wellness: Theory and practice. *Journal of Counseling & Development, 71,* 168–75.

Cousins, E (General ed) (1986) *World Spirituality. An encyclopedic history of the religious quest.* See for instance Volume 16: *Christian Spirituality: Origins to the twelfth century.* B McGinn & J Meyendorff (eds), (1986). London: Routledge and Kegan Paul.

Fukuyama, M & Sevig, T (1999) *Integrating Spirituality into Multicultural Counseling.* Thousand Oaks, California USA: Sage.

Grof, S & Grof, C (1989) *Spiritual Emergency: When personal transformation becomes a crisis.* New York: Tarcher.

Hanegraaff, W (1996) *New Age Religion and Western Culture. Esotericism in the mirror of secular thought.* Leiden: Brill.

Kelly, E (1995) *Spirituality and Religion in Counseling and Psychotherapy: Diversity in theory and practice.* Alexandria, VA: American Counseling Association.

Maso, I & Smaling, A (1998) *Kwalitatief onderzoek: Praktijk en theorie.* Amsterdam: Boom.

Miller, G (2002) *Incorporating Spirituality in Counseling and Psychotherapy. Theory and technique.* New Jersey: John Wiley & Sons.

Richards, P & Bergin, A (1997) *A Spiritual Strategy for Counseling and Psychotherapy.* Washington, DC: American Psychological Association.

Schreurs, A (2001) *Psychotherapie en Spiritualiteit. Integratie van de spirituele dimensie in de therapeutische praktijk.* Assen: Koninklijke Van Gorkum.

Sperry, L (2001) *Spirituality in Clinical Practice. Incorporating the spiritual dimension in psychotherapy and counseling.* Philadelphia PA: Brunner-Routledge.

Tiemersma, D (ed) (2003) *Psychotherapie & non-dualiteit. 3e Advaita Symposium.* Leusden: Uitgeverij Advaita Centrum.

Van Houten, D & Mooren, J (2002) Humanist counseling in the Netherlands. In A Halsema & D van Houten (eds) *Empowering Humanity. State of the art in humanistics.* Utrecht:

Tijdstroom.

Van Kalmthout, M (2001) Psychotherapie: een hedendaags zingevingssysteem? In M van Kalmthout, T Festen, B-P De Roeck, H De Dijn, A Schreurs & F Maas (eds) *Spiritualiteit in Psychotherapie?* (pp. 12–28). Tilburg: KSGV.

Van Kalmthout, M (2002) Psychotherapie: Tussen wetenschap en religie (I&II) In GAMMA, jaargang 9 nr. 3&4.

Waaijman, K (2000) *Spiritualiteit: Vormen, grondslagen, methoden.* Kampen: Kok.

West, W (2000) *Psychotherapy and Spirituality: Crossing the line between therapy and religion.* London: Sage.

Wiggins Frame, M (2003) *Integrating Religion and Spirituality into Counseling. A comprehensive approach.* Toronto: Brooks/Cole.

Wilber, K (2000) *Integral Psychology: Consciousness, spirit, psychology, therapy.* Boston: Shambhala.

Young-Eisendrath, P & Miller, M (eds) (2000) *The Psychology of Mature Spirituality: Integrity, wisdom, transcendence.* London: Routledge.

Young-Eisendrath, P & Muramoto, S (eds) (2002) *Awakening and Insight: Zen Buddhism and psychotherapy.* Hove: Brunner-Routledge.

CHAPTER 22

AN EXPLORATION OF THE RELATIONSHIP BETWEEN HUMANISM AND CHRISTIANITY IN THE PRACTICE OF COUNSELLING

JACK EARL

INTRODUCTION

This paper is based on a study carried out by my late wife, Anne Earl, ten years ago at the St Barnabas Counselling Centre in Norwich. The Centre is still active—it has just celebrated its thirtieth anniversary—and, while there have inevitably been changes, its basic principles remain the same as they were then.

The Centre was started by a group of Christians interested in healing and developed under the guidance of Denis Duncan and Brian Thorne into a Christian counselling centre operating on the principles of Rogerian person-centred counselling. It was not run by any church or denomination. There was (and is) an unobtrusive ecumenical chapel. And we worked on the principle that religion would not be mentioned unless it came up spontaneously—but if it did we were all prepared to follow wherever it led. We found that we were treated by secular referral bodies as a normal centre but we also found that we received very few referrals from the churches—the church members who came were almost all self-referrals. It became clear that some Christian bodies were uneasy about our allegedly humanist approach and it was this area of unease and suspicion that Anne decided to explore.

There is, of course, a long tradition, dating back to Erasmus and beyond, of Christian humanism, but 'humanist' is here taken as referring to a world-view which excludes religious and spiritual considerations, as in Erich Fromm's statement that humanism 'is the belief in the unity of the human race and man's ability to perfect himself by his own efforts' (Fromm, 1965: ix).

Anne based her work on 30 taped interviews of ex-clients, counsellors and local clergy, in approximately equal numbers. Most, but not all, were connected with St Barnabas.

EXPECTATIONS

All the ex-clients interviewed had been to St Barnabas. Their answers were interestingly varied.

Q What was your reaction to the idea of going to a Christian centre?
1 (ex-client) When a friend suggested St Barnabas I said 'Oh, no. They're going to lay hands on me and pray!'

In spite of this reaction she did come, but presumably a lot of other people felt much the same and did not come—and we can say nothing more about them.

2 (ex-client) I think I thought of St Barnabas first, and only thought of Christian counselling then.
Q The fact that it was a Christian centre seemed to you a plus?
2 (ex-client) It didn't at the time because it was the only counselling centre I knew of and although I always had deep Christian feelings my faith wasn't really strong at that time. It's got stronger since then actually.
Q Did you meet anyone who took the other view—you know, they didn't want the Christian outlook?
2 (ex-client) Oh yes, I have, definitely. It did make people wary. I have got a friend, actually, who was going into counselling but she didn't want any connection with St Barnabas because of the Christian connection. Although I explained that it's Christian only as far as you want it to be, she just didn't want any connection.

Q Did you want Christian counselling?
3 (ex-client) Yes. In fact if it hadn't been Christian counselling I wouldn't have considered it. The fact that it was Christian was very important.
Q You would have turned down the idea of another sort?
3 (ex-client) Yes. I think I would have felt very apprehensive because I wouldn't have been sure that the person doing the counselling would have been sympathetic towards Christian belief, and I don't think I could have coped at that stage with anybody who wasn't.

4 (ex-client) Yes, I think probably a Christian counselling centre is more caring; they are more able to reach individuals and help them achieve the best in their lives. I thought of an occasion when I did have counselling with a psychiatric nurse, and she wasn't a believer, and when I said that when I read in church, actually God helped me to do that, she said: 'You can't even take that, that you did it yourself.'
Q How did that make you feel?
4 (ex-client) I felt a little bit angry, and a little bit sorry, and it was hard for me to go on from there, to express much more about that. I don't often talk about my Christian feelings to people who I know haven't got them, anyway, which may not be a very good thing to be doing but—

5 (ex-client) I don't think it made any difference. I'd heard about St Barnabas and I knew its reputation so I chose it because I felt it would be a good place to go to. I never thought about the Christian side of it. Actually I'd met quite a few people from there—that was through youth work. I hadn't really thought of having counselling myself, but I

> *recognized, because of sort of looking at things more deeply, there were some areas in my life I needed to talk through with somebody. I don't think I even thought about the Christian side of it. It certainly wasn't what attracted me to going there.*
> *Q It didn't put you off?*
> *5 (ex-client) No, because I had a sense that if I wanted to talk about the Christian side of it, it would be all right, and if I didn't want to, that would be all right as well. I don't know where I got this sense from, but I suppose it was from the people I knew. I didn't want to be preached to, I knew that. I don't want people to preach to me. I like to find my own way.*

> *6 (ex-client) I first came to know of St Barnabas through a leaflet pinned to a noticeboard inside Norwich Cathedral. I think the fact that it was ecumenical relaxed me because I thought it would be open-minded and not narrowly religious or fundamentalist. It definitely hooked up the leaflet with the calm, cool, stately reassurance and tradition of the cathedral, and this was somehow merging St Barnabas and the cathedral in my mind. There was never a strict or severe religious atmosphere at St B's, but one I always appreciated as very tolerant and at the same time sacramental. I loved the fact that although religion was never mentioned in the waiting area, and for someone coming in it might be looked on as strictly secular, I felt there was a lovely silent undergirding, a thread that gave the counsellors and clients and staff a sense of a security and a firm foundation.*

There is a clear divide observable here—clients who come with a Christian faith already developed and are anxious about attacks on their faith which they fear they might meet in a secular setting, while others come without any clear religious affiliation and are sometimes anxious about unwelcome attacks on their undecided stance. Both the Christian and the agnostic seem to expect the 'other side' to launch an attack which in their vulnerable state they fear. Unfortunately such fears are by no means always unjustified. A friend (who had not been to St Barnabas) spoke of an unhappy encounter in another Christian centre with a clergyman who 'told me if I didn't know what was wrong with me; he did'. And 4 (ex-client) above gives an example from the other side. The authoritative approach is normally unwelcome and unproductive, even to a troubled soul. As we shall see later, there may be exceptions to this, but most clients, whether Christian or agnostic, would echo 5 (ex-client)'s words 'I don't want people to preach to me. I like to find my own way.'

The counsellors they met naturally had rather different expectations and might see both the task and the aim differently.

> *7 (counsellor) The clients' expectations vary enormously. Some people want you to wave a magic wand and make them better; others want to explore themselves, and others come for a solution to particular crises and problems.*
> *Q Do you think the title 'Christian' has any implications, negative or positive?*
> *7 (counsellor) If it puts people off—but then it doesn't arise.*
> *Q Because then they don't come?*
> *7 (counsellor) Yes. Some people have said that they were perhaps slightly put off by it, and*

had all sorts of expectations about that. The other thing that happens is of course that people come wanting Christian counselling—a particular idea of what that will mean.
Q Do you think they sometimes have the wrong idea?
7 (counsellor) I think they do, yes, well, as far as I'm concerned. I was just thinking of one lady who expected that I would pray with her in every session—and that might have been appropriate. It didn't feel appropriate because I think she'd always used that as a way of avoiding what she was feeling.

8 (counsellor) Well, generally, I think people are asking for several things. They are asking for you to take the pain away, asking to feel better, asking to have a problem solved, and sometimes they are asking for all those things to happen without them having to change—I always have this feeling and what I often say to people who talk about the Christian dimension is that when I say I am a Christian what I'm really saying is that it's something about how I try to value people.

9 (counsellor) Yes. I think I've had experience of clients who have wanted answers. No matter how many times I've said to them: 'It's self-direction here', there's still an undercurrent of 'So what do you think?' So in that sense they've come with a different understanding of counselling. But they've worked with that, and I've batted it back to them quite a lot, till they've actually heard it and said, 'Well I know it's no use me asking. I'll have to think about it myself.' What they've found out is that they actually do know exactly what they want.

The fear that clients may have, that their beliefs, their stances, will be attacked, is evident to counsellors, but they distinguish a more disabling expectation: that the problems of their lives will be solved for them 'without them having to change'. This can be true of both the believer and the agnostic and is due, as 9 (counsellor) says, to 'a different understanding of counselling'. The counsellor's expectation is that, as the relationship develops, the client will find the courage to explore his or her self and discover their own directions. The faith of the counsellor, whether Christian or not, is that within the client's essential self there is an inner wisdom; that 'they actually do know exactly what they want'.

THE GOAL OF COUNSELLING

Of the following answers three come from St Barnabas staff, one (11) comes from a counsellor who is an atheist and one (14) from a Christian counsellor working in a secular setting. There seems to be considerable agreement.

Q What do you consider to be the goal of counselling?
10 (counsellor) For me the goal is self-acceptance by the person. That will enable them to go forward and go on and not see any particular set of obsessions as an end in itself. They can do that, I feel, when they've accepted themselves.

11 (counsellor) I suppose that I see it as helping people to come to terms with themselves as they are, and making them perhaps feel more at home with themselves. I think that's what counselling's about. It's about making people feel at ease with themselves and, where possible, changing things so that they can be. If not, perhaps accepting that that's how they are, but they can still manage.

12 (counsellor) I think the goal of counselling is to try and help someone to find their own way through and out into a better situation, which is their answer and may not be mine.

13 (counsellor) The overall goal for me is to seek to help the client become more in touch with their own strength and their own wisdom, so that they may have more hands on and eyes on their own life.

14 (counsellor) It's actually to enable a person to discover more about the essential nature of their own being, and to move towards the fulfilment of that being. That's what I see to be the goal. It's a very broad goal indeed, and I, at the start of any counselling relationship, do not have any goals. And that's quite interesting, because I think that quite a number of counsellors do have goals. The only goal I have, in a sense, is to accompany my client towards his or her goals, and I haven't the remotest idea what those are. They may change. They may come with the goal of stopping the pain—a goal which may well change as time goes on.

The humanist counsellor and the Christian counsellor do seem to have very similar ideas about the goal of counselling even though clients who come to a Christian centre may not expect this. If we go on to consider the replies from a group of interested clergy to the same question we get more theological answers.

Q What is the wholeness towards which a human being is striving and growing? What is *a human being?*
15 (clergy) Wholeness for the individual; that is quite likely to have ramifications for the social setting of the individual; it's not merely doing good for the counselled individual. Wholeness has a spin-off right across the spectrum. One—a person who is at one with themselves and with those that they are in relationship with, family and community, and ultimately at one, at peace, with God. That's a state which, I suspect, one hardly, if ever, achieves. But I think that is the state to which we are called.

16 (clergy) I think spiritual direction is very often understood to be about growth or development in your religious beliefs, but I would not separate that from development in your personal growth because I think both of them go hand in hand. It's one person; I think we've for much too long given in to the old Hellenistic division between soul and body and spirit; a human being is one unit. And everything affects everything else.

17 (clergy) At some point a human being comes into contact with the divine, the eternal. Presumably a humanist can have a tremendous sense of the value of a person, which is why some humanists are more humane than a lot of Christians, though not necessarily; some humanists are very cynical about human life. But it starts at birth and finishes at death; on that view that's it, it finishes—and looking vertically, well, there's no vertical, there's no upwards to God. It's just us together on earth. 'Upwards' is a bit old-fashioned but you know what I mean. You look outside yourself and there is God, who is incomparably greater than yourself, which doesn't actually diminish your personal meaning; in the long run it enhances it, because you are subordinate to an almighty God. And on the time continuum, your life moves into the eternal.

18 (clergy) There's a modern way of expressing it—an open-ended proposition: someone with a transcendental destiny, and someone who, in relationship, is always open to the transcendent. And I suppose here Freud has helped me—(and I have taken fully on board the business of neurotic religion, I suppose we're all captive to it to some extent because there's a great deal of it about). I think that view is present in the New Testament. Where Christianity might disagree with Freud is in holding that healthy religion is actually a truth, in the divine calling of the soul, which is what we were made to orient ourselves towards. That's truly what we're about, and in doing that we take up our complete humanity—so it's not a cop-out from being human. It's flourishing as a human, in the process of being restored through Christ.

Humanist and Christian have something in common in their view of human beings, something which can be called respect or reverence, an exalted view of human possibility summed up in two ancient sayings. The humanist Protagorus is reported to have said: 'Man is the measure of all things' (Plato: *Theaetetus* 160d) and the Christian Irenaeus wrote: 'The glory of God is man fully alive' (*Adversus Haereses* iv. 20. 7). But there is a difference, which is brought out by the speakers who refer to the 'vertical dimension' and 'the divine calling of the soul' in which 'we take up our complete humanity'.

Some of us believe that there can be a positive side to this conflict. One Christian counsellor who worked in a secular setting, with clients of every sort, after expressing his vision of his clients as spiritual entities, went on to speak of the creative aspect of this tension thus:

19 (counsellor) I think one of the most exciting things about counselling is how individuals can, from the most unlikely starting points, gradually get towards that perception for themselves, in their own ways—they may not be Christian ways at all—a way of apprehending themselves really as having infinite value, and therefore being part of something which is infinite.

Not all Christians involved in counselling and not all clergy are prepared to take such an open-ended approach.

One parish priest—who has brought spiritual help to many—said:

> *20 (clergy) I see how counselling has developed, but actually I see myself standing in a much older tradition, and if they want to find a new-fangled word to talk about it, that's all right with me. But people are coming to see me because I'm a priest, and the God dimension has got something to do with it. Obviously if someone goes along to a secular agency and wants to talk about the situation they're in, and their own growth, etc., that's fine. But if they come to me as a priest, and want to talk about the difficult circumstances they're in, or how they're going to grow, then that becomes spiritual direction. Much, I think, of what secular agencies do is based on a misunderstanding. There are clearly those people who have had bad experiences, and, yes, they do need people alongside them as they come to terms with, and deal with the consequences of, those experiences. I wouldn't want to say that helping agencies are not a good thing. But sometimes people will talk round and round again, and I think there's a sense in which they're talking themselves deeper into depression.*

And to the couple who run a respected Christian healing centre there is no doubt that they can offer more than the secular counsellor can:

> *21 (clergy) We start then into some positive ministry. We're not secular counsellors. All they can say at that point is, 'OK—well we can see what your problem is, now can you shrug your shoulders—and own it and go on ahead?' Well, I don't think that is the truth. So there has to be a positive stage of handing them over to God. And that will take place in a variety of ways.*

We may feel tempted to dismiss some of these comments as caricatures of person-centred counselling but it is as well to remember that they do represent the views of a number of our Christian friends. It may also be as well to remember that a number of those seeking counselling are looking for an authoritative figure (wearing a dog-collar or a white coat) to free them from their pain—as some earlier quotations from counsellors have indicated. These comments also indicate why self-designated Christian centres and counsellors are sometimes regarded with suspicion by others. Several such suspicions were recorded—and they do not all come from non-Christians.

> *22 (counsellor) I see us all as being incredibly subjective, as human beings, and that subjectivity is there lurking, and I think sometimes it can be poisonous. I mean you might actually behave in a manipulative way with a client and not know it. So if there's no organisational back-up and supervision, we're putting ourselves at risk, not only putting clients at risk.*
> *Q But if an agency or a person offers what they call 'Christian counselling'?*
> *22 (counsellor) I would be anxious until I actually knew the people who were doing it, and who were supervising those who were offering it. I do know that there are times when Christians can be rather directive, and rather too powerful, actually. It's not telling you what to do, it's more as though their scheme of things must be the right way forward, and their interpretation of Christianity must be the model. I do have an anxiety about people who adopt a religion, and can sometimes not be allowing that religion to permeate them*

> *in a deep sense; it's simply helping them with their identity. I think some followers of religious beliefs are searching madly, because they find relationships a failure. So on both scores I would have some anxiety unless I knew the organization and the people running it.*

A Christian counsellor sums up the secular view thus:

> *23 (counsellor) I think the fear is that these people aren't counsellors at all. Rightly or wrongly, they* [secular counsellors] *see them very often as plying a particular belief system, and they see them essentially as operating from a basis which doesn't offer the individual proper freedom.*
> *Q From the secular side, is there a feeling that these people have a hidden agenda?*
> *23 (counsellor) Yes, I think that's right, that sums it up quite nicely, and the hidden agenda is that this counsellor would really prefer it if this person believed in God, and would really prefer it, further, if this client were able to own allegiance to Christ and the church. But by sticking the word 'Christian' in front of you at least you're being honest in a way because you say, 'This is my agenda'; it's not so hidden.*

Another counsellor who is a Christian comments in this way:

> *24 (counsellor) I feel in a lot of the secular centres a lot of the participants have found a spiritual ingredient. I think that the area we're working in has a spiritual ingredient.*
> *Q How does that relate to the people who want to make the area more precise, who want to define what's Christian and what isn't?*
> *24 (counsellor) Well that's much more to do with their needs than with the needs of those who come to them for help. There's a place for it, but I think it can often encourage a dependency, somebody else providing the absolutes and the truths, rather than working them out for yourself.*

We've already had evidence of the way in which many of our clients feel anxiety in the face of dogmatism, fear of judgement, fear of pressure on their own, sometimes fragile, ego-strength: 'Oh no. They're going to lay hands on me and pray!'; 'I don't want people to preach to me'. One of Anne's friends (already mentioned) had the experience of being assailed from both sides.

> *25 (ex-client)* Having escaped from the parson who 'knew what was wrong with me though I didn't', she landed in a group which '*felt very uneasy with me. I actually got called "the enemy within" because I was bringing the churchy, destructive thing. There was no way ever you could get them to notice that other dimension.*'

The whole spirit of these exchanges is well expressed by a remark made to Anne in an informal conversation after a church meeting. Someone had quoted Frances Havergal's (1836–1879) hymn (in *Hymns and Psalms*, 1983):

O strengthen me, that while I stand
Firm on the rock, and strong in thee
I may stretch out a loving hand
To wrestlers with the troubled sea.

In relation to this, a friend whom Anne knew to be deeply disturbed said to her,

> *26 (ex-client) No, I don't want someone on a rock. I want someone in the sea with me—but they can swim.*

It does indeed seem that one thing that most humanist and Christian counsellors have in common is a conviction that rocks are out and swimmers are in. But how does this work out in practice?

REACHING THE GOAL

Well, for a start, it means real openness to one another and that leads to all sorts of exciting possibilities. A freelance counsellor with a strong interest in Indian religions speaks very positively of this:

> *27 (counsellor) That process of unconditional positive regard for their world-view—and they're doing the same for me, because they come back even though they know I'm not a Christian in their terms, so they are actually doing me the honour of looking at my world and accepting it—it's that process that somehow seems to me to be the door—those wordless moments when all that structure falls away, and what I'm trying to do becomes possible because I cannot name what is nameless. I can only say, 'Come with me to that place'.*

Other counsellors have stressed that their acceptance of a client's world-view does not mean that they share it. The counsellor remains a separate person and this can make the resulting interaction all the more fruitful.

> *28 (counsellor) I also have to make sure that I do not take on board for me personally the value system from which they are working, because if I do that and my value system is different, I'm colluding with them and I'm not a separate person. And part of the essence of the way we're working is the interaction between the two of us, so there's a place for disagreement. I think to acknowledge that two people can come from different places but can still do business together, that would be valuable for both of us.*

It is not the presence of a value system that prevents people from finding themselves but rather the sense of dogmatism and pressure in their surroundings.

One ex-client described her experience like this:

29 (ex-client) I found the same thing when I went, because the first person I met, who did my intake—I was conscious that she was a Christian but it didn't get in the way. I think what was so creative about the whole thing was the freedom in it; that I knew that they were Christian-based, that once the counselling got under way the presence of God was there. And I think it was the first time that I've felt that in such a profound way, and that I valued the Christian base more and more as time went on.
Q Did any of the concepts which came up in counselling seem wrong to you, or challenge your previous ideas?
29 (ex-client) No, nothing. It really was exactly what I was looking for, it was very creative. It was almost as if it was just the right thing at the right time for me, and that I was allowed to grow and be myself.

Another ex-client, one who later became a counsellor, was even more eloquent:

Q Did your own feelings and values change when you started counselling training?
*30 (counsellor and ex-client) Values, I think. My values have been the important change, that's what I'm trying to say. I think I became freer to be me. I think, before, I used to put on an act or image of what I was supposed to be, and it was like being set free. And I found the more I was more real with people, the more I got back. It was very rewarding. I'm not sure about the word '*real*'. I don't know what 'real' means, but I found freedom with people. I've been touched by people, and I think I've touched them, and I think that's what my religion is. I went into an encounter group. Now I didn't know what an encounter group was. I knew very little about this Carl Rogers person. I can remember just sitting there and somebody said something. I can remember thinking, 'We can be real!' And I can remember feeling such a relief. It was just like someone had opened the doors for the first time. I don't think I'd been pretending all my life, but—it just felt as if I'd made human contact with people, real human contact. So that was what started it, that was valuable—and, I think, sharing at a different level. It must be something to do with inside, how you feel about yourself inside.*
Q How you feel about yourself?
30 (counsellor and ex-client) Yes, I'm much more comfortable with myself now. Not all the time—and that's like—I've heard people say it's like something that I can't explain. It's like this Godlike—whatever word you use. It's like this important thing. It's something I can't get hold of, I suppose.

Words often fail us—as postmodernism has reminded us. Can we get beyond words? In one sense the conflict we are discussing is about language; it's a conflict between those to whom God-language has no meaning and those to whom God-language has all the meaning there is, those to whom, in fact, God *is* meaning. This is the biggest problem of modern theology: can we talk about God at all?

One of Anne's clerical friends puts this very clearly:

31 (clergy) The Church's language is either so alien, or so worked to death, or so emptied of its fundamental meaning, which I think it sometimes is. I think tremendous words of theological thrust and religious power are used in such a flat, shallow way that it's not surprising that people have parted company with trying to give them credibility. For a lot of people religious language is airy-fairy; it doesn't apply to reality, it's a psychological choice of interpretative language—so that there is 'my spirituality' and 'your spirituality', and this is a language of considerable integrity, granted where we all start from today. But it begs many awe-full questions about the common journey and destiny of human beings, and the kind of language of communal experience and sharing which we desperately need and are finding it very difficult to locate, because all the traditional languages of that kind have been dishonoured, or the doors have been shut in so many people's faces that they have no access to them.

Some of the remarks made by ex-clients certainly bear this out:

32 (ex-client) I can look around, you know, at the sky and the trees and all things like that, and especially out in the wilderness somewhere, especially somewhere that's not been cultivated—I can really feel that there is something really enormous, something that I don't understand and don't know about, but I'm not so sure that I believe the stories. I don't think I believe the stories behind religion, but I believe that there is something, you know—that I can't explain. Perhaps I don't even want to. Perhaps it doesn't matter. Someone has written that they've been striving all their lives to get somewhere, and arrive, and then they realized that that was what life was, striving towards something, and that's what it was, each day was—it. And that sort of made sense. It encouraged me. So I don't really know what will happen, I don't even know if that matters.

One counsellor feels that language by itself is bound to be divisive, and that if we human beings are to meet and understand one another we must meet 'outside', without 'naming':

33 (counsellor) As I was thinking about it, the quality of the experience I've sometimes had when I've been counselling or, indeed, have had when I've been counselled (it's a mutual experience) is the same, it's a timeless moment. And in counselling, when I'm struggling after unconditional positive regard, or experiencing it from someone else, there comes a moment when it seems to me that even my failure to have it is held by this process of regarding. We are both looking at our thoughts, feelings, everything that is moving within us—and we're just looking, just gazing. That moment to me is the moment of healing. In my experience there is a point at which being with a Christian or being with someone who doesn't share that world view ... the quality of the meeting can be the same—and it is at that moment that we're enabled to stand back, see what we are, accept what we are, and not even name it.

He speaks of the 'timeless moment' when the exchange of speech is abandoned for a different kind of understanding. Several ex-clients have also spoken of non-speech experiences.

34 (ex-client) I loved the fact that though religion was never mentioned—and for someone coming in it might be looked on as strictly secular, I felt that there was a lovely silent undergirding.

35 (ex-client) Although I didn't actually go into the chapel, I liked the fact that it was there, for some reason.

36 (ex-client) It was the presence of God that became known in an unspoken way.

Can the principles of counselling bring insights to these experiences of encounter between opposing world-views? This is a claim often made for it and it has a sound basis in one of the 'core conditions', empathy or understanding, which is defined by Mearns and Thorne as follows:

> The third element which is necessary in the therapeutic relationship is *empathic understanding*. When this is present the counsellor demonstrates a capacity to track and sense accurately the feelings and personal meanings of the client; she is able to learn what it feels like to be in the client's skin and to perceive the world as the client perceives it. What is more, she develops the ability to communicate to the client this sensitive and expectant understanding. (Mearns & Thorne, 1988: 15, original emphasis)

And Rogers says:

> It is the counselor's function to assume, in so far as he is able, the internal frame of reference of the client, to perceive the world as the client sees it, to perceive the client himself as he is seen by himself ... and to communicate something of this empathic understanding to the client. (Rogers, 1951: 29)

Naturally the counsellor is not always successful, but the attempt to understand may itself be reassuring to the client, and may help him or her to clarify their own confused feelings.

As one counsellor said:

37 (counsellor) I don't know that I have to understand a person necessarily; I've heard what they said, and I suppose mirroring it is an invitation to them to look again at what they've said, to go down another layer. It's not necessarily to show whether I understood it, but to clarify it in their own minds.

There are illuminated moments in human interaction, whether in a counselling interview, or a group discussion, or an ordinary conversation—when one is really attending, when one says the tentative, 'You mean ... ?' and the other replies, 'Yes, That's it!' It creates a space, sometimes a long space, a silence, a timeless moment. It is a moment of disclosure, what Gestalt therapists call an 'Aha! moment'. It is in that silence that change—healing—takes place.

One counsellor says:

> *38 (counsellor) It's an awareness, I suppose, of something happening between the counsellor and the client, of something above and beyond the counsellor and the client; that those moments are actually not the result of the work of either but of something bigger—the personal history of the client, and of the counsellor, seem to be kind of used—there is something more going on.*

One ex-client describes the profound healing of this exchange—understanding and being understood:

> *39 (ex-client) It was the sheer quality of the thing that I enjoyed as well, because I knew that she was getting almost as much out of it as me, and that made it more valuable to me. I rather expected that I would be talked to a lot, and that didn't happen—I found that very good, that I was able to give something as well. It wasn't just the time that I spent there; sometimes I'd be walking along the road afterwards, something completely new would occur to me, that I'd never thought about before. It was quite a profound moment, afterwards.*

Wittgenstein says: 'Only in the stream of thought and life do words have meaning' (Thiselton, 1980: 374), and Thiselton, commenting on this, says, 'What speaking is and what meaning is, depends on the surroundings in which language is spoken' (1980: 375). Thus those who try to establish the 'surroundings' of a relationship of unconditional positive regard are experimenting with new creative exchanges which bypass the difficulties we have in understanding one another's language.

Both Christian and secular counsellors see healing as coming through unconditional acceptance and forgiveness. Some Christians consider forgiveness as mediated only through Christian thought-forms and Christian words, but this does not seem to be how Jesus himself spoke of forgiveness. He gave it a central place in his teaching and told his followers to pray: 'Forgive us our sins as we also forgive everyone who sins against us' (Luke 11: 4).[1] This has always been a cornerstone of the Christian faith. Paul says, 'Forgive as the Lord forgave you' (Colossians 3: 13). Forgiveness does not seem to be a matter of ritual words or actions but of restored relationships, both human and divine, of reconciliation. The theologian Paul Tillich sums up the Christian gospel thus: 'You are accepted, accepted by that which is greater than you—simply accept the fact that you are accepted' (Tillich, 1962: 163). These words could almost (as he himself implies) be used by a non-Christian counsellor as well as by a Christian one, as (with a few amendments) could John Taylor's: 'Not in our greater goodness, then, but in our openness to one another, in Christ's name, the Spirit possesses us' (Taylor, 1972: 127).

---

1. Biblical quotations are from The New International Version (1979), London: Hodder & Stoughton.

It is true that the humanist and the Christian may not believe the same about the origin of sin or of forgiveness or, indeed, use the same words, but both believe in the importance of mutual openness and acceptance for healing—for salvation. Conflict may arise if language obscures this agreement—the dogmatic use of religious or psychological language. It is in action, very often without words, that healing comes; when a human being, acknowledging his or her own inner reality, meets another with real understanding and acceptance.

Thus Lambourne, writing as a Christian, says of humanist psychotherapy:

> The therapy is a matter of 'involvement', 'self-exposure', and the limits of the willingness of those concerned to suffer creatively are the limits of therapy attainable. There is real insight here into the Christian affirmation that fullness of life is a life of self-committal to others from the depths of one's being to the depths of another's being, and that this involves suffering love. (Lambourne, 1963: 119)

This is echoed on the humanist side by writers such as Peter Lomas, who stresses the central importance of human relationships in counselling, commenting: 'I am not alone in openly stating that the therapist's love often plays a significant part in healing, and may even be the crucial factor' (Lomas, 1981: 7).

That Lomas was certainly not alone was demonstrated by the publication of *The Faith of the Counsellors*, in which Paul Halmos produced an impressive weight of evidence to show that, even though it often hid behind a screen of respectable scientific terminology, the counselling profession was in fact expressing a tremendous faith in the power of love, often astonishingly similar to certain kinds of Christian mysticism—not least in its acceptance of paradox. It is surprising, but perhaps salutary, to find that he felt it necessary to end by expressing concern at the inroads of what he called 'mechanistic' therapies:

> The question is primarily not whether the mechanistic account of love is true, but how shall we continue our progress in love and, indeed, survive when everybody thinks it true? And how shall we be able to administer help to others without the Faith of the Counsellors? (Halmos, 1965: 200)

This conference is, surely, ample evidence that the faith of the counsellors is still very much alive forty years later, and if we are looking for twenty-first century testimony to the healing power of love we have only to turn to two recent books by one of our conference organizing committee, Brian Thorne (Thorne, 2002, 2003).

In fact, testimony to that power can be found throughout the whole history of psychotherapy for, as far back as the 6th December 1906, Freud wrote to Jung: 'Essentially, one might say, the cure is effected by love' (McGuire, 1974: 12–13). Is, then, the basic conflict simply about the Christian saying, 'Love? Hey, that's my magic!' and the humanist replying, 'Yes, I daresay, but you haven't done very well with it, so move over and let us have a turn'?

There may be an element of such feelings in the picture we have uncovered but fortunately the general situation is much happier than that. Ten years ago Anne wrote: 'The outstanding feature of the present scene, at least in my experience, seems to be how much we learn from each other, and how freely we help each other in the great endeavour to help those among whom we live.' In my own experience these words are even more true today, as this conference abundantly demonstrates.

After all, the question to all counsellors, be they Christian or humanist, believer or atheist, is 'Can you help?' And we can only help if we have a profound respect for our clients, as for all human beings, the humanist a profound respect for human possibility and a desire for every human being to reach his or her full potential, to be themselves; for the Christian a profound respect for God the creator and for this most wonderful and puzzling inhabitant of his creation, again that each should be enabled to be the person he or she is called to be.

Towards the end of the first century, Pliny the Elder wrote, in words which modern humanists like to quote: '*Deus est mortali iuvare mortalem*'—'A mortal's God lies in helping his fellow mortal'—or possibly, 'God is when a mortal helps a fellow-mortal' (Bibby, 1968: 13). At about the same time the author of The First Epistle of John wrote: '*ean agapomen allelous ho Theos en hemin menei*'—'If we love each other God lives in us' (1 John 4: 12). I hope I am not alone in feeling that these two insights, from very different starting points, come astonishingly close together.

There is a difference, of course, the difference which, in conscious thought and language at least, divides modern humanists from modern Christians. Pliny, who died investigating the eruption of Vesuvius, believed that he was celebrating the warmth and glory of human love in the face of a fascinating but unfeeling universe. John believed that he was celebrating the love at the heart of reality which had been manifested supremely in the life and death of a man whom he regarded as the embodiment of reality, able, even beyond death, to open people's hearts and minds to themselves and to one another. The differences seem to be deep, even fundamental, but it also seems that both men could, literally, have used the words with which Anne ended her paper: '*Ubi caritas, ibi Deus*': 'Where love is, there God is'.

REFERENCES

Bibby, C (1968) Towards a scientific humanist culture. In AJ Ayer (ed) *The Humanist Outlook*. London: Pemberton.

Fromm, E (1965) *Introduction to Socialist Humanism*. New York: Doubleday.

Halmos, P (1965) *The Faith of the Counsellors*. London: Constable.

Hymns and Psalms (1983). F Havergal (1836–1879), 'Lord, speak to me, that I may speak. London: Methodist Publishing House.

Lambourne, R (1963) *Community, Church and Healing*. London: Darton, Longman & Todd.

Lomas, P (1981) *The Case for a Personal Psychotherapy*. Oxford: OUP. Republished (1993) as *The Psychotherapy of Everyday Life*. New Brunswick, NJ: Transaction.

McGuire, W (ed) (1974) *The Freud–Jung letters: The correspondence between Sigmund Freud and CG Jung*. (Trans R Mannheim and RFC Hull). London: The Hogarth Press and Routledge & Kegan Paul.

Mearns, D & Thorne, B (1988) *Person-Centred Counselling in Action*. London: Sage.

Rogers, CR (1951) *Client-Centred Therapy*. London: Constable.

Taylor, J (1972) *The Go-between God*. London: SCM Press.

Thiselton, A (1980) *The Two Horizons*. Carlisle: Paternoster Press.

Thorne, B (2002) *The Mystical Power of Person-Centred Therapy*. London: Whurr.

Thorne, B (2003) *Infinitely Beloved*. London: Darton, Longman & Todd.

Tillich, P (1962) *The Shaking of the Foundations*. London: Penguin Books. Originally published: London: SCM Press (1949).

CONTRIBUTORS

Jack Earl was born in 1913 and educated at the Norwich School and Corpus Christi College, Cambridge. He then spent twelve years as a schoolmaster, four as a Naval meteorological officer, and twenty-four years as one of HM Inspectors of Schools, ending as Staff Inspector for Religious Education. After retirement (in 1975) he joined his wife, Anne, on the staff of the St Barnabas Counselling Centre in Norwich. Anne herself was a Froebel-trained primary school teacher and one of the first students of the Open University. Both trained as counsellors under the direction of Brian Thorne.

Ivan Ellingham spent six years in a boys' secondary school as a teacher of Religious Education, after studying theology at Kings College, London. He subsequently gained a diploma in counselling at the University of Aston where he met Professor C. H. Patterson, a fervent advocate of client-centred therapy. Ivan continued his counselling studies with Professor Patterson at the University of Illinois in the USA, eventually gaining a PhD in counselling psychology. Ivan currently lives in Hertfordshire where he works as a counselling psychologist in the NHS and as a tutor on the counselling diploma course at North Herts College.

Mary Green is a person-centred counsellor working privately and in association with Norwich Cathedral, rather drawn to a sense of being a 'wild' Christian and aspiring to honour the holiness in all people. She is particularly intrigued in the nurture and challenge of the relationships that a child needs in their early years, the effect this has on their emotional and spiritual buoyancy and, consequently, their energy and desire to learn. Before having a family and working as a counsellor, she trained as a paediatric nurse. She has recently discovered the sheer pleasure of learning out of school with her youngest son; and she accompanies her husband when he leads treks in the Indian Himalayas. She can be contacted on email at <maryhalsey@lineone.net>.

Mary Hill trained as a counsellor at UEA where spirituality was an integral part of the Diploma in Counselling, and has since gained experience as a counsellor in the workplace in a prison setting and with emergency services personnel. She now manages a welfare and counselling service in a large London theatre. She is attracted to Western Sufism as a contemporary expression of a perennial spiritual path, and its practices that deepen the capacity for inner stillness.

Stephen Hitchcock lives in Cumbria and works as a counsellor and supervisor in private practice, primary care and education. He trained in the person-centred approach at the University of East Anglia, Norwich. He has been significantly influenced by Brian Thorne and his writings, particularly with regard to self-worth and the realization of being 'infinitely beloved'. Stephen is a practising Christian and central to his faith is the concept of the Incarnation of God—not only in the person of Jesus (Emmanuel, *God with us*), but in humankind. Stephen is fascinated by the continuity, as he sees it, between the human and the divine, brokenness and wholeness, and life and death. He seeks to recognize in others, and to reflect in his own life, something of the image of God in which, he believes, we are all created.

Richard Holloway was Bishop of Edinburgh and Primus of the Scottish Episcopal Church until his retirement in 2000. He is now a writer and broadcaster. Author of twenty-six books, the latest are *Looking in the Distance*, published by Canongate, and *How to Read the Bible*, to be published by Granta this summer (2006). He is a Fellow of the Royal Society of Edinburgh, a former Gresham Professor of Divinity, and is currently Chairman of the Scottish Arts Council.

Dora Iseli Schudel is a psychotherapist working in private practice with individuals and couples. She also supervises staff of clinical as well as educational institutions. As a member of the training staff of the Swiss Association for Person-Centred Psychotherapy (SGGT) she is involved in the postgraduate training of PC therapists. She is a graduate (DiplPsych) of the University of Hamburg (Germany) and has lived and worked in different cultures after her Interdisciplinary Studies at the Swiss Federal Institute of Technology in Zurich, always returning to her Swiss roots. Her life as a wife and a mother of two adult children continues to be a challenge, joy and source of meaning. People, poetry, music, nature and deep silence are at present her favourite teachers for what her life is all about. Dora can be contacted at <d.iseli@tiscali.ch>.

Chris Jenkins has been a priest for almost twenty years. For the last nine years, having trained in rich multicultural settings in Margate (St Anselm's) and London (with Petruska Clarkson), he has been professionally involved in the world of counselling, as a therapist and group facilitator. He is on the executive of the Association for Pastoral and Spiritual Care and Counselling. His research focuses on clients' experience of the exclusion or pathologizing of their spirituality in counselling and he is due to submit his PhD thesis the week this book is published! Chris was formerly Director of St Joseph's Centre, Malpas, Cheshire. He continues to work as a therapist, facilitator and spiritual director. Chris can be contacted on <chrisjenkins148@btinternet.com>.

Suzanne Keys works as a psychotherapist and supervisor in private practice and in a sixth-form college in London. She is also involved in training courses in Martinique and France. She is a practising and struggling Anglican Christian and has worked with the Methodist Church in the Ivory Coast, West Africa. She edited *Idiosyncratic Person-Centred Therapy: From the personal to the universal* (PCCS Books, 2003) and has written articles and chapters on her experiences of training and working in different settings looking at human rights, ethics, politics, love and prayer. She is currently interested in writing and dialoguing about the interconnections between the political, spiritual, sexual and therapeutic. She is also curious about how becoming a mother for the first time affects it all.

Jeff Leonardi is Bishop's Adviser for Pastoral Care and Counselling in the Anglican Diocese of Lichfield, England, a post which combines counselling, supervision, training and priestly ministry. He trained in the person-centred approach in 1978 and, from the beginning, that experience was for him both psychological and spiritual. That same year he made a mature commitment to Christian faith and has continued to explore the relationship between faith and therapy ever since, working first as a counsellor and trainer, and then, following ordination, as a parish priest. For the past six years he has been pursuing doctoral research at the University of East Anglia into the spirituality of the person-centred approach. Email <jeff.leonardi@btinternet.com>.

Sarah Luczaj was born in 1970, in Somerset. After graduating in literature from UEA, and a few years of travelling around, she has been living in the Polish countryside with husband and daughter since 1997. She is a person-centred counsellor, poet, translator, English teacher, sometime workshop facilitator and sloppy Buddhist, working in private practice and for the 'Before Tomorrow Comes' centre for women based in Sanok, which somehow survives despite constant political/police interference. Her main interest is the work of Gendlin, but in day-to-day practice—in the given conditions— whatever works! Sarah can be contacted at <sluczaj@box43.pl.>.

Judy Moore is Director of Counselling and Director of the Centre for Counselling Studies at the University of East Anglia. She originally trained with FDI (Britain) (subsequently PCT) in the mid 1980s and has been engaged in the theory and practice of the person-centred approach since then. She taught for several years on the UEA postgraduate Diploma in Counselling and currently teaches on the postgraduate Diploma in Focusing. She is particularly interested in experiencing levels and the integration of focusing within the person-centred approach and is involved in the development of research in this area at UEA. She has practised Sōtō Zen meditation for the past ten years.

Daishin Morgan was ordained as a monk in the Soto Zen Buddhist tradition at Throssel Hole Buddhist Abbey in Northumberland in 1974, not long after the monastery was established by his teacher Reverend Master Jiyu-Kennett. He went on to study with her at Shasta Abbey in California and became a master in 1981.

In 1982 he returned to the UK to take up the position of Abbot at Throssel and since then the community has grown and become well established. All are welcome to take part in the retreats offered by the monastery, you don't have to be a Buddhist to come. For more information see <www.throssel.org.uk> or ring 01434 345 204.

Matis Nimetz has been a practitioner, trainer and supervisor in person-centred counselling/ psychotherapy in Norwich for several years. She moved to Norwich from France in 1985 and trained on the Postgraduate Diploma in Counselling at UEA. It was during the writing of her Masters thesis in Counselling Research that she became interested in the concept of acceptance as it applies both to therapeutic work and to the human lived experiences and relationships at large. She is interested in psychotherapy and body work and in psychosomatic illness. She is also interested, as a group facilitator, in the development of the person through groupwork.

Clive Perraton Mountford teaches environmental ethics by distance education for the University of British Columbia, is senior lecturer in counselling and coordinator of the person-centred training program at Buckinghamshire Chilterns University College, and is a therapist in private practice at Counselling People in Norwich. His life has been divided between Western Canada and the UK, and although at present his professional life is mostly in England, he has a home in both jurisdictions. Clive has published on issues in environmental ethics, education, and counselling.

Stephen Platten has taught theology now for some twenty-five years. He was a tutor at Lincoln Theological College and then Secretary for Ecumenical Affairs to the Archbishop of Canterbury at Lambeth Palace when he was also the Anglican Co-Secretary of the Anglican-Roman Catholic International Commission. On leaving Lambeth he became Dean of Norwich and is now Bishop of Wakefield. His main specialisms have been Moral Theology, Ecclesiology and Christian Doctrine. He is the author and editor of a number of books including two on the role of cathedrals in the contemporary world, and Chair of the Church of England's Liturgical Commission.

Veronika Prüller-Jagenteufel has a doctoral degree in pastoral theology. She works as editor of the theological magazine *Diakonia—Internationale Zeitschrift für die Praxis der Kirche* <www.diakonia-online.net>. She gives seminars in the field of theology and spirituality and offers spiritual counselling for individuals. She has undergone training for person-centred counselling in Vienna. She is Austrian and lives in Vienna. Veronika can be contacted at <v.pj@utanet.at>.

Campbell Purton is the Director of the postgraduate Diploma Course in Focusing and Experiential Psychotherapy at the University of East Anglia, where he also works as a student counsellor. He has been a lecturer in philosophy at universities in Britain and Canada, a therapist in private practice and Director of the UEA Postgraduate Diploma in Counselling. He is a Certifying Coordinator for the Focusing Institute, and has published many articles in the areas of counselling, focusing and Buddhist studies. He is the author of *Person-centred Therapy: The Focusing-oriented Approach.* His current interests are in the philosophical work of Eugene Gendlin, and its relationship to both Buddhist thought and the theory of psychotherapy.

Peter F. Schmid PhD, is Universitätsdozent (Associate Professor) at the Institute for Pastoral Theology and Pastoral Psychology of the University of Graz in Austria; faculty member of Saybrook Graduate School and Research Center in San Francisco, California; practical theologian, pastoral psychologist and person-centred psychotherapist; founder of person-centred training in Austria; co-director of the Academy for Counselling and Psychotherapy (Institute for Person-Centered Studies—IPS of APG) in Vienna; co-founder of both the Person-Centered and Experiential PsychotherapiesWorld Association (WAPCEPC) and the European Network (NEAPCEPC). He is author of fourteen books and numerous publications in the fields of theology and person-centred psychotherapy. His main concern is with the anthropological and epistemological foundations of PCT and its further development towards a dialogical understanding of psychotherapy and counselling.

Hans Julius Schneider is Professor of Philosophy at the University of Potsdam. He has held teaching positions in Konstanz, Erlangen, Potsdam, and has been a Visiting Professor at the University of Georgia, The School of the Art Institute (Chicago) and Fudan University (Shanghai). Selected publications are: *Phantasie und Kalkül,* 1992; The Situatedness of Thinking, Knowing and Speaking: Wittgenstein and Gendlin, in David M Levin (ed), *Language beyond Postmodernism,* 1997; Creation and re-creation. The interplay of activity and structure in language, in *Journal of Pragmatics,* 1999; Metaphors and Theoretical Terms: Problems in Referring to the Mental, in M Carrier, GJ Massey, L Ruetsche (eds), *Science at Century's End,* 2000; Liberating Language in Linji and Wittgenstein, in *Asian Philosophy,* 2003 (co-author JD Sellmann); Metaphor and the Limits of Language, in George Allan, Merle F Allshouse (eds), *Nature, Truth and Value,* 2005. Contact: <hschneid@rz.uni-potsdam.de>.

Robina Scott BA (Joint Hons) PGCE, PGDipCouns has been accompanying people on their personal and spiritual growth journeys for ten years. Whilst she is the only PRH (Personality and Human Relations) educator in England, she feels privileged to be part of an international organisation which helps people to discover who they are in their essence and to liberate themselves from the obstacles to living this way. She is proud that this method is universally accessible, regardless of race, creed, religion, or educational background.

She feels blessed to be working in this school of research into the phenomenon of human growth and happiness. Here she can combine her therapeutic and pedagogical skills as well as her fascination for the human person, their transpersonal dimension and their process of transformation towards full actualization. Despite being on a radical search, she is deeply at peace with what is.

She can be contacted at: <robina.scott@prhengland.co.uk>
<www.prhengland.co.uk> <www.prh-international.com>

Jon Sharp is the Faculty Manager within the School of Education and Lifelong Learning at UEA. He is an associate member of the Keswick Hall Centre and makes a contribution to the MA in Counselling. Jon's interest in spirituality is based in his own experience of occultism, and he has had a number of books published which explore practical applications of the hermetic tradition. His academic interests include experiential spirituality, philosophical implications of the occult and the phenomenology of the self. He can be contacted at <jon.sharp@uea.ac.uk>.

Tess Sturrock writes: As a child the moments for me that were most filled with life were often those in which I was involved in some way with the arts: I felt fulfilled through having an avenue for my expression. Typically, caught up in the event with others, I also experienced a sense of connection. Working as an Expressive Therapist, using writing, art, movement and sound in connection with each other, provides some of the most 'coloured in' parts of my life. Helping others to discover whatever lies within is tremendously satisfying. Twinned with my own exploration, this is what constitutes the spiritual for me.

Brian Thorne is Emeritus Professor of Counselling at the University of East Anglia and Co-founder of the Norwich Centre. He is also a Lay Canon of Norwich Anglican Cathedral. Brian is an international figure in the world of person-centred therapy and has done much to explore the understanding of the approach as an essentially spiritual discipline. He is the author of *The Mystical Power of Person-Centred Therapy* (Whurr, 2002) and of *Love's Embrace* (PCCS Books, 2005). The latter is an autobiographical study.

Jan van Blarikom works as a psychologist at an institution of mental health (Emergis) in the Netherlands. He works especially with persons with enduring mental illnesses and people with borderline personality disorder. He has published in *Maandblad Geestelijke Volksgezonheid* 'About the meaning of suffering in psychiatry'. He has written a book review of *Psychology for the Other* for a forthcoming issue of the WAPCEPC journal and in this journal is a series of three articles planned about person-centered psychiatry (schizophrenia, borderline personality disorder and mood disorders). In the summer of 2006 he will deliver a lecture at the PCE 2006 conference in Potsdam: 'Beautiful mind revisited: Towards a person-centered psychiatry'. He can be contacted at <janvanblarikom@gmail.com>.

Suzette van IJssel graduated from the University of Utrecht (the Netherlands) in Womens Studies with a thesis on spirituality and (feminist) philosophy of science. Her PhD thesis, based on both qualitative and quantitative research on spirituality and humanist counselling at the University for Humanistics, will be finished near the end of 2006. The objective of this research is to gather insight into what forms or aspects of spirituality interest humanist counsellors and what the impact of this interest is in their counselling practice. Dr van IJssel also works as a teacher in philosophy, spirituality and religions.

Martin van Kalmthout is a person-centred therapist in private practice in the Netherlands. He has published widely on the history and foundations of psychotherapy in general and person-centered therapy in particular. Currently he is exploring the thesis that person-centred therapy is a modern system of meaning which might be of help to many people in our secularized world who are in search of life meaning. He can be contacted at <M.vankalmthout@planet.nl>.

William West is a Reader in Counselling Studies at the University of Manchester where he is Director of the Counselling Studies Programme, including the Doctorate programme in counselling. He is a registered practitioner and Fellow of BACP. William has researched, practised and written extensively on spirituality and therapy, including books: *Psychotherapy and Spirituality* (Sage 2000) and *Spiritual Issues in Therapy* (Palgrave MacMillan 2004). William is also gripped by, and has written on, qualitative research, supervision, culture, and traditional healing and has recently co-edited a book with Roy Moodley *Integrating Traditional Healing Practices into Counseling and Psychotherapy* (Sage 2005).

INDEX